Great Disciples of the Buddha

GREAT DISCIPLES OF THE BUDDHA

Their Lives, Their Works, Their Legacy

Nyanaponika Thera and Hellmuth Hecker

Edited with an Introduction by Bhikkhu Bodhi

Wisdom Publications • Boston

in collaboration with the

Buddhist Publication Society of Kandy, Sri Lanka

WISDOM PUBLICATIONS
199 Elm Street
Somerville, Massachusetts 02144
USA

Library of Congress Cataloging-in-Publication Data

Nyanaponika, Thera.
Great disciples of the Buddha : their lives, their works, their legacy / Nyanaponika Thera and Hellmuth Hecker ; edited and with an introduction by Bhikkhu Bodhi.
p. cm.
Includes bibliographical references and index.
ISBN 0-86171-128-9 (alk. paper)
1. Gautama Buddha—Disciples—Biography. I. Hecker, Hellmuth.
II. Bodhi, Bhikkhu. III. Title.
BQ900.N93 1997
294.3'092'2
[B]—DC21 97–19024

0 86171 128 9

02 01 00 99 98
6 5 4 3 2

Cover Art: Votive plaque with seated Buddha Shakyamuni and attendant bodhisattvas and monks. China, Sui Dynasty, 581–618; gilt bronze; 15.2 x 15.2 cm. Courtesy of the Arthur M. Sackler Museum, Harvard University Art Museum; bequest of Grenville L. Winthrop.

Design by: L·J·SAWLIT & STEPHANIE SHAIMAN

Wisdom Publications' books are printed on acid-free paper and meet the guidelines for permanence and durability of the Committee on Production Guidelines for Book Longevity of the Council on Library Resources.

Printed in the United States of America.

Contents

Preface

WHILE IN RECENT YEARS in the West oceans of ink have been expended on books dealing with the Buddha and his Teaching, the first two Jewels of Buddhism, the coverage given to the third Jewel, the Sangha, has been far from adequate. Even the meaning of the word "sangha" has been a matter of dispute, while for those without access to the original Pāli texts a dense cloud of obscurity still hangs over the Buddha's original nucleus of disciples. This gap is all the more glaring because the very measure of the Buddha's success as a spiritual teacher is to be determined by his skill in training his disciples. The canonical verse of homage to the Buddha hails him as "the unsurpassed trainer of persons to be tamed," and thus the acid test for the validity of this claim must be the mettle of the men and women who submitted to his guidance. Just as the sun is valued not only for its own intrinsic radiance but also for its ability to illuminate the world, so the brilliance of the Buddha as a spiritual master is determined not only by the clarity of his Teaching but by his ability to illuminate those who came to him for refuge and to make them luminaries in their own right. Without a community of disciples to testify to its transformative power, the Teaching, the Dhamma, would be merely a package of doctrines and formal practices, admirably lucid and intellectually rigorous, but remote from vital human concerns. The Dhamma comes to life only to the extent that it touches life, ennobling its followers and turning them into models of wisdom, compassion, and purity.

The present book is an attempt to fill this gap in Western Buddhist literature with living portraits of twenty-four of the most distinguished disciples of the Buddha. The book evolved from a series of individual tracts on the great disciples issued by the Buddhist Publication Society (BPS) under its well-known imprint, The Wheel. The first biography to appear was *The Life of Sāriputta* by the Venerable Nyanaponika Thera. This was first published in 1966 as an independent monograph, with no intention to initiate an ongoing series. In the same year, however, the German Buddhist author Hellmuth Hecker began publishing short biographical profiles of the great disciples in the German Buddhist periodical *Wissen und Wandel* (established in 1955 by Paul Debes). Over the next twenty years *Wissen und Wandel* carried forty-one such portraits, many quite short.

In the late 1970s the idea occurred to Ven. Nyanaponika, then the editor of the BPS, to follow up his study of Sāriputta with a line of Wheel titles on the other great disciples, using the articles by Dr. Hecker as a basis. Thus between 1979 and 1989 there appeared, as individual Wheel booklets, portraits of Mahāmoggallāna, Ānanda, Aṅgulimāla, Anāthapiṇḍika, Mahākassapa, Anuruddha, and eight prominent women disciples. These had been translated into English either by Ven. Nyanaponika himself or by others at his request. Finally, in 1995 I wrote a booklet on the Elder Mahākaccāna, which was the last to appear in the series.

Almost all the original articles by Dr. Hecker were considerably enlarged by Ven. Nyanaponika with additional material gathered from the Pāli Canon and its commentaries, and deepened with his own insightful reflections. In preparing this comprehensive volume from the original booklets I have made substantial alterations in almost all the older versions and added still more material to give a fuller picture of the disciple under scrutiny. The chapter on the women disciples has been expanded by the addition of four profiles that were not in the original Wheel, although a full-length treatment of individual women comparable to the studies of the leading male disciples was not possible owing to the sparsity of source material. A thorough stylistic revision of the original portraits was also necessary.

I have retranslated almost all the verses, which in the Wheel booklets were often quoted from older translations composed in a style that would strike present-day readers as stilted. To leaven the prose accounts I have added still more verses, particularly from the *Theragāthā* and *Therīgāthā.* Unless indicated otherwise all verse translations are my own, though my verse renderings from the two collections just named lean heavily upon the literal prose translations by K.R. Norman, published as *Elders' Verses,* parts 1 and 2.

I would like to thank my long-time assistant at the BPS, Ayyā Nyanasirī, who first reviewed the original Wheels with the idea of reissuing them in a single volume. I also thank Mrs. Savithri Chandraratne, who diligently and accurately typed the manuscripts into the computer. I am grateful to Wisdom Publications for its collaboration in the publication of this book, particularly to Sara McClintock, whose editorial comments led to major improvements.

Bhikkhu Bodhi

Credits

"Sāriputta: The Marshal of the Dhamma," by Nyanaponika Thera. First published as *The Life of Sāriputta*, BPS Wheel No. 90/92 (1966).

"Mahākaccāna: Master of Doctrinal Exposition," by Bhikkhu Bodhi. First published as BPS Wheel No. 405/406 (1995).

The following biographies are all by Hellmuth Hecker, translated into English from the German:

"Mahāmoggallāna: Master of Psychic Powers." Trans. by Nyanaponika Thera. First published as *Mahā-Moggallāna*, BPS Wheel No. 263/264 (1979).

"Mahākassapa: Father of the Sangha." Revised and enlarged trans. by Nyanaponika Thera. First published as BPS Wheel No. 345 (1987).

"Ānanda: Guardian of the Dhamma." Trans. by Sister Khemā. First published as BPS Wheel No. 273/274 (1980).

"Anuruddha: Master of the Divine Eye." Revised and enlarged trans. by Nyanaponika Thera. First published as BPS Wheel No. 362 (1989).

"Great Women Disciples of the Buddha." Trans. by Sister Khemā. First published as *Buddhist Women at the Time of the Buddha*, BPS Wheel No. 292/293 (1982). The following stories are new to this volume: "Visākhā: The Buddha's Chief Patroness" (trans. by Friedgard Lottermoser, enlarged by Bhikkhu Bodhi); "Ambapālī: The Generous Courtesan," "Sirimā and Uttarā," and "Isidāsī: A Journey through Saṁsāra" (trans. by Amadeo Solé-Leris).

"Aṅgulimāla: A Murderer's Road to Sainthood." Enlarged trans. by Nyanaponika Thera. First published as BPS Wheel No. 312 (1984).

"Anāthapiṇḍika: The Buddha's Chief Patron." Trans. under supervision of Nyanaponika Thera. First published as *Anāthapiṇḍika: The Great Benefactor*, BPS Wheel No. 334 (1986).

"Shorter Lives of the Disciples." Adapted from a translation by Mudita Ebert. First published as BPS Wheel No. 115 (1967).

Translations from the Pāli sources are by the respective authors, unless otherwise noted. Verse translations are by Bhikkhu Bodhi, unless otherwise noted.

ABBREVIATIONS

AN	Aṅguttara Nikāya (by section and sutta)
Ap.	Apadāna (i = Thera-apadāna, ii = Therī-apadāna; by chapter and section; Burmese-script ed.)
BL	*Buddhist Legends* (Dhp. Comy.)
BPS	Buddhist Publication Society (Kandy, Sri Lanka)
Comy.	Commentary
Dhp.	Dhammapada (by verse)
DN	Dīgha Nikāya (by sutta number)
Jāt.	Jātaka (by number)
Mil.	Milindapañha
MN	Majjhima Nikāya (by sutta number)
PTS	Pali Text Society (Oxford, England)
Pv.	Petavatthu
SN	Saṁyutta Nikāya (by chapter and sutta)
Snp.	Suttanipāta (by verse, or sutta)
Thag.	Theragāthā (by verse)
Thig.	Therīgāthā (by verse)
Ud.	Udāna (by chapter and sutta)
Vin.	Vinaya (by volume and page)
Vism.	Visuddhimagga (chapter and paragraph of *The Path of Purification*)
Vv.	Vimānavatthu (by verse)

All references are to PTS editions unless otherwise noted.

Publisher's Acknowledgment

The publisher gratefully acknowledges the generous help of the Hershey Family Foundation in sponsoring the printing of this book.

Editor's Introduction

The Place of Discipleship in Buddhism

As a religious founder the Buddha did not claim to be a divinely inspired prophet, a personal savior, or a deity incarnate in flesh. Within the framework of his Teaching, the Dhamma, his special role is that of a teacher, the Supreme Teacher who reveals the unique path to final deliverance. In the earliest form of the Teaching, as represented by the Pāli Canon, no essential difference divides the goal attained by the Buddha himself from that realized by his disciples. For both the goal is the same, *Nibbāna*, the perfect liberation of the mind from all constricting bonds and the consequent release from *saṁsāra*, the round of repeated birth and death.

The differences between the Buddha and his disciples concern, first, the temporal sequence of their attainment and, second, the personal qualities which they acquire through their realization of the goal. In terms of temporal sequence, the Buddha is the discoverer of the path to Nibbāna, while his disciples are those who tread the path under his guidance and thereby gain the fruit: "The Tathāgata, monks, is the originator of the path unarisen before, the producer of the path unproduced before, the declarer of the path undeclared before. He is the knower of the path, the finder of the path, the one skilled in the path. And his disciples now dwell following that path and become possessed of it afterwards. This, monks, is the distinction, the disparity, the difference between the Tathāgata, the Arahant, the Fully Enlightened One, and a monk liberated by wisdom" (SN 22:58).

In terms of personal qualities, the Buddha, as the founder of the *sāsana*, the teaching or "Dispensation," possesses a vast array of skills and modes of knowledge that are not fully shared by his disciples. These cognitive faculties include not only certain thaumaturgical powers but also the unimpeded knowledge of the constitution of the world with its many planes of existence and a thorough understanding of the diverse mental proclivities of sentient beings.[1] Such faculties are necessary to enable the Buddha to fulfill his essential mission of establishing the Dispensation in the world at large and of guiding countless beings to liberation from suffering.

Since the Buddha's aim when he first "set in motion the Wheel of the Dhamma" was to lead sentient beings to Nibbāna, the very structure of his Teaching presupposes a relationship of discipleship between himself and those who hearken to his message. The Buddha is the fully enlightened teacher (*satthā*); his Teaching (*sāsana*) is an injunction to undergo a particular course of training; and those who conform to the demands of discipleship do so by following his injunction (*sāsanakara*) and complying with his advice (*ovādapaṭikara*). Even at the close of his ministry, as he lay on his deathbed between the twin *sāla* trees at Kusinārā, he declared that it was not by external acts of homage that the Tathāgata, the Perfect One, was properly worshipped, but by the consistent and dedicated practice of the Dhamma (DN 16).

The course of discipleship under the Buddha begins with an act of faith (*saddhā*). Faith, for Buddhism, is not an unquestioning assent to propositions beyond the range of possible verification but a readiness to accept on trust the claim that the Buddha makes about himself: that he is the Fully Enlightened One, who has awakened to the deepest, most crucial truths about the nature of sentient existence and who can show the path to the supreme goal. The placing of faith in the Buddha's Enlightenment is manifested by the process of "going for refuge" to the Three Jewels of Buddhism (*tiratana*): to the Buddha as one's mentor and spiritual guide; to his Teaching, the Dhamma, as the most perfect expression of existential truth and the flawless path to liberation; and to the Ariya Sangha, the community of noble ones, as the corporate embodiment of wisdom and spiritual purity. Faith necessarily leads to action, to the undertaking of the training, which in concrete terms means the implementation in one's life of the guidelines the Buddha has laid down for his followers. These guidelines vary widely in dependence on the situation and aptitude of the disciple. Certain sets of guidelines are more appropriate for lay followers, others more appropriate for monastics, and it is the disciple's task to make the right choice among them. But all such guidelines, originating from different starting points, eventually converge upon a single path, universal and unique, leading infallibly to the final goal. This is the Noble Eightfold Path, the way to the cessation of suffering, with its three divisions of virtue (*sīla*: right speech, right action, right livelihood), concentration (*samādhi*: right effort, right mindfulness, right concentration), and wisdom (*paññā*: right view, right intention).

Those who accept the Buddha as teacher and attempt to follow his path are his *sāvaka* (Skt. *śrāvaka*), his disciples. The category of discipleship cuts across the conventional distinction between the monastic order and the lay community and thus embraces the traditional "four assemblies" of Buddhist followers: *bhikkhus* and *bhikkhunīs* (monks and nuns) and *upāsakas* and *upāsikās* (laymen and laywomen). Although later texts of the Mahāyāna tradition speak of the *sāvakas* as if they formed a distinct class of disciples—a class contrasted unfavorably with the bodhisattvas—the early Buddhist scriptures do not know any such distinction but use the word *sāvaka* broadly to refer to all those who accept the Buddha as their master. The word is derived from the causative verb *sāveti*, "to inform, to declare," and thus means those who declare the Buddha to be their master (or perhaps those to whom the Dhamma has been declared). In the early texts *sāvaka* is used not only as a designation for the Buddha's disciples but also for the followers of other spiritual systems in relation to their own mentors.

TWO TYPES OF DISCIPLES

Within the wide circle of the Buddha's followers a critical distinction is drawn between two types of disciples, the ordinary disciples and the noble disciples. The differences that divide them do not pertain to outward form and mode of life but to inward spiritual stature. Such differences will become clearer if we discuss them in the light of the worldview that underlies both the Buddhist tradition as a whole and the biographical profiles that constitute the substance of the present volume.

The compilers of the Buddhist scriptures accept as axiomatic a worldview that differs significantly from the picture of the universe bequeathed to us by modern science. This worldview is characterized by three basic and interrelated premises. The first is that the sentient universe is a multitiered edifice, with three primary realms divided into a number of subsidiary planes. The grossest tier is the *sense-desire realm* (*kāmadhātu*), which consists of eleven planes: the hells, the animal kingdom, the sphere of ghosts, the human realm, the sphere of titans, and the six sensuous heavens; of these, only the human realm and the animal kingdom are normally accessible to our natural sense faculties. Above the sense-desire realm is the *fine-material realm*, or the realm of subtle form (*rūpadhātu*), an ascending series of some sixteen exalted planes which are the ontological counterparts of the *jhānas*, the meditative absorptions; here the grosser aspects of matter have faded away and the beings enjoy far greater bliss, peace, and power than is ordinarily accessible in the terrestrial realm. Finally, at the pinnacle of the Buddhist cosmos is the *immaterial realm* (*arūpadhātu*), four planes of extremely attenuated nature corresponding to the four immaterial meditative absorptions (*āruppajhāna*); here matter has disappeared completely and the denizens are of a purely mental constitution.[2]

The second axiom concerns rebirth. Buddhism holds that all unenlightened beings, those who have not eradicated ignorance and craving, are bound to be reborn within the three realms. The course of transmigration is without discoverable beginning. It is propelled from within by ignorance and craving, which drive the stream of consciousness from death to new birth in a repeatedly self-sustaining process. This uninterrupted succession of births and deaths is called saṁsāra, "the wandering on," the round of repeated existence.

The third axiom is the principle that determines the sphere of rebirth. This is what the Buddha calls *kamma*, action, specifically volitional action. According to the Buddha, all our morally determinate volitional actions are subject to an inescapable law of retribution. Our deeds leave behind, in the ongoing stream of consciousness, a potential to produce results (*vipāka*), to bring forth fruits (*phala*), which appear when the accumulated kamma meets with external conditions congenial to its germination. Kamma determines not only the specific plane into which one is reborn but also our inherent capacities and propensities and the basic direction of our lives. The mode by which kamma operates is an ethical one: unwholesome kamma—deeds motivated by greed, aversion, and delusion—brings a bad rebirth and engenders pain and suffering; wholesome kamma—deeds inspired by generosity, kindness, and wisdom—leads to a good rebirth and to happiness and well-being.[3]

Since all experience within the round of rebirth is impermanent and unsatisfactory, the ultimate aim for early Buddhism is to break free from this self-generating cycle and thereby win the unconditioned state, Nibbāna, where there is no more birth, aging, and death. This is the goal the Buddha himself attained as the culmination of his own noble quest, and it is also the goal he constantly set before his disciples. The distinction between the two types of disciples pertains to their relationship to this goal. The class of ordinary disciples, which is by far the more numerous of the two, consists of those who are still technically classed as worldlings or commoners (*puthujjana*). Such disciples may have sincerely gone for refuge to the Three Jewels and may be fully devoted to the practice of the Dhamma, but despite their earnestness they have not yet reached the plane where liberation is irrevocably assured. They have not yet seen the Dhamma for themselves, nor eliminated the mental fetters, nor entered irreversibly upon the path to final emancipation. Their present mode of practice is preparatory in character: it is intended to bring their spiritual faculties to maturity so that, in due course, they may enter upon the supramundane path. Until that experience dawns, however, they must wander on through the round of rebirths, uncertain of their future destination, still liable to moral lapses and even to rebirth in the lower realms.

In contrast to this class stands the class of noble disciples, the *ariyasāvaka*.[4] These disciples have surmounted the plane of the worldlings, have arrived at the stage of irreversibility, and are assured of reaching the final goal in a maximum of seven more births. What has raised them from the status of a worldling to the plane of spiritual nobility is a radical transformation that has occurred at the very base of the mind. This transformation may be viewed from two complementary perspectives, one cognitive, the other psychological. The suttas refer to the cognitive aspect as the gaining of the vision of the Dhamma (*dhammacakkhu-paṭilābha*) and the breakthrough to the Dhamma (*dhammābhisamaya*).[5] Such an event, altering one's destiny for all time, generally takes place after the disciple has fulfilled the preliminary requisites of the training and has been engaged in the practice of insight meditation (*vipassanā-bhāvanā*). As deepening insights into the true nature of phenomena bring to maturity the faculty of wisdom (*paññā*), at a certain point, when all conditions are ripe, the mists of ignorance momentarily disperse, affording the disciple an immediate glimpse of the unconditioned element, the Deathless, which is the precondition and final term of the whole process of liberation.

When this vision dawns the disciple becomes a true heir to the Buddha's message. The texts describe such a disciple as "one who has seen the Dhamma, reached the Dhamma, understood the Dhamma, fathomed the Dhamma, who has overcome all doubt and perplexity, and become self-sufficient in the Master's Teaching" (e.g., at MN 74). Even though the vision may still be clouded and imperfect, the disciple has won access to the ultimate truth and it is only a matter of time until, by diligent practice, he or she brings this vision to its culmination in enlightenment (*sambodhi*), the complete experiential understanding of the Four Noble Truths.

The other aspect of the transformation which the disciple undergoes pertains to the constitution of the psyche. It consists in the permanent elimination of certain unwholesome mental dispositions called defilements (*kilesa*). For purposes of exposition, the defilements are usually classified into a set of ten fetters (*saṁyojana*), called thus because they hold beings in bondage to the round of rebirths. From the suttas it appears that in exceptional cases a disciple with a high degree of wisdom from previous lives can cut off all ten fetters at a single stroke, thereby advancing in one leap from the stage of a worldling to that of an *arahant*, a fully liberated one. The more typical process of attainment, however, is a calibrated one whereby the fetters are cut off sequentially, in discrete clusters, on four different occasions of awakening. This results in a fourfold gradation among the noble disciples, with each major stage subdivided in turn into two phases: a phase of the path (*magga*), when the disciple is practicing for the elimination of the particular cluster of fetters; and a phase of the fruit (*phala*), when the breakthrough is complete and the fetters have been destroyed. This subdivision explains the classical formula of the Ariya Sangha as made up of four pairs and eight types of noble persons (*yadidaṁ cattāri purisayugāni aṭṭhapurisapuggalā esa bhagavato sāvakasaṅgho*).

The first stage of awakening is called *stream-entry* (*sotāpatti*), because it is with this attainment that the disciple can properly be said to have entered "the stream of the Dhamma" (*dhammasota*), i.e., the Noble Eightfold Path that leads irreversibly to Nibbāna. Stream-entry is won with the first arising of the vision of the Dhamma and is marked by the eradication of the coarsest three fetters: personality view (*sakkāyadiṭṭhi*), the view of a substantial self within the empirical person; doubt in the Buddha and his Teaching; and wrong grasp of rules and vows (*sīlabbataparāmāsa*), the belief that mere external observances (including religious rituals and penitential forms of asceticism) can lead to salvation. With the cutting off of these three fetters the stream-enterer is freed from the prospect of rebirth in the plane of misery (*apāyabhūmi*), the three lower realms of the hells, the animal kingdom, and the sphere of spirits or "hungry ghosts." Such a one is certain to attain final liberation in at most seven more lifetimes passed either in the human world or in the heavens.

The next major stage of awakening is that of the *once-returner* (*sakadāgāmi*), who will be reborn only one more time in the human realm or in the sense-sphere heavens and there reach the ultimate goal. The path of once-returning does not eradicate any fetters beyond those already eliminated by the path of stream-entry. It does, however, attenuate the three root defilements—greed, hatred, and delusion—so that they arise only sporadically and then only in a mild degree.

The third path, that of the *non-returner* (*anāgāmī*), cuts off two deep roots of emotional turbulence within the psyche: the defilements of sensual lust and ill will, the fourth and fifth fetters, which are removed in all their manifold guises, even the subtlest. Because these two fetters are the principal ties that keep living beings bound to the sense-desire realm, the non-returner, as the name implies, never returns to this realm. Rather, such a one is spontaneously reborn in one of the exalted form-realm heavens called the Pure Abodes (*suddhāvāsa*), accessible only to non-returners, and there attains final Nibbāna without ever coming back to this world.

The fourth and final stage of noble discipleship is that of arahantship (*arahatta*), which is attained by the elimination of the five subtle fetters that remain unabandoned even in the non-returner: desire for existence in the form realm and formless realm, conceit, restlessness, and ignorance. As ignorance is the most deeply grounded of all the defilements, when the path of arahantship arises fully fathoming the Four Noble Truths, ignorance collapses, bringing all the other residual defilements along with it. The mind then enters upon "the taintless liberation of mind, liberation by wisdom, attained by the destruction of the taints"—the state that the Buddha calls the unsurpassed consummation of the holy life.

The arahant is the fully accomplished disciple of early Buddhism, the perfect model for the entire Buddhist community. Even the Buddha himself, with respect to his liberation, is described as an arahant, and he declared the arahants to be his equals in regard to the destruction of defilements. For the arahant there is no further task to be achieved and no falling away from what has been achieved. He or she has completed the development of the noble path, has fully understood the true nature of existence, and has eradicated all the mind's bonds and fetters. For the duration of life the arahant abides in unruffled peace, in the experiential realization of Nibbāna, with a mind stainless and secure. Then, with the breakup of the body at the end of the life span, he or she reaches the end of the entire process of re-becoming. For the arahant death is not the passageway to a new rebirth, as it is for all others, but the doorway to the unconditioned state itself, the Nibbāna-element without residue of conditioned existence (*anupādisesa-nibbānadhātu*). This is the true cessation of suffering to which the Buddha's Teaching points, the final termination of the beginningless round of birth and death.

THE GREAT DISCIPLES

It is often believed that early Buddhism recognized only one Buddha—the Buddha Gotama, Sakyamuni—and that the conception of multiple Buddhas was an innovation belonging to the stage of Buddhist thought preceding the rise of the Mahāyāna. The Pāli Nikāyas, our oldest integral source for the most archaic phase of Buddhism, belie this assumption. The suttas regularly mention six Buddhas of antiquity, the predecessors of Gotama, and in one text (DN 14) the Buddha gives detailed information about their careers. Elsewhere he prophesies the arising of a future Buddha to be named Metteyya, who will rekindle the light of the true Dhamma in an age of spiritual darkness (DN 26). In the later literature of the Theravāda school the list of past Buddhas is increased to twenty-seven. It was under the twenty-fourth of these (counting backwards), a Buddha named Dīpaṅkara, that the being who was to become the Buddha Gotama received his original prediction to future Buddhahood.[6]

The specific function of a Buddha within the historical and cosmic process is to rediscover and proclaim the lost path to Nibbāna. For Buddhism, history does not unfold in a straight line from creation to apocalypse. It develops, rather, in repetitive cycles of growth and decline nested within the wider cycles of the cosmic process. World systems arise, evolve, and disintegrate, replaced by new world systems arisen from the ashes of the old. Against this background, boundless in space and time, sentient beings migrate from life to life within the three realms of existence. All existence within the round is burdened with suffering: it is transient, unstable, insubstantial, beginning with pain at birth and ending with pain in old age, sickness, and death. Periodically, however, from amid the dark labyrinths of saṁsāra, a being arises—always in the human realm—who unravels the intricate tangle of conditions that sustain this process of bondage and thereby discovers, by his own unaided wisdom, the lost path to Nibbāna, the unconditioned state of perfect bliss, peace, and freedom. This being is a Buddha.

A Buddha not only rediscovers the path to Nibbāna but he also establishes a sāsana, a Dispensation, to give countless other beings the opportunity to learn the Dhamma and to tread the path to the goal. To facilitate progress along the path each Buddha founds a Sangha, an order of renunciant monks and nuns, who leave behind the household life to take upon themselves the full yoke of his discipline, the *brahmacariya* or holy life. Each Buddha teaches the Dhamma freely and openly to all four classes of disciples—monks and nuns, laymen and laywomen—showing them the courses of conduct that lead to higher rebirths within the round of existence and the path to release from the entire vicious cycle. Even for those who fail to reach the first stage of noble discipleship, the arising of a Buddha is still an auspicious event; for by going for refuge to the Three Jewels, making offerings to the Buddha and his Sangha, and undertaking the practice of his Teaching, beings plant seeds of merit with the most sublime potency for producing favorable fruits. Such seeds of merit, when they mature, not only bring lofty forms of rebirth, but lead these beings into contact with future Buddhas, thereby enabling them to hear the Dhamma again and, when their faculties are fully ripened, to attain realization of the paths and fruits of liberation.

From among their retinues of noble disciples every Buddha appoints a number of particular disciples as the most eminent in certain special fields.

First the Buddha appoints, at the head of the entire Sangha, two bhikkhus as chief disciples (*aggasāvaka*), who share with him the major responsibilities for the instruction of the monks and the administration of the Sangha as a whole. Of these two, one is also the foremost in wisdom, the other in the exercise of psychic powers. In the Dispensation of our present Buddha, Gotama, these two posts were held by the arahants Sāriputta and Mahāmoggallāna. In addition, every Buddha appoints one bhikkhu as his personal attendant (*upaṭṭhāka*) to look after his needs, to function as the intermediary between himself and the general public, and to accompany him on his preaching rounds. For our present Buddha, this post was held by the Venerable Ānanda, who was also known as the Guardian of the Dhamma for his role in preserving the Buddha's discourses.

These most elevated and intimate posts by no means exhaust the range of great discipleship. The Pāli Canon contains one chapter in the Aṅguttara Nikāya called the *Etadaggavagga* ("This-One-Is-Chief" Chapter; AN 1; chap.14) in which the Buddha creates eighty categories of great disciples: forty-seven among the bhikkhus, thirteen among the bhikkhunīs, and ten each among the male and female lay followers. For each of these posts he appoints a foremost disciple, though in a few instances a single disciple excels in several categories. For example, among the monks there is one who is foremost among "those with a gentle voice"—Lakuṇṭaka Bhaddiya; one who is foremost among those who compose spontaneous verse—Vaṅgīsa; one who is foremost among those who have gone forth out of faith—Raṭṭhapāla, etc. The Bhikkhunī Sangha is headed by two chief bhikkhunīs: Khemā, who is foremost in wisdom, and Uppalavaṇṇā, who is foremost in psychic powers. But there is also a nun who excels in mastery over the discipline—Paṭācārā; one foremost in energy—Soṇā; one foremost in the recollection of past lives—Bhaddā Kapilānī, etc. Among the laymen there is a chief patron—Anāthapiṇḍika; a foremost preacher—Citta the householder; one foremost in attracting a retinue—Hatthaka of Āḷavi, etc. And among the laywomen there is a chief patroness—Visākhā; one foremost in learning—Khujjuttarā; one foremost in spreading lovingkindness, Sāmāvatī, etc.

The canonical chapter on the great disciples is extremely terse, mentioning only the category and the name of the disciple appointed as preeminent in that sphere. It is to the Pāli commentaries, and in particular to the commentary on the Etadaggavagga, that we must turn to learn the background to these appointments. Such commentarial accounts certainly stem from a later period than the suttas, but although they betray their later origins with their profusion of legend and hyperbole, they indicate clearly enough that the appointments related in the canon itself in each case consummate a process of spiritual growth that began long ago in the dim recesses of the past.

Each story, though differing in details, conforms to the same paradigm. During the Dispensation of a past Buddha a certain supporter of his sees him designate one of his disciples as preeminent in a particular field. Rather than strive for immediate attainment of the supramundane path under that Buddha, the devotee forms an aspiration (*patthanā*, *abhinīhāra*) to attain, under a future Buddha, the same post of preeminence as that to which the great disciple was assigned. To prepare for the announcement of this aspiration, the devotee makes abundant offerings to the Buddha and his Sangha, pays homage at the Master's feet, and then declares his or her heart's resolve. The Blessed One then directs his mind into the future and sees, with his knowledge of omniscience, that the aspiration will succeed under a future Buddha to be named Gotama. Thereupon he gives the disciple the prediction (*veyyākaraṇa*) that the aspiration will be fulfilled. In the case of the two chief disciples, Sāriputta and Mahāmoggallāna, the initial aspiration was made under the past Buddha Anomadassī, the eighteenth Buddha preceding Gotama; in the case of the other great disciples, it was made under the Buddha Padumuttara, the fifteenth Buddha of antiquity.

After forming the aspiration and receiving the prediction, the aspirant to great discipleship must devote successive lives to the accumulation of the merits and knowledge necessary for its fulfillment. This requires the assiduous practice of ten sublime virtues called the *pāramī*, the Pāli counterpart of the *pāramitā* of Sanskrit Buddhism. The Pāli sources enumerate ten pāramī: giving, virtue, renunciation, wisdom, energy, patience, truthfulness, determination, loving-kindness, and equanimity.[7] While the Mahāyāna systems regard the practice of the six pāramitā as the specific chore of the bodhisattvas, the candidates for supreme Buddhahood, later Theravāda doctrine (as represented by the Pāli commentaries) considers them as in some measure obligatory for all aspirants to enlightenment, whether as supreme Buddhas, *paccekabuddhas*, or arahant disciples.[8]

The difference between these three classes of enlightened beings concerns the length of time the pāramīs must be fulfilled and the demands involved in bringing them to perfection. Candidates for supreme Buddhahood must practice the pāramī for a minimum of four incalculables (*asaṅkheyya*) and one hundred thousand aeons, and must fulfill them in three degrees of severity: ordinary, superior, and supreme. Candidates for the enlightenment of a paccekabuddha must fulfill the pāramī for two incalculables and one hundred thousand aeons. In the case of arahant disciples the requirements vary considerably depending on the mode in which the final goal is to be realized. Those who aspire to be chief disciples must practice them for one incalculable and one hundred thousand aeons; candidates for great discipleship, for one hundred thousand aeons; and candidates for arahantship of lesser stature, for a correspondingly lesser period of time.[9]

This stipulation helps us to understand one particularly striking feature which runs through many of the biographical sketches that we will encounter in this volume: the astonishing speed and suddenness with which the great disciples attain realization. The wanderer Sāriputta, for example, on his first meeting with a Buddhist monk, became a stream-enterer while listening to a four-line stanza. Mahākaccāna, while still a court brahmin, attained arahantship at the end of a discourse by the Buddha. The royal consort Khemā attained arahantship even while still wearing her regal attire. At first impulse one might be tempted to dismiss such rapid attainments as just another example of hagiographic fervor, but when we take the saṁsāric background into account we can then see that such instances of "sudden enlightenment" are by no means as fortuitous as they might appear. Their abrupt occurrence is not a defiance of the normal laws of spiritual growth but the culmination of a long, slow process of prior preparation—spread out over countless lives against a vast cosmic backdrop—that nurtured all the requisites of enlightenment to maturity. It was because the disciples brought along, unknown even to themselves, such rich accumulations of merit and wisdom from their past existences that their initial encounter with the Buddha and his Dhamma could prove so immediately efficacious.

THE PRESENT BOOK

The present book is a collection of biographical profiles, of varying length, of twenty-four eminent disciples of the Buddha: one authored by the late Venerable Nyanaponika Thera (the life of Sāriputta), one by myself (the life of Mahākaccāna), the others all by Hellmuth Hecker.[10] While we aim to be as informative as the scope of this volume will allow, our underlying purpose is not so much to weave together reams of factual data as it is to provide a source of inspiration and edification for those devoted to the spiritual ideals of early Buddhism. Our profiles rarely attempt to evaluate the various accounts of the disciples' lives from an objective standpoint in order to distinguish fact from pious fiction, and thus we make no pretense to unimpeachable historical authenticity. The approach we have adopted places the author's perspective within the material, as that of an empathetic witness and advocate, rather than outside it as a disinterested scholar and judge. Whether or not all the events recorded in the texts actually occurred in the way they are reported is for us of less importance than the insights our sources give us into how the early Buddhist community viewed its models of the spiritual life. Thus, instead of attempting to sift through the material from a historicist point of view, we have recorded exactly what the texts themselves tell us about the great disciples and their careers, linking together the disconnected source citations with our own reflections and comments.

The proper way to approach this book, then, is as an exercise in contemplation rather than as an enterprise of objective scholarship. The Buddha says that contemplation of the noble disciples is an essential part of the meditative life. It is an aspect of the contemplation of the Sangha (*saṅghānussati*), one of the six recollections he frequently recommended to his followers.[11] To contemplate the noble ones, who broke the bonds of egotism and reached the heights of purity and wisdom, is a great encouragement for those who still find themselves far from deliverance. By their example these exalted persons inspire us with confidence in the emancipating power of the Dhamma. Their lives demonstrate to us that the spiritual ideals posited in the Teaching are not mere fantasy but can be achieved by real human beings struggling against the same human infirmities that we find within ourselves. When we study their lives we see that those great disciples had begun as ordinary human beings like ourselves, beset by the same hindrances, the same difficulties, that beset us. But by placing trust in the Buddha and his Teaching and by wholehearted application to the practice of the path they could surmount all the limitations we blandly take for granted and rise to a dimension of true spiritual nobility.

In the pages that follow we will explore the careers and characters of these great Buddhist disciples, who stand at the very fountainhead of the entire Buddhist tradition. We will examine their past-life backgrounds and early experiences, their struggles for enlightenment, their attainments and teachings, their activities as members of the Buddha's retinue, and (when known) the manner of their death. All this is just as much a part of the Buddhist heritage as the formal doctrines and practices of Buddhism: not mere fragments of ancient history, dead and vapid, but a living and luminous legacy that has come down to us at this critical juncture of human history, when our very survival hinges on the capacity for self-transcendence of the kind that these disciples so vividly demonstrate by their lives.

The principal criterion on which we relied in selecting disciples for study was their spiritual stature and prominence within the Dispensation. This criterion, however, had to be balanced by another factor which severely limited our choices, namely, the availability of relevant source material. Contrary to expectations based on present-day attitudes, the amount of biographical data the classical texts contain on a particular disciple is not always proportional to his or her spiritual eminence and role in the Buddha's ministry. The Buddha's circle of great disciples included monks and nuns, laymen and laywomen, who are extolled most highly by the Master, yet about whom hardly any noteworthy information has been handed down. To take but one example: the Venerable Upāli was the chief specialist in the Vinaya, the monastic discipline, and the monk responsible for the codification of the original *Vinaya Piṭaka*, the Compilation of Discipline, at the First Buddhist Council; yet the biographical information that has been preserved about him would barely fill a page. The problem of sparse source material becomes even more acute when we turn to the women disciples, as I will discuss at greater length below. But with the men as well, once we leave the circle of monks whose lives intersected most closely with the Buddha's, the accounts become terse even to the point of silence. Apparently, with their insight sharpened by the contemplation of the non-self nature of all phenomena, the ancient Buddhists were not particularly keen on compiling biographies of "selfless persons."

Despite this formidable limitation, by combing the canonical texts and commentaries we were able to collect sufficient material for biographical studies of twenty-four disciples. We begin with six chapters on elder bhikkhus or monks: Sāriputta and Mahāmoggallāna, the two chief disciples, who shared most fully the Buddha's burden of establishing the Dispensation through the forty-five years of his ministry; Mahākassapa, who became the de facto leader of the Sangha after the Master's demise and whose foresight ensured that the Dispensation would survive; Ānanda, the Buddha's cousin and personal attendant, whose prodigious memory enabled him to preserve the vast treasures of the Dhamma and protect it from the ravages of time; Anuruddha, another cousin of the Buddha, who excelled in the exercise of the divine eye, the faculty of supernormal vision; and Mahākaccāna, the foremost disciple in the detailed analysis of the Master's brief utterances. Although, in two or more of these biographies, accounts of the same incidents are sometimes repeated—for example, the early careers of Sāriputta and Moggallāna, and the preliminaries to the First Council in the lives of Mahākassapa and Ānanda—we have retained these repetitions in order to keep each individual biography intact. Such repetition also serves to highlight the same incident from the personal perspectives of the different disciples involved and thus offers us a more complete picture of events.

The next chapter is a study of twelve outstanding women disciples, including both bhikkhunīs and laywomen. A sensitive reader might protest that by relegating all the women disciples to a single chapter, while devoting nine chapters to male disciples, the authors have shown an unfair sense of gender balance. To this complaint I, as editor, can only reply that the lack of proportion in the treatment of the male and female disciples does not stem from any bias on the part of the authors but reflects the distribution of material in the sources. While we would have liked to include studies of individual women comparable in depth and detail to the studies of the men, the material seldom lent itself to anything fuller than short sketches focusing on the events that led the women to seek refuge in the Buddha and their experiences of awakening. Sometimes, sadly, not even that much material was at hand. For example, Uppalavaṇṇā was the second chief disciple in the Bhikkhunī Sangha, yet her biographical sketch (in the commentaries) consists almost entirely of a long story of a previous life—straining on contemporary sensibilities—followed by a few terse paragraphs on her historical life as a nun in the Buddhist Order. The chapter on women disciples also includes one laywoman who did not reach any stage of noble attainment. This is Mallikā, the chief queen of King Pasenadi of Kosala. Although Mallikā did not attain stream-entry, and by reason of one bizarre moral lapse was even briefly reborn in hell, she was one of the most deeply devoted of the Buddha's supporters whose conduct was in all other respects exemplary. The nun Isidāsī, whose story concludes the chapter, was probably not a direct disciple of the Buddha, as internal evidence suggests her poem may have been composed even a century after the Master's demise; but as her story is found in the canonical *Therīgāthā,* and is of intrinsic interest, we have included it in this volume.

The chapter on the women disciples is followed by a portrait of a bhikkhu who does not rank among the eighty great disciples but whose life story is still of almost mythical stature. This is the monk Aṅgulimāla. In his early years he had been a serial killer of the cruelest and most brutal kind, but through the intercession of the Buddha he was converted from a life of crime to a life of sanctity and became the virtual "patron saint" of pregnant women. Next we will study the life and achievements of the Buddha's chief patron, the householder Anāthapiṇḍika, who offered the Buddha his favorite monastic residence and who represents in many respects the ideal lay Buddhist. Finally we will conclude our survey with a series of short sketches of four disciples, including the other prominent lay disciple, Citta the householder, whose understanding of the Dhamma and skills in meditation won the admiration of many monks.

SOURCES

The principal source from which we have drawn material for our portraits of the great disciples is the Pāli Canon, the scriptural collection of Theravāda Buddhism, preserved in the Middle Indo-Aryan language now known as Pāli. This collection consists of three "baskets" or compilations: the *Sutta Piṭaka* or Compilation of Discourses, the *Vinaya Piṭaka* or Compilation of Discipline, and the *Abhidhamma Piṭaka* or Compilation of Philosophical Treatises.[12] This last compilation, consisting of technical tracts of psycho-philosophical analysis, was almost completely irrelevant to our purposes, while the Vinaya Piṭaka was of use primarily on account of its background stories to the disciplinary rules rather than its own proper subject matter, the rules and regulations of the monastic order.

The Sutta Piṭaka has thus turned out to be the foundation stone of our biographical studies. This compilation consists of four major collections: the *Dīgha Nikāya* or Long Discourses; the *Majjhima Nikāya* or Middle Length Discourses; the *Saṁyutta Nikāya* or Connected Discourses, short suttas in fifty-six chapters united by a common theme; and the *Aṅguttara Nikāya* or Numerical Discourses, short suttas structured according to a numerical pattern ranging from the Ones to the Elevens. It is in the Ones Division of the Aṅguttara Nikāya that we find the *Etadaggavagga*, the "This-One-Is-Chief" Chapter, where the Buddha designates the eighty foremost disciples.

Besides the four main collections the Sutta Piṭaka includes a fifth collection called the *Khuddaka Nikāya*, literally the Minor Collection, which yet turns out to be the most voluminous portion of this "basket." Within this miscellaneous collection of texts we find four works especially relevant to the lives of the great disciples. Two of these form a pair: the *Theragāthā,* the Verses of the Elder Monks, consisting of 1279 verses ascribed to 264 bhikkhus; and the *Therīgāthā,* the Verses of the Elder Nuns, consisting of 494 verses ascribed to seventy-three bhikkhunīs. In these works the elders of the ancient Buddhist Sangha relate in verse the events that led them to a life of renunciation, their attainment of enlightenment, and their insights into the Dhamma. Although many of these verses are purely didactic (and have parallels elsewhere in the canon) a significant portion are at least vaguely autobiographical, while even the didactic verses afford us glimpses into the personality of the disciple who utters them.

The third work of the Minor Collection that contributed to this book is the *Jātaka* collection. While the canonical Jātaka book consists solely of verses barely intelligible when read alone, the full Jātaka collection (found in the Jātaka Commentary) contains 547 "birth stories" in which the canonical verses are embedded. These stories relate the exploits and adventures of the Bodhisatta, the future Buddha Gotama, during his past existences as he fared from life to life accumulating the virtues that would flower with his attainment of Buddhahood. Nurtured by the luxuriant Indian imagination, these tales draw fable and fantasy into the service of the Dhamma as a medium for conveying lessons in Buddhist ethics. The stories become relevant to a study of the great disciples through their preambles and epilogues. The preamble relates the incident in the Buddha's ministry which elicted from him the story to follow; often these incidents mirror events from the distant past that involved previous incarnations of his prominent disciples. In the epilogue the Buddha identifies the characters from the past birth with those dwelling in his present milieu (e.g., "Moggallāna was the elephant of those days, Sāriputta was the monkey, and I myself was the wise partridge"), thereby enabling us to discover the saṁsāric background of the disciples.

A fourth book of the Minor Collection, being entirely in verse and of late origins, has been used sparingly. This is the *Apadāna*, an anthology in which the monks and nuns who gained arahantship under the Buddha speak about their meritorious deeds in past lives and, occasionally, about their attainment of liberation in their last existence. The work has two main divisions: the *Thera-apadāna* or Tales of the Elder Monks (fify-five chapters with ten tales each), and a much shorter *Therī-apadāna* or Tales of the Elder Nuns (four chapters with ten tales each).

The next body of source material we have drawn upon, second in importance only to the canon, is the Pāli commentaries. Among the numerous commentaries to the canon, four were of special value to our undertaking, apart from the Jātaka Commentary mentioned just above, which is in a class of its own. One is the commentary to the Etadaggavagga of the Aṅguttara Nikāya, found in the *Manorathapūraṇī*, the complete commentary to the Aṅguttara. This is ascribed to Ācariya Buddhaghosa, the greatest of the Pāli commentators, who based his work on the ancient Sinhala commentaries (no longer extant) that had been preserved at the Mahāvihāra (the Great Monastery) in Anurādhapura, Sri Lanka. The commentary to this chapter gives biographical reports on each of the disciples declared preeminent in a particular sphere. Each story is molded upon a similar pattern. It begins with the occasion in the past existence when the disciple made his or her original aspiration to chief discipleship, highlights incidents from a few past lives when he or she performed some deed of exalted merit, and then relates the events in the last life that brought the disciple into contact with the Buddha. Usually the story culminates in their appointment to the post of great disciple, but occasionally it continues beyond to relate incidents in their career as members of the Master's entourage.

Two other commentaries of biographical interest are those to the *Theragāthā* and *Therīgāthā.* These are both entitled *Paramatthadīpanī* and are attributed to Ācariya Dhammapāla of Badaratittha, who worked in South India, perhaps a century later than Buddhaghosa; they are evidently based on older documents and reflect the exegetical principles of the Mahāvihāra. These two commentaries partly replicate the material in the commentary to the Aṅguttara Nikāya (sometimes with interesting variations), incorporate substantial excerpts from the *Apadāna*, and also explain the incidents that prompted the disciples to utter the particular verses assigned to them.

Still a fourth commentary that proved to be a mine of useful material, even though often fanciful, was the Dhammapada Commentary. The authorship of this work is traditionally ascribed to Buddhaghosa, though this claim is sometimes questioned by present-day scholars. Underlying this commentary is the premise that each verse (or string of verses) found in the *Dhammapada* was uttered by the Buddha in response to a particular incident. The purpose of the commentary is to narrate the course of events that prompted the Buddha to speak that verse, but often it takes us back in time beyond the immediate background incident to the whole complex web of circumstances that culminated in the verse. Sometimes the commentary relates a cycle of background stories that even extends into previous lives, thereby revealing the kammic background to the happenings that unfolded around the Buddha and his disciples.

A Note on Method

It should be stressed that apart from the background stories in the commentaries, none of the source material at our disposal contains anything even approximating connected, coherent biographies of the great disciples. Indeed, in the entire Pāli Canon we do not find even a connected biography of the Buddha; the earliest attempt at this, in the Pāli tradition, seems to be the *Jātaka-nidāna*, the introduction to the Jātaka Commentary. The commentary to the Etadaggavagga, which is our fullest source of biographical information on the disciples, tends to place greater emphasis on their past saṁsāric history than on their careers under the Buddha, and other commentaries offer at most explanations of particular incidents rather than of entire lives. Thus the biographical profiles that make up this book had to be constructed piecemeal from the bricks and beams of the textual heritage, which we have attempted to fashion into orderly wholes with the cement of our own personal reflections and interpretative comments.

Further, to make our task even more difficult, the redactors of the Pāli Canon did not structure their narratives according to a principle of continuous flow, such as we would expect from a modern biography or even a news report. Being participants in an essentially oral tradition rather than a literary one, they preferred to treat events in a staccato manner, subordinating fluid literary grace to the pedagogical and mnemonic demands of their discipline. We can only hope that the narratives we have fashioned out of the abrupt, discontinuous flashes of events recorded in the ancient texts do not show too many obtrusive seams.

In our treatment of the material at our disposal we have tried to be as comprehensive as is realistically possible within the limits of a single volume such as this. We did, however, rely upon certain specific criteria to govern the selection of events to be included. In all likelihood these are basically the same as the criteria that the redactors of the Pāli Canon looked to when compiling the texts: namely, to select those incidents and anecdotes which most clearly convey a vivid picture of the disciple's character as a model for the Buddhist community to emulate, or which reveal distinctive aspects of his or her approach to the practice and understanding of the Dhamma. We also wanted to include some of the material on the past lives of the disciple; for although this is almost certainly legendary, it does disclose the way the early Buddhist community perceived the formative influences at work in that disciple's life. But as this material often had to be drawn from later texts like the Apadāna and Jātakas, we did not want to include so much that it would drive the more historically based material from the ancient Nikāyas into the background. The verses from the *Theragāthā* and *Therīgāthā* were also used. Sometimes, in a given biography, these are discussed all together in a section of their own, sometimes they are integrated into the general profile.

This book can be used most effectively if the biographical profiles are read for the purpose for which they were originally written, namely, for spiritual inspiration and edification. They should not be read in the same frame of mind with which one reads a novel. It is suggested that the reader should not try to read more than one chapter per day. One should "make friends" with the particular disciple one is learning about, reflect on his or her life and teachings, and seek to discover the universal implications that life story has for present-day humanity. Only on the next day, at the earliest, should one take up the next chapter. As these accounts can cast a spell of fascination over the mind, it is important to curb one's curiosity and repeatedly remind oneself why one is reading this collection. The proper reason should be: not for the sake of interesting anecdotes and romantic images of a bygone period, but to uplift one's spiritual vision with the living portraits of those who fulfilled the early Buddhist ideals of human perfection.

CHAPTER 1

SĀRIPUTTA

The Marshal of the Dhamma

Nyanaponika Thera

PROLOGUE

IN MANY TEMPLES OF SRI LANKA you will find, on either side of the Buddha image, the statues of two monks. Their robes are draped over one shoulder and they stand in the attitude of reverence, with joined palms. Quite often there are a few flowers at their feet, laid there by some pious devotee.

If you ask who they are, you will be told that they are the Enlightened One's two chief disciples, the arahants Sāriputta and Mahāmoggallāna. They stand in the positions they occupied in life, Sāriputta on the Buddha's right, Mahāmoggallāna on his left. When the great *stūpa* at Sāñchi was opened up in the middle of the last century, the relic chamber was found to contain two stone receptacles; the one to the north held the bodily relics of Mahāmoggallāna, while that on the south enclosed those of Sāriputta. Thus they had lain while the centuries rolled past and the history of two thousand years and more played out the drama of impermanence in human life. The Roman Empire rose and fell, the glories of ancient Greece became a distant memory; new religions wrote their names, often with blood and fire, on the changing face of the earth, only to mingle at last with legends of Thebes and Babylon; and gradually the tides of commerce shifted the great centers of civilization from East to West, while generations that had never heard the Teaching of the Buddha arose and passed away. But all the time that the ashes of the holy disciples lay undisturbed, forgotten in the land that gave them birth, their memory was held dear wherever the Buddha's message spread, and the record of their lives was passed down from one generation to another, first by word of mouth, then in the written pages of the Buddhist Tipiṭaka, the most voluminous and detailed scripture of any religion. Next to the Enlightened One himself, it is these two disciples of his who stand highest in the veneration of Buddhists in the Theravāda lands. Their names are as inseparable from the annals of Buddhism as that of the Buddha himself. If it has come about that in the course of time many legends have been woven into the tradition of their lives, this is but the natural outcome of the devotion that has always been felt for them.

And that high esteem was fully justified. Few religious teachers have been so well served by their immediate disciples as was the Buddha. This you will see as you read these pages, for they tell the story of one of the two greatest of them, the Venerable Sāriputta, who was second only to the Buddha in the depth and range of his understanding and in his ability to teach the doctrine of deliverance. In the Tipiṭaka there is no connected account of his life, but it can be pieced together from the various incidents, scattered throughout the canonical texts and commentaries, in which he figures. Some of them are more than incidents, for his life is so closely interwoven with the life and ministry of the Buddha that he plays an essential part in it, and on a number of occasions it is Sāriputta himself who takes the leading role—as skilled preceptor and exemplar, as kind and considerate friend, as guardian of the welfare of the bhikkhus under his charge, as faithful repository of his Master's doctrine, the function which earned him the title of *Dhammasenāpati*, Marshal of the Dhamma. And always as himself, a man unique in his patience and steadfastness, modest and upright in thought, word, and deed, a man to whom one act of kindness was a thing to be remembered with gratitude so long as life endured. Even among the arahants, those freed from all defilements of passion and delusion, he shone like the full moon in a starry sky.

This then is the man, of profound intellect and sublime nature, a true disciple of the Great Teacher, whose story we have set down, to the best of our ability, in the pages that follow. If you, the reader, can gather from this imperfect record something of the qualities of a perfected human being, fully liberated and raised to the highest level of realization, and of how such a person acts and speaks and comports himself toward his fellows, and if the reading of it gives you strength and faith in the assurance of *what a human being may become*, then our work has been worthwhile and is fully rewarded.

THE QUEST FOR THE DHAMMA

EARLY LIFE

The story begins at two brahmanical villages in India, called Upatissa and Kolita, which lay not far from the city of Rājagaha.[1] Before our Buddha had appeared in the world, a brahmin woman named Rūpasārī, living in Upatissa village,[2] conceived; and so too, on the same day at Kolita village, did another brahmin woman whose name was Moggallī. The two families were closely connected, having been friends with one another for seven generations. From the first day of their pregnancy the families gave due care to the mothers-to-be, and after ten months both women gave birth to boys, on the same day. On the name-giving day Rūpasārī's child received the name Upatissa, as he was a son of the foremost family of that village; and for the same reason Moggallī's son was named Kolita.

When the boys grew up they were educated and acquired mastery of all the sciences. Each of them had a following of five hundred brahmin youths, and when they went to the river or park for sport and recreation, Upatissa used to go with five hundred palanquins, and Kolita with five hundred horse carriages.

Now at Rājagaha there was an annual event called the Hilltop Festival. Seats were arranged for both youths and they sat together to witness the celebrations. When there was an occasion for laughter, they laughed; when the spectacle was exciting, they became excited; and they paid their fees for the extra shows. In this manner they enjoyed the festival for a second day. On the third day, however, strange thoughts cast their shadows across their hearts, and they could no longer laugh or share in the excitement. As they sat there, watching the plays and dances, for just a moment the specter of human mortality revealed itself to their inner vision, and once they had caught a glimpse of it their attitude could never again be the same. For each, this somber mood gradually crystallized into a compelling question: "What is there to look at here? Before these people have reached a hundred years they will all be dead. Shouldn't we go seek a teaching of deliverance?"

It was with such thoughts in mind that on this third day they sat through the festival. Kolita noticed that his friend seemed pensive and withdrawn and asked him: "What is the matter, my dear Upatissa? Today you are not happy and joyous as you were on the other days, but you seem to be troubled about something. Tell me, what is on your mind?"

"My dear Kolita, I have been thinking that there is no benefit at all for us in enjoying these hollow shows. Instead of wasting my time on such festivals, what I really ought to do is to seek a path to deliverance from the entire round of rebirths. But you too, Kolita, seem to be discontented."

And Kolita replied: "My thoughts are exactly the same as yours." When he knew that his friend shared his inclination, Upatissa said: "That was a good thought of ours. However, for those who seek a teaching of deliverance there is only one thing to do: to leave home and become ascetics. But under whom shall we live the ascetic life?"

At that time, there lived at Rājagaha a wandering ascetic (*paribbājaka*) named Sañjaya, who had a great following of pupils. Deciding to take ordination under him, Upatissa and Kolita approached him, each with his own following of five hundred brahmin youths, and all of them received ordination from Sañjaya. And from the time of their ordination under him, Sañjaya's reputation and support increased abundantly.

Within a short time the two friends had learned Sañjaya's entire doctrine. They then went to him and asked: "Master, does your doctrine go so far only, or is there something beyond?"

Sañjaya replied: "So far only does it go. You know it completely."

Hearing this, they thought to themselves: "If that is the case, it is useless to continue the holy life under him. We have gone forth from home to seek a teaching of deliverance, but under him we cannot find it. India is vast, and if we wander through villages, towns, and cities we shall certainly find a master who can show us the path we are seeking." And from then on, whenever they heard that there were wise ascetics or brahmins in this place or that, they went to meet them and learn their doctrines. There was none, however, who could answer all their questions, while they were able to reply to those who questioned them.

Having thus traveled through the whole of India, they returned to Rājagaha. There they made an agreement that whichever of them should find the Deathless first would inform the other. It was a pact of brotherhood, born of the deep friendship between the two young men.

Sometime after they had made that agreement, the Blessed One, the Buddha, set out for Rājagaha. He had, shortly before, completed the first rainy season retreat following his Enlightenment, and now the time had arrived for wandering and preaching. Before his Enlightenment he had promised King Bimbisāra that he would return to Rājagaha after attaining his goal, and now he set forth to fulfill that promise. So in stages the Blessed One journeyed from Gayā to Rājagaha, and having received from King Bimbisāra the Bamboo Grove Monastery (Veḷuvana), he took up residence there.

Among the first sixty-one arahants whom the Master had sent forth to proclaim the message of deliverance to the world was an elder named Assaji. Assaji had belonged to the group of five ascetics who had attended upon the Bodhisatta while he was engaged in his ascetic practices, and he was also one of the first five disciples. One morning when Assaji was walking on alms round in Rājagaha, Upatissa saw him calmly wending his way from door to door with his bowl in hand.[3] Struck by Assaji's dignified and serene appearance, Upatissa thought: "Never before have I seen such a monk. He must be one of those who are arahants, or who are on the way to arahantship. Should I not approach him and question him?" But then he considered: "It is not the proper time now for putting questions to this monk, as he is going for alms through the streets. I had better follow behind him after the manner of supplicants." And he did so.

Then, when the elder had finished his alms round and was seeking a quiet place to eat his meal, Upatissa spread out his own sitting cloth and offered the seat to the elder. The Elder Assaji sat down and took his meal, after which Upatissa served him with water from his own water-container, and in this way performed toward Assaji the duties of a pupil to a teacher.

After they had exchanged the usual courteous greetings, Upatissa said: "Serene are your features, friend. Pure and bright is your complexion. Under whom have you gone forth as an ascetic? Who is your teacher and whose doctrine do you profess?"

Assaji replied: "There is, friend, a great recluse, a scion of the Sākyas, who has gone forth from the Sākya clan. I have gone forth under him, the Blessed One. That Blessed One is my teacher and it is his Dhamma that I profess."

"What does the venerable one's master teach, what does he proclaim?"

Questioned thus, the Elder Assaji thought to himself: "These wandering ascetics are opposed to the Buddha's teaching. I shall show him how profound this teaching is." So he said: "I am but new to the training, friend. It is not long since I went forth from home, and I came but recently to this doctrine and discipline. I cannot explain the Dhamma in detail to you."

The wanderer replied: "I am called Upatissa, friend. Please tell me according to your ability, be it much or little. It will be my task to penetrate its meaning by way of a hundred or a thousand methods." And he added:

Be it little or much that you can tell,
The meaning only, please proclaim to me!
To know the meaning is my sole desire;
Of no use to me are many words.

In response, the Elder Assaji uttered this stanza:

Of those things that arise from a cause,
The Tathāgata has told the cause,
And also what their cessation is:
This is the doctrine of the Great Recluse.[4]

Upon hearing the first two lines, there arose in the wanderer Upatissa the dust-free, stainless vision of the Dhamma—the first glimpse of the Deathless, the path of stream-entry—and to the ending of the last two lines he already listened as a stream-enterer.

At once he knew: "Here the means of deliverance is to be found!" And he said to the elder: "Do not enlarge upon this exposition of the Dhamma, venerable sir. This much will suffice. But where does our Master live?"

"In the Bamboo Grove, wanderer."

"Then please go ahead, venerable sir. I have a friend with whom I have made an agreement to share the Dhamma. I shall inform him, and together we shall follow you and come into the Master's presence." Upatissa then prostrated himself at the elder's feet and went back to the park of the wanderers.

Kolita saw him approaching and immediately knew: "Today my friend's appearance is quite changed. Surely, he must have found the Deathless." And when he inquired, Upatissa replied: "Yes, friend, the Deathless has been found!" He told him all about his meeting with the Elder Assaji, and when he recited the stanza he had heard, Kolita too was established in the fruit of stream-entry.

"Where, my dear, does the Master live?" he asked.

"I learned from our teacher, the Elder Assaji, that he lives at the Bamboo Grove."

"Then let us go, Upatissa, and see the Master," said Kolita.

But Sāriputta was one who always respected his teacher, and therefore he said to his friend: "First, my dear, we should go to our teacher, the wanderer Sañjaya, and tell him that we have found the Deathless. If he can grasp it, he will penetrate to the truth. And even if he does not, he may, out of confidence in us, come with us to see the Master; and hearing the Buddha's teaching, he will attain to the penetration of the path and fruition."

So both of them went to Sañjaya and said: "O teacher! A Buddha has appeared in the world! His doctrine is well proclaimed and his community of monks is following the right path. Let us go and see the Master."

"What are you saying, my dear?" Sañjaya exclaimed. And refusing to go with them, he offered to appoint them as co-leaders of his community, speaking of the gain and fame such a position would bring them. But the two wanderers refused to be deflected from their decision, saying: "Oh, we would not mind always remaining pupils. But you, teacher, must know for yourself whether to go or not."

Then Sañjaya thought: "If they know so much, they will not listen to what I say." And realizing this, he replied: "You may go, then, but I cannot."

"Why not, teacher?"

"I am a teacher of many. If I were to revert to the state of a disciple, it would be as if a huge water tank were to change into a small pitcher. I cannot live the life of a pupil now."

"Do not think like that, teacher!" they urged.

"Let it be, my dear. You may go, but I cannot."

"O teacher! When a Buddha has appeared in the world, people flock to him in large crowds and pay homage to him, carrying incense and flowers. We too shall go there. And then what will happen to you?"

To which Sañjaya replied: "What do you think, my pupils: are there more fools in this world, or more wise people?"

"Fools there are many, O teacher, and the wise are few."

"If that is so, my friends, then the wise ones will go to the wise recluse Gotama, and the fools will come to me, the fool. You may go now, but I shall not."

So the two friends left, saying: "You will come to understand your mistake, teacher!" And after they had gone there was a split among Sañjaya's pupils, and his monastery became almost empty. Seeing his place deserted, Sañjaya vomited hot blood. Five hundred of his disciples had left along with Upatissa and Kolita, out of whom 250 returned to Sañjaya. With the remaining 250, and their own following, the two friends arrived at the Bamboo Grove Monastery.

There the Master, seated among the fourfold assembly,[5] was preaching the Dhamma, and when he saw the two wanderers coming he addressed the monks: "These two friends, Upatissa and Kolita, who are now approaching, will be my two chief disciples, an excellent pair."

Having arrived, the friends bowed low in homage to the Blessed One and sat down at one side. When they were seated they said to the Master: "May we obtain, Lord, the going forth under the Blessed One, may we obtain the higher ordination."

And the Blessed One said: "Come, bhikkhus! Well proclaimed is the Dhamma. Now live the life of purity to make an end of suffering." This alone served as the ordination of these venerable ones.

Then the Master continued his discourse, taking the individual temperaments of the listeners into consideration; and with the exception of Upatissa and Kolita all of them attained to arahantship. But on that occasion the two friends did not attain the higher paths and fruits. For them a longer period of preparatory training was needed in order that they could fulfill their personal destiny, that of serving as the Blessed One's chief disciples.

After their entry into the Buddhist Order, the texts always refer to Upatissa by the name Sāriputta, while Kolita is always called Mahāmoggallāna. For his intensive training Moggallāna went to live at a village near

Magadha named Kallavālaputta, on which he depended for alms. On the seventh day after his ordination, when he was engaged in intense meditation, he was troubled by fatigue and torpor. But spurred on by the Master, he dispelled his fatigue, and while listening to the Master expound the meditation subject of the elements (*dhātukammaṭṭhāna*), he won the three higher paths and reached the acme of a chief disciple's perfection.

But the Venerable Sāriputta continued to stay near the Master at a cave called the Boar's Shelter (*sūkarakhata-leṇa*), depending on Rājagaha for his alms. Half a month after his ordination the Blessed One gave a discourse to Sāriputta's nephew, the wandering ascetic Dīghanakha.[6] Sāriputta was standing behind the Master, fanning him. While listening to the discourse and following it attentively with his mind, as though sharing the food prepared for another, Sāriputta reached the acme of "knowledge pertaining to a disciple's perfection" and attained to arahantship together with the four analytical knowledges (*paṭisambhidā-ñāṇa*).[7] His nephew, at the end of the sermon, was established in the fruit of stream-entry.

Now it may be asked: "Did not Sāriputta possess great wisdom? And if so, why did he attain arahantship later than Moggallāna?" The answer, according to the commentaries, is because of the greatness of the preparations required. When poor people want to go anywhere they take to the road at once; but in the case of kings, extensive preparations must be made, and these require time. And so too is it in order to become the first chief disciple of a Buddha.

On that same day, when the evening shadows had lengthened, the Master called his disciples to assembly and bestowed upon the two elders the rank of chief disciples. At this, some monks were displeased and murmured among themselves: "The Master should have given the rank of chief disciples to those who were ordained first, that is, the group of five disciples; or if not to them, then either to the group of fifty-five bhikkhus headed by Yasa, or to the thirty of the auspicious group (*bhaddavaggiya*), or else to the three Kassapa brothers.[8] But passing over all these great elders, he has given it to those whose ordination was the very last of all."

The Master inquired about the subject of their talk. When they told him, he said: "I do not show preference, but give to each what he has aspired to. When, for instance, Aññā Koṇḍañña in a previous life gave alms nine times during a single harvest, he did not aspire to chief discipleship; his aspiration was to be the very first to penetrate to the highest state, arahantship. And so it came about. But many aeons ago, at the time of the Buddha Anomadassī, Sāriputta and Moggallāna made the aspiration for chief discipleship, and now the conditions for the fulfillment of that aspiration have ripened. Hence I have given them just what they aspired to, and did not do so out of preference."

THE ORIGINAL ASPIRATION

The Buddha's statement underscores a fundamental tenet of Buddhist thought: that who we are, and what we reap as our life's destiny, is not the product simply of our intentions and activities within the brief span of time that began with our physical birth, but reflects a deep wellspring of past experience accumulated in the beginningless round of rebirths, saṁsāra. Thus the story of Sāriputta, the great disciple, properly begins in the distant past, with events that have been preserved for us in the form of legend. Such legends, however, are not mere fictions spun by an excessively vibrant imagination. They are, rather, narrative representations of principles that are too profound and universal to be reduced to mere matters of historical fact, principles that can be adequately conveyed only by turning facts into sacred archetypes and archetypes into spiritual ideals.

This particular legend unfolds one incalculable period (*asaṅkheyya*) and one hundred thousand aeons in the past.[9] At that time the being who was to become the Venerable Sāriputta was born into a rich brahmin family and was given the name Sarada. At the same time the future Moggallāna was born into a wealthy householder family and was named Sirivaddhana. The two families were acquainted, and the boys became playmates and close friends.

On the death of his father, Sarada inherited the vast family fortune. But before long, reflecting in solitude on his own inevitable mortality, he decided to abandon all his property and go forth seeking a path to deliverance. Sarada approached his friend Sirivaddhana and invited him to join him on this quest, but Sirivaddhana, still too strongly attached to the world, refused. Sarada, however, was firm in his decision. He gave away all his wealth, left the household, and took up the life of a matted-hair ascetic. Quickly, and without difficulty, he mastered the mundane meditative attainments and supernormal powers and attracted to himself a band of disciples. Thus his hermitage gradually became home to a large community of ascetics.

At this time the Buddha Anomadassī—the eighteenth Buddha counting back from the present Buddha Gotama—had arisen in the world. One day, on emerging from meditative absorption, the Buddha Anomadassī cast his "net of knowledge" out upon the world and beheld the ascetic Sarada and his retinue. Realizing that a visit to this community would bring great benefits to many beings, he left behind his monks and journeyed to their hermitage alone. Sarada noticed the marks of physical excellence on the body of his visitor and at once understood that his guest was a Fully Enlightened One. He humbly offered him a seat of honor and provided him with a meal from the food gathered by his disciples.

Meanwhile the Buddha's monks had come to join him at the hermitage—one hundred thousand arahants free from all defilements, led by the two chief disciples, Nisabha and Anoma. To honor the Buddha the ascetic Sarada took a large canopy of flowers and, standing behind the Blessed One, held it over his head. The Master entered the attainment of cessation (*nirodhasamāpatti*)—the meditative state wherein perception, feeling, and other mental processes utterly cease. He remained absorbed in this state for a full week, while throughout that entire week Sarada stood behind him holding aloft the canopy of flowers.

At the end of the week the Buddha emerged from the attainment of cessation and requested his two chief disciples to give talks to the community of ascetics. When they had finished speaking he himself spoke, and at the end of his discourse all the ascetic pupils of Sarada attained arahantship and asked to be admitted to the Buddha's order of monks. Sarada, however, did not attain arahantship, nor any other stage of sanctity. For as he listened to the discourse of the chief disciple Nisabha, and observed his pleasing deportment, the aspiration arose in his mind to become the first chief disciple of a Buddha in the future. Thus, when the proceedings were finished, he approached the Buddha Anomadassī, prostrated himself at his feet, and declared: "Lord, as the fruit of the act of homage I performed toward you by holding the canopy of flowers over you for a week, I do not aspire for rulership over the gods, nor for the status of Mahābrahmā, nor for any other fruit but this: that in the future I might become the chief disciple of a Fully Enlightened One."

The Master thought, "Will his aspiration succeed?" And sending out his knowledge into the future, he saw that it would. Then he spoke to Sarada thus: "This aspiration of yours will not be barren. In the future, after an incalculable age and one hundred thousand aeons, a Buddha by the name of Gotama will arise in the world, and you will be his first chief disciple, the Marshal of the Dhamma, named Sāriputta."

After the Buddha left, Sarada went to his friend Sirivaddhana and urged him to make an aspiration to become the second chief disciple of the Buddha Gotama. Sirivaddhana had a lavish alms hall built and, after all the preparations were complete, invited the Master and his monks to come for an alms meal. For a full week Sirivaddhana provided the Buddha and the monks with their daily meal. At the end of the festivities, having offered costly robes to all the monks, he approached the Buddha and announced: "By the power of this merit, may I become the second chief disciple of the same Buddha under whom my friend Sarada will become the first chief disciple!" The Master looked into the future, and seeing that the aspiration would be fulfilled, he gave Sirivaddhana the prediction: he would become the second chief disciple of the Buddha Gotama, a monk of great power and might known by the name Moggallāna.

After the two friends had received their respective predictions, each devoted himself to good deeds in his own proper sphere. Sirivaddhana, as a lay devotee, looked after the needs of the Sangha and performed various works of charity. Sarada, as an ascetic, continued with his meditative life. On their deaths Sirivaddhana was reborn in a sense-sphere heavenly world, while Sarada, having mastered the meditative attainments and the divine abodes (*brahmavihāra*), was reborn in the Brahma-world.

SĀRIPUTTA IN THE *JĀTAKAS*

From this point on there is no continuous narrative of their activities, but at a certain point in their wandering through the cycle of birth and death the two friends must have crossed paths with another being who much earlier, at the feet of the twenty-fourth Buddha of antiquity, had vowed to win supreme Buddhahood. This was the Bodhisatta, the being who was to become the Buddha Gotama, the Enlightened One of our own historical era. The Jātaka stories record the deeds of the Bodhisatta in some five hundred and fifty of his former births, and in these stories Sāriputta plays a prominent role, appearing more often than any other disciple of the Buddha with the possible exception of Ānanda. Only a representative sampling of these stories can be considered here. Since the process of rebirth does not respect divisions between realms of existence but flows up from the animal realm to the human and celestial realms, and down from the heavens to the human and animal realms, we find that the specific forms of relationship between Sāriputta and the Bodhisatta vary from life to life. We may take these diverse relationships as the outline for our survey.

In several of their past births both the Bodhisatta and Sāriputta were animals. Once the Bodhisatta was a chief stag who had two sons, both of whom he instructed in the art of leadership. One son (Sāriputta) followed his father's advice and led his herd to prosperity; the other, who was to become the Buddha's jealous cousin Devadatta, spurned his father's advice in favor of his own ideas and thereby brought his herd to disaster (Jāt. 11). When the Bodhisatta was a royal goose his two young sons (Sāriputta and Moggallāna) tried to outrace the sun; when they grew weary and were about to collapse in midflight, the Bodhisatta came to their rescue (476). In a birth as a partridge the Bodhisatta was senior to his two friends, a monkey (Sāriputta) and an elephant (Moggallāna); thus he became their teacher and preceptor, a foretoken of their relationship in their final existence (37). The Bodhisatta again figures as a preceptor in the *Sasa Jātaka* (316), where he is a wise hare who teaches a monkey (Sāriputta), a jackal (Moggallāna), and an otter (Ānanda) the value of morality and generosity. When Sakka, king of the devas, comes to him in the guise of a hungry brahmin to test his resolve, the hare is ready to throw himself into a fire to provide the brahmin with a meal.

On several occasions the two future disciples rendered vital help to the Bodhisatta. When the Great Being, as a deer, was caught in a snare, his companions—a woodpecker (Sāriputta) and a tortoise (Moggallāna)—saved him by breaking the trap. Although the hunter (Devadatta) caught the tortoise, the other two animals came to his rescue and succeeded in freeing him (206). The Bodhisatta was not, however, always so fortunate, and the Jātakas record their share of tragedies. Thus in one birth story (438), when the Bodhisatta was a partridge who taught the Vedas to young brahmins, a wicked ascetic (Devadatta) killed him and made a meal of him. His friends, a lion (Sāriputta) and a tiger (Moggallāna), came to visit him, and on seeing a feather in the ascetic's beard, they understood the enormity of his deed. The lion wanted to show mercy, but the tiger slew the ascetic and threw his body in a pit. This incident already discloses a difference in temperament between the two disciples: Sāriputta, though mighty as a lion, is gentle and soft, while Moggallāna, though harmless in his last life as an enlightened monk, can still exhibit the fierceness of a tiger.

In other Jātakas one of the two—the Bodhisatta and Sāriputta—is human and the other an animal, and their roles as benefactor and beneficiary also undergo reversals. Thus we encounter the Bodhisatta as a war steed and Sāriputta as his warrior (23); the Bodhisatta as a peerless white elephant who enters the service of the king of Benares (Sāriputta) (122); the Bodhisatta as a partridge and Sāriputta as a wise ascetic who instructs him (277). But in other births the Bodhisatta is human and Sāriputta an animal. In one story, for example, the Bodhisatta is a hermit who rescues an evil prince (Devadatta) and three animals from a flood. The animals—a snake (Sāriputta), a rat (Moggallāna), and a parrot (Ānanda)—show their gratitude by offering the hermit hidden treasures, but the envious prince tries to have him executed (73).

Sometimes the future spiritual heroes were reborn in celestial form. Once, when the Bodhisatta was Sakka, Sāriputta and Moggallāna were respectively Canda the moon god and Suriya the sun god. Together with several other deities they visited a notorious miser and converted him to a life of generosity (450). Often it is the Bodhisatta who benefits the future disciples, but sometimes we see Sāriputta come to the Bodhisatta's aid. When they were both reborn as princes of the *nāgas*, semidivine serpents, the Bodhisatta was captured by a cruel brahmin who made him perform tricks in public. His elder brother, Sāriputta, set out in search of him and delivered him from this humiliating fate (543). When the Bodhisatta was the virtuous Prince Mahāpaduma, maligned by his step-mother for refusing her seductive advances, his father the king tried to have him hurled from a precipice; but Sāriputta, as a spirit of the mountain, caught him before he hit the ground and led him to safety (472).

Most often in the Jātakas the Bodhisatta and Sāriputta appear in human births. In such stories the Bodhisatta is invariably the hero, the supreme exemplar of virtue and wisdom, while Sāriputta appears as his friend, pupil, son, or brother, and often serves as his benefactor. In one life the Bodhisatta was a king and Sāriputta his charioteer (151). When they crossed paths with a chariot carrying a rival king (Ānanda), Sāriputta and the rival charioteer (Moggallāna) compared their respective kings' merits. The rival had to admit the superiority of Sāriputta's master, who ruled by bestowing benefits on both the good and the wicked while his own master rewarded the good and punished the wicked. In the influential *Khantivādī Jātaka* (313) the Bodhisatta, as the saintly "preacher of patience," is reviled and tortured by the wicked King Kālabu (Devadatta). After the king has severed the Bodhisatta's limbs to test his patience, the king's general (Sāriputta) bandages the Bodhisatta's wounds and begs him not to take revenge.

Often in the longer Jātakas the Bodhisatta enters upon the ascetic life, and Sāriputta usually joins him in this quest. Such an inclination would have been deeply implanted in the temperaments of both men, who in their last existence would consummate their spiritual careers only after going forth into homelessness. When the Bodhisatta was the chaplain's son Hatthipāla he was named the heir to the throne by the childless king. Recognizing the danger in worldly life, he decided to become an ascetic and was soon joined by his three brothers, the eldest of whom was the future Sāriputta (509). In the *Indriya Jātaka* (423) the Bodhisatta is an ascetic with seven chief disciples, six of whom, including the eldest

(Sāriputta), eventually leave him to establish their own hermitages, but Anusissa (Ānanda) remains behind as his attendant; this presages the relationship between the Buddha and Ānanda in their last existence. Sāriputta did not always concur with the Bodhisatta's decision to renounce the world. When the Bodhisatta, as a king, decided to enter the ascetic life, his eldest son (Sāriputta) and youngest son (Rāhula) pleaded with him to give up this idea, and he had to struggle inwardly to overcome his attachment to his sons (525). In still another birth, however, the Bodhisatta wavered in his decision to go forth, and this time Sāriputta, as an ascetic named Nārada, appeared to him by mystic power and encouraged him to remain firm in his decision (539).

Thus, buffeted by the winds of kamma, the two noble beings migrated from life to life and from realm to realm through the round of re-becoming. Unlike blind worldlings, however, their wandering was not purposeless and devoid of direction but was guided by aspirations they had formed in the far distant past. After countless lives during which they had practiced the ten perfections, matured their virtue, and forged increasingly closer bonds of comradeship and mutual trust, the time had come for them to actualize the goal for which they had struggled so long. Thus, in their final birth in Middle India some 2500 years ago, the one emerged as the Buddha Gotama, teacher of devas and humans, the other as his most eminent disciple, the Venerable Sāriputta, Marshal of the Dhamma.

SĀRIPUTTA THE MAN

The Chief Disciple

In the *Mahāpadāna Sutta* (DN 14) the Buddha relates various details about the six Buddhas who preceded him, beginning with the Buddha Vipassī ninety-one aeons ago. He mentions their names, the periods in which they arose, their caste and clan, their life span, and the milestones of their teaching careers. He also states the names of their two chief disciples, who are in each case described as "the chief pair of disciples, the excellent pair" (*sāvakayugaṁ aggaṁ bhaddayugaṁ*). Elsewhere in the Pāli Canon (e.g., at SN 47:14) the Buddha declares that all the Buddhas of the past had a pair of chief disciples such as he had in Sāriputta and Moggallāna, and all the Buddhas to arise in the future will likewise have such a pair. From such statements we can see that the posts of chief discipleship are inherent in the very nature of the Buddha's Dispensation. Thus in appointing two monks as chief disciples our Buddha Gotama was not acting according to his own caprice but was conforming to a timeless paradigm—a paradigm followed by all the Fully Enlightened Ones of the past and to be followed by all their successors in the future.

The basic functions of the chief disciples within the Dispensation may be enumerated as threefold: to help the Master in consolidating the Dhamma and thereby in making it a vehicle of spiritual transformation and deliverance for as many beings as possible, both human and celestial; to serve as models for the other monks to emulate and to supervise their training; and to assist in the administration of the Sangha, particularly when the Blessed One goes into solitary retreat or travels alone on an urgent mission. Always the Buddha remains the final authority at the head of the Dispensation, and the appointment of chief disciples does not represent in any way a democratic "devolution of powers": the Blessed One is the sole source of the teachings, the revealer of the path, the "supreme charioteer of persons to be tamed." But just as a king requires ministers to supervise the affairs of state, so the Buddha, the King of the Dhamma (*dhammarājā*), delegates responsibility for particular spheres of training to his best-qualified disciples in each area. Naturally, the most demanding tasks fall on the two chief disciples, who possess the acumen and ability needed to discharge them most effectively. We thus can see that appointment to chief discipleship is far from being an entitlement to special perks and privileges. To be appointed a chief disciple is to shoulder an immensely heavy responsibility in all areas of the Dispensation. It is to share the Buddha's burden of compassion and to work in closest cooperation with him to ensure that the Dhamma becomes "successful and prosperous, extended, popular, widespread, well proclaimed among devas and humans" (DN 16; SN 51:10).

The reason the Buddhas always appoint *two* chief disciples seems to be to achieve an optimal balance between the spheres of responsibility and the human aptitudes available to meet them. A Buddha unites in his own person all perfections; he is "the sage perfect in all respects" (*sabbaṅgasampanna muni*). But human beings of lesser stature, even enlightened arahants, will display diversities in their characters and talents which qualify them for different tasks. Thus, to supervise the main areas of responsibility, a Buddha is invariably attended by two chief disciples, one constantly at his right hand, the other at his left. Of the two, the right-hand disciple, the one regarded as closest to the Blessed One, is the disciple distinguished by excellence of wisdom (*mahāpaññā*). In the case of the Buddha Gotama, this was the Venerable Sāriputta. His special task in the

Dispensation is the systematization of the doctrine and the detailed analysis of its content. By means of his deep insight into the ultimate truth and his sharp discernment of the sphere of differentiated phenomena (*dhammadhātu*) he is responsible for drawing out the subtle implications of the Dhamma and for explicating its meaning with a wealth of detail that the Buddha, as head of the Dispensation, cannot personally attend to himself. The other chief disciple, who stands at the Buddha's left hand, is distinguished by his versatility in the exercise of spiritual power (*iddhi*). In the Buddha Gotama's Sangha this position was held by the Venerable Mahāmoggallāna. Such spiritual power is not a means of dominating others or of self-aggrandizement but must be founded upon a perfect realization of selflessness. The power springs specifically from mastery over the sphere of concentration (*samādhi*), which opens up a profound comprehension of the fundamental forces that govern mind and matter and their subtle interconnections. Guided by the compassionate ideals of the Dhamma, this power is used to remove obstacles to the secure establishment of the Dispensation in the world and to transform other beings who cannot be easily reached by the gentler transformative approach of verbal instruction.

Detailed discussion of the Venerable Sāriputta's first major task as chief disciple, the systematization of the Dhamma, will be undertaken in the next chapter, when we examine his role as "turner of the Wheel." Here we will focus upon the ways Sāriputta and Moggallāna jointly fulfilled the other two roles of chief disciples, serving as exemplars and mentors for the monks and assisting in the administration of the Sangha.

In an injunction given to the Sangha the Buddha held up the two chief disciples as models for the other monks to follow: "A monk of faith, O bhikkhus, should cherish this right aspiration: 'Oh, may I become such as Sāriputta and Moggallāna!' For Sāriputta and Moggallāna are the model and standard for my bhikkhu disciples" (AN 2:131). In their mastery over the three aspects of the path—virtue, concentration, and wisdom—they embodied the qualities the monks still in training were to acquire for themselves. But even more, because they both possessed the analytical knowledges and skill in speech, they were ideal teachers to whom the younger monks could turn for guidance and instruction.

The relationship in which the two chief disciples stood to one another in the matter of teaching was explained by the Buddha in the *Saccavibhaṅga Sutta*:

> Associate, O monks, with Sāriputta and Moggallāna, and keep company with them! They are wise bhikkhus and helpers of their

fellow monks. Sāriputta is like a mother who brings forth, and Moggallāna is like a nurse to the newborn child. Sāriputta trains (his pupils) in the fruition of stream-entry, and Moggallāna trains them for the highest goal. (MN 141)

In explanation of this passage, the Majjhima Commentary says: "When Sāriputta accepted pupils for training, whether they were ordained by him or by others, he favored them with his material and spiritual help, looked after them in sickness, gave them a subject of meditation, and at last, when he knew that they had become stream-enterers and had risen above the dangers of the lower worlds, he dismissed them in the confident knowledge, 'now they can, by their own manly strength, produce the higher stages of holiness.' Having thus become free from concern about their future, he instructed new groups of pupils. But Moggallāna, when training pupils in the same way, did not give up concern for them until they had attained arahantship. This was because he felt, as was said by the Master: 'As even a little excrement is of evil smell, I do not praise even the shortest spell of existence, be it no longer than a snap of the fingers.'"

It is said that whenever Sāriputta gave advice, he showed infinite patience; he would admonish and instruct up to a hundred or a thousand times, until his pupil was established in the fruition of stream-entry. Only then did he discharge him and give his advice to others. Very great was the number of those who, after receiving his instruction and following it faithfully, attained to arahantship. But although the Majjhima Commentary states that Sāriputta used to lead his regular pupils only up to stream-entry, in individual cases he helped monks to attain the higher stages. The Udāna Commentary, for example, says that "at that time bhikkhus in higher training often used to approach the Venerable Sāriputta for a subject of meditation that could help them to attain the three higher paths." It was after taking instruction from Sāriputta that the Elder Lakuṇṭika Bhaddiya attained arahantship (Ud. 7:1), having been a stream-enterer at the time.

As chief disciples, Sāriputta and Mahāmoggallāna shared the responsibility for supervising the affairs of the Sangha under the immediate direction of the Blessed One, and they were the ones expected to take charge in the Master's absence. On one occasion, recorded in the *Cātumā Sutta* (MN 67), the Buddha makes this point clear by reproaching the Venerable Sāriputta for failing to recognize his responsibility. Once a large number of monks (newly ordained, as the commentary tells us, by Sāriputta and Moggallāna) had come to pay their respects to the Buddha for the first time. On arrival they were allotted quarters and started chatting with the resident monks of Cātumā. Hearing the noise, the Buddha summoned the resident monks to question them about it, and was told that the commotion was caused by the new arrivals. The text does not say the visiting monks were present at the time, but they must have been, for the Buddha addressed them with the words: "Go away, monks, I dismiss you. You should not stay with me."

The newly ordained monks left, but some lay supporters intervened on their behalf and they were allowed to return. The Buddha then said to Sāriputta: "What did you think, Sāriputta, when I dismissed that group of monks?"

Sāriputta replied: "I thought: 'The Blessed One wishes to live at ease and to abide in the state of happiness here-and-now; so we too shall live at ease and abide in the state of happiness here-and-now.'"

"Wait, Sāriputta! Do not allow such a thought ever to arise in you again!" the Buddha said. Then turning to Moggallāna, he put the same question to him. "When the Blessed One dismissed those monks," replied Moggallāna, "I thought: 'The Blessed One wishes to live at ease and to abide in the state of happiness here-and-now. Then Sāriputta and I should now look after the community of monks.'"

"Well spoken, Moggallāna, well spoken!" said the Master. "It is either I myself or Sāriputta and Moggallāna who should look after the community of monks."

It was the Venerable Sāriputta too who first appealed to the Buddha to lay down the code of monastic rules. He had asked the Buddha why it was that the Dispensation of some of the Buddhas of the past did not last very long while that of others did, and the Buddha had replied that the Dispensation did not last long in the case of those Buddhas who did not preach much Dhamma, nor lay down regulations for the disciples, nor institute the recital of the Pātimokkha; but the Dispensation of those Buddhas who took these precautions endured. Sāriputta then got up, saluted the Master respectfully, and said, "It is now time for the Blessed One to promulgate the regulations and to lay down the Pātimokkha, so that the holy life might last for a long time." But the Buddha replied: "Let it be, Sāriputta! The Tathāgata himself will know the occasion for that. The Master will not lay down regulations for the disciples nor recite the Pātimokkha until signs of corruption have appeared in the Sangha" (Vin. 3:9–10).

This concern that the Dispensation should endure as long as possible is characteristic of Sāriputta; equally characteristic was it of the Buddha that he did not wish to lay down regulations until such time as it was absolutely necessary to do so. He went on to explain that at that time the least-advanced member of the Sangha was a stream-enterer (perhaps a fact of which Sāriputta was not aware), and therefore it was not yet necessary to lay down the rules of the bhikkhu life.

Often the Buddha charged the two chief disciples with special missions arising out of pressing circumstances. One such occasion was when he dispatched them to win back a group of young monks who were being led astray by Devadatta, the Buddha's ambitious cousin. After Devadatta had formally split the Sangha by declaring that he would conduct Sangha acts separately, he went to Vultures' Peak with five hundred young monks whom he had persuaded to become his followers. The Buddha sent Sāriputta and Moggallāna to Vultures' Peak in order to win them back. When Devadatta saw the two elders approach, he assumed that they had decided to forsake the Buddha and join his faction. He extended to them a warm welcome and treated them as if they were now *his* chief disciples. In the evening, while Devadatta was resting, the two elders preached to the monks, led them to the attainment of stream-entry, and convinced them to return to the Blessed One (Vin. 2:199–200).

Another time that Sāriputta and Moggallāna worked together to restore order in the Sangha was when a group of monks led by Assaji (not the Elder Assaji referred to earlier) and Punabbasu, living at Kīṭāgiri, were misbehaving. They ate in the evening, sang and danced with young girls in the town, and mingled with laypeople in ways that besmirched the dignity of the Sangha. In spite of repeated admonitions these monks would not mend their ways, so the two chief disciples were sent to pronounce the penalty of banishment (*pabbājaniya-kamma*) on them for refusing to submit to the discipline (Vin. 2:12; 3:182–83).

THE HELPER

Among the bhikkhus Sāriputta was outstanding as one who helped others. In the *Devadaha Sutta* (SN 22:2) the Buddha himself said of his great disciple, "Sāriputta, bhikkhus, is wise, and a helper of his fellow monks." The commentary, in explanation of these words, refers to a traditional distinction among the ways of helping others: "Sāriputta was a helper in two ways: by giving material help (*āmisānuggaha*) and by giving the help of the Dhamma (*dhammānuggaha*)."

Elaborating on the way he provided "material help," the commentary says that the elder did not go on alms round in the early morning hours as the other bhikkhus did. Instead, when they had all gone, he walked around the entire monastery grounds, and wherever he saw an unswept place, he swept it; wherever refuse had not been removed, he threw it away; where furniture such as beds and chairs or earthenware had not been properly arranged, he put them in order. He did this so that the non-Buddhist ascetics who might visit the monastery would not see any disorderliness and speak in contempt of the bhikkhus.

Then he used to go to the hall for the sick, and having spoken consoling words to the patients, he would ask them about their needs. To procure their requirements he took with him young novices and went in search of medicine either by way of the customary alms round or to some appropriate place. When the medicine was obtained he would give it to the novices, saying: "Caring for the sick has been praised by the Master. Go now, good people, and be heedful!" After sending them back to the monastery sick room he would go on the alms round or take his meal at a supporter's house.

The above was his routine when staying for some time at a monastery. But when going on a journey on foot with the Blessed One, he did not walk at the head of the procession, shod with sandals and umbrella in hand, as one who thinks: "I am the chief disciple." Rather, he would let the young novices take his bowl and robes and go on ahead with the others, while he himself would first attend to those who were old, very young, or unwell, making them apply oil to any sores they might have on their bodies. Then, either later on the same day or on the next day, he would leave together with them.

Because of his solicitude for others, on one occasion Sāriputta arrived particularly late at the place where the others were resting. For this reason he did not get proper quarters and had to pass the night seated under a tent made from robes. Having seen this, the next day the Master caused the monks to assemble and told them the *Tittira Jātaka* (Jāt. 37), the story of the elephant, the monkey, and the partridge who, after deciding which was the eldest of them, lived together showing respect for the most senior. He then laid down the rule that "lodgings should be allocated according to seniority" (Vin. 2:160–61).

Sometimes Sāriputta would give material help and the help of the Dhamma together. For example, when the monk Samitigutta was suffering from leprosy in the infirmary, Sāriputta went to visit him and spoke to him thus: "Friend, so long as the five aggregates (*khandhā*) continue, all feeling is just suffering. Only when the aggregates are no more is there no more suffering." Having thus given him the contemplation of feelings as a subject of meditation, Sāriputta left. Samitigutta followed the elder's instruction, developed insight, and realized the six supernormal powers (*chaḷabhiññā*) as an arahant (Thag. 81 and Comy.).

A sickbed sermon given by the elder to Anāthapiṇḍika, the Buddha's chief patron, is preserved in the Sotāpatti Saṁyutta (SN 55:26). In this discourse, given when Anāthapiṇḍika was afflicted by such severe pain that he felt as if his head was being crushed, Sāriputta consoled the great lay disciple by reminding him that as a stream-enterer he was utterly free of the bad qualities that lead to rebirth in states of woe and that he possessed the four factors of stream-entry (*sotāpattiyaṅga*): unwavering confidence in the Buddha, the Dhamma, and the Sangha, and "the virtues dear to the noble ones." Moreover, he was securely established on the Noble Eightfold Path and thus was certain to reach the fruits of the path, enlightenment and deliverance. As Anāthapiṇḍika listened to him, his pains subsided and right on the spot he recovered from his illness. As a mark of gratitude he then offered Sāriputta the food that had been prepared for himself.

On one occasion, however, the Buddha mildly reproved Sāriputta for not having carried his teaching far enough. When the brahmin Dhānañjāni was on his deathbed he was visited by the Venerable Sāriputta. The elder, reflecting that brahmins are bent on the Brahma-world, taught the dying man the four *brahma-vihāra*—the meditations on universal love, compassion, altruistic joy, and equanimity—the path to the Brahma-world, but ended his discourse there without teaching the path of insight.

When the Venerable Sāriputta returned from the visit, the Master asked him: "Why, Sāriputta, while there was more to do, did you set the brahmin Dhānañjāni's thoughts on the inferior Brahma-world, and then rising from your seat, leave him?" Sāriputta replied: "I thought: 'These brahmins are bent on the Brahma-world. Should I not show the brahmin Dhānañjāni the way to union with Brahmā?'"

"The brahmin Dhānañjāni has died, Sāriputta," said the Buddha, "and he has been reborn in the Brahma-world."

This story, which is found in the *Dhānañjāni Sutta* (MN 97), is interesting as an illustration of the undesirability of rebirth in an inferior Brahma-world for one who is capable of bringing rebirth to an end. For while the Buddha himself sometimes showed only the way to Brahmā, as for example in the *Tevijja Sutta*, it seems probable that in this case he saw that Dhānañjāni was fit to receive a higher teaching, while Sāriputta, lacking a Buddha's unique knowledge of others' faculties, was unaware of this. As a consequence Dhānañjāni would have to spend a long time in the Brahma-world and might have to take human birth again before he could achieve the goal.

Once the Elder Channa was lying ill and in great pain. The Venerable Sāriputta paid him a visit, in company with the Elder Mahācunda. Seeing the sick monk's agonies, Sāriputta at once offered to go in search of medicines and suitable food for him. But Channa told them he had decided to take his life. They appealed to him to abandon such thoughts, but were not successful; after they retired Channa "used the knife." Later the Buddha explained that in this matter the Elder Channa was blameless, since he had attained arahantship while dying and had passed away into final Nibbāna. This story is found in the *Channovāda Sutta* (MN 144; SN 35:87).

When Anāthapiṇḍika was lying on his deathbed, he requested the Venerable Sāriputta to visit him "out of compassion." Sāriputta came at once, accompanied by Ānanda, and preached to the dying man a stirring sermon on nonattachment (MN 143). He told the lay disciple that he should put away clinging to all the phenomena of the conditioned world: to the six sense faculties, the six sense objects, the six kinds of consciousness, the six kinds of contact, the six kinds of feeling—in brief, to everything seen, heard, sensed, and thought. Anāthapiṇḍika was moved to tears by this profound discourse, the likes of which, he said, he had never before heard.

Shortly after this encounter Anāthapiṇḍika died and was reborn in the Tusita heaven. One night, while the rest of the world slept, the new deva Anāthapiṇḍika paid a visit to Jetavana in his celestial body and in the presence of the Blessed One recited a verse in praise of the chief disciple:

> Sāriputta truly is endowed with wisdom,
> With virtue and with inner peace.
> Even a monk who has gone beyond
> At best can only equal him.

The next day the Buddha informed the monks what had happened, but he did not mention the identity of his visitor. Ānanda then said to the Master: "Venerable sir, that young deva must surely have been Anāthapiṇḍika. For Anāthapiṇḍika had full confidence in the Venerable Sāriputta." The Buddha confirmed that Ānanda's inference was correct.

It was in this manner that the Venerable Sāriputta gave the help of the Dhamma. A great leader and outstanding spiritual adviser, he brought to the task of guiding others not only a keen and perceptive understanding of the human mind, but also a warm sympathetic interest in other people, which must have been a great encouragement to those under his guidance. Administering to the physical as well as to the spiritual needs of the monks under his charge, restraining them with kindly admonitions and encouraging them with the praise their efforts deserved, Sāriputta combined the qualities of a perfect teacher with those of a perfect friend. He was ready to help in every way, in small things as in great. Filled with the virtue of the holy life himself, he was quick to see virtue in others, was expert in developing it in those in whom it was latent, and was among the first to extol it where it was in full flower. His was no cold, aloof perfection, but the richest intermingling of spiritual exaltation with the qualities that are finest and most endearing in a human being.

THE UNRESENTFUL

The Dhammapada Commentary (to vv. 389–90) records an incident that epitomizes still another outstanding trait of the chief disciple, his patience and forbearance. In the neighborhood of the Jetavana monastery, where the Buddha was residing, a group of men were praising the noble qualities of Sāriputta. "Such great patience has our elder," they said, "that even when people abuse him and strike him, he feels no trace of anger."

"Who is this that never gets angry?" The question came from a brahmin, a holder of false views. And when they told him, "It is our elder, Sāriputta," he retorted: "That must be because nobody has ever provoked him."

"That is not so, brahmin," they replied. "Well, then, I will provoke him to anger." "Provoke him to anger if you can!" "Leave it to me," said the brahmin. "I know just what to do to him."

When the Venerable Sāriputta entered the city on his alms round, the brahmin approached him from behind and gave him a tremendous blow on the back. "What was that?" said Sāriputta; and without so much as turning to look, he continued on his way.

The fire of remorse leapt up in every part of the brahmin's body. Prostrating himself at the elder's feet, he begged for pardon. "For what?" asked the elder, mildly. "To test your patience I struck you," the penitent brahmin replied. "Very well, I pardon you."

"Venerable sir," the brahmin said, "if you are willing to pardon me, please take your food at my house." When the elder silently consented, the brahmin took his bowl and led him to his house, where he served him a meal.

But those who saw the assault were enraged. They gathered at the brahmin's house, armed with sticks and stones, ready to kill him. When Sāriputta emerged, accompanied by the brahmin carrying his bowl, they cried out: "Venerable sir, order this brahmin to turn back!"

"Why, lay disciples?" asked the elder. They replied: "The man struck you, and we are going to give him what he deserves!"

"But what do you mean? Was it you or me that he struck?"

"It was you, venerable sir."

"Well, if it was me he struck, he has begged my pardon. Go your ways." And so, dismissing the people and permitting the brahmin to return, the great elder calmly made his way back to the monastery.

The Venerable Sāriputta's humility was as great as his patience. He was willing to receive correction from anyone, not only with submission but with gratitude. It is told in the commentary to the *Susīma Sutta* (SN 2:29) that once, through momentary negligence, a corner of the elder's under-robe was hanging down, and a seven-year-old novice, seeing this, pointed it out to him. Sāriputta stepped aside at once and arranged the garment in the proper way, and then he stood before the novice with folded hands, saying: "Now it is correct, teacher!"[10]

There is a reference to this incident in the *Milindapañha*, where these verses are ascribed to Sāriputta:

If one who has gone forth this day at the age of seven
Should teach me, I accept it with lowered head;
At sight of him I show my zeal and respect;
May I always set him in the teacher's place.

(Mil. 397)

It was no wonder, therefore, that throughout his life he continued to show respect for the Venerable Assaji, from whom he had gained his introduction to the Buddha's Teaching. We are told in the commentary to the *Nāvā Sutta* (*Suttanipāta*), and also in the commentary to the *Dhammapada* (to v. 392), that whenever Sāriputta lived in the same monastery as the Elder Assaji, immediately after having paid homage to the Blessed One, he always went to venerate the great elder, thinking: "This venerable one was my first teacher. It was through him that I came to know the Buddha's Dispensation." And when the Elder Assaji lived in another monastery, Sāriputta used to face the direction in which he was living and pay homage to him by touching the ground at five places (with the head, hands, and feet), and saluting him with joined palms.

But this led to misunderstanding, for when other monks saw Sāriputta acting thus they said: "After becoming a chief disciple, Sāriputta still worships the heavenly quarters! Even today he cannot give up his brahmanical views!" When these complaints reached the Blessed One, he said: "It is not so, bhikkhus. Sāriputta does not worship the heavenly quarters. He salutes the one through whom he first learned the Dhamma, and worships and reveres him as his teacher. Sāriputta is one who gives devout respect to his teacher." It was then that the Master preached to the monks the *Nāvā Sutta*,[11] which starts with the words:

> As the devas pay devout homage to Indra,
> So one should revere the person
> Through whom one has learnt the Dhamma.

Another example of the Venerable Sāriputta's gratitude is given in the story of the Elder Rādha. The commentary to the *Dhammapada* (to v. 76) relates that Rādha was a poor brahmin who stayed at the Jetavana monastery at Sāvatthī. He served as a temple hand, performing little services such as weeding, sweeping, and the like, and the monks supported him with food. When he asked to be ordained, however, the monks did not want to ordain him. One day the Blessed One, in his mental survey of the world, saw that this brahmin was mature for arahantship. He inquired about him from the assembled monks, and asked whether any one of them remembered ever receiving some help from the poor brahmin. Sāriputta said that he remembered an occasion when he was going for alms in Rājagaha and this poor brahmin had given him a ladleful of alms food that he had begged for himself. The Master asked Sāriputta to ordain the man, which he did. Sāriputta then advised him time and again as to what things should be done and what should be avoided. Rādha always received his admonitions gladly, without resentment, and in a short time he attained arahantship. On this occasion the bhikkhus extolled Sāriputta's sense of gratitude and said that he who himself willingly accepts advice obtains pupils who do the same. Commenting on this, the Buddha said that not only then but also formerly Sāriputta had shown gratitude and remembered any good deed done to him. And in that connection the Master told the *Alīnacitta Jātaka* (Jāt. 156), in which Sāriputta was a grateful elephant who dedicated his life to helping a team of carpenters that had nursed him when he was wounded.

The Venerable Sāriputta's powers of forbearance and humility came to the fore on an occasion when he was the victim of a false accusation.[12] This incident took place when he was dwelling at Jetavana. At the end of the rains retreat the elder took leave of the Master and departed with his own retinue of monks on a journey. A large number of monks also took leave of Sāriputta, and in dismissing them he addressed by name those who were known to him by their personal and family names. Among them there was a monk who was not known by his personal and family name, but a strong desire arose in him that the chief disciple should address him by those names in taking his departure. In the great throng of monks, however, Sāriputta did not give him this distinction, and the monk was aggrieved. "He does not greet me as he does the other monks," he thought, and conceived a grudge against Sāriputta.

At the same time it chanced that the hem of the elder's robe brushed against him, and this added to his grievance. He approached the Buddha and complained: "Lord, the Venerable Sāriputta, doubtless thinking to himself, 'I am the chief disciple,' struck me a blow that almost damaged my ear. And having done that, without so much as begging my pardon, he set out on his journey." The Buddha summoned Sāriputta into his presence. Meanwhile, Mahāmoggallāna and Ānanda, knowing that a calumny was about to be exposed, summoned all the monks, convoking an assembly. "Approach, venerable sirs!" they called. "When the Venerable Sāriputta is face to face with the Master, he will roar his lion's roar."

And so it came about. When the Master questioned the great elder, instead of denying the charge he said: "O Lord, one who is not firmly established in the contemplation of the body with regard to his body, such a one may be able to hurt a fellow monk and leave without apologizing." Then followed Sāriputta's lion's roar. He compared his freedom from anger and hatred with the patience of the earth which receives all things, clean and unclean; his tranquillity of mind to a bull with severed horns, to a lowly outcast youth, to water, fire and wind, and to the removal of impurity; he compared the oppression he felt from his own body to the oppression of snakes and corpses, and the maintenance of his body to that of fatty excrescences. In nine similes he described his own virtues, and nine times the great earth responded to the words of truth. The entire assembly was moved by the majestic force of his utterance.

As the elder proclaimed his virtues, remorse filled the monk who had unjustly maligned him. Immediately, he fell at the feet of the Blessed One, admitting his slander and confessing his fault. Thereupon the Buddha said: "Sāriputta, pardon this deluded man, lest his head should split into seven pieces." Sāriputta's reply was: "Venerable sir, I freely pardon this venerable monk." And, with joined palms, he added, "May this venerable monk also pardon me if I have in any way offended him." In this way they were reconciled. The other monks were filled with admiration, saying: "See, brethren, the extraordinary goodness of the elder! He cherishes neither anger nor hatred against this lying, slanderous monk! Instead, he crouches before him, stretches his hands in reverence, and asks his pardon."

The Buddha's comment was: "Monks, it is impossible for Sāriputta and his like to cherish anger or hatred. Sāriputta's mind is like the great earth, firm like a gate post, like a pool of still water." He then recited the following verse:

> Unresentful like the earth, firm like a gate post,
> Equipoised and strong in vows,
> Mind without impurities like a pool:
> For such a one the round of births exists no more.
>
> (Dhp. 95)

Another incident of this nature did not end so happily, for the slanderer refused to admit his fault. He was a monk named Kokālika, who approached the Buddha with a slander against the two chief disciples: "Sāriputta and Moggallāna have bad intentions, Lord," he said. "They are in the grip of evil ambition."

The Master replied: "Do not say so, Kokālika! Do not say so! Have friendly and trustful thoughts towards Sāriputta and Moggallāna! They are of good and lovable behavior!" But the misguided Kokālika paid no heed to the Buddha's words. He persisted with his false accusation, and soon after that his whole body became covered with boils, which continued to grow until eventually he died of his illness and was reborn in hell.

This incident was well known. It is recorded in the following places in the Sutta Piṭaka: Saṁyutta Nikāya (SN 6:10); *Suttanipāta*: *Mahāvagga* (10); Aṅguttara Nikāya (10:89); and *Takkāriya Jātaka* (Jāt. 481). A comparison of these two incidents reveals the importance of penitence. Neither Sāriputta nor Moggallāna bore the monk Kokālika any ill will for his malice, and his apologies, had he offered them, would have made no difference to the attitude of the two chief disciples. But they would have benefited the erring monk himself, averting the consequences of his bad kamma. Evil rebounds upon those who direct it toward the innocent, and so Kokālika was judged and punished by himself, through his own deeds.

FRIENDSHIPS AND RELATIVES

Such personal qualities as gratitude, kindness, helpfulness, and patience won for the Venerable Sāriputta many deep friendships which endured throughout his life as a monk. With Moggallāna, the friend and companion of his youth, he maintained intimate ties until death separated them in the very last year of the Buddha's life. But Sāriputta's friendships were in no way exclusive. According to the commentary to the *Mahāgosiṅga Sutta* there was also a bond of mutual affection between Sāriputta and the Elder Ānanda. On Sāriputta's part it was because he thought: "He is attending on the Master—a duty which should have been performed by me"; and Ānanda's affection was due to the fact that Sāriputta had been declared by the Buddha as his foremost disciple. When Ānanda gave novice ordination to young pupils, he used to take them to Sāriputta to obtain higher ordination under him. Sāriputta did the same in regard to Ānanda, and in that way they had five hundred pupils in common.

Whenever Ānanda received choice robes or other requisites he would offer them to Sāriputta, and in the same way, Sāriputta passed on to Ānanda any special offerings that were made to him. Once Ānanda received from a certain brahmin a very valuable robe, and with the Master's permission he kept it for ten days, awaiting Sāriputta's return. The subcommentary says that later teachers commented on this: "There may be those who say: 'We can well understand that Ānanda, who had not yet attained to arahantship, felt such affection. But how is it in the case of Sāriputta, who was a canker-free arahant?' To this we answer: 'Sāriputta's affection was not one of worldly attachment, but a love for Ānanda's virtues (*guṇa-bhatti*).'"

The Buddha once asked Ānanda: "Do you, too, approve of Sāriputta?" And Ānanda replied: "Who, Lord, would not approve of Sāriputta, unless he were childish, corrupt, stupid, or of perverted mind! Sāriputta is wise, of great wisdom, of broad, bright, quick, keen, and penetrative wisdom. Sāriputta is of few wants and contented, inclined to seclusion, not fond of company, energetic, eloquent, willing to listen, an exhorter who censures what is evil" (SN 2:29).

In the *Theragāthā* (1034 f.) we find Ānanda describing his emotion at the time of Sāriputta's death. "When the noble friend (Sāriputta) had gone," he declares, "the world was plunged in darkness for me." But he adds that after the companion had left him behind, and the Master had also passed away, there was no other friend like mindfulness directed to the body. Ānanda's sorrow on learning of Sāriputta's death is also described very movingly in the *Cunda Sutta*.[13]

Sāriputta was a true friend in the fullest sense of the word. He well understood how to bring out the best in others, and in doing so did not hesitate sometimes to speak straightforwardly and critically, like the ideal friend described by the Buddha, who points out his friend's faults. It was through such honest criticism that he helped the Venerable Anuruddha in his final breakthrough to arahantship, as recorded in the Aṅguttara Nikāya (3:128):

> Once the Venerable Anuruddha went to see the Venerable Sāriputta. When they had exchanged courteous greetings he sat down and said to the Venerable Sāriputta: "Friend Sāriputta, with the divine eye that is purified, transcending human sight, I can see the thousandfold world-system. Firm is my energy, unremitting; my mindfulness is alert and unconfused; my body is tranquil and unperturbed; my mind is concentrated and one-pointed. And yet, my mind is not freed from the cankers, not freed from clinging."
>
> "Friend Anuruddha," said the Venerable Sāriputta, "that you think thus of your divine eye, this is conceit in you. That you think thus of your firm energy, your alert mindfulness, your unperturbed body, and your concentrated mind, this is restlessness in you. That you think of your mind not being freed from the cankers, this is worrying in you.[14] It would be good, indeed, if you would abandon these three states of mind and, paying no attention to them, direct your mind to the deathless element."

The Venerable Anuruddha followed Sāriputta's advice and in a short time he attained the destruction of the cankers.

Sāriputta must have been stimulating company, as he was sought after by many. What attracted people of quite different temperaments to him and his conversation can be well understood from the incident described in the *Mahāgosiṅga Sutta* (MN 32). One evening the Elders Mahāmoggallāna, Mahākassapa, Anuruddha, Revata, and Ānanda went to Sāriputta to listen to the Dhamma. Sāriputta welcomed them, saying: "Delightful is this Gosiṅga sāla-tree forest, it is a clear moonlit night, the sāla trees are in full bloom, and it seems as if celestial scents are being wafted around. What kind of monk, do you think, Ānanda, will lend more luster to this Gosiṅga sāla-tree forest?"

The same question was put to the others as well, and each replied according to his personal temperament. Finally, Sāriputta gave his own answer, which was as follows:

> There is a monk who has control over his mind, who is not under the control of his mind. In whatever (mental) abiding or attainment he wishes to dwell in the forenoon, he can dwell in it at that time. In whatever (mental) abiding or attainment he

> wishes to dwell at noon, he can dwell in it at that time. In whatever (mental) abiding or attainment he wishes to dwell in the evening, he can dwell in it at that time. It is as though a king's or royal minister's cloth chest were full of many-colored garments, so that whatever pair of garments he wishes to wear in the morning, or at noon, or in the evening, he can wear it at will at those times. Similarly it is with a monk who has control over his mind, who is not under the control of his mind; in whatever (mental) abiding or attainment he wishes to dwell in the morning, or at noon, or in the evening, he can do so at will at those times. Such a monk, friend Moggallāna, can lend lustre to this Gosiṅga sāla-tree forest.

They then went to the Buddha and reported the course of their discussion. The Master approved of all their answers and added his own.

We see from this episode that, despite his powerful intellect and his status in the Sangha, Sāriputta was far from being a domineering type who tried to impose his views on others. He understood well how to stimulate self-expression in his companions in a natural way, conveying to them the pensive mood evoked by the enchanting scenery. His own sensitive nature responded to natural beauty and drew a similar response from his friends.

There are many such conversations recorded between Sāriputta and other monks, not only with Moggallāna, Ānanda, and Anuruddha, but also with Mahākoṭṭhita, Upavāṇa, Samiddhi, Savittha, Bhūmija, and many more. Sāriputta was also keen to meet noble monks, particularly those whom the Master had commended. One such was the Elder Puṇṇa Mantāniputta, whom he had not met before the Buddha praised him before the Sangha. When Sāriputta learned that Puṇṇa had come on a visit he went to meet him and, without revealing his own identity, engaged him in a profound discussion on the successive stages of purification and their relation to Nibbāna. His questions elicited from Puṇṇa a great discourse, the *Rathavinīta Sutta* (The Stage Coach Simile; MN 24), which delineates the stages of the Buddhist path later used by Ācariya Buddhaghosa as the framework for his monumental treatise, the *Visuddhimagga.*

It seems that the Buddha himself liked to talk to Sāriputta, for he often did so, and many of his discourses were addressed to his "Marshal of the Dhamma." Once Sāriputta approached the Buddha and repeated some words the Master had spoken to Ānanda on another occasion: "This is the whole of the holy life (*brahmacariya*); namely, noble friendship, noble companionship, noble association" (SN 45:2). There could be no better exemplification of that teaching than the life of the chief disciple himself.

As we have already seen, Sāriputta was born into a brahmin family of Upatissa village (or Nālaka), near Rājagaha. His father's name was Vaganta and his mother's Rūpasārī. No mention is made of his relationship with his father, and we may thus presume that his father died in Sāriputta's youth. He had three brothers: Cunda, Upasena, and Revata, and three sisters named Cālā, Upacālā, and Sīsūpacālā. All six took ordination into the Buddhist Order and attained arahantship.

Cunda was known by the name Samaṇuddesa, meaning "the novice" in the Sangha, even after becoming a bhikkhu; this was to distinguish him from the Elder Mahācunda. At the time of Sāriputta's death, Cunda was his attendant, and it was he who informed the Buddha of his passing away, bringing with him the chief disciple's relics. The story is told in the *Cunda Sutta*, recounted below.

Upasena, who came to be known as Vagantaputta, or "Son of Vaganta," as Sāriputta is "Son of Sārī," was said by the Buddha to be foremost among those of all-pleasing deportment (*samantapāsādika*). He died of a snakebite, as is related in the Saḷāyatana Saṁyutta (SN 35:69). Revata was the youngest of the brothers. Their mother, wishing to prevent him from seeking ordination, had him married when he was a very young boy. But on the wedding day he saw the grandmother of his future wife, an old woman of 120, stricken with all the signs of decrepitude. At once he became disgusted with worldly life. Escaping from the wedding procession by a ruse, he fled to a monastery and was ordained. In later years he was on his way to see the Buddha when he stopped at a forest of acacia trees (*khadīravana*), and while spending the rainy season there he attained arahantship. After that he became known as Revata Khadīravaniya—"Revata of the Acacia Forest." The Buddha distinguished him as being the foremost among forest dwellers.

The three sisters, Cālā, Upacālā, and Sīsūpacālā, wishing to follow their brothers' example, became nuns after their marriages. In marriage, each of them had a son who was named after his mother, Cālā (or Cālī) and so on. These three sons were also ordained, being received as novices by Revata Khadīravaniya, and their good conduct was praised by Sāriputta (in the commentary to Thag. 42). When Cālā, Upacālā, and Sīsūpacālā became nuns they were approached by Māra, who tried to taunt and tempt them. Their excellent replies are recorded in the *Therīgāthā* and the Bhikkhunī Saṁyutta.

In contrast to all these, Sāriputta's mother was a staunch brahmin who, throughout the years, remained hostile to the Buddha's Teaching and his followers. In the commentary to the *Dhammapada* (v. 400) it is related that once, when the Venerable Sāriputta was in his own village of Nālaka with a large retinue of monks, he came to his mother's house in the course of his alms round. His mother gave him a seat and served him with food, but while she did so she uttered abusive words: "Oh, you eater of others' leavings!" she said. "When you fail to get leavings of sour rice gruel, you go from house to house among strangers, licking the leavings off the backs of ladles! And so it was for this that you gave up eighty crores of wealth and became a monk! You have ruined me! Now go on and eat!"

Likewise, when she was serving food to the monks, she said: "So! You are the men who have made my son your page boy! Go on, eat now!"

Thus she continued reviling them, but Sāriputta spoke not a word. He took his food, ate it, and in silence returned to the monastery. The Buddha learned of the incident from his son Rāhula, who had been among the monks at the time. All the bhikkhus who heard of it wondered at the elder's great forbearance, and in the midst of the assembly the Buddha praised him, uttering the stanza:

> He that is free from anger, who performs his duties faithfully,
> He that guards the precepts and is free from lust;
> He that has subdued himself, he that wears his last body—
> He it is I call a brahmin.
>
> (Dhp. 400)

It was not until the very close of Sāriputta's life that he was able to convert his mother; that story will be told below. But the incident just related reminds us again of the great elder's most pleasing characteristics—his humility, patience, and forbearance.

THE MEDITATOR

When the Bodhisatta had left the household life in search of a path to enlightenment he first entered upon discipleship under two distinguished meditation masters of the time, through whose guidance he reached the two highest formless attainments, the base of nothingness and the base of neither-perception-nor-nonperception (see MN 26). From the account of Sāriputta's quest it seems that his inclinations took him along a different route, not to the feet of those who had mastered the domain of superconscious states but to those who excelled in philosophical discourse and intellectual analysis. His initiation into the Dhamma, too, as we have seen, came about not through the path of the meditative absorptions but through a direct, spontaneous insight into the conditionality of all phenomena and into the unconditioned element beyond the network of causes and effects. Nevertheless, once Sāriputta became a disciple of the Buddha, he quickly attained mastery over all the stages of meditative absorption and harnessed his meditative experience as a tool for the final breakthrough to full enlightenment.

The process by which Sāriputta advanced from the stage of stream-enterer to that of arahantship is related by the Buddha in the *Anupada Sutta* (MN 111). In this revealing discourse the Blessed One declares that during the two-week period of his striving for the final goal, Sāriputta had practiced "insight into states one by one as they occurred" (*anupadadhamma-vipassanā*). He mastered in succession the nine meditative attainments: the four fine-material jhānas, the four immaterial states, and the cessation of perception and feeling. On mastering each attainment except the last two (which are too subtle for introspective investigation), he would analyze it into its constituent factors, define each of these factors in turn, and then consider how they arose, how they persisted, and how they disappeared. Abiding "unattracted, unrepelled, independent, detached, free, dissociated, with a mind rid of barriers," he would then cultivate the next higher attainment until he reached the cessation of perception and feeling.

His actual breakthrough to arahantship, as mentioned above, took place while he was standing behind the Buddha, fanning him as the Master gave a discourse to the wanderer Dīghanakha, Sāriputta's nephew. The theme of the Buddha's talk was the comprehension of feelings. The Buddha began by explaining the nature of the body, instructing Dīghanakha to contemplate the body in such a way that desire, affection, and concern for the body would be abandoned. Then he explained the contemplation of feeling: all feeling should be seen as impermanent, conditioned, and dependently arisen, as subject to break up, vanish, disappear, and cease. As Sāriputta listened to the Buddha's words, he reflected: "The Blessed One speaks about the abandonment of these things through direct knowledge; he speaks about the relinquishment of these things through direct knowledge." As he reflected thus, suddenly final knowledge arose and his mind was liberated from the cankers by nonclinging.

In his stanzas in the *Theragāthā*, Sāriputta recalls the way he attained arahantship:

> The Blessed One, the Buddha, the One with Vision,
> Was teaching the Dhamma to another.
> While the Dhamma was being taught

I lent an ear, keen on the goal.
That listening of mine was not in vain,
For I am released, free from cankers.

(Thag. 995–96)

Although Sāriputta ranked first among the Buddha's disciples in overall comprehension of the Dhamma, unlike many other monks he did not strive after the supernormal modes of knowledge and psychic powers that were often accessories of an arahant. Thus in the next verses of the *Theragāthā* (996–97) he states that he felt no inclination (*paṇidhi*) for the five supernormal powers (*abhiññā*), qualities in which his friend Mahāmoggallāna excelled. Nevertheless, the commentary to these verses tells us that while Sāriputta made no deliberate effort to obtain the supernormal powers, they "came into his hands" spontaneously along with his attainment of arahantship, being inherent qualifications of a chief disciple.

The "Treatise on Psychic Power" of the *Paṭisambhidāmagga* (2:212) also credits Sāriputta with "the power of intervention by concentration" (*samādhivipphāra-iddhi*), which is capable of intervening in certain normal physiological processes or other natural events. The canonical basis for this ascription is a story in the *Udāna* (4:4). Once, when Sāriputta was living with Moggallāna at Kapotakandarā, he was sitting in meditation out in the open air on a full-moon night, his head freshly shaved. A malicious demon (*yakkha*) passing overhead, in a spiteful mood, descended and gave the elder a severe blow on the head, but he was so deeply absorbed in meditation that he suffered no harm. The story continues:

> The Venerable Mahāmoggallāna saw the incident, approached the Venerable Sāriputta, and asked him: "Friend, are you comfortable? Are you doing well? Does nothing trouble you?"
>
> "I am comfortable, friend Moggallāna," said the Venerable Sāriputta. "I am doing well, but I have a slight headache."
>
> Thereupon the Venerable Mahāmoggallāna said: "It is wonderful, friend Sāriputta! It is marvellous, friend Sāriputta! How great is the psychic power and might of the Venerable Sāriputta! For just now, friend Sāriputta, a certain demon gave you a blow on the head. And such a mighty blow it was that it might have felled an elephant or split a mountain peak. But the Venerable Sāriputta says only this, 'I am comfortable, friend Moggallāna. I am doing well, friend Moggallāna, but I have a slight headache.'"
>
> Then the Venerable Sāriputta replied: "It is wonderful, friend

> Moggallāna! It is marvellous, friend Moggallāna! How great is the psychic power and might of the Venerable Moggallāna, that he should see any demon at all! As for me, I have not seen so much as a mud-sprite."

Meanwhile the Blessed One had been listening in, with his divine ear, to this discussion between the two elders, and he then spoke the following "inspired utterance" in praise of Sāriputta:

> Whose mind stands unmoving as a rock,
> Unattached to things that arouse attachment,
> Unangered by things that provoke anger.
> How can suffering come to one
> Whose mind has been cultivated thus?

After he had become securely established in the highest goal, meditation became for Sāriputta a natural expression of his realization rather than a means toward some higher attainment. In the Sāriputta Saṁyutta, the Venerable Ānanda questioned Sāriputta on several occasions about how he had passed his day, and Sāriputta replied that he had spent the day dwelling in the various stages of meditative absorption. But in the case of each stage, he added, he was utterly free of self-reference: "I had no such thoughts as 'I am entering the jhāna; I have entered it; I am rising from it'" (SN 28:1–9).

On another occasion Sāriputta described to Ānanda how he could enter a unique state of concentration in which he would not be cognizant of any familiar object of cognition. In regard to the earth element he was without perception of earth, and so also in regard to the other three elements, the four immaterial objects, and everything else pertaining to this world or even to the world beyond. And yet, he said, he was not entirely without perception. His only perception was: "Nibbāna is the cessation of becoming" (*bhavanirodho nibbānaṁ*) (AN 10:7).

This inscrutable attainment seems to be identical with the meditative "abiding in voidness" (*suññatāvihāra*) that the Venerable Sāriputta regularly cultivated. We read in the *Piṇḍapāta-pārisuddhi Sutta* (MN 151) that the Buddha once noticed that Sāriputta's features were serene and radiant and asked him how he had acquired such radiance.[15] Sāriputta replied that he frequently practiced the abiding in voidness. Thereupon the Buddha exclaimed that this was the abode of great men and proceeded to describe it in detail. The commentary identifies this "abiding in voidness" with the fruition attainment of arahantship (*arahattaphala-samāpatti*), entered upon by focusing on Nibbāna's aspect of voidness (*suññatā*). When Sāriputta became absorbed in this meditative state, even the gods from the highest heavens descended to venerate him, as the Venerable Mahākassapa testifies in the following verses:

> These many devas powerful and glorious,
> Ten thousands devas from Brahmā's company,
> Stand with joined hands worshipping him,
> Sāriputta, wise Marshal of the Dhamma,
> The great meditator in concentration:
> "Homage to you, O thoroughbred man,
> Homage to you, O supreme man.
> We do not know what it is
> In dependence on which you meditate."
>
> (Thag. 1082–84)

For Sāriputta proficiency in meditative absorption was skilfully balanced by a capacity for thorough and exact analysis that had been honed through his practice of insight meditation. Among the Buddha's bhikkhu disciples Sāriputta was the foremost of those with great wisdom (*etadaggaṁ mahāpaññānaṁ*), and in the exercise of wisdom he stood second only to the Enlightened One himself. The chief expression of Sāriputta's wisdom was his facility in the four analytical knowledges (*paṭisambhida-ñāṇa*), which he acquired during the two-week period following his ordination:

> It was half a month after my ordination, friends, that I realized, in all their parts and details, the analytical knowledge of meaning, the analytical knowledge of the doctrine, the analytical knowledge of language, the analytical knowledge of perspicacity. These I expound in many ways, teach them and make them known, establish and reveal them, explain and clarify them. If anyone has any doubt or uncertainty, he may ask me and I shall explain (the matter). Present is the Master who is well acquainted with our attainments. (AN 4:173)

The first analytical knowledge confers special insight into the meaning of the doctrines, their implications and ramifications, as well as into the effects that might arise from specified causes. The second gives special insight into the doctrines themselves, their interconnections within the total framework of the Dhamma, as well as into the causes from which certain effects might spring. The third is skill in the understanding of language, grammar, and etymology. The fourth is the ability to marshal the former three types of knowledge when expounding the Dhamma in order to awaken understanding in others. Through his endowment with the four analytical knowledges Sāriputta excelled not only in personal understanding but also in the tasks of teaching and explaining the Dhamma. Because he was so versatile in all these respects, at the conclusion of the *Anupada Sutta* (MN 111), the Buddha could declare him to be his true spiritual son and his chief assistant in the work of "turning the Wheel of the Dhamma":

> If one could ever say rightly of one that he has come to mastery and perfection in noble virtue, in noble concentration, in noble wisdom, and noble liberation, it is of Sāriputta that one could thus rightly declare.
>
> If one could ever say rightly of one that he is the Blessed One's true son, born of his speech, born of the Dhamma, formed of the Dhamma, heir to the Dhamma, not heir to worldly benefit, it is of Sāriputta that one could thus rightly declare.
>
> After me, O monks, Sāriputta rightly turns the supreme Wheel of the Dhamma, even as I have turned it.

THE TURNER OF THE WHEEL

The discourses of the Venerable Sāriputta and the books attributed to him form a comprehensive body of teaching that for scope and variety of exposition can stand beside that of the Master himself. Sāriputta understood in a unique way how to organize and present the rich material of the Dhamma lucidly, in a manner that was intellectually stimulating and also an inspiration to practical effort. In the Theravāda tradition he is regarded not only as the progenitor of many suttas of prime importance but also as the original inspiration behind three substantial exegetical treatises and the individual responsible for the final codification of the Abhidhamma. We will discuss each of these contributions in turn.

THE SUTTAS

We find the Venerable Sāriputta's skill as an expositor of the Dhamma exemplified, firstly, in two classic discourses of the Majjhima Nikāya, the *Mahāhatthipadopama Sutta* (The Greater Discourse on the Simile of the

Elephant's Footprint; MN 28) and the *Sammādiṭṭhi Sutta* (Discourse on Right View; MN 9).

The Greater Discourse on the Simile of the Elephant's Footprint[16] is a masterpiece of methodical treatment. Sāriputta begins by stating that just as the elephant's footprint can contain the footprints of all other animals, so the Four Noble Truths comprise everything wholesome. He then singles out, from the four truths, *the truth of suffering* for detailed analysis, ending with the five aggregates, or personality factors. He next enumerates the five aggregates—material form, feeling, perception, volitional formations, and consciousness—and then singles out, for closer attention, the aggregate of material form. This he explains as twofold: the four great elements and the secondary types of matter derived from the four elements. Each of the elements in turn, he declares, is found both internally, in one's own body, and externally, in the outer world. He enumerates the bodily parts and functions belonging to the internal elements, and declares of both the internal and external elements that they neither belong to a self nor constitute a self. Seeing them thus, one becomes disenchanted with the elements and overcomes one's attachment to this body.

Sāriputta then goes on to show the impermanence of the mighty external elements: they are all destined for destruction in the great cataclysms of nature, and when one realizes this one can never again consider this tiny body, the product of craving, as "I" or "mine." If a monk who has seen the elements in such a way is abused, blamed, and attacked by others, he will analyze the situation soberly and remain imperturbable. He recognizes that the painful feeling that has arisen in him is produced by ear-contact, which is in itself no more than a conditioned phenomenon; and he knows that all the elements of this experience of abuse—contact, feeling, perception, volitional formations, and consciousness—are impermanent. At this point we see that Sāriputta has introduced the other four aggregates, the mental components of personality, in an organic way, so that the meditator can resolve the entire experience into the five impermanent, selfless aggregates. He continues: "Then his mind, just by taking only the elements as its object, becomes elated, gladdened, firm, and intent; and even if he is beaten and injured he will think: 'This body is of such a nature that it is liable to these injuries.'" Thereupon he will recollect the Master's *Kakacūpama Sutta* (Simile of the Saw; MN 21) and will resolve to follow the Buddha's injunction to bear all injuries with patience and without regard even for his life.

But, the elder continues, if while he is recollecting the Buddha, Dhamma, and Sangha the monk cannot maintain his equanimity, he will be stirred by a sense of urgency and feel ashamed that despite his recollection of the Triple Gem he could not remain undisturbed. On the other hand, if his endurance persists, he will experience abundant happiness. "Even to this extent, much has been achieved by that monk," he says.

Sāriputta applies the same method of analysis in turn to each of the other three great elements. He then compares the body and its constituent parts to a house, which is made up of bricks, timber, shingles, etc. and has no independent nature apart from its components. Then, in the concluding portion of the sutta, he launches into a perspicacious account of the conditioned origination of consciousness through the six sense faculties. The five sense organs and sense objects, the basic conditions for the arising of the fivefold sense consciousness, are species of matter derived from the four elements, and thus he completes the analysis of the aggregate of material form by including secondary matter. Each section of consciousness that arises from an object and sense faculty includes an associated feeling, a perception, and various volitional formations, and thus all five aggregates are implicated. These five aggregates, the elder declares, are dependently arisen, and thus with these words he introduces the doctrine of dependent origination (*paṭicca-samuppāda*). Then he quotes the Master: "One who sees dependent origination sees the Dhamma; and one who sees the Dhamma sees dependent origination." Desire, inclination, and attachment in regard to the five aggregates are the *origin of suffering*. Removal of desire, inclination, and attachment is the *cessation of suffering*. And of the monk who has understood this, he says: "Even to this extent, much has been achieved by that monk." Thus he rounds off the exposition with the Four Noble Truths. This discourse is indeed like an intricate and beautifully constructed piece of music ending on a solemn and majestic chord.

A second model exposition of Sāriputta's is the *Discourse on Right View*.[17] This is a masterpiece of teaching, which also provides a framework for further elaboration, such as given in the extensive commentary to it. The commentary says: "In the Buddha Word as collected in the five great Nikāyas there is no discourse other than the Discourse on Right View, wherein the Four Noble Truths are stated thirty-two times, and thirty-two times the state of arahantship." In this discourse Sāriputta includes an original exposition of dependent origination, with slight, but very instructive, variations. The wholesome and unwholesome courses of action, the four kinds of nutriment, and each factor of dependent origination are used to illustrate the Four Noble Truths, which is also treated in its own right; thus the range of the four truths is greatly enhanced, broadened, and deepened. This discourse has been widely used for instructional purposes in Buddhist lands throughout the centuries down to the present day.

Another discourse of Sāriputta's that has been held in high esteem is the *Samacitta Sutta,* which was listened to by the "devas of tranquil mind" (AN 2:35). Its theme is the residuum of rebirths awaiting disciples on the first three stages of sanctity—the stream-enterer, the once-returner, and the non-returner—and its purpose is to clarify whether their rebirths are to take place in the sensual world or in the fine-material and immaterial worlds. Although the discourse is very short, it had a singular impact on the vast assembly of devas who, according to tradition, had gathered to hear it. It is said that many devas in the assembly attained arahantship, while those who reached stream-entry were countless. This discourse is, in fact, one of the few which had such unusually far-reaching results among beings of the higher worlds; and though it is brief and rather cryptic without the commentarial explanation, it has been revered and studied through the centuries. It was this sermon that the arahant Mahinda preached on the evening of his arrival in Sri Lanka, and the *Mahāvaṁsa* (14:34 ff.), the island's famous chronicle, relates that on this occasion, too, numerous devas listened to it and achieved penetration of the Dhamma.

The veneration accorded to the discourse, and the strong impact ascribed to it, may stem from the fact that it helps those on the path to determine the kind of rebirths they may expect. Devas on higher levels of development are sometimes inclined to regard their heavenly status as final, and do not expect to be reborn in the five-sense world, as may sometimes be the case. The great elder's discourse gave them a criterion by which to judge their position. For worldlings still outside the paths as well it must have offered valuable orientation for the direction of their efforts.

The *Saṅgīti Sutta* (The Recital) and *Dasuttara Sutta* (The Tenfold Series), two more of Sāriputta's sermons, are the last two texts of the Dīgha Nikāya (nos. 33 and 34). They are both compilations of doctrinal terms which classify a large number of topics according to a numerical scheme ranging from one to ten members. The reason for stopping the compilation at ten may have been that the groups of doctrinal terms extending beyond ten members are very few in number, and these would have been well known and easily remembered. The *Saṅgīti Sutta* was preached in the presence of the Buddha, and at its conclusion he gave it his express approval.

While the *Saṅgīti Sutta* arranges the doctrinal terms solely in numerical groups of one to ten, the *Dasuttara Sutta* classifies each numerical set in accordance with a tenfold scheme which serves to bring out the practical significance of these groups. For example:

> One thing (1) is of great importance, (2) should be developed, (3) should be fully known, (4) should be abandoned, (5) implies decline, (6) implies progress, (7) is hard to penetrate, (8) should be made to arise, (9) should be directly known, (10) should be realized. What is the one thing of great importance? Heedfulness in wholesome qualities.... What is the one thing that should be abandoned? The conceit "I am".... What is the one thing that should be realized? Unshakable liberation of mind.

These texts must have been compiled at a fairly late period of the Buddha's ministry, when there was already in existence a large body of doctrine and carefully transmitted discourses which required organizing for ready use, and also where anthologies of salient features of the Dhamma had become a useful aid in a comprehensive study of the Teaching. The *Saṅgīti Sutta* was delivered shortly after the death of Nigaṇṭha Nātaputta, the leader of the Jains, otherwise known as Mahāvīra. It was, in fact, this event that occasioned the preaching of the sutta, for it speaks of the dissensions, schisms, and doctrinal disagreements that arose among the Jains immediately after the death of their master. Sāriputta took the eruption of internal conflict in the Jain camp as a warning for the Buddhists, and in his discourse he stresses that this text "should be recited by all in concord and without dissension, so that the holy life should last long for the welfare and happiness of gods and men." The commentators say that the *Saṅgīti Sutta* is meant to convey the "flavor of concord" (*sāmaggirasa*) in the Teaching, which is strengthened by doctrinal proficiency (*desanākusalatā*).

The practical purpose of the *Dasuttara Sutta* is indicated in Sāriputta's introductory verses:

> The Dasuttara (Discourse) I shall proclaim
> A teaching for the attainment of Nibbāna
> And the ending of suffering,
> The release from all bondage.

It seems likely that these two suttas served as a kind of index to selected teachings. They may have been useful also to those monks who did not memorize a great many texts, granting them quick access to numerous aspects of the Teaching in a form that was easily memorized and assimilated. Both of these discourses admirably illustrate Sāriputta's concern with the preservation of the Dhamma and his systematic way of ensuring that it would be transmitted intact in all its details. It was for that purpose that he provided "study aids" such as these and other discourses, together with works like the *Niddesa.*

EXPOSITORY WORKS

A summary of other discourses given by the Venerable Sāriputta is included at the end of this study. We shall now turn to a consideration of larger canonical works attributed to him.

The first is the *Niddesa,* which belongs to the Khuddaka Nikāya of the Sutta Piṭaka. It is the only work of an exclusively commentarial character included in the Pāli Tipiṭaka. Of its two parts, the *Mahāniddesa* is a commentary to the Aṭṭhakavagga of the *Suttanipāta,* while the *Cūḷaniddesa* comments on the Pārāyanavagga and the *Khaggavisāṇa Sutta,* also included in the *Suttanipāta.*

The Aṭṭhakavagga and the Pārāyanavagga are the last two books of the *Suttanipāta* and doubtlessly belong to the oldest parts of the entire Sutta Piṭaka. They were highly appreciated even from the earliest days both by monks and laity, as is clear from the fact that the *Udāna* records a recital of the Aṭṭhakavagga by Soṇa Thera, while the Aṅguttara Nikāya mentions a recital of the Pārāyanavagga by the female lay disciple Nandamātā. On at least five occasions the Buddha himself has given explanations of verses contained in these two parts of the *Suttanipāta.* Apart from the high esteem in which they were evidently held, the fact that these two verse collections contain numerous archaic words and terse aphoristic sayings makes it understandable that in very early days a commentary on them was composed which was later included in the Sutta Piṭaka. The traditional ascription of it to the Venerable Sāriputta must be regarded as highly plausible, at least with respect to the original nucleus of the work if not to the literary document now found in the Pāli Canon.[18] It is quite in character with the great elder's concern for the methodical instruction of bhikkhus that the *Niddesa* contains not only word explanations, clarifications of the context, and supporting quotations from the Buddha Word, but also material obviously meant for linguistic instruction, such as the addition of many synonyms of the word explained.[19]

The *Mahāniddesa* also contains a commentary on the *Sāriputta Sutta* (also called the *Therapañha Sutta*), the last text of the Aṭṭhakavagga. The first part of this sutta consists of verses in praise of the Master and a series of questions put to him, which the commentaries ascribe to Sāriputta. The *Mahāniddesa* explains the opening stanza as referring to the Buddha's return from the Tāvatiṁsa heaven after he had preached the Abhidhamma there. Apart from that it contains only the questions, assigned to Sāriputta, and the replies, which are obviously spoken by the Buddha.

The *Paṭisambhidāmagga* appears to have been a manual of higher Buddhist studies, and its range is as broad as that of the mind of its reputed author.[20] The work consists of thirty treatises of varying length. The first, a long treatise on seventy-two types of knowledge (*ñāṇa*), and the second, on the types of wrong speculative views (*diṭṭhi*), both show the working of a methodical and penetrative mind such as was characteristic of Sāriputta. The "Treatise on Knowledge," as well as other chapters of the work, contains a large number of doctrinal terms unique to the *Paṭisambhidāmagga*. It also elaborates upon terms and teachings that are mentioned only briefly in the older parts of the Sutta Piṭaka, and includes material of great practical value dealing with meditation, as for example on mindfulness of breathing, the meditation on loving-kindness (*mettā*), and numerous exercises for the development of insight. In the middle of the text, giving variety to the subject matter, we find a passage of hymnic character and striking beauty on the great compassion of the Tathāgata. Mahānāma Thera, who wrote the *Saddhamma-ppakāsinī*, the commentary to the work, confidently ascribes it to Sāriputta, and in the introductory stanzas he eloquently praises the great elder. In the *Paṭisambhidāmagga* itself, Sāriputta is mentioned twice, once as being one who possesses "the power of intervention by concentration" (*samādhivipphāra-iddhi*) in the "Treatise on Psychic Power" (see above, p. 36) and again in the "Treatise on Great Wisdom" (2:196), where it is said: "Those whose wisdom is equal to that of Sāriputta, they partake to some extent of the Buddha-knowledge."

THE ABHIDHAMMA

We come now to one of the most important contributions made by the Venerable Sāriputta to the Buddhist teaching, namely, his codification of the Abhidhamma. According to the *Atthasālinī*, the commentary to the *Dhammasaṅgaṇī*, the Buddha preached the Abhidhamma in the Tāvatiṁsa heaven—the heaven of the Thirty-three—to the devas who had gathered from the ten-thousandfold world-system; at the head of this celestial assembly was his mother, Queen Māyā, who had been reborn as a deva in the Tusita heaven. The Buddha taught the Abhidhamma for three months, returning briefly to the human realm each day to collect his alms food. It was then that he would meet Sāriputta and transmit to him the "method" (*naya*) of that portion of Abhidhamma he had just preached. The *Atthasālinī* says: "Thus the giving of the method was to the chief disciple, who was endowed with analytical knowledge, as though the Buddha stood on the edge of the shore and pointed out the ocean with his open hand. To the elder the doctrine taught by the Blessed One in hundreds and thousands of methods became very clear."[21] Thereafter the elder passed on what he had learned to his five hundred disciples.

Further it is said: "The textual order of the Abhidhamma originated with Sāriputta; the numerical series in the Great Book (*Paṭṭhāna*) was also determined by him. In this way the elder, without spoiling the unique doctrine, laid down the numerical series in order to make it easy to learn, remember, study, and teach the Dhamma."[22]

The *Atthasālinī* also ascribes to Sāriputta the following contributions to the canonical Abhidhamma: (a) the forty-two couplets (dyads; *duka*) of the *Suttanta Mātikā*, which follows the *Abhidhamma Mātikā*, both of which preface the seven Abhidhamma books. The forty-two *Suttanta* couplets are explained in the *Dhammasaṅgaṇī* and this likewise has probably to be ascribed to the elder; (b) the fourth and last part of the *Dhammasaṅgaṇī*, the *Atthuddhārakaṇḍa*, the "Synopsis"; (c) the arrangement for the recitation of the Abhidhamma (*vācanamagga*); (d) the numerical section (*gaṇanacāra*) of the *Paṭṭhāna*.

In the *Anupada Sutta* (MN 111) the Buddha himself speaks of Sāriputta's analysis of meditative consciousness into its chief mental concomitants, which the elder undertook from his own experience, after rising from each of the meditative attainments in succession. This analysis may well be either a precursor or an abridgment of the detailed analysis of meditative consciousness found in the *Dhammasaṅgaṇī*.

Concerning the Venerable Sāriputta's mastery of the Dhamma and his skill in exposition, the Buddha said (SN 12:32):

> The essence of Dhamma (*dhammadhātu*) has been so well penetrated by Sāriputta, O monks, that if I were to question him about it for one day in different words and phrases, Sāriputta would reply for one day in various words and phrases. And if I were to question him for one night, or a day and a night, or for two days and nights, even up to seven days and nights, Sāriputta would expound the matter for the same period of time, in various words and phrases.

And on another occasion the Master compared the great elder to a crown prince (AN 5:132):

> If he is endowed with five qualities, O monks, the eldest son of a world monarch righteously turns the Wheel of Sovereignty that had been turned by his father.[23] And that Wheel of Sovereignty cannot be overturned by any hostile human being. What are the five qualities? The eldest son of a world monarch knows what is beneficial, knows the law, knows the right measure, knows the right time, and knows the society (with which he has to deal, *parisā*).
>
> Similarly, O monks, is Sāriputta endowed with five qualities and rightly turns the supreme Wheel of Dhamma, even as I have turned it. And this Wheel of Dhamma cannot be overturned by ascetics, or priests, by deities or Brahmā, nor by anyone else in the world. What are those five qualities? Sāriputta, O monks, knows what is beneficial, knows the Dhamma, knows the right measure, knows the right time, and knows the assembly (he is to address).

That Sāriputta's great reputation as a teacher of the Dhamma long survived him, to become a tradition among later Buddhists, is shown by the concluding passage of the *Milindapañha*, written some three hundred years later. There King Milinda compares the Elder Nāgasena to the Venerable Sāriputta, saying: "In this Buddha's Dispensation there is none other like yourself for answering questions, except the Elder Sāriputta, the Marshal of the Dhamma" (Mil. 420).

That grand reputation still lives today, upheld by the cherished teachings of the great disciple, preserved and enshrined in some of the oldest books of Buddhism alongside the words of his Master.

THE FURTHER SHORE

THE LAST DEBT PAID

We now come to the year of the Master's Parinibbāna, his complete passing away. The Blessed One had spent the rainy season at Beluvagāma, a village near Vesālī,[24] and when the retreat was over he left that place and returned by stages to Sāvatthī, arriving back at the Jetavana monastery.

There the Elder Sāriputta, the Marshal of the Dhamma, paid homage to the Blessed One and went to his day quarters. When his own disciples had saluted him and left, he swept the place and spread his leather mat. Then, having rinsed his feet, he sat down cross-legged and entered into the fruition attainment of arahantship (*arahattaphala-samāpatti*).

At the time predetermined by him, he arose from the meditation, and this thought occurred to him: "Do the Enlightened Ones pass away into final Nibbāna first, or do the chief disciples do so?" And he saw that it is the chief disciples who pass away first. Thereupon he considered his own life force and saw that its residue would sustain him for only one more week.

He then considered: "Where shall I attain final Nibbāna?" And he thought: "Rāhula attained final Nibbāna among the deities of the Thirty-three, and the Elder Aññā Koṇḍañña at the Chaddanta Lake in the Himalayas. Where, then, shall I pass away?"

While thinking this over repeatedly he remembered his mother, and the thought came to him: "Although she is the mother of seven arahants, she has no faith in the Buddha, the Dhamma, and the Sangha. Has she the supportive conditions in her to acquire that faith or has she not?"

Investigating the matter he discerned that she had the supportive conditions for the path of stream-entry. Then he asked himself: "Through whose instruction can she win to the penetration of truth?" He saw that it could not come about through anyone else's instruction in the Dhamma but his own. And following upon that there came the thought: "If I now remain indifferent, people will say: 'Sāriputta has been a helper to so many others; on the day, for instance, when he preached the Discourse to the Deities of Tranquil Mind a large number of devas attained arahantship, and still more of them penetrated to the first three paths; and on other occasions there were many who attained to stream-entry, and there were thousands of families who were reborn in heavenly worlds after the elder had inspired them with joyous confidence in the Triple Gem. Yet despite this he cannot remove the wrong views of his own mother!' Thus people may speak of me. Therefore I shall free my mother from her wrong views, and shall attain final Nibbāna in the very chamber where I was born."

Having made that decision, he thought: "This very day I shall ask the Master's permission and then leave for Nālaka." And calling the Elder Cunda, who was his attendant, he said: "Friend Cunda, please ask our group of five hundred bhikkhus to take their bowls and robes, for I wish to go to Nālaka." And the Elder Cunda did as he was bidden.

The bhikkhus put their lodgings in order, took their bowls and robes, and presented themselves before the Elder Sāriputta. He, for his own part, had tidied up his living quarters and swept the place where he used to spend the day. Then, standing at the gate, he looked back at the place, thinking: "This is my last sight of it. There will be no more coming back."

Then, together with the five hundred bhikkhus, he went to the Blessed One, saluted him, and spoke: "O Lord, may the Blessed One permit, may the Exalted One consent: the time has come for me to attain final Nibbāna. I have relinquished the life force."

> Lord of the world, O greatest sage!
> I soon shall be released from life.
> Going and coming shall be no more;
> This is the last time I worship you.
> Short is the life that now remains to me;
> But seven days from now, and I shall lay
> This body down, throwing the burden off.
> Grant it, O Master! Give permission, Lord!
> At last the time has come for my Nibbāna;
> Now I have relinquished the will to live.

Now, says the text, if the Enlightened One were to have replied, "You may attain final Nibbāna," hostile sectarians would say that he was speaking in praise of death; and if he had replied, "Do not attain final Nibbāna," they would say that he extolled the continuation of the round of existence. Therefore the Blessed One did not speak in either way, but asked: "Where will you attain final Nibbāna?"

Sāriputta replied: "In the Magadha country, in the village called Nālaka, in the chamber where I was born."

Then the Blessed One said: "Do, Sāriputta, what you think timely. But now your elder and younger brethren in the Sangha will no longer have the chance to see a bhikkhu like you. Give them one last discourse on the Dhamma."

The great elder then gave a discourse in which he displayed all his wondrous powers. Rising to the loftiest heights of truth, descending to mundane truth, rising again, and again descending, he expounded the Dhamma directly and with similes. And when he had ended his discourse he paid homage at the feet of the Master. Embracing his legs, he said: "So that I might worship these feet I have fulfilled the ten perfections throughout an incalculable period and a hundred thousand aeons.[25] My heart's wish has found fulfillment. From now on there will be no more contact or meeting; that intimate connection is now severed. I shall soon enter the City of Nibbāna, the unaging, undying, peaceful, blissful, heat-assuaging and secure, which has been entered by many hundreds of thousands of Buddhas. If any deed or word of mine did not please you, O Lord, may the Blessed One forgive me! It is now time for me to go."

Now, once before, the Buddha had answered this, when he said: "There is nothing, be it in deeds or words, for which I should have to reproach you, Sāriputta. For you are learned, Sāriputta, of great wisdom, of broad and bright wisdom, of quick, keen, and penetrative wisdom" (SN 8:7).

So now he answered in the same way: "I forgive you, Sāriputta," he said. "But there was not a single word or deed of yours that was displeasing to me. Do now, Sāriputta, what you think timely." From this we see that on those few occasions when the Master seemed to reproach his chief disciple, it was not that he was displeased with him in any way, but rather that he was pointing out another approach to a situation, another way of viewing a problem.

Immediately after the Master had given his permission and Sāriputta had risen from paying homage at his feet, the great earth cried out, and with a single huge tremor shook to its watery boundaries. It was as though the great earth wished to say: "Though I bear these girdling mountain ranges with Mount Meru, the encircling mountain walls and the Himalayas, I cannot sustain on this day so vast an accumulation of virtue!" And mighty thunder split the heavens, a vast cloud appeared, and heavy rain poured down.

Then the Blessed One thought: "I shall now permit the Marshal of the Dhamma to depart." And he rose from the seat of the Dhamma, went to his Perfumed Cell, and there stood on the Jewel Slab. Three times Sāriputta circumambulated the cell, keeping it to his right, and paid reverence at four places. And this thought was in his mind: "It was an incalculable period and a hundred thousand aeons ago that I prostrated at the feet of the Buddha Anomadassī and made the aspiration to see you. This aspiration has been realized, and I have seen you. At the first meeting it was my first sight of you; now it is my last, and there will be none in the future." And with raised hands joined in salutation he departed, going backwards until the Blessed One was out of sight. And yet again the great earth, unable to bear it, trembled to its watery boundaries.

The Blessed One then addressed the bhikkhus who surrounded him. "Go, bhikkhus," he said. "Accompany your elder brother." At these words, all the four assemblies of devotees at once went out of Jetavana, leaving the Blessed One there alone. The citizens of Sāvatthī also, having heard the news, went out of the city in an unending stream carrying incense and flowers in their hands; and with their hair wet (the sign of mourning), they followed the elder, lamenting and weeping.

Sāriputta then admonished the crowd, saying: "This is a road that none can avoid," and asked them to return. And to the monks who had accompanied him, he said: "You may turn back now. Do not neglect the Master."

Thus he made them go back, and with only his own group of disciples, he continued on his way. Yet still some of the people followed him, lamenting, "Formerly our noble monk went on journeys and returned. But this is a journey without return!" To them the elder said: "Be heedful, friends! Of such nature, indeed, are all things that are formed and conditioned." And he made them turn back.

During his journey Sāriputta spent one night wherever he stopped, and thus for one week he favored many people with a last sight of him. Reaching Nālaka village in the evening, he stopped near a banyan tree at the village gate. It happened that at the time a nephew of the elder, Uparevata by name, had gone outside the village and there he saw Sāriputta. He approached the elder, saluted him, and remained standing.

The elder asked him: "Is your grand-aunt at home?"

"Yes, venerable sir," he replied.

"Then go and announce our coming," said the elder. "And if she asks why I have come, tell her that I shall stay in the village for one day, and ask her to prepare my birth chamber and provide lodgings for five hundred bhikkhus."

Uparevata went to his grand-aunt and said: "Grand-aunt, my uncle has come."

"Where is he now?" she asked.

"At the village gate."

"Is he alone, or has someone else come with him?"

"He has come with five hundred bhikkhus."

And when she asked him, "Why has he come?" he gave her the message the elder had entrusted to him. Then she thought: "Why does he ask me to provide lodgings for so many? After becoming a monk in his youth, does he want to be a layman again in his old age?" But she arranged the birth chamber for the elder and lodgings for the bhikkhus, had torches lit, and then sent for the elder.

Sāriputta, accompanied by the bhikkhus, then went up to the terrace of the house and entered his birth chamber. After sitting down, he asked the bhikkhus to go to their quarters. They had hardly left when a grave illness, dysentery, fell upon the elder, and he felt severe pains. When one pail was brought in, another was carried out. The brahmin woman thought: "The news of my son is not good," and she stood leaning by the door of her own room.

And then it happened, the text tells us, that the Four Great Divine Kings asked themselves: "Where may he now be dwelling, the Marshal of the Dhamma?"[26] And they perceived that he was at Nālaka, in his birth chamber, lying on the bed of his final passing away. "Let us go for a last sight of him," they said.

When they reached the birth chamber, they saluted the elder and remained standing.

"Who are you?" asked the elder.

"We are the Great Divine Kings, venerable sir."

"Why have you come?"

"We want to attend on you during your illness."

"Let it be!" said Sāriputta. "There is an attendant here. You may go."

When they had left, there came in the same manner Sakka, the king of the devas, and after him, Mahābrahmā, and all of them the elder dismissed in the same way.

The brahmin woman, seeing the coming and going of these deities, asked herself: "Who could they have been who paid homage to my son and then left?" And she went to the door of the elder's room and asked the Venerable Cunda for news about the elder's condition. Cunda conveyed the inquiry to the elder, telling him: "The great upāsikā (lay devotee) has come."

Sāriputta asked her: "Why have you come at this unusual hour?"

"To see you, dear," she replied. "Tell me, who were those who came first?"

"The Four Great Divine Kings, upāsikā."

"Are you, then, greater than they?" she asked.

"They are like temple attendants," said the elder. "Ever since our Master took rebirth they have stood guard over him with swords in hand."

"After they had left, who was it that came then, dear?"

"It was Sakka, the king of the devas."

"Are you, then, greater than the king of the devas, dear?"

"He is like a novice who carries a bhikkhu's belongings," answered Sāriputta. "When our Master returned from the heaven of the Thirty-three, Sakka took his bowl and robe and descended to earth together with him."

"And when Sakka had gone, who was it that came after him, filling the room with his radiance?"

"Upāsikā, that was your own lord and master, Mahābrahmā."

"Then are you greater, my son, even than my lord, Mahābrahmā?"

"Yes, upāsikā. On the day when our master was born, it is said that four Mahābrahmās received the Great Being in a golden net."

Upon hearing this, the brahmin woman thought: "If my son's power is such as this, what must be the majestic power of my son's master and lord?" And while she was thinking this, suddenly rapture and joy arose in her, suffusing her entire body.

The elder thought: "Rapture and joy have arisen in my mother. Now is the time to preach the Dhamma to her." And he said: "What was it you were thinking about, upāsikā?"

"I was thinking," she replied, "if my son has such virtue, what must be the virtue of his master?"

Sāriputta answered: "At the moment of my master's birth, at his great renunciation of worldly life, on his attaining Enlightenment, and at his first turning of the Dhamma Wheel—on all these occasions the ten-thousandfold world-system quaked and shook. None is there who equals him in virtue, in concentration, in wisdom, in deliverance, and in the knowledge and vision of deliverance." And he then explained to her in detail the words of homage: "Such indeed is that Blessed One... (*Iti pi so Bhagavā...*)." And thus he gave her an exposition of the Dhamma, basing it on the virtues of the Buddha.

When the Dhamma talk given by her beloved son had come to an end, the brahmin woman was firmly established in the fruit of stream-entry, and she said: "Oh, my dear Upatissa, why did you act like that? Why, during all these years, did you not bestow on me this ambrosial knowledge of the Deathless?"

The elder thought: "Now I have given my mother, the brahmin woman Rūpasārī, the nursing-fee for bringing me up. This should suffice." And he dismissed her with the words: "You may go now, upāsikā."

When she was gone, he asked: "What is the time now, Cunda?"

"Venerable sir, it is early dawn."

And the elder said: "Let the community of bhikkhus assemble."

When the bhikkhus had assembled, he said to Cunda: "Lift me up to a sitting position, Cunda." And Cunda did so.

Then the elder spoke to the bhikkhus, saying: "For forty-four years I have lived and traveled with you, my brethren. If any deed or word of mine was unpleasant to you, forgive me, brethren."

And they replied: "Venerable sir, you have never given us the least displeasure, although we have followed you inseparably like your shadow. But may you, venerable sir, grant forgiveness to us."

After that the elder gathered his large robe around him, covered his face, and lay down on his right side. Then, just as the Master was to do at his own Parinibbāna, he entered into the nine successive attainments of meditation, in forward and reverse order, and beginning again with the first absorption he led his meditation up to the fourth absorption. And at the moment after he had entered it, just as the crest of the rising sun appeared over the horizon, he utterly passed away into the Nibbāna-element without residue.

And it was the full-moon day of the month Kattika, which by the solar calendar corresponds to October/November.

The brahmin lady in her room thought: "How is my son? He does not say anything." She rose, and going into the elder's room she massaged his legs. Then, seeing that he had passed away, she fell at his feet, loudly lamenting; "O my dear son! Before this, we did not know of your virtue. Because of that, we did not gain the good fortune to have offered hospitality and alms to hundreds of bhikkhus! We did not gain the good fortune to have built many monasteries!" And she lamented thus up to sunrise.

As soon as the sun was up, she sent for goldsmiths and had the treasure room opened and had the pots full of gold weighed on a large scale. Then she gave the gold to the goldsmiths with the order to prepare funeral ornaments. Columns and arches were erected, and in the center of the village the upāsikā had a pavilion of heartwood built. In the middle of the pavilion a large, gabled structure was raised, surrounded by a parapet of golden arches and columns. Then they began the sacred ceremony, in which human beings and deities mingled.

After the great assembly of people had celebrated the sacred rites for a full week, they made a pyre with many kinds of fragrant wood. They placed the body of the Venerable Sāriputta on the pyre and kindled the wood with bundles of fragrant roots. Throughout the night of the cremation the concourse listened to sermons on the Dhamma. After that the flames of the pyre were extinguished by the Elder Anuruddha with scented water. The Elder Cunda gathered together the relics and placed them in a filter cloth.

Then the Elder Cunda thought: "I cannot delay here any longer. I must tell the Fully Enlightened One of the final passing away of my elder brother, the Venerable Sāriputta, the Marshal of the Dhamma." So he took the filter cloth with the relics, and Sāriputta's bowl and robes, and went to Sāvatthī, spending only one night at each stage of the journey.

These are the events related in the commentary to the *Cunda Sutta* of the Satipaṭṭhāna Saṁyutta, with additions from the parallel version in the commentary to the *Mahāparinibbāna Sutta.* The narrative is taken up in the *Cunda Sutta* (SN 47:13).

CUNDA SUTTA

Once the Blessed One was dwelling at Sāvatthī, in Jetavana, the monastery of Anāthapiṇḍika. At that time the Venerable Sāriputta was at Nālaka village in the Magadha country, and was sick, suffering, gravely ill. The novice Cunda was his attendant.[27]

And the Venerable Sāriputta passed away through that very illness. Then the novice Cunda took the almsbowl and robes of the Venerable Sāriputta and went to Sāvatthī, to Jetavana, Anāthapiṇḍika's Park. There he approached the Venerable Ānanda and, having saluted him, sat down at one side and said: "Venerable sir, the Venerable Sāriputta has passed away. These are his bowl and robes."

"On this matter, friend Cunda, we ought to see the Blessed One. Let us go, friend Cunda, and meet the Master. Having met him, we shall report this to the Blessed One."

"Yes, venerable sir," said the novice Cunda.

They went to see the Blessed One, and having arrived there and saluted the Master, they sat down at one side. Then the Venerable Ānanda addressed the Blessed One:

"Lord, the novice Cunda has told me this: 'The Venerable Sāriputta has passed away. These are his bowl and robes.' Then, Lord, my own body became weak as a creeper; everything around became dim and things were no longer clear to me, when I heard about the final passing away of the Venerable Sāriputta."

"How is this, Ānanda? When Sāriputta passed away, did he take from you your portion of virtue, or your portion of concentration, or your portion of wisdom, or your portion of deliverance, or your portion of the knowledge and vision of deliverance?"

"Not so, Lord. When the Venerable Sāriputta passed away he did not take my portion of virtue...of concentration...of wisdom...of deliverance, or of the knowledge and vision of deliverance. But, Lord, the Venerable Sāriputta has been to me a mentor, a teacher, an instructor, one who rouses, inspires and gladdens, untiring in preaching the Dhamma, a helper of his fellow monks. And we remember how vitalizing, enjoyable, and helpful his Dhamma instruction was."

"Have I not taught you already, Ānanda, that it is the nature of all things near and dear to us that we must suffer separation from them and be severed from them? Of that which is born, come into being, put together, and so is subject to dissolution, how should it be said that it should not depart? That, indeed, is not possible. It is, Ānanda, as though from a mighty hardwood tree a large branch should break off, so has Sāriputta now passed away from this great and sound community of bhikkhus. Indeed, Ānanda, of that which is born, come into being, put together, and so is subject to dissolution, how should it be said that it should not depart? That, indeed, is not possible.

"Therefore, Ānanda, be an island unto yourself, a refuge unto yourself, seeking no external refuge; with the Dhamma as your island, the Dhamma as your refuge, seeking no other refuge."

The commentary takes up the narrative thus:

The Master stretched forth his hand, and taking the filter with the relics, placed it on his palm, and said to the monks:

> These, O monks, are the shell-colored relics of the bhikkhu who, not long ago, asked for permission to attain final Nibbāna. He who fulfilled the ten perfections for an incalculable period and a hundred thousand aeons—this was that bhikkhu. He who helped me in turning the Wheel of the Dhamma that was first turned by me—this was that bhikkhu. He who obtained the seat next to me—this was that bhikkhu. He who, apart from me, had none to equal him in wisdom throughout the whole ten-thousandfold universe—this was that bhikkhu. Of great wisdom was this bhikkhu, of broad wisdom, of bright wisdom, of quick wisdom, of penetrative wisdom was this bhikkhu. Few wants had this bhikkhu; he was contented, bent on seclusion, not fond of company, full of energy, an exhorter of his fellow monks, censuring what is evil. He who went forth into homelessness, abandoning the great fortune obtained through his merits in five hundred existences—this was that bhikkhu. He who, in my Dispensation, was patient like the earth—this was that bhikkhu. Harmless like a bull whose horns have been cut—this was that bhikkhu. Of humble mind like an outcast boy—this was that bhikkhu.
>
> See here, O monks, the relics of him who was of great wisdom, of broad, bright, quick, keen, and penetrative wisdom; who had few wants and was contented, bent on seclusion, not fond of company, energetic—see here the relics of him who was an exhorter of his fellow monks, who censured evil!

Then the Buddha spoke the following verses in praise of his great disciple:[28]

To him who in five times a hundred lives
Went forth to homelessness, casting away
Pleasures the heart holds dear, from passion free,
With faculties controlled—now homage pay
To Sāriputta who has passed away!

To him who, strong in patience like the earth
Over his own mind had absolute sway,
Who was compassionate, kind, serenely cool,
And firm as the great earth—now homage pay
To Sāriputta who has passed away!

Who, like an outcast boy of humble mind,
Enters the town and slowly wends his way
From door to door with begging bowl in hand,
Such was this Sāriputta—now homage pay
To Sāriputta who has passed away!

One who in town or jungle, hurting none,
Lived like a bull whose horns are cut away,
Such was this Sāriputta, who had won
Mastery of himself—now homage pay
To Sāriputta who has passed away!

When the Blessed One had thus lauded the virtues of the Venerable Sāriputta, he asked for a stūpa to be built for the relics.[29]

After that, he indicated to the Elder Ānanda his wish to go to Rājagaha. Ānanda informed the monks, and the Blessed One, together with a large body of bhikkhus, journeyed to Rājagaha. At the time he arrived there, the Venerable Mahāmoggallāna had also passed away. The Blessed One took his relics likewise and had a stūpa raised for them.

Then he departed from Rājagaha, and going by stages toward the Ganges, he reached Ukkacelā. There he went to the bank of the Ganges, and seated with his following of monks, he preached the *Ukkacelā Sutta* (SN 47:14), on the Parinibbāna of Sāriputta and Mahāmoggallāna.

UKKACELĀ SUTTA

Once the Blessed One was dwelling in the Vajji country, at Ukkacelā on the bank of the river Ganges, not long after Sāriputta and Moggallāna had passed away. And at that time the Blessed One was seated in the open, surrounded by the company of bhikkhus.

The Blessed One surveyed the silent gathering of bhikkhus, and then spoke to them, saying:

"This assembly, O bhikkhus, appears indeed empty to me, now that Sāriputta and Moggallāna have passed away. Not empty for me is an assembly, nor need I have concern for a place where Sāriputta and Moggallāna dwell.

"Those who in the past have been Holy Ones, Fully Enlightened Ones, those Blessed Ones, too, had such excellent pairs of disciples as I had in Sāriputta and Moggallāna. Those who in the future will be Holy Ones, Fully Enlightened Ones, those Blessed Ones, too, will have such excellent pairs of disciples as I had in Sāriputta and Moggallāna.

"Marvelous it is, most wonderful it is, bhikkhus, concerning those disciples, that they will act in accordance with the Master's teaching, will act in accordance with his advice; that they will be dear to the four assemblies, will be loved, respected, and honored by them. Marvelous it is, most wonderful it is, bhikkhus, concerning the Perfect One, that when such a pair of disciples has passed away there is no grief, no lamentation on the part of the Perfect One. For of that which is born, come into being, put together, and so is subject to dissolution, how should it be said that it should not depart? That, indeed, is not possible.

"Therefore, bhikkhus, be an island unto yourselves, a refuge unto yourselves, seeking no external refuge; with the Dhamma as your island, the Dhamma as your refuge, seeking no other refuge."

And with that profound and deeply moving exhortation, which echoes again and again through the Buddha's Teaching up to the time of his own final passing away, ends the story of the youth Upatissa who became the Master's chief disciple, the beloved Marshal of the Dhamma. The Venerable Sāriputta died on the full-moon day of the month Kattika, which begins in October and ends in November of the solar calendar. The death of Mahāmoggallāna followed a half-month later, on the day of the new moon.[30] Half a year later, according to tradition, came the Parinibbāna of the Buddha himself.

Could such an auspicious combination of three great personages, so fruitful in blessings to gods and humans, have been brought about purely by chance? We find the answer to that question in the *Milindapañha* where the Elder Nāgasena says: "In many hu.ndred thousands of births, too, sire, the Elder Sāriputta was the Bodhisatta's father, grandfather, uncle, brother, son, nephew, or friend."[31]

So the weary round of becoming, which linked them together in time, came at last to its end. Time, which is but the succession of fleeting events, became for them the Timeless, and the round of birth and death gave place to the Deathless. And in their final lives they kindled a glory that has illumined the world. Long may it continue to do so!

DISCOURSES OF SĀRIPUTTA

The suttas attributed to the Venerable Sāriputta cover a wide range of subjects connected with the holy life, from simple morality up to abstruse points of doctrine and meditation practice. A list of them, together with a brief description of the subject matter of each, is given below. Their arrangement in the Sutta Piṭaka does not give any indication of the chronological order in which they were delivered. Some few, however, contain references to particular events which make it possible to assign them to a period in the Buddha's ministry. One such is the *Anāthapiṇḍika Sutta,* preached just before the great lay disciple's death.

THE MAJJHIMA NIKĀYA

3: Heirs in Dhamma *(Dhammadāyāda Sutta)*
After the Buddha has discoursed on "heirs of Dhamma" and "heirs of worldliness" and then retired into his cell, Sāriputta addresses the monks on how they should conduct themselves, and how not, when the Master goes into seclusion. They likewise should cultivate seclusion, should reject what they are told to give up, and should be modest and lovers of solitude. He concludes by speaking on the evil of the sixteen defilements of mind (see MN 7) and says that the middle way by which they can be eradicated is the Noble Eightfold Path.

5: Without Blemishes (*Anaṅgaṇa Sutta)*
On four types of persons: those who are guilty of an offense and know it, and those who are guilty and unaware of it; those who are guiltless and know it, and those who are guiltless and unaware of it. The first of each pair is said to be the better one of the two, and the reason is explained. This discourse shows the importance of self-examination for moral and spiritual progress.

9: Right View (*Sammādiṭṭhi Sutta*). Summarized above, p. 41.

28: The Greater Discourse on the Simile of the Elephant's Footprint (*Mahāhatthipadopama Sutta*). Summarized above, pp. 40–41.

43: The Greater Series of Questions and Answers (*Mahāvedalla Sutta*)
The elder answers a number of questions put by the Venerable Mahākoṭṭhita, who was foremost in analytical knowledge. Sāriputta matches the excellence of the questions with the clarity and profundity of his answers. The questions and answers extend from analytical examination of terms, through the position of wisdom and right understanding, to subtle aspects of meditation.

69: Discourse to Gulissāni (*Gulissāni Sutta*)
On the conduct and Dhamma practice to be followed by a forest-dwelling monk. Questioned by the Venerable Mahāmoggallāna, the elder confirms that the same duties apply also to monks living in the vicinity of towns and villages.

97: Discourse to Dhānañjāni (*Dhānañjāni Sutta*)
Sāriputta explains to the brahmin Dhānañjāni that the multifarious duties of a layman are no excuse for wrong moral conduct, nor do they exempt one from painful consequences of such conduct in a future existence. Later, when Dhānañjāni was on his deathbed, he requested the elder to visit him, and Sāriputta spoke to him on the way to Brahmā through the brahma-vihāra. The Buddha mildly reproached the elder for not having led Dhānañjāni to a higher understanding. (See p. 23.)

114: To be Cultivated and Not to be Cultivated (*Sevitabbāsevitabba Sutta*)
Sāriputta elaborates upon brief indications given by the Buddha on what should be practiced, cultivated, or used, and what should not. This is shown with regard to threefold action in deed, word, and thought; in relation to mental attitudes and views, the six sense objects, and the monk's requisites.

143: Discourse to Anāthapiṇḍika (*Anāthapiṇḍikovāda Sutta*)
Sāriputta is called to Anāthapiṇḍika's deathbed and admonishes him to free his mind from any attachment whatsoever, beginning with the six sense faculties: "Thus should you train yourself, householder: 'I shall not cling to the eye, and my consciousness will not attach itself to the eye.' Thus, householder, should you train yourself." This is repeated in full for

each of the other five sense faculties, the six sense objects, the sixfold consciousness, sixfold contact, sixfold feeling born of contact, the six elements, the five aggregates, the four formless spheres, and concludes with detachment from this world and all other worlds; detachment from all things seen, heard, sensed, and thought; from all that is encountered, sought, and pursued in mind. In short, detachment should be practiced as to the entire range of experience, beginning with what for a dying person will be his immediate concern: his sense faculties and their function.

This call for detachment drawing ever wider circles and repeating the same mighty chord of thought must have had a deeply penetrating impact and a calming, liberating, even cheering influence on the dying devotee's mind. This was what Sāriputta, the skilled teacher, obviously intended. And in fact his words had that impact because our text says that Anāthapiṇḍika was moved to tears by the loftiness of the discourse, one in profundity unlike any he had ever heard before. Anāthapiṇḍika passed away soon after, and was reborn as a deity in Tusita heaven.

DĪGHA NIKĀYA

28: Faith-Inspiring Discourse (*Sampasādanīya Sutta*)
An eloquent eulogy of the Buddha by Sāriputta, spoken in the Buddha's presence and proclaiming the peerless qualities (*anuttariya*) of his Teaching. It is an expression and at the same time a justification of Sāriputta's deep confidence in the Buddha. The first section of the discourse is also found in the *Mahāparinibbāna Sutta.*

33: Doctrinal Recitation (*Saṅgīti Sutta*), and 34: Tenfold Series Discourse (*Dasuttara Sutta*). See above, pp. 42–44.

AṄGUTTARA NIKĀYA

2:35: *Samacitta Sutta.* On the stream-enterer, the once-returner, and the non-returner, and on what determines the places of the rebirths they have still before them. See above, p. 42.

3:21: On another classification of noble persons (*ariyapuggala*): the body-witness (*kāyasakkhī*), the one attained to right understanding (*diṭṭhippatta*), and the one liberated through faith (*saddhāvimutta*).

4:79: Sāriputta asks the Buddha why the enterprises of some people fail, those of others succeed, and those of others even surpass their expectations. The Buddha replies that one of the reasons is generosity, or lack of it, shown to ascetics, priests, and monks.

4:158: On four qualities indicative of loss or maintenance of wholesome states of mind. If one finds in oneself four qualities, one can know for certain that one has lost wholesome qualities; this is what has been called deterioration by the Blessed One. These four are: excessive greed, excessive hate, excessive delusion, and lack of knowledge and wisdom concerning the diverse profound subjects (relating to wisdom). If, on the other hand, one finds in oneself four other qualities, one can know for certain that one has not lost one's wholesome qualities; this is what has been called progress by the Blessed One. These four other qualities are: attenuated greed, attenuated hate, attenuated delusion, and the possession of knowledge and wisdom concerning the diverse profound subjects.

4:167–68: The four types of progress on the path. See above, pp. xx–xxi.

4:172: Sāriputta elaborates a brief statement made by the Buddha on the four forms of personalized existence (*attabhāva*) and puts an additional question. The Buddha's reply to it was later elaborated by Sāriputta in the *Samacitta Sutta* (see above).

4:173: Sāriputta states that he attained to the fourfold analytical knowledge (*paṭisambhidā-ñāṇa*) two weeks after his ordination (i.e., at his attainment of arahantship). He appeals to the Buddha for confirmation. See p. 10.

4:174: Discussion with the Venerable Mahākoṭṭhita on the limits of the explainable. Sāriputta says: "As far, friend, as the six bases of sense-contact (*phassāyatana*) reach, so far reaches the (explainable) world of diffuseness (*papañca*); and as far as the world of diffuseness reaches, so far reach the six bases of sense-contact. Through the entire fading away and cessation of the six bases of sense-contact, the world of diffuseness ceases and is stilled."

4:175: On the need for both knowledge and right conduct (*vijjācaraṇa*) for the ending of suffering.

4:179: On the reasons for obtaining, and not obtaining, Nibbāna in the present life.

5:165: Five reasons why people ask questions: through stupidity and foolishness; with evil intentions and through covetousness; with a desire to know; out of contempt; with the thought: "If he answers my question correctly, it is good; if not, then I shall give the correct answer."

5:167: On how to censure fellow monks.

6:14–15: Causes of a monk's good or bad dying.

6:41: Sāriputta explains that a monk with supernormal powers may, if he so wishes, regard a tree trunk merely as being solid, or as liquid, fiery (calorific), or airy (vibratory), or as being either pure or impure (beautiful or ugly), because all these elements are to be found in the tree.

7:66: On respect and reverence. Sāriputta says that these are helpful in overcoming what is unwholesome and developing what is wholesome: that is, respect and reverence toward the Master, the Teaching, the community of monks, the training, meditation, heedfulness (*appamāda*), and the spirit of kindliness and courtesy (*paṭisanthāra*). Each of these factors is said to be a condition of the one following it.

9:6: On the two things one should know about people, robes, alms, lodgings, villages, towns, and countries: whether or not one should associate with them, use them, or live in them.

9:11: The "lion's roar" of Sāriputta, uttered in the Master's presence on the occasion of a monk's false accusation; with nine similes proclaiming his freedom from anger, detachment from the body, and his inability to hurt others. See p. 28.

9:13: A discussion with Mahākoṭṭhita about the purpose of living the holy life.

9:14: Sāriputta questions the Venerable Samiddhi about the essentials of the Dhamma and approves of his answers.

9:26: This text illustrates Sāriputta's scrupulous fairness even toward antagonists. He corrects a statement attributed to Devadatta that was probably wrongly formulated by one of Devadatta's followers, who reported it to Sāriputta. Later, Sāriputta speaks to that monk on the fully developed and steadfast mind, which is not shaken by even the most attractive sense impressions.

9:34: On Nibbāna, which is described as happiness beyond feelings.

10:7: Sāriputta describes his meditations, during which he had only the single perception that "Nibbāna is the cessation of becoming." See p. 37.

10:65: To be reborn is misery; not to be reborn is happiness.

10:66: To have delight in the Buddha's Teaching and discipline is happiness; not to have delight in them is misery.

10:67–68: Causes of progress and decline in the cultivation of what is wholesome.

10:90: On the ten powers of a canker-free arahant that entitle him to proclaim his attainment.

SAṀYUTTA NIKĀYA

Nidāna Saṁyutta

24: Sāriputta rejects the alternatives that suffering is produced either by oneself or by another and explains the conditioned arising of suffering through sense contact.

25: The same is stated with regard to both happiness and suffering (*sukha-dukkha*).

31: On the conditioned arising of existence from nutriment.

32: *Kaḷāra Sutta.* Questioned by the Buddha, Sāriputta says that the knowledge inducing him to declare his attainment of arahantship was that he knew this: the cause of birth being extinct, the result—i.e., future birth—becomes extinct. Hence he was able to say, in the words of the stock formula declaring arahantship: "Extinct is birth..." (*khīṇā jāti*). He then replies to further questions of the Buddha about the cause and origin of birth, becoming, and the other terms of dependent origination, leading up to feeling, the contemplation of which had served

Sāriputta as the starting point for his attainment of arahantship. He says that since he sees impermanence and suffering in all three kinds of feeling, there is in him no arising of any hedonic gratification (*nandī*).

22. Khandha Saṁyutta

1: Sāriputta explains in detail the Buddha's saying: "Even if the body is ill, the mind should not be ill."

2: Monks going to distant border districts are instructed by Sāriputta on how to answer questions posed to them by non-Buddhists. He tells them that the removal of desire for the five aggregates is the core of the Teaching.

122–23: On the importance of reflecting on the five aggregates. If a monk who possesses virtue or learning contemplates the five aggregates as impermanent, bound up with suffering, and void of self, he may be able to attain to stream-entry. If a stream-enterer, once-returner, or non-returner thus contemplates, he may be able to win the next higher stage. An arahant should also contemplate the five aggregates thus, as it will conduce to his happiness here and now, as well as to mindfulness and clear comprehension.

126: On ignorance and knowledge.

28. Sāriputta Saṁyutta

1–9: In these nine texts Sāriputta speaks of his having developed all nine meditative attainments, i.e. from the first jhāna up to the cessation of perception and feeling; and states that in doing so he was always free of any self-affirmation. See p. 35.

10: Once, at Rājagaha, after the alms round Sāriputta was taking his food near a wall. A female ascetic called Sucimukhī (Bright Face) approached him and asked whether when eating he turned to one or other of the directions, as was done by some non-Buddhist ascetics. Sāriputta interpreted her questions as referring to wrong means of livelihood. He denied following any of these and said that he sought his alms in the right manner; and what he had thus obtained righteously, that he would eat. Sucimukhī, deeply impressed, thereafter went from street to street and square to square loudly proclaiming: "The Buddhist ascetics take their food righteously! They take their food blamelessly! Please give almsfood to the Buddhist ascetics!"

35. Saḷāyatana Saṁyutta

232: Not the senses and their objects, but the desire for them is the fetter that binds to existence.

38. Jambukhādaka Saṁyutta
Sāriputta replies to questions put by his nephew, Jambukhādaka, who was a non-Buddhist ascetic.

1–2: He defines Nibbāna and arahantship as the elimination of greed, hatred, and delusion.

3–16: He replies to questions about those who proclaim truth; about the purpose of the holy life; about those who have found true solace. He explains feeling, ignorance, the taints, personality, etc. and speaks on what is difficult in the Buddha's doctrine and discipline.

48. Indriya Saṁyutta

44: Questioned by the Buddha, Sāriputta says that not out of faith in him, but from his own experience he knows that the five spiritual faculties (confidence, etc.) lead to the Deathless.

48–50: On the five spiritual faculties.[32]

55. Sotāpatti Saṁyutta

55: On the four conditioning factors of stream-entry (*sotāpattiyaṅga*).

CHAPTER 2

MAHĀMOGGALLĀNA

Master of Psychic Powers

Hellmuth Hecker

YOUTH

IN A SMALL TOWN NAMED KOLITA, near Rājagaha, capital of the kingdom of Magadha, a child was born who was destined to become the second chief disciple of the Buddha.[1] The boy's parents named him Kolita, after the town. The family belonged to the Moggallāna clan, one of the most illustrious brahmin clans of the period, which claimed direct descent from the ancient Vedic seer Mudgala. The town was inhabited entirely by brahmins, and in its religious attitudes and social customs it was extremely conservative. Kolita's father was born of the most prominent family, from which the town's mayor was usually appointed. Being a member of such a high caste and of the town's most respected family, his father was almost a petty king. Thus Kolita was raised in an environment of wealth and honor, and his favorable circumstances shielded him from direct contact with the sorrows of life. He was educated entirely in the brahmanic tradition, which upheld the belief in the reality of an afterlife and in the law of kamma and its fruits. These beliefs permeated the everyday life of the brahmins and determined the form and content of their rituals, which governed all aspects of their lives.

Kolita's family lived on very friendly terms with another brahmin family from a neighboring village. On the very day of Kolita's birth, a son was born to this other family, whom they named Upatissa. When the children grew up they became fast friends and before long were inseparable. Whatever they did, they did together, whether it was play or study, pleasure or work. Always the two boys were seen together, and their undisturbed friendship was to last until the end of their lives.

In their temperaments the two were quite different. Upatissa was more adventuresome, daring, and enterprising, while Kolita's tendency was to preserve, to cultivate, and to enrich what he had gained. Their places within their families were also different: Kolita was the only child, but Upatissa had three brothers and three sisters. Yet, despite the differences in their characters, they never quarreled or came into conflict but always dwelt on amicable terms, maintaining a steadfast loyalty and self-sacrificing devotion.

To both youths, their friendship meant so much and filled their daily life to such an extent that they displayed little interest in the opposite sex. Nevertheless, like other young men of their background—wealthy and high ranking brahmins—the two friends were enamored with the intoxications of youth, health, and life. Each was the leader of a group of friends with whom he engaged in play and sport. When they went to the river, Kolita's companions came on horseback and those of Upatissa were carried in palanquins.

Each year Rājagaha hosted a grand public celebration called the Hilltop Festival, which featured popular shows and amusements. The two friends looked forward to this event with keen anticipation and reserved seats from which they could comfortably watch the entertainment, a mixture of folk comedies and old legends. On the first day of the festival they were fully engrossed in the entertainment. When there was something to laugh at, they joined in the laughter; and when there was something exciting, they became excited. They enjoyed the show so much that they returned on the second day and closely followed all the performances. Inexplicably, however, far from satisfying them, the entertainment left them with a deep feeling of discontent. Nevertheless, they made reservations for the third day too, as a new program had been announced in glowing terms.

That night strange thoughts haunted their hearts and disturbed their sleep. As Kolita tossed and turned in his bed, he kept on asking himself: "What is the use to us of this frivolity? Is there anything here really worth seeing? What benefit comes from a life devoted to enjoyment and pleasure seeking? After a few years, these glamorous actors will all be old and feeble; they will leave the stage of life and continue their migrations through existence, driven on by craving, and we too will also have to move on. These actors cannot even help themselves to solve the problem of existence. How then can they help us? Instead of wasting our time with these festivities we should seek a path to deliverance!"

Upatissa, too, had spent a restless night, disturbed by quite similar thoughts. He reflected how the ancient myths and legends dramatized in those performances presupposed the reality of rebirth; but the jokes and frolics overlaying those ideas in the plays insinuated that one need be concerned with this present life alone. Was this not an artificial suppression of truth by pretense and vain illusions?

The next morning, when they took their seats, Kolita said to his friend: "What is the matter with you? You are not your usual merry self. Is something troubling you?" His friend replied: "Last night, while I lay in bed, I kept on asking myself, 'What is the use to us of all these pleasures of eye and ear? They are absolutely worthless! Shouldn't we rather seek to find release from the devastating law of impermanence, to liberate ourselves from the fleeting illusions of life, which lure us on yet leave us empty?' That is what has been weighing on my mind. But you, too, dear Kolita, seem morose today." Kolita replied: "I have been thinking exactly the same thoughts. Why should we stay here any longer, in this unholy vanity show? We should seek the way to deliverance!" When Upatissa heard that his friend had the very same wish, he happily exclaimed: "That was a good thought that came to us both, independent of each other. We have wasted our time long enough with worthless frivolities. But if we earnestly seek a teaching of deliverance, we shall have to give up home and possessions and go forth as homeless wanderers, free of worldly and sensual bonds, rising above them like birds on the wing."

So the two friends decided to undertake the life of ascetics—homeless mendicants who then wandered along the roads of India, as they still do now, in search of a spiritual teacher, a guru who could guide them to the liberating knowledge of enlightenment. When they told their followers about their decision, these young men were so deeply impressed that most decided to join their friends in their spiritual quest. So all of them said farewell to their families, took off the sacred brahmanic thread, cut off their hair and beards, and put on the pale saffron garments of religious wanderers. Discarding all distinguishing marks and privileges of their caste, they entered the classless society of ascetics.

WANDERING AND SPIRITUAL SEARCH

At about the same time that Prince Siddhattha, the future Buddha, married—and thus for the time at least stepped more deeply into worldly life—the two friends Kolita and Upatissa left behind their homes and embarked upon the difficult quest for inner peace and salvation. Together with their retinues, they began a period of training under a spiritual teacher, just as the Bodhisatta did later.

At that time, northern India teemed with spiritual teachers and philosophers whose views ranged from the demonic to the superdivine. Some taught amoralism, others fatalism, still others materialism. Both friends realized the hollowness of such teachings early enough and thus felt no attraction towards them. In Rājagaha, however, there was one teacher who appealed to them. His name was Sañjaya, who, according to tradition, was identical with Sañjaya Belaṭṭhaputta, mentioned in the Pāli Canon as one of six non-Buddhist teachers. Under him the group of friends were ordained, which added considerably to Sañjaya's reputation.

The texts do not give us detailed information about Sañjaya's teachings, but from a number of brief indications we can roughly reconstruct the substance of his doctrine. Unlike other ascetic teachers who made definite dogmatic statements about specific topics, Sañjaya maintained a rigorous skepticism in regard to the deep existential problems with which the thinkers of the period wrestled. He formulated this skepticism around the chief questions debated by his philosophical contemporaries: Is there another world beyond the visible order? After the death of this material body, does one appear in the world beyond by way of a purely mental birth process as a spontaneously arisen being? Will the good and bad actions one has performed in this present existence bear good and bad fruits in the next life? What, finally, is the destiny of a Tathāgata or Perfect One after death? How are we to conceive and describe his postmortem condition?

Whenever such questions were raised by the Indian thinkers of this period, four alternative types of answers were thought possible: affirmation, negation, partial affirmation and partial negation, and neither affirmation nor negation. Sañjaya, however, taught that with regard to the questions mentioned, none of those four positions was acceptable as a solution; they all contained unresolvable contradictions or antinomies, and therefore, he held, one should refrain from any judgment about these problems. Here it may be noted that, of the four sets of antinomies which often occur in the Pāli scriptures (e.g., at MN 63 and MN 72), only the fourth set is identical with Sañjaya's problems, namely, the one concerning the afterdeath state of a Perfect One.

While other ascetic teachers always advocated one of the four logical alternatives as a solution to these problems—yes, no, yes and no, neither yes nor no—Sañjaya did not commit himself to any of them. He especially did not commit himself dogmatically to the unprovable assertion (made, for instance, by popular natural science) that there is no world beyond, no mind-made (astral) body, no law of kamma, and no survival after death. In that attitude, he clearly differed from the materialists of his time. He taught rather that, in view of the unresolvable nature of these problems, one should keep to a stance of detachment and impartiality, not tolerating the slightest bias toward approval or disapproval of any of these theories and their consequences. From this we can see that he was a confirmed agnostic who tried to develop a consistent skepticism built upon a recognition of the dialectic tensions inherent in speculative thought.

In the *Sāmaññaphala Sutta*, the king of Magadha, Ajātasattu, reported to the Buddha the following talk he had with the ascetic Sañjaya.

Although this account may reflect the way the Buddhists understood Sañjaya rather than his own way of formulating his doctrine, it offers us a glimpse into his philosophical stance:

> One day I went to Sañjaya of the Belaṭṭha clan and I asked him: "Can you, sir, declare to me an immediate fruit, visible in this very world, of the life of a recluse?"
>
> Being thus asked, Sañjaya said: "If you ask me whether there is another world—well, if I thought there were, I would say so. But I don't say so. And I don't think it is thus or thus. And I don't think it is otherwise. And I don't deny it. And I don't say there neither is nor is not another world. And if you ask me whether there are beings reborn spontaneously; or whether there is any fruit, any result, of good or bad actions; or whether a Tathāgata exists or not after death—to each and all of these questions do I give the same reply."
>
> Thus, Lord, when asked about the immediate fruit and advantage in the life of a recluse, Sañjaya of the Belaṭṭha clan showed his manner of prevarication.[2]

Kolita and Upatissa initially must have felt that Sañjaya's philosophy was something more than mere evasion. Not having met a better teacher, they were probably attracted to him because of his apparent freedom from dogmatism and his dialectical skills. After a short time, however, they clearly realized that Sañjaya could not offer them what they were really searching for: a cure for the illness of universal suffering. Besides, we may suppose that by reason of their mental formations from past existences they must have intuitively felt that there actually was another world, that there were mind-born beings (e.g., deities), and that there was moral recompense of actions. In this respect their understanding went beyond that of their skeptical teacher. Hence one day the two friends approached Sañjaya and asked him whether he had still other teachings more advanced than those they had already learned from him. To this he replied: "That is all. You know my entire teaching." Hearing this, they decided to leave and to continue their search elsewhere. After all, they had not left their families for the sake of endless and futile agnostic arguments but to find a path to final deliverance from suffering.

Thus, for a second time, they took up the life of wanderers in search of truth. They walked across India for many years, from north to south, from east to west. They endured the dust of the road and the tormenting heat, the rain and the wind, spurred on by thoughts that moved deep within the Indian soul: "I am a victim of birth, aging and death, of sorrow, lamentation, pain, grief, and despair. I am a victim of suffering, a prey of suffering. Surely, an end to this whole mass of suffering can be discovered!" (MN 29).

In their travels they met many ascetics and brahmins who were reputed to be exceptionally wise. With them they had religious discussions on God and the world, on heaven and hell, on the meaning of life and the way to salvation. But with their keen and critical minds trained by Sañjaya's skepticism, they very soon realized the emptiness of all those assertions and the learned ignorance of these philosophers. None of these teachers could answer their probing questions, while the two friends themselves were quite able to reply when questioned.

The records do not tell us who their other teachers were, but it would be surprising if the two truth-seekers had not met such mystics and sages as, for instance, Bāvarī, a seer of great meditative power, or Āḷāra Kālāma and Uddaka Rāmaputta, the two teachers of formless infinity under whom the Bodhisatta had studied. From their life story, however, one thing is clear: until they encountered the Buddha the two had failed to find even the tracks of a path to the world-transcending experience of liberation. What may have been the reason?

Spiritual seekers at the time of the Buddha pursued either of two aims: to gain inner peace and serenity by deep meditation (samādhi) or to acquire a clear view of the ultimate meaning of existence. Those who sought to understand the nature of existence generally proceeded through speculative flights of the intellect and tended to spurn the path of meditative absorption. In contrast, those who had achieved inner peace through the meditative path for the most part remained content with their attainment, believing this to be the final goal. Lacking the guidance of a Buddha, they did not even suspect that this meditative peace, so tranquil and sublime, was still mundane and thus merely a force of kammic construction within the cycle of repeated birth and death. Their meditative attainments would bring them a blissful rebirth in one of the supersensual Brahma-worlds, where the life span is inconceivably longer than in the sensual world; but eventually such kammic force would be depleted, followed by a rebirth elsewhere, leaving the meditators in the same saṁsāric imprisonment as before. In their former lives as meditating hermits, this must have happened often to the Bodhisatta as well as to Kolita and Upatissa. This is one aspect of existential misery, of prisonlike ignorance: either, like the mystics, one settles down at the gate, regarding it as one's true home of peace and bliss; or, like the speculative thinkers, one bypasses it quickly and becomes lost within the labyrinths of the intellect.

Though the two friends had no recollection of jhānic experiences from previous lives, they obviously had an intuitive feeling that meditative bliss and its rewards were not the final goal but only a temporary relief within the continuing cycle of suffering. Hence their foremost quest was for clarity about the concatenation of existence, for understanding how things hang together in the complex web of saṁsāra. In ages devoid of a Buddha's appearance, their search would have been as futile as the recurring attainment, enjoyment, and loss of samādhi. It may have been an undefinable inner urge within them that did not allow them to rest until they had found the Enlightened One who, like them, had gone forth in search of liberation during the last years of their own quest. If even the Bodhisatta, the future Buddha, could discover how to integrate meditative absorption with penetrating insight only when he reached a critical impasse in his own spiritual search, it was not to be expected that the two friends on their own could find the subtle key to mind's emancipation, for they had neither the wide meditative experience nor the far-reaching independent mental range of a Buddha. In retrospect, the friends' wandering in search of truth was just a running in circles, which would end only when their uncompromising integrity and insatiable thirst for truth finally led them to the feet of the Enlightened One.

FINDING THE DHAMMA

Without knowing anything of the Buddha, the two friends gave up their life of wandering and returned to their home country of Magadha. Both were about forty years of age.[3] Despite their many disappointments they still had not given up hope. Having made a pact that the one who found a genuine path to the Deathless first would quickly inform the other, they set out on their search separately, thereby doubling their chances of meeting a competent spiritual guide.

It was shortly before this happened that the Buddha had set in motion the Wheel of the Dhamma at Benares, and after his first rains retreat he sent out his first batch of disciples, sixty arahants, to proclaim the Dhamma for the well-being and happiness of the world. The Buddha himself had gone to Rājagaha, where the king of Magadha soon became his follower and donated to him the Bamboo Grove Monastery. He was living at that monastery when Kolita and Upatissa returned to Rājagaha, where they were offered accommodations at Sañjaya's place.

One day Upatissa had gone to the town while Kolita had stayed at their dwelling. When Kolita saw his friend returning in the afternoon, he was struck with awe at the change in his friend's manner. Never before had he seen him so beatific; his entire being seemed to have been transformed, and his face shone with a sublime radiance. Eagerly Kolita asked him: "Your features are so serene, dear friend, and your complexion is so bright and clear. Have you found the way to the Deathless?"

Upatissa then replied: "It is so, dear friend, the Deathless has been found." He then reported what had happened. In town, he had seen a monk whose behavior impressed him so deeply that he was immediately convinced he was an arahant, or at least one well advanced on the path to arahantship. He approached him and started a conversation. The monk, whose name was Assaji, replied that he was a disciple of the ascetic Gotama of the Sakyan clan, whom he referred to as "the Enlightened One." When Upatissa begged him to explain his teacher's doctrine, Assaji modestly said that he was only a beginner and could not explain it in detail, but he could briefly tell him the gist of the teaching. When Upatissa assured him that he would be satisfied with that, Assaji recited a short stanza that summed up the main points—a stanza that in the centuries and millennia to follow was to become famous wherever the Buddha's Teaching spread:

> Of those things that arise from a cause,
> The Tathāgata has told the cause,
> And also what their cessation is:
> This is the doctrine of the Great Recluse.[4]

When Assaji spoke this stanza, right on the spot there arose in Upatissa the dust-free, stainless vision of the Dhamma: "All that has the nature of arising has the nature of cessation." And the very same thing happened to Kolita when Upatissa repeated the stanza to him. Such sudden experiences of enlightenment may fascinate us and baffle us, particularly when they are triggered by sayings that to us seem so opaque and enigmatic. But the power of the Dhamma to ignite realization of ultimate truth is proportional to the receptivity and earnestness of the disciple. For those who have long trained themselves in the disciplines of contemplation and renunciation, who have reflected deeply upon the impermanent and the Deathless, and who are ready to relinquish everything for the sake of final deliverance, even a concise four-line stanza can reveal more truth than volumes of systematic exposition. The two friends Upatissa and Kolita were amply endowed with these qualifications. Single-minded in their quest for final freedom, they had learned to investigate things solely in terms of the conditioned and the unconditioned, and their faculties were ripe to the bursting point. All they lacked was the key to direct insight. Assaji's stanza was that key. Having swiftly cut through the subtle screens of ignorance that covered their mental eyes, in a flash it bestowed on them the first vision of the Deathless. They had penetrated the Four Noble Truths and seen the Uncreated, Nibbāna, beyond the transience of phenomenal existence where death ever reigns. They now stood securely in the stream of the Dhamma (*sotāpatti*), assured that the goal was within their grasp.[5]

After Kolita had listened to that potent stanza, he asked at once where the Great Ascetic, the Tathāgata, was staying. Hearing that he was staying not far away at the Bamboo Grove Monastery, he wished to go there immediately, but Upatissa asked him to wait, saying, "Let us first go to Sañjaya and tell him that we have found the Deathless. If he can understand, he is sure to make progress toward the truth. But if he cannot comprehend at once, he may perhaps have confidence enough to join us when we go to see the Master. Then, on listening to the Buddha himself, he will certainly understand."

Thus the friends went to their former Master and said: "Listen, teacher, listen! A Fully Enlightened One has appeared in the world. Well proclaimed is his teaching, and his monks live the fully purified life. Come with us to see him!" Sañjaya, however, declined their invitation, but instead offered to share with them the leadership of his community. "If you will accept my offer," he said, "you will enjoy abundant gain and fame and you will be held in the highest respect." But the two friends would not swerve from their course and firmly replied, "We would not mind remaining pupils for life, but you should make up your mind now, as our own decision is final." Sañjaya, however, torn by indecision, lamented: "I cannot go! For so many years I have been a teacher and have had a large following of disciples. If I were to become a pupil again, it would be as if a mighty lake were to change into a pitcher!" Thus conflicting motives contended within his heart: on one side, his longing for truth, on the other the desire to preserve his superior status. But the latter prevailed, and he stayed behind.

At that time, Sañjaya had about five hundred disciples. When they learned that the two friends had decided to follow the Buddha, spontaneously all of them wanted to join. But when they noticed that Sañjaya would not go, half of them wavered and returned to their teacher. Sañjaya, seeing that he had lost so many of his disciples, was so stricken by grief and despair that, as the texts tell us, "hot blood spurted from his mouth."

THE STRUGGLE FOR REALIZATION OF THE TEACHING

Now the two friends, at the head of 250 fellow ascetics, approached the Bamboo Grove. There the Buddha was teaching the Dhamma to his monks, and when he saw the two friends approaching, he announced: "Here, monks, they are coming, the two friends, Kolita and Upatissa. They will be my chief disciples, a blessed pair!" Having arrived, the whole company respectfully saluted the Buddha, raised their joined palms to the forehead, and bowed at his feet. Then the two friends spoke: "May we be permitted, Lord, to obtain under the Blessed One the going forth and the full admission?" Then the Blessed One responded: "Come, monks, well proclaimed is the Dhamma. Live now the holy life for making an end of suffering!" These brief words served to bestow ordination on the two friends and their following.[6]

From that point on the texts refer to Upatissa by the name Sāriputta, "the son of Sārī," after the name of his mother, and to Kolita as Mahāmoggallāna, "Moggallāna the Great," to distinguish him from others of the same brahmanic clan, such as Gaṇaka Moggallāna and Gopaka Moggallāna.

After all of them had obtained ordination, the Buddha addressed the 250 disciples and explained to them the Teaching in such a way that before long they attained to the first stage of emancipation, stream-entry, and in due course all became arahants except Sāriputta and Moggallāna. These two went into solitude, in separate places, to continue their striving for the highest goal.

Sāriputta remained in the vicinity of Rājagaha and went to meditate in a cave called the Boar's Den. From there he walked to the city for his alms, which often gave him the opportunity to listen to the Buddha's discourses. What he heard from the Master he independently worked over in his own mind and he methodically penetrated to clear understanding of the fundamental nature of phenomena. He needed fourteen days to reach arahantship, the utter destruction of all cankers (*āsavakkhaya*).

Moggallāna, however, for reasons not specified in the texts, resorted to a forest near the village of Kallavālaputta in Magadha. With great zeal, he meditated there while sitting or walking up and down, but despite his determination he was often overcome by sleepiness. Though he struggled to keep his body erect and his head upright, he kept on drooping and nodding. There were times when he could keep his eyes open only by sheer force of will. The tropical heat, the strain of his long years of a wandering life, and the inner tensions he had gone through all bore down on him at once, and thus, at the very end of his quest, his body reacted by fatigue.

But the Awakened One, with a great teacher's solicitude for his disciples, did not lose sight of him. With his supernormal vision he perceived the difficulties of the new monk, and by psychic power he appeared before him. When Moggallāna saw the Master standing before him, a good part of his fatigue had already vanished. Now the Awakened One asked him:

> "Are you nodding, Moggallāna, are you nodding?"
>
> "Yes, Lord."
>
> "Well then, Moggallāna, at whatever thought drowsiness descends upon you, you should not give attention to that thought or dwell on it. Then, by doing so, it is possible that your drowsiness will vanish. But if, by doing so, drowsiness does not vanish, then you should reflect upon the Teaching as you have heard it and learned it, you should ponder over it and examine it closely in your mind. Then, by doing so, it is possible that your drowsiness will vanish. But if, by doing so, drowsiness does not vanish, then you should repeat in full detail the Teaching as you have heard it and learned it...you should pull both ear-lobes and rub your limbs with your hands...you should get up from your seat and, after washing your eyes with water, you should look around in all directions and upwards to the stars and constellations...you should give attention to the perception of light, to the perception of day: as by day so by night, as by night so by day; thus, with your mind clear and unclouded, you should cultivate a mind that is full of brightness...with your senses turned inward and your mind not straying outward, you should walk up and down, being aware of going to and fro. Then, by doing so, it is possible that your drowsiness will vanish. But if, by doing so, drowsiness does not vanish, you may, mindfully and clearly aware, lie down lionlike on your right side, placing foot on foot, keeping in mind the thought of rising; and on awakening, you should quickly get up, thinking, 'I must not indulge in the comfort of resting and reclining, in the pleasure of sleep.'
>
> "Thus, Moggallāna, should you train yourself."[7]

Here the Buddha gives Moggallāna a graded sequence of advice on how to overcome drowsiness. The first and best device is not to pay attention to the thought causing or preceding the state of drowsiness. This, however, is the most difficult method. If one does not succeed with it, one may summon some energizing thoughts or one may reflect upon the excellence of the Teaching, or recite parts of it by heart. If these mental remedies do not help, one should turn to bodily activity such as, for instance, pulling one's ears, shaking the body, activating the circulation by rubbing one's limbs, refreshing one's eyes with cold water, and, at night, looking at the grandeur of the starry sky. This may make one forget one's petty drowsiness.

If these measures are of no avail, then one may try to arouse an inner vision of light, suffusing the entire mind with luminosity. With this self-radiant mind, one will then be able to leave behind, like a Brahmā deity, the whole realm of days and nights as perceived by the senses. This line of advice suggests that Moggallāna had experienced such states before, so that the Buddha could refer to them as something known to Moggallāna. This "perception of light" (*ālokasaññā*) is mentioned in the texts as one of four ways of developing samādhi and as leading to "knowledge and vision" (*ñāṇadassana*) (DN 33).

If this method, too, does not help, one should walk up and down mindfully, and thus, by resorting to bodily movement, try to get rid of fatigue. If, however, none of these seven devices proves helpful, one may just lie down and rest for a short while. But as soon as one feels refreshed, one should quickly get up, without allowing drowsiness to return.

The Buddha's instruction on that occasion, however, did not stop here, but continued as follows:

> Further, Moggallāna, you should train yourself in this way. You should think, "When calling at families (on the alms round), I shall not be given to pride." Thus should you train yourself. For in families it may happen that people are busy with work and may not notice that a monk has come. Then a monk (if given to pride) may think, "Who, I wonder, has estranged me from this family? These people seem to be displeased with me." Thus, by not receiving an offering from them, he is perturbed; being perturbed he becomes excited; being excited he loses self-control; and if he is uncontrolled, his mind will be far from finding concentration.
>
> Further, Moggallāna, you should train yourself in this way: "I shall not speak contentious talk." Thus should you train yourself. If there is contentious talk, there is sure to be much wordiness; with much wordiness, there will be excitement; one who is excited will lose self-control; and if he is uncontrolled, his mind will be far from finding concentration.

Here the Buddha points out two kinds of behavior that lead to excitement and restlessness. In the first case, the monk is proud of his status and counts on respect from the laity, but if the laypeople pay more attention to their own business than to him, he becomes perturbed and falls away from concentration. In the other case, he takes intellectual delight in discussions, becomes aroused by differences of opinion, and finds pleasure in defeating others in debate. By all this, his mental energy is diverted into futile and unprofitable channels. If one cannot keep one's senses under control, or easily allows one's mind to become excited or diverted, one grows slack and careless in the practice and thus cannot find the unification of mind and inner peace to be obtained in meditation.

After the Buddha had given him these instructions on the overcoming of drowsiness and the avoidance of excitement, Moggallāna asked the following question:

> "In what way, Lord, can it be briefly explained how a monk becomes liberated by the elimination of craving; how he becomes one who has reached the final end, the final security from bondage, the final holy life, the final consummation, and is foremost among devas and humans?"
>
> "Here, Moggallāna, a monk has learned this: 'Nothing is fit to be clung to!' When a monk has learnt that nothing is fit to be clung to, he directly knows everything; by directly knowing everything, he fully comprehends everything; when he fully comprehends everything, whatever feeling he experiences, be it pleasant, painful, or neutral, he abides contemplating impermanence in these feelings, contemplating dispassion, contemplating cessation, contemplating relinquishment. When thus abiding, he does not cling to anything in the world; without clinging he is not agitated; and without agitation he personally attains the complete extinction of defilements. He knows: 'Rebirth has ceased, the holy life has been lived, the task has been done, there is no more of this or that state.'"

After Moggallāna had received all these personal instructions of the Master (as recorded in AN 7:58), he resumed his training with great ardor, fighting vigorously against the inner hindrances of the mind. During his many years of ascetic life he already had, to a great extent, suppressed sensual desire and ill will, the first and the second of the five hindrances. Now, with the help given by the Buddha, he fought against sloth-and-torpor and restlessness-and-worry, the third and fourth hindrances. By overcoming these hindrances he was able to attain meditative states transcending the world of material form, which prepared the way for the penetrative knowledge of reality.

He first attained and enjoyed the overwhelming bliss of the first jhāna, a state of profound absorption and concentration. Yet, gradually, some worldly thoughts arose and claimed his attention, dragging him down to the level of sensory consciousness. The Buddha came to his aid, this time, however, not with detailed instructions as before, but with a brief indication that helped him to break through the impasse. The Exalted One warned him that he should not lightheartedly believe himself to be secure in the attainment of the first jhāna, but should strive to master it and bring it fully under his control. When Moggallāna followed this advice he became proficient in the first jhāna and could no longer be disturbed by mundane thoughts.

Having thus gained a firm footing in the first jhāna, he next gained the second jhāna, which is called "the noble silence" (SN 21:1) because within this absorption all discursive thought is silenced. Thus, in stages, he advanced to the fourth jhāna. From there he proceeded still further in the scale of concentration to the four formless or immaterial absorptions (*arūpajjhāna*) and the cessation of perception and feeling (*saññāvedayita-nirodha*). Then he gained the "signless concentration of mind," which is free from all that "marks" or signifies conditioned existence (SN 40:2–9).[8]

But this attainment, too, was not final. For even here he developed a subtle attachment to his refined experience—an attachment which is still a delusive "sign" or "mark" superimposed on a high spiritual attainment of greatest purity. But aided by the Master's instructions, he broke through these last, most subtle fetters and attained to the final fruit, perfect liberation of mind and liberation by wisdom in all their fullness and depth. The Venerable Mahāmoggallāna had become an arahant.

Like Sāriputta, Moggallāna was an arahant of the type called "liberated in both ways" (*ubhatobhāgavimutta*). Although all arahants are identical in their perfect liberation from ignorance and suffering, they are distinguished into two types on the basis of their proficiency in concentration. Those who can attain the eight deliverances (*aṭṭha vimokkhā*), which include the four formless attainments and the attainment of cessation, are called "liberated in both ways"—liberated from the material body by means of the formless absorptions, and from all defilements by the path of arahantship. Those who lack this mastery over the eight deliverances but have destroyed all defilements through wisdom are called "liberated by wisdom" (*paññāvimutta*).[9] Even more, Moggallāna had not only mastered the successive planes of meditative concentration but had also explored the "roads of psychic power" (*iddhipāda*), and thus had achieved facility in the modes of supernormal knowledge (*abhiññā*). In his own words, he was one of whom it could be declared, "Supported by the Master the disciple attained to greatness of the superknowledges."[10]

This entire development took place within a single week. These were, indeed, seven days of tremendous internal transformation, packed with dramatic ordeals, struggles, and triumphs. The intensity and depth of Moggallāna's determination during this short period must have been staggering. A person like him, endowed with such an active mind and such a wide range of natural gifts, would have had to make a truly valiant effort to cut through all the fetters binding him to this world of vast potentialities. For such an immensity of inner experience to have been compressed into one short week, the dimensions of space and time must have virtually contracted and dissolved. It is reported that on the occasion of his own Enlightenment the Buddha had recollected ninety-one aeons in the first watch of the night. Moggallāna too, in perfecting his superknowledges, would have called up before his mind's eye many past aeons of world contraction and expansion. Here notions of the measurable duration of time fail entirely. For an ordinary person, immured in the prison of the senses, one week is no more that seven days, but for one who has pierced the veil of manifest phenomena and reached the subliminal depths of reality, infinities can burst through the very boundaries of finitude.

Moggallāna later said that he attained arahantship by quick penetration (*khippābhiññā*), that is, in one week, but his progress was difficult (*dukkha-paṭipadā*), requiring the helpful assistance of the Master. Sāriputta, too, attained arahantship by quick penetration, in two weeks, but his progress was smooth (*sukha-paṭipadā*).[11] Moggallāna had advanced to the goal more speedily than Sāriputta because the Buddha directed and inspired him personally and intensively, and also because he had a lesser range to comprehend. Sāriputta was superior to him in regard to the independence of his progress and also in the detailed scope of his knowledge.

THE MOST EXCELLENT PAIR OF DISCIPLES

For a Fully Enlightened One his two chief disciples and his personal attendant are as necessary as the ministers of war, of the interior, and of finance are to a king. The Buddha himself used this comparison with a state's administration. He spoke of Ānanda, who could remember all the discourses, as the treasurer of the Dhamma (the minister of finance), of Sāriputta as its marshal or general-in-command, and of Moggallāna as "the child's nurse" (the minister of the interior).

Of these four (including the Buddha), two groups of two had certain things in common: both the Buddha and Ānanda belonged to the warrior caste (*khattiya*), Sāriputta and Moggallāna to the brahmin caste. This affinity showed itself also in their lives. Ānanda was always with the Buddha; from the time when he was appointed his attendant, he followed him like a shadow. Similarly, Moggallāna was almost inseparable from Sāriputta and nearly always dwelt together with him. Whenever the Buddha, in advancing years, felt physically tired, these three disciples were the only ones whom he asked to expound the Dhamma on his behalf. This happened, for instance, at Kapilavatthu when Moggallāna gave a long discourse on sense control as the remedy against being submerged in the flood of the six senses.[12]

After Sāriputta and Mahāmoggallāna had attained arahantship, the Buddha announced to the Order that they would now be his chief disciples. Some of the monks were surprised and began to grumble, asking why the Master did not treat with such distinction those ordained first, the "men of the first hour," as for instance, the first five disciples, or Yasa, or the three Kassapas. Why did he overlook them and give prominence to those who had entered the Order last and were of junior standing? To this, the Awakened One replied that each reaps according to his merit. For aeons Sāriputta and Moggallāna had been progressing towards this state by gradually cultivating the necessary faculties. Others, however, had developed along different lines. Although both chief disciples were of another caste and from another region than the Buddha's, their special position within the Noble Order was an outcome of the law of kamma.

In many ways the Buddha had spoken in praise of this noble pair of disciples:[13]

> If a devout lay woman should admonish her only son whom she dearly loves, she would rightly do so by saying: "My dear son, you should be like Citta the householder or Hatthaka of Ālavi!"—because these two are models and exemplars for my lay devotees. (And she should further say:) "But if, my dear, you go forth from home into the homeless life of a monk, you should be like Sāriputta and Moggallāna!"—because they are models and exemplars for my bhikkhu disciples.
>
> O monks, seek and cultivate the company of Sāriputta and Moggallāna! They are wise and are helpful to their fellows in the

holy life. Sāriputta is like a mother, and Moggallāna is like a nurse. Sāriputta trains the monks for the fruit of stream-entry, and Moggallāna for the supreme goal.

The characterization of the two in the last text may be interpreted as follows: Sāriputta, like a mother, gives birth to the path of emancipation in his pupils, urging them to cut through the first, most basic fetters and thus attain to stream-entry. In this way he "converts" his pupils by vigorously diverting them from the futility of the round of existence and guiding them into the zone of safety. At this point Moggallāna takes over and leads the pupils further along the upwards path, supporting them in their struggle for arahantship in the same way that he himself had been helped by the Master. Thus he is like a wet-nurse, nourishing the pupils' strength and sustaining their growth.

Both these aspects are found perfectly united in a Fully Awakened One, but in Sāriputta and Moggallāna they were separate qualifications. Though both were "liberated in both ways," for Sāriputta the major emphasis was on wisdom, and for Moggallāna on the meditative "liberation of the mind" (*cetovimutti*). For this reason Sāriputta guided disciples to the intuitive understanding of liberating truth, the breakthrough to the Dhamma (*dhammābhisamaya*), the vision of things in their real undistorted nature. With Moggallāna, who knew well the subtle and tortuous labyrinths of the mind, the stress was on harnessing the forces of concentration toward the removal of all remaining defilements and fetters. This fact found perfect expression when these two spiritual sons of the Buddha had to look after Rāhula, the Buddha's own son. Like every newly ordained monk, Rāhula had two teachers, one in knowledge and one in conduct. Sāriputta was appointed as his teacher in knowledge, and Moggallāna as his teacher in conduct and spiritual practice.

Once Sāriputta said to his friend that, compared with Moggallāna in regard to supernormal powers, he was like a small splinter of rock set against the mighty Himalayas. Moggallāna, however, replied that, compared with Sāriputta in regard to the power of wisdom, he was like a tiny grain of salt set against a big salt barrel (SN 21:3). About the differing range of wisdom, the Buddha said that there are questions that only he could conceive and answer, but not Sāriputta; there are other questions that only Sāriputta could clarify, but not Moggallāna; and there are those questions that only Moggallāna could solve, but not the other disciples (Jāt. 483). Thus the two chief disciples were like a bridge between the supreme qualities of the Buddha and the capacities of the other disciples.

When Devadatta voiced his claim to lead the Order, the Buddha said that he would not entrust anybody with the leadership of the Sangha, not even his two chief disciples, let alone Devadatta (Vin. 2:188). Between the extremes of discipleship—with Sāriputta and Moggallāna at one end of the scale and Devadatta, the most depraved of the disciples, at the other—there is a long and varied line of disciples with different degrees of accomplishments and virtues. It is characteristic that the only slander uttered against the chief disciples came from a follower of Devadatta. The monk Kokālika, wishing to malign them, told the Buddha that the two had evil intentions, which, in fact, was the case with Devadatta. The Buddha, however, replied: "Don't say so, Kokālika, don't speak like that! Let your heart have glad confidence in Sāriputta and Moggallāna! They are virtuous monks." But Kokālika, in spite of this emphatic admonition, persisted in his slander.[14] According to the old texts, Devadatta and Kokālika were reborn in a state of utter suffering, in the deepest hell, while Sāriputta and Moggallāna won the highest bliss, Nibbāna.

In the Pāli Canon there are many reports about the common activities of the two chief disciples as they assisted the Master in looking after the community of monks. Both worked tirelessly for the advancement and benefit of the Order, and their activities aimed at maintaining its inner concord, stability, and discipline deserve special mention. At the request of the Buddha they brought about the banishment of a clique of monks known as "the group of six" (*chabbhaggiya*), after their six leaders, whose reckless and scandalous behavior was threatening to tarnish the entire image of the Buddha's Dispensation in the eyes of the wider populace of the Ganges Valley. The Vinaya Piṭaka records many instances when the Buddha had to promulgate rules of discipline on account of their misconduct. One major upheaval they brought about is reported in the *Kīṭāgiri Sutta* (MN 70), when they flaunted the Buddha's regulations regarding the proper times for meals. Finally they behaved in such a frenzied way that the Buddha sent Sāriputta and Moggallāna, at the head of a group of virtuous monks, to banish these six from their seat of residence, which was near Kīṭāgiri. Thereafter most of them left the Order (Vin. 2:12–14).

The most noteworthy mission the two great disciples performed together was to induce the newly ordained monks led astray by Devadatta to return to the Buddha's fold and to the right conduct of the monk's life. At that time, when Sāriputta gave his exhortation to those misguided monks, he spoke about the power of thought reading, while Moggallāna spoke on psychic powers (Vin. 2:199–200).[15] On another occasion, when a junior monk came to the Buddha and complained that the Venerable Sāriputta had treated him rudely, Moggallāna and Ānanda called together all the monks, so that, for their instruction and edification, they could hear Sāriputta's dignified reply to those accusations (AN 6:11).[16]

The two chief disciples often lived together in the same cell of the monastery, and they held many dialogues for the benefit of their fellow monks. An example of this is the *Anaṅgaṇa Sutta* (Discourse on No Blemishes; MN 5), Sāriputta's great sermon on the removal of "evil wishes," which was inspired by questions from Moggallāna. At the end of the sermon Moggallāna applauded Sāriputta's eloquence, comparing his discourse to a garland of flowers which one might place on one's head as an ornament. On another occasion, when a group of leading disciples had gathered in the Gosiṅga sāla-tree forest on a full-moon night, Sāriputta asked them each in turn to describe what they considered to be the ideal monk, "one who could illuminate this forest" (MN 32). Moggallāna replied:

> Here, friend Sāriputta, two monks engage in a talk on the higher Dhamma (*abhidhamma*), and they question each other, and each being questioned by the other answers without foundering, and their talk rolls on in accordance with the Dhamma. That kind of monk could illuminate this Gosiṅga sāla-tree forest.

Later the Buddha confirmed that Moggallāna was indeed a very capable speaker on the Dhamma, as is evident from his discourses in the canon. Talks on the Dhamma gain in range and depth when they issue from an experience that transcends the realm of the senses. The more one has widened one's consciousness by deep meditation and personal insight into truth, the more convincing one's words will be, and when one can speak from the heights of wisdom, one's understanding will be contagious.[17]

The Buddha often extolled his chief disciples for their personal qualities as much as for their contributions to his mission. One particularly striking instance is recorded in the *Udāna*. When the two were seated near the Master, immersed in deep concentration based on contemplation of the body, first the Buddha spoke an "inspired utterance" (*udāna*) in praise of Sāriputta:[18]

> Just as a mountain made of solid rock
> Stands firm and unshakable,

Even so, when delusion is destroyed,
A bhikkhu, like a mountain, is not perturbed.

Then he applauded Moggallāna:

With mindfulness of the body established,
Controlled over contact's sixfold base,
A bhikkhu who is always concentrated
Can know Nibbāna for himself.

It happened only once that the Buddha preferred Moggallāna's attitude in a certain matter to that of Sāriputta. After he had dismissed from his presence a band of noisy, unmannerly monks, just recently ordained, the Master later asked his two chief disciples what they had thought when he sent those monks away. Sāriputta said he thought that the Master wanted to enjoy a blissful abiding in meditation and that they, the chief disciples, were to do the same. But the Buddha reproached him, saying that he should never again entertain such thoughts. Then he turned to Moggallāna with the same question. Moggallāna replied that he, too, had thought the Master wanted to enjoy the bliss of meditation; but if so, then the responsibility for looking after the community of monks would have devolved on Sāriputta and himself. The Buddha praised him and said that if both his chief disciples took care of the community, it would be as good as if he himself looked after the monks (MN 67).

MOGGALLĀNA'S PSYCHIC POWERS

In the eyes of its early Western interpreters, many of whom saw in Buddhism a rational alternative to Christian dogmatism, Buddhism was essentially a pragmatic code of psychological ethics free from the traditional trappings of religion. In their understanding the suprarational side of Buddhism was dispensable, and the wonders and marvels so conspicuous in the canon and commentaries, when not overlooked, were explained away as later interpolations. But while it is true that early Buddhism does not ascribe the same significance to supernatural events as does Christianity, to insist on expunging the miraculous altogether from Buddhism is to tailor the Dhamma to fit external standards rather than to accept it on its own terms. The Pāli suttas, as a matter of course, frequently ascribe supernormal powers to the Buddha and his arahant disciples, and there is little ground apart from personal prejudice for supposing such passages to be interpolations. Although the Buddha compares the miracle of psychic powers unfavorably with "the miracle of instruction," he does so not to detract from their reality but only to highlight their limited value. Nevertheless, when the suttas are considered in their totality, the clear conclusion emerges that the acquisition of paranormal powers was regarded as a positive good which serves to enhance the stature and completeness of the spiritually accomplished person.

The suttas frequently mention a set of six paranormal faculties—called the six superknowledges (*chaḷabhiññā*)—which were possessed by many arahants. The sixth of these, the knowledge of the destruction of the cankers (*āsavakkhaya-ñāṇa*), is the supramundane realization that all defilements have been eradicated and can never arise again; this knowledge is shared by all arahants, being their guarantee of final deliverance. The other five kinds of superknowledge, however, are all mundane. They include the knowledge of the modes of psychic power (*iddhividha-ñāṇa*), the knowledge of the divine ear-element (*dibbasotadhātu-ñāṇa*), the knowledge encompassing the minds of others (*cetopariya-ñāṇa*), the knowledge of recollection of past lives (*pubbe-nivāsānussati-ñāṇa*), and the divine eye, or the knowledge of the passing away and rebirth of beings (*dibbacakkhu, cutūpāta-ñāṇa*). These faculties may be found outside the Buddha's Dispensation, among mystics and yogis who have mastered meditative absorption, and their attainment does not certify that their possessor has reached a state of true sanctity. They are neither requirements for nor indications of liberation. In the Buddhist texts even Devadatta, the most evil of the monks, had acquired such powers early in his spiritual career and lost them only when he tried to use them against the Buddha.

The Buddha was well aware of the dangers of being sidetracked by a fascination with psychic powers. For those whose minds were still fired by personal ambition, they could be a frightful pitfall, serving to enhance the delusion of separate selfhood and the drive for domination. But for those who had seen through the unreality of "I" and "mine" and whose hearts were rich in compassion, such powers could be valuable tools in the service of the Dispensation. Hence the Buddha includes the five mundane superknowledges among "the fruits of recluseship" in which his system of mental training culminates (DN 2), and he also counts them among the benefits that come from the observance of the precepts (MN 6). He declares that he himself had totally mastered the bases of psychic power, by reason of which, if he had so wished, he could have lived on until the end of the aeon (DN 2; SN 51:10). For the first generation of monks after the Buddha's Parinibbāna the five superknowledges were also given high regard, being included among "the ten qualities that inspire confidence" which the orphaned Sangha, deprived of its Master, used as its criteria for choosing its spiritual guides (MN 108).

While the sixth superknowledge, the knowledge of the destruction of the defilements, is the fruit of insight, the five mundane superknowledges result from concentration. In the suttas the Buddha usually introduces them only after he has explained the four jhānas. The jhānas are the prerequisite for the superknowledges because they transform the tone and clarity of consciousness in ways that open up the channels through which such knowledges become accessible. In its undeveloped condition the mind is soiled by defiled thoughts and moods, which cloud its intrinsic luminosity, drain its potency, and make it rigid and unworkable. But by systematic training in the practice of the four jhānas the mind is cleansed and purified. When it becomes "bright, unblemished, rid of defilement, malleable, wieldy, steady, and imperturbable" (DN 2), it can then function as a mighty instrument capable of uncovering domains of knowledge normally concealed from us by impenetrable screens. Those who have gained access to those hidden dimensions, like the Buddha and Moggallāna, will realize a vast extension of their experience in space and time. Their horizons will grow universal and immeasurable, transcending all boundaries and limitations.

The Buddha particularly stresses a set of practices called "the four roads to power" (*iddhipādā*, or "bases of success") as the means to winning the superknowledges. They are often described in the texts by a set formula that runs as follows:

> Here, bhikkhus, a bhikkhu develops the basis for spiritual power that possesses concentration due to desire and volitional forces of striving. He develops the basis for spiritual power that possesses concentration due to energy and volitional forces of striving. He develops the basis for spiritual power that possesses concentration due to mind and volitional forces of striving. He develops the basis for spiritual power that possesses concentration due to investigation and volitional forces of striving.

Here four separate mental factors are singled out as the main agents for developing concentration: desire, energy, mind, and investigation (*chanda, viriya, citta, vīmaṁsā*). To ensure that the jhāna attained will not merely engender a state of calm but will also serve as a repository of energy, each has to be accompanied by "volitional forces of striving" (*padhānasaṅkhāra*). These forces build up immense psychic energy which can then be tapped, by a suitable determination, to exercise the supernormal powers.

To appreciate the traditional account of the psychic faculties we must grasp the fact that the material world perceived through the senses—which today's physicists declare to be a manifestation of energy—is only a small portion of experiential reality. Beyond the domain of solid, sensible objects exist other vibrational levels which we can scarcely even conceive, let alone understand. Inklings of this wider reality occasionally trickle through the filters that sustain our rational, coherent picture of the world, appearing to us as psychic phenomena or as "wonders" and "miracles." Because disruptions to the regular patterns of the natural order are so rare, we are inclined to regard these familiar patterns as laws, absolutely binding and inviolable. We then insist on ignoring whatever transcends our limited sense faculties, even when the evidence for these other forces is clear and compelling. But the universe as experienced by the wise is much vaster than that known by the common person. The wise can perceive dimensions of reality that others do not even suspect exist, and their insight into the underlying relations between mind and matter gives them a control over phenomena that defies the limits set by our consensual understanding of the world.

The Venerable Mahāmoggallāna was the bhikkhu who had been most assiduous in developing and cultivating the four roads to power, and thus the Buddha named him the foremost disciple among those who possessed the psychic powers (AN 1:14). There were, of course, other prominent disciples who were highly skilled in psychic power, but they were usually proficient in only one or two areas. Thus, for instance, the monk Anuruddha and the nun Sakulā possessed the supernormal vision of the divine eye; the monk Sobhita and the nun Bhaddā Kapilānī could recollect their previous lives far back into the past; the monk Sāgala was skilled in the exercise of the fire element; Cūḷa Panthaka excelled in the ability to manifest himself in multiple bodies; and Pilindavaccha was foremost in communicating with heavenly beings. Mahāmoggallāna, however, had a comprehensive master over the psychic faculties that no other disciple shared, not even the nun Uppalavaṇṇā, who was foremost among the bhikkhunīs in the exercise of the psychic powers.

We shall now turn to what the Buddhist canonical texts relate about Moggallāna's supernormal faculties. We will not follow the familiar sequence of the five superknowledges, but instead will single out the particular faculties demonstrated by Moggallāna in incidents and anecdotes related in the suttas.

PENETRATION OF OTHERS' MINDS (THOUGHT READING)

Once on an Uposatha day, the Buddha sat silently in front of the assembly of monks.[19] At each watch of the night Ānanda requested him to recite the code of monastic discipline, the Pātimokkha, but the Buddha remained silent. Finally, when dawn came, he only said: "This assembly is impure." Thereupon Moggallāna surveyed with his mind the entire assembly and saw one monk sitting there who was "immoral, wicked, of impure and suspect behavior,...rotten within, lustful and corrupt." He went up to him and told him to leave three times. When the monk did not move even after the third request, Moggallāna took him by the arm, led him out of the hall, and bolted the door. Then he begged the Exalted One to recite the Pātimokkha, as the assembly was now pure again.

Once the Master was dwelling together with a community of five hundred monks all of whom were arahants. When Moggallāna joined them, he searched their minds with his own mind and saw that they were arahants, released and free from all defilements. Then the Venerable Vaṅgīsa, the foremost poet in the Sangha, realizing what had taken place, rose from his seat, and in the Buddha's presence praised Moggallāna in verse:

> While the sage is seated on the mountain slope,
> Gone beyond to the far shore of suffering,
> His disciples sit in attendance on him,
> Triple-knowledge men who have left Death behind.
>
> Moggallāna, great in spiritual power,
> Encompassed their minds with his own,
> And searching (he came to see) their minds:
> Fully released, without acquisitions![20]

A third report tells us that once, while the Venerable Anuruddha was meditating in solitude, he considered how the noble path that leads to the extinction of suffering can be perfected by means of the four foundations of mindfulness (*satipaṭṭhāna*). Then Moggallāna, penetrating Anuruddha's mind by his own, appeared before him through supernormal power and requested him to describe in detail this method of practice (SN 52:1–2).

THE DIVINE EAR (CLAIRAUDIENCE)

One evening when Sāriputta went to see Moggallāna he found that his features had such a strikingly serene expression that he felt moved to ask Moggallāna whether he had dwelt in one of the peaceful abodes of mind. Moggallāna replied that he had dwelt only in a coarse abode, but that he had been engaged in a talk on the Dhamma. On being asked with whom he had such a talk, Moggallāna replied that it had been with the Exalted One. Sāriputta remarked that the Master was now dwelling very far away, in Sāvatthī, while they themselves were in Rājagaha. Had Moggallāna gone to the Buddha by way of supernormal power, or had the Buddha come to him? Moggallāna replied that neither had been the case; rather, they had directed toward each other their divine eye and divine ear, which enabled them to engage in a Dhamma talk on the mental faculty of energy. Then Sāriputta exclaimed that Moggallāna, being endowed with powers so great, might be able to live through an entire aeon, like the Buddha, if he so wished (SN 21:3).

With the divine ear Moggallāna could also hear the voices of nonhuman beings, deities, spirits, etc., and receive messages from them. So, for instance, a spirit had warned him against Devadatta, who harbored evil intentions toward the Buddha and was plotting against him (Vin. 2:185).

THE DIVINE EYE (CLAIRVOYANCE)

As mentioned above, Moggallāna, with his divine eye, was able to perceive the Buddha over a long distance. The texts describe other occasions when the Elder made use of this faculty. Once, while Sāriputta was sitting in meditation, a malicious demon (*yakkha*) pounded him on the head. Moggallāna saw this and asked his friend how he was feeling. Sāriputta, who had not seen the demon, said that he was feeling generally well, but was troubled by a slight touch of headache. Then Moggallāna praised his strength of concentration, but Sāriputta said that Moggallāna had been able to see that demon while he himself could not (Ud. 4:4).

Once Moggallāna saw with the divine eye how King Pasenadi had been defeated in battle by the Licchavis and how afterwards he had gathered his troops again and vanquished them. When Moggallāna reported this, some monks accused him of falsely boasting about his supernormal faculties, which is a disciplinary offense making a monk subject to expulsion from the Order. The Buddha, however, explained that Moggallāna had reported only what he had seen and what had actually happened (Vin. 3:108–9).

Above all, Moggallāna used his divine eye to observe the operation of the law of kamma and its fruits. Again and again he saw how human beings, through their evil actions that harmed their fellow beings, were reborn among the *petas*, miserable ghosts, and had to undergo much suffering, while others, who practiced charity and virtue, rose upwards to the heavenly abodes. He often reported such cases to exemplify the law of kamma. These reports are collected in two books of the Pāli Canon, one dealing with the ghost realm (the *Petavatthu*, fifty-one reports) and one with the heavenly abodes (the *Vimānavatthu*, eighty-five). From this it can be readily understood why Moggallāna was famous as one who knew the worlds beyond as well as the workings of kamma. The reports are too numerous to discuss here, but at least one of his visions, recorded in the Saṁyutta Nikāya, should be mentioned.[21]

Once Moggallāna lived on Vulture's Peak, near Rājagaha, together with the monk Lakkhaṇa, one of the thousand brahmin ascetics who had been converted together with Uruvela Kassapa. One morning, when they had descended from the peak to go on alms round in the town, Moggallāna smiled when they reached a certain place on the road. When his companion asked him the reason, Moggallāna said that this was not the right time to explain; he would explain later in the presence of the Master. When they later met the Buddha, Lakkhaṇa repeated his question, and Moggallāna now said that at that spot he had seen many miserable ghosts flying through the air, chased around by predators and tormented by various kinds of afflictions. The Buddha confirmed this as absolutely true and added that he himself spoke only reluctantly about such matters because people with skeptical minds would not believe it. Then the Buddha, out of his universal knowledge, explained what propensities and behavior had brought those ghosts to their present pitiable position.

Travel by Mind-made Body (Astral Travel)

"Just as a person might bend his stretched arm or stretch his bent arm," so quickly could Moggallāna depart bodily from the human world and reappear in a celestial realm. Repeatedly he made use of this capacity to instruct other beings and to look after the affairs of the Order. Thus he taught the devas in the realm of the Thirty-three the factors of stream-entry, and tested Sakka, their king, to determine whether he had understood the teaching about the extinction of craving (MN 37). When the Buddha was preaching the Abhidhamma for three months in one of the heavenly worlds, Moggallāna appeared in that heaven, informed him of happenings in the Order, and asked for instructions (Jāt. 483). He visited not only the gods of the sense sphere, but also those of the Brahma-world. Thus he appeared before a Brahmā deity who believed that there were no ascetics capable of entering his realm, and through questioning and supernormal feats Moggallāna shook that deity's self-assurance (SN 6:5). On another occasion he appeared in front of a Brahmā named Tissa—who formerly had been a monk and had died recently—and gave him instructions about stream-entry and the realization of final deliverance (AN 4:34, 7:53).

TELEKINESIS (SUPERNORMAL LOCOMOTION)

Moggallāna also had mastery over what appears to be solid matter. Once the monks staying at a monastery were negligent, busying themselves too much with material trifles. Learning of this, the Buddha asked Moggallāna to use a feat of supernormal power in order to shake them out of their complacency and inspire them to return to serious striving. In response, Moggallāna pushed the building with his big toe, so that the entire monastery, called the Mansion of Migāra's Mother, shook and trembled as if there was an earthquake. The monks were so deeply stirred by this event that they shook off their worldly interests and again became receptive to the Buddha's instructions. The Buddha explained to them that the source of Moggallāna's great supernormal prowess was the development of the four roads to power (SN 51:14; Jāt. 299).

Once Moggallāna visited Sakka in his heavenly realm and saw that he was living rather lightheartedly. Captivated by heavenly sense pleasures, he had become forgetful of the Dhamma. To dispel his vanity Moggallāna used his toe to shake Sakka's celestial palace, the Banner of Victory, in which Sakka took much pride. This had a shock effect on Sakka too, and he now recalled the teaching on the extinction of craving, which the Buddha had briefly taught him not long ago. It was the same teaching that the Buddha had given to Moggallāna as a spur to attaining arahantship (MN 37).

Once there was a famine in the area where the Buddha and his community of monks were residing, and the monks could not obtain sufficient almsfood. On that occasion Moggallāna asked the Buddha whether he might overturn the ground so that the nourishing substance underneath would be accessible and could be eaten. But the Buddha prohibited him, as this would cause the destruction of a large number of living beings. Then Moggallāna offered to use his psychic power to open a road to the Uttarakuru country so that the monks could go there for alms. This, too, the Buddha prohibited. But all survived the famine unharmed, even without such supernormal devices (Vin. 3:7). This was the only occasion when the Buddha disapproved of Moggallāna's suggestions.

Moggallāna's supernormal power expressed itself too in his ability to bring things from far distances by magical locomotion. Thus, for instance, he brought lotus stalks from the Himalayas when Sāriputta was ill and needed them for medicine (Vin. 1:214–15; 2:140). He also fetched a shoot of the Bodhi tree for Anāthapiṇḍika to be planted at the Jetavana Monastery (Jāt. 78). However, when his fellow-monk Piṇḍola asked him to prove the superiority of the Buddha's Sangha over the sectarians by magically bringing down a precious bowl that had been hung up in town so high that nobody could take it down, Moggallāna refused, saying that Piṇḍola himself possessed sufficient powers to do it. But when Piṇḍola actually performed that feat, the Buddha rebuked him: a monk should not display supernormal powers merely to impress the laity (Vin. 2:110–12).

THE POWER OF TRANSFORMATION

Although we have confined the preceding discussion to incidents mentioned in the Pāli Canon, this account would be deficient if we did not mention what the commentaries regard as Moggallāna's most formidable display of psychic power, his triumph over the divine serpent, the royal nāga Nandopananda. This incident is recorded in the *Visuddhimagga* (XII, 106–16). On one occasion, when the Buddha together with five hundred monks visited the heaven of the Thirty-three, they passed just above the abode of Nandopananda. This infuriated the royal nāga, who sought to take revenge by surrounding Mount Sineru with his coils and spreading his hood so that the entire world was enveloped in darkness. Several eminent monks offered to subdue the nāga, but the Buddha, aware of his ferocity, would not permit them. It was only to Moggallāna, the last to volunteer, that he granted permission. Moggallāna then transformed himself into a huge royal nāga and engaged Nandopananda in a terrible battle of flame and smoke. Drawing upon one power after another, appearing in a variety of shapes and sizes, he shattered his rival's defenses. In the last phase of the battle he assumed the form of a *supaṇṇa*, the celestial eagle, arch-enemy of the nāga. At this point Nandopananda capitulated, and the elder, assuming once again the form of a monk, brought him to the Buddha in triumph and elicited from him an apology.

MOGGALLĀNA'S PREVIOUS LIVES

About his recollection of his own former existences, Moggallāna spoke only once, in the *Māratajjaniya Sutta* (MN 50). With that text we shall deal later.

In the Jātakas, the stories about the Buddha's former existences, it is reported that the Bodhisatta and Moggallāna had lived together quite often. In no less than thirty-one lives the two had met, and in thirty of them Moggallāna and Sāriputta had lived together; the bond that had connected these three was already strong in previous lives. Although these thirty-one lives are but an infinitesimal fraction of the infinity of lives through which every being in saṁsāra has passed, they enable us to draw some substantive conclusions concerning Moggallāna's life and personality.

The first thing we find from the Jātakas is his close relationship to the Bodhisatta. Moggallāna and Sāriputta were often the Bodhisatta's brothers (Jāt. 488, 509, 542, 543), his friends (326), or his ministers (401). Sometimes they were his disciples as ascetics (423, 522), or even his teachers (539). Sometimes Sāriputta is the son and Moggallāna the general of the royal Bodhisatta (525). When the Buddha was Sakka, king of the gods, they were the moon-god and the sun-god respectively (450).

The second point worth noting is the relationship of Sāriputta to Moggallāna. When, in the Jātakas, both are seen to traverse all the heights and depths of saṁsāra, they sometimes play quite inferior parts in relation to the main figures of the respective stories. There appears a certain lawfulness in the stories insofar as the difference between them (e.g., in status) is usually greater when their level of rebirth is lower, and smaller when their rebirth is on a higher level. When reborn as animals, they rarely were equals (only as swans, in Jāt. 160, 187, 215, 476), and Sāriputta was most often born in a higher species of animals. Thus they were snake and rat (73), bird and tortoise (206, 486), lion and tiger (272, 361, 438), monkey and elephant (37), monkey and jackal (316), man and jackal (490). When born as human beings in worldly careers, Sāriputta was always in a higher position than Moggallāna: as a royal prince and royal minister (525), royal minister and son of a slave (544), charioteer of the royal Bodhisatta and charioteer of king Ānanda (151). Once Moggallāna was the moon god and Sāriputta the wise ascetic Nārada (535). But when both were ascetics or deities, they were generally of equal status. Once it happened that Sāriputta was only the moon-god and Moggallāna the superior sun-god (450); once Sāriputta was the king of the nāgas and Moggallāna the king of their foes, the supaṇṇas (545).

The only time when Moggallāna appears in the Jātakas without Sāriputta is a life in which he holds the office of Sakka, king of the gods. At that time, as Sakka, he also appeared on earth to a miser in order to urge on him the virtue of giving and thus to lead him to a better rebirth (78). But another time when Sāriputta and Moggallāna lived on earth they were stingy merchants who had buried much money. After death, they were reborn close to their buried treasure, but as a snake and a rat (73).

There is also a story in which Moggallāna was reborn as a jackal. Seeing a dead elephant, he was so greedy for its flesh that he crept through an intestinal aperture right into the elephant's belly, ate as much as he could, but was then unable to get out again, suffering mortal fear—an impressive symbol of the perils of sensual enjoyment (490).

Finally, in the famous Jātaka about the law of the Kuru people (276), Moggallāna is a keeper of grain stores and Sāriputta a merchant. Both were very careful in observing the law of non-stealing.

MOGGALLĀNA'S VERSES

Like many other arahant disciples of the Buddha, the Venerable Moggallāna has left us, in the *Theragāthā*, a testament in verse in which he celebrates his triumphs over the vicissitudes of life. His chapter, containing sixty-three verses (1146–1208), is the second longest in the collection. The overriding theme of these verses is his equipoise in the face of saṁsāra's temptations and upheavals. The suffering of worldly affairs no longer touched him, as he dwelt in a peace that transcended all the pain and restlessness of becoming.

His verses begin with four stanzas (1146–49), apparently addressed to himself, extolling the life of a forest hermit devoted to the struggle against the forces of mortality:

> Living in the forest, subsisting on almsfood,
> Delighting in the scraps that come into our bowl,
> Let us tear apart the army of Death
> Firmly concentrated within ourselves.
>
> Living in the forest, subsisting on almsfood,
> Delighting in the scraps that come into our bowl,
> Let us shatter the army of Death
> As an elephant does a hut of reeds.

The next two verses differ only in replacing "subsisting on almsfood" with "persevering."

The next eight verses (1150–57) are spoken to a prostitute who tried to seduce him. Although their tone, and their depreciation of the body, may strike the contemporary reader as abrasive, it must be remembered that the Buddha himself was emphatic about the need to contemplate the wretchedness of physical existence, not from a morbid loathing of life but as an antidote to sensual lust, the most powerful bond tying beings to the sense sphere. The next two verses were spoken with reference to the death of the Venerable Sāriputta. Whereas Ānanda, who was not yet an arahant, was stricken with fear and terror, Moggallāna reflected on the impermanence of all conditioned things and thereby remained calm (1158–59).

In two piquant verses (1167–68) Moggallāna's extols his prowess in meditation:

> Flashes of lightning fall upon the cleft
> Of the mountains Vebhāra and Paṇḍava,
> But gone within the cleft he meditates—
> The son of the peerless Stable One.
>
> Tranquil, still, the sage resorts
> To remote places for his lodging;
> A true heir of the supreme Buddha,
> He is venerated even by Brahmā.

The following verses (1169–73) are addressed to a superstitious brahmin of wrong views who had abused the Venerable Mahākassapa when the latter was walking on alms round. Moggallāna warns him against the dangers of such conduct and urges him to respect the holy ones. He then praises Sāriputta (1176–77). The commentary says that the next four verses (1178–81) are Sāriputta's own praise of Moggallāna.

After Moggallāna reciprocates with a verse in praise of Sāriputta, he then reviews his attainments and rejoices in his consummation of the goal of his monk's life (1182–86):

> In but a moment I can create
> A hundred thousand koṭis of bodies;
> I am skilled in transformations,
> I am the master of psychic powers.

A master of concentration and knowledge,
Moggallāna, gone to perfection,
A sage in the Dispensation of the Detached One,
With concentrated faculties has cut off his bonds
As an elephant bursts a rotten creeper.

The Teacher has been served by me,
The Buddha's Teaching has been done.
The heavy burden has been dropped,
The conduit to becoming has been uprooted.

That goal has been attained by me
For the sake of which I have gone forth
From the home life into homelessness—
The destruction of all the fetters.

The last verses (1187–1208) are identical with those concluding his encounter with Māra, recorded in MN 50, to which we shall now turn.

THE LAST DAYS OF MOGGALLĀNA

Half a year before the Buddha's Parinibbāna, on the full-moon day of the month Kattika (October/November), death separated the two chief disciples for the last time. It was on this day that Sāriputta passed away in his birth chamber in his parental home—surrounded by his many pupils, but far away from Moggallāna. Even though during life the two had been almost inseparable, their deaths, like their attainment of arahantship, occurred at different places.

Soon after the passing away of Sāriputta, Moggallāna had a bizarre encounter with Māra, the Evil One, the Tempter and Lord of Death,[22] which may well have been a premonition of his own imminent demise. One night, while the elder was walking back and forth for exercise, Māra slipped into his body and entered his bowels. Moggallāna sat down and attended to his abdomen, which suddenly felt as heavy as a bag of beans. He then discovered the Evil One lodged within his own belly. Calmly he told Māra to get out. Māra was astonished that he had been detected so soon, and in his delusion thought that even the Buddha would not have recognized him so quickly. But Moggallāna read his thoughts and again ordered him to depart. Māra now escaped through Moggallāna's mouth and stood at the door of the hut. Moggallāna told him that he knew him not only on that day but had also known him in the past, for their kammic connection was old and deep.

The following is the gist of what he said: The first of the five Buddhas appearing in our "fortunate aeon" (*bhaddakappa*) was Kakusandha, whose chief disciples were the arahants Vidhura and Sañjīva. At that time, Moggallāna was Māra, by name Māra Dūsī. For Māra too, like Mahābrahmā and Sakka, is not a permanent being but a cosmic post or office—chief of demons, lord of the lower world—which is filled by different individuals migrating through the round of existence. At that time Māra Dūsī had a sister named Kālī, whose son was to become the Māra of our age. Hence Moggallāna's own nephew then was now standing in front of him in his hut as the present Māra. When, in that past age, Moggallāna was Māra, he had taken possession of a boy and made him throw a potsherd at the head of the Buddha Kakusandha's chief disciple, the arahant Vidhura. The wound was a severe one, which caused blood to flow.

When the Buddha Kakusandha turned around and saw this, he said: "Indeed, Māra knows no moderation here"—for even in diabolical actions there might be moderation—and under the Perfect One's glance Māra Dūsī's body dissolved and reappeared in the deepest hell. Just a moment earlier he had been the overlord of all the hellish worlds, and now he himself was one of hell's victims. For many thousands of years Moggallāna had to suffer in hell as the kammic result of attacking an arahant. He was condemned to spend ten thousand years alone in the Great Hell, having a human body and the head of a fish, just like the beings in Pieter Breughel's pictures of the hells. Whenever two lances of his torturers crossed in his heart, he would know that a thousand years of his torment had passed.

This encounter with Māra once more brought to Moggallāna's mind the terrors of saṁsāra from which he was now forever free. Soon afterwards Moggallāna felt that the time of his last existence was running out. Being an arahant he saw no reason to extend his life span to the end of the aeon by an act of will,[23] and he calmly allowed impermanence to take its lawful course.

MOGGALLĀNA'S DEATH

Surrounded by many of his monks, the Buddha passed away peacefully during a meditative absorption which he entered with perfect mastery. Sāriputta's death in his parental home, likewise with fellow monks in attendance, was similarly serene. Ānanda died at the age of 120; as he did not wish to burden anyone by his funeral, he entered meditative concentration on the fire element so that his body vanished in a blaze. Considering the serene death of the Master and of these two disciples, one would have expected that Mahāmoggallāna, too, would have undergone the final dissolution of the body under peaceful circumstances. But Moggallāna's end was very different, though the gruesome nature of his death did not shake his firm and serene mind.

Moggallāna passed away a fortnight after his friend Sāriputta, on the new-moon day of the month Kattika (October/November), in the autumn. The "great decease" of the Buddha took place on the full-moon night of the month Vesākha (May), half a year after the death of his two chief disciples. The Buddha was in his eightieth year when he passed away, while both Sāriputta and Mahāmoggallāna died at the age of eighty-four.

The circumstances of Moggallāna's death are related in two sources, the Dhammapada Commentary (to vv. 137–40) and the Jātaka Commentary (to Jāt. 523). Although these two sources share a common core, they differ in details, which no doubt stem from embellishments in the course of oral transmission. The account here will be based on the Dhammapada Commentary, with the differences in the Jātaka Commentary noted parenthetically.[24]

Because the Buddha was so skillful as a teacher, leading countless people to the gates of deliverance, the populace of Magadha for the most part had transferred its allegiance from the various rival ascetic orders to the Enlightened One and his Sangha. A group of naked ascetics, resentful over this loss of prestige, pinned the prime responsibility for their hard times on the Venerable Mahāmoggallāna. They believed that Moggallāna had won over their own adherents to the Buddha's Dhamma with his reports of his celestial travels, in which he related how he had seen the virtuous devotees of the Buddha enjoying rebirth in heaven and the followers of other sects, lacking moral conduct, suffering in miserable subhuman states of existence. These ascetics were so enraged about their loss of popularity that they wanted to eliminate Moggallāna. Without accepting responsibility for their own misfortune, they projected the blame externally and concentrated their envy and hate on the great disciple.

While the ascetics were hesitant to kill Moggallāna by their own hand, they had no scruples about employing others to carry out their nefarious deed. Having procured a thousand gold coins from their followers, they approached a band of brigands and offered them the money in exchange for the great disciple's life. At that time Moggallāna was living alone in a forest hut at the Black Rock, on the slope of Mount Isigili outside Rājagaha.

After his encounter with Māra he knew that the end of his days was near. Having enjoyed the bliss of liberation, he now felt the body to be an obstruction and burden and had no desire to use his psychic faculties to keep it alive for the rest of the aeon. Yet, when he saw the brigands approach, he knew they were coming to kill him, and he used his supernormal powers to slip through the keyhole. The gangsters arrived at an empty hut, and though they searched everywhere, they could not find him. They returned the following day too, but this time the elder soared up into the air and escaped through the roof. The next month too the bandits came, but again they could not catch the elder. (In the Jātaka version the bandits return on six consecutive days and catch him only on the seventh day.)

Moggallāna's motivation in escaping was not fear of death. The reason he used his psychic powers to elude the gangsters was not to protect his body but to spare the would-be assassins the frightful kammic consequences of such a murderous deed, necessarily leading to rebirth in the hells. He wanted to spare them such a fate by giving them time to reconsider and abstain from their crime. But their greed for the promised money was so great that they persisted and returned again the following month (or on the seventh day in the Jātaka account). This time their persistence was "rewarded," for at that moment Moggallāna suddenly lost his psychic mastery over the body.

The reason for this sudden change in fate lay in a terrible deed he had committed in the distant past. Many aeons ago, in a previous birth, Moggallāna had brought about the death of his parents (in the Jātaka version, however, he relents at the last moment and spares them). That heinous kamma had brought him to a rebirth in hell for countless years, but it had not yet fully matured. A residue remained, and now, when he was in mortal danger, that residue suddenly ripened and confronted him with its fruit. Moggallāna realized that he had no choice but to submit to destiny. The brigands entered, knocked him down, and "pounded his bones until they were as small as grains of rice." Then, thinking that he was dead, they threw his body behind a clump of bushes and fled, keen on collecting their reward.

But Moggallāna's physical and mental strength was formidable and he had not yet capitulated to death. He regained consciousness and, by the power of meditation, he soared through the air and came into the presence of the Master. There he announced that he would attain final Nibbāna. The Buddha asked him to give a final sermon to the community of monks, which he did, with an additional display of wonders and marvels. Then he paid homage to the Blessed One, returned to the Black Rock, and passed into the Nibbana element without residue. (The Jātaka account more realistically omits the final sermon and has Moggallāna expire right at the Buddha's feet.)

In this last turbulent phase of his life, the kamma of the past that had ripened so suddenly could affect only his body but could not shake his mind, for he no longer identified himself with his empirical personality. For him the five aggregates that others identified as "Moggallāna" were as foreign as an inanimate body:

> They penetrate the subtle truth
> As the tip of a hair with an arrow
> Who see the five aggregates as alien
> And do not regard them as self.
>
> Those who see conditioned things
> As alien and not as self
> Have pierced right through the subtle truth
> As the tip of a hair with an arrow.
>
> (Thag. 1160–61)

This last episode of Moggallāna's life, however, did show that the law of moral causality has even greater potency than the supernormal feats of a master of psychic power. Only a Buddha can control the kammic consequences acting upon his body to such an extent that nothing might cause his premature death.

Speaking about his chief disciples shortly after their deaths, the Buddha declared:

> Those who in the past have been Holy Ones, Fully Enlightened Ones, those Blessed Ones, too, had such excellent pairs of disciples as I had in Sāriputta and Moggallāna. Those who in the future will be Holy Ones, Fully Enlightened Ones, those Blessed Ones, too, will have such excellent pairs of disciples as I had in Sāriputta and Moggallāna.
>
> Marvellous it is, most wonderful it is, bhikkhus, concerning those disciples, that they will act in accordance with the Master's teaching, will act in accordance with his advice; that they will be dear to the four assemblies, will be loved, respected, and honored by them.

Sāriputta and Mahāmoggallāna were such wonderful disciples, the Buddha said, that the assembly of monks appeared empty to him after their death. It was marvelous that such an excellent pair of disciples existed, but it was marvelous, too, that, in spite of their excellence, when the two had passed away there was no grief, no lamentation on the part of the Master.[25]

Therefore, the Buddha continued, inspired by the greatness of the two chief disciples, let dedicated followers of the Dhamma strive to be their own island of refuge, with the Dhamma as their island of refuge, not looking for any other refuge. Let them rely entirely on the powerful help of the four foundations of mindfulness (*satipaṭṭhāna*). Those who, with keen desire, thus train themselves along the Noble Eightfold Path will certainly pass beyond all the realms of darkness which abound in saṁsāra. So the Master assures us.

CHAPTER 3

MAHĀKASSAPA

FATHER OF THE SANGHA

Hellmuth Hecker

KASSAPA'S EARLY YEARS

SHORTLY BEFORE HIS PARINIBBĀNA the Buddha had refused to appoint a personal successor. Instead he urged the monks to look upon the Dhamma and the Vinaya—the doctrine and the discipline—as their Master, for within the teachings proclaimed during his forty-five year ministry they could find all the instructions they needed to tread the path to deliverance. Nevertheless, though the monks did not select a successor, in the period immediately following the Blessed One's demise the community came to regard with increasing reverence one solitary elder whose person emanated a natural aura of strength and authority. This figure, whom the Pāli commentaries describe as "the disciple who was the Buddha's counterpart" (*buddhapaṭibhāga-sāvaka*), was known as the Venerable Mahākassapa, Kassapa the Great.

There were many factors that contributed to Mahākassapa's rise to preeminence in the newly orphaned Sangha. He shared with the Buddha seven of the thirty-two "marks of a great man" and had been praised by the Master for his meditative attainments and realizations.[1] He was the only monk with whom the Buddha had exchanged robes, a special honor. Mahākassapa possessed to the highest degree the "ten qualities that inspire confidence."[2] He was also a model of a disciplined and austere life devoted to meditation. So it is hardly surprising that he assumed the presidency of the First Council of the Sangha, which had been summoned on his urgent advice. Evidently it was for the same reasons that, much later in China and Japan, this redoubtable elder came to be regarded as the first patriarch of Ch'an or Zen Buddhism.

Like the two chief disciples, Sāriputta and Moggallāna, Mahākassapa was of brahmin descent. Some years before the Bodhisatta's own birth he was born in the Magadha country, in the village Mahātittha, as the son of the brahmin Kapila and his wife Sumanādevī.[3] He was named Pipphali. His father owned sixteen villages over which he ruled like a little king, so Pipphali grew up in the midst of wealth and luxury. Yet already in his youth he felt a longing to leave the worldly life behind and hence he did not want to marry. When his parents repeatedly urged him to take a wife, he told them that he would look after them as long as they lived but that after their deaths he would become an ascetic. Yet they insisted again and again that he should take a wife, and thus just to comfort his mother he finally agreed to marry—on the condition that a girl could be found who conformed to his idea of perfection.

For that purpose he commissioned goldsmiths to fashion for him a golden statue of a beautiful maiden. He had it bedecked with fine garments and ornaments and showed it to his parents, saying: "If you can find a maiden like this for me, I shall remain in the home life." But his mother was a clever woman and thought: "Surely my son must have done deeds of merit in the past, and he must have done them together with a woman who is the counterpart of this golden image." Thus she approached eight brahmins, showered them with rich gifts, and asked them to take the image and travel around in search of a human likeness of it. The brahmins thought: "Let us first go to the Madda country, which is a gold mine of beautiful women." There they found at Sāgala a girl whose beauty equaled that of the image. She was Bhaddā Kapilānī, a wealthy brahmin's daughter, aged sixteen, four years younger than Pipphali Kassapa. Her parents agreed to the marriage proposal, and the brahmins returned to tell of their success.

Yet Bhaddā Kapilānī too did not wish to marry. Like Pipphali, she longed to live a religious life and wished to leave home as a female ascetic. Such correspondence between her aspiration and that of Pipphali was not due to chance but sprang from the strong kammic bond they had forged in previous lives. Maturing in the present life, this bond was to unite them in marriage in their youth and to lead to a decisive separation later on—a separation which was again to be resolved by a union at a still higher level, when both consummated their spiritual endeavors by winning the supreme fruit of holiness under the Enlightened One.

Pipphali was most distressed to hear that his plot had been foiled and that his parents had actually found a girl who matched the golden statue. Still intent on escaping from his agreement, he sent the following letter to the girl: "Bhaddā, please marry someone else of equal status and live a happy home life with him. As for myself, I shall become an ascetic. Please do not have regrets." Bhaddā Kapilānī, like-minded as she was, independently sent him a similar letter. But their parents, suspecting such an exchange would take place, had both letters intercepted on the way and replaced by letters of welcome.

So Bhaddā was taken to Magadha and the young couple were married. However, in accordance with their ascetic yearning, both agreed to maintain a life of celibacy. To give expression to their decision, each night they would lay a garland of flowers between them before they went to bed, resolving, "If on either side the flowers wilt, we shall understand that the person on whose side they wilted had given rise to a lustful thought." At night they lay awake all night long from fear of making bodily contact; during the day they did not even smile at one another. As long as their parents lived they remained aloof from worldly enjoyment, and they did not even have to look after the estate's farms.

When Pipphali's parents died, the couple took charge of the large property. It was then that they felt the spur that set them on the course of renunciation. One day, as Pipphali was inspecting the fields, he saw as if with new eyes something that he had seen so often before. He observed that when his farm hands plowed the land, many birds gathered and eagerly picked the worms from the furrows. This sight, so common to a farmer, now startled him. It struck him forcefully that what brought him his wealth, the produce of his fields, was bound up with the suffering of other living beings. His livelihood was purchased with the death of so many worms and other little creatures living in the soil. Thinking about this, he asked one of his laborers: "Who will have to bear the consequences of such an evil action?"

"You yourself, sir," was the answer.[4]

Shaken by that insight into kammic retribution, Pipphali went home and reflected: "If I have to carry along the burden of guilt for this killing, of what use to me is all my wealth? I would be better off giving it all to Bhaddā and going forth into the ascetic life."

But at home, at about the same time, Bhaddā had a similar experience, seeing afresh with a deeper understanding something she had very often seen before. Her servants had spread out sesamum seeds to dry in the sun, and crows and other birds ate the insects that had been attracted by the seeds. When Bhaddā asked her servants who had to account morally for the violent death of so many creatures, she was told that the kammic responsibility was hers. Then she thought: "If even by this much I commit evil, I won't be able to lift my head above the ocean of rebirths even in a thousand lives. As soon as Pipphali returns, I shall hand over everything to him and leave to take up the ascetic life."

When both found themselves in accord, they had saffron cloth and clay bowls brought for them from the bazaar and then shaved each other's head. They thus became like ascetic wanderers, and they made the aspiration: "We dedicate our going forth to the arahants in the world!" Even though they had not yet encountered the Buddha or his Teaching, they knew instinctively that they should follow the ascetic life in a state of "adopted discipleship" to the truly wise and holy ones, whoever they might be. Then, slinging their alms bowls over their shoulders, they left the manor house, unnoticed by the servants. When, however, they reached the next village, which belonged to the estate, the laborers and their families saw them. Crying and lamenting, they fell at the feet of the two ascetics and exclaimed: "Oh, dear and noble ones! Why do you want to make us helpless orphans?"

"It is because we have seen the three worlds to be like a house afire that we go forth into the homeless life." To those who were serfs, Pipphali Kassapa granted freedom, and he and Bhaddā continued on, leaving the villagers behind still weeping.

As they walked, Kassapa went ahead while Bhaddā followed behind him. Then the thought occurred to Kassapa: "Now, this Bhaddā Kapilānī follows me close behind, and she is a woman of great beauty. Some people could easily think: 'Though they are ascetics, they still cannot live without each other! What they are doing is unseemly!' If they spoil their minds by such false thoughts or even spread evil rumors, they will cause great harm to themselves. It is better that we separate." Thus, when they reached a crossroads, Kassapa told her what he had been thinking and said to her: "Bhaddā, you take one of these roads, and I shall go the other way." She replied: "It is true, for ascetics a woman is an obstacle. People might suspect us of misconduct and slander us, so let us part. You go your way and I'll go my way."

She then respectfully circumambulated him three times, saluted his feet, and with folded hands she spoke: "Our close companionship and friendship that had lasted for an unfathomable past comes to an end today. Please take the path to the right and I shall take the other road." Thus they parted and went their individual ways, seeking the high goal of arahantship, final deliverance from suffering. It is said that the earth, shaken by the power of their virtue, quaked and trembled, and peals of thunder came forth from the sky, and the mountains at the edge of the world system resounded.

BHADDĀ KAPILĀNĪ

Let us first follow Bhaddā Kapilānī. Her road led her to Sāvatthī where she listened to the Buddha's discourses at the Jetavana monastery. As the Bhikkhunī Sangha, the order of nuns, did not yet exist at that time, she took up residence at a nunnery of non-Buddhist female ascetics not far from Jetavana. There she lived for five years until she could obtain ordination as a bhikkhunī. It was not long afterward that she attained the goal of the holy life, arahantship. The Buddha praised Bhaddā as being the foremost among the nuns who could recollect their past lives (AN 1, chap. 14). The Pali commentaries and the Jātaka stories leave us a record of some of her former existences in which she had been Kassapa's wife.

One day she uttered the following verses in which she praised Mahākassapa and declared her own attainment:

A son of the Buddha and his rightful heir,
Kassapa who is well concentrated
Knows his abodes in previous lives
And sees the heavens and planes of woe.

He too has attained the destruction of birth,
A sage consummate in direct knowledge;
Endowed with these three modes of knowledge,
The brahmin is a triple-knowledge bearer.

Just so is Bhaddā Kapilānī
A triple-knowledge nun who has left Death behind.
Having conquered Māra and his mount,
She lives bearing her final body.

Having seen the grave danger in the world,
We both went forth into homelessness.
Now we are destroyers of the cankers;
Tamed and cool, we have won Nibbāna.

(Thig. 63–66)

As an arahant bhikkhunī, Bhaddā devoted herself chiefly to the education of the younger nuns and their instruction in monastic discipline. In the Bhikkhunī Vibhaṅga (Analysis of Nuns' Discipline), instances are recorded involving her pupils which led to the prescribing of certain disciplinary rules for bhikkhunīs.[5] There were also two instances when Bhaddā Kapilānī had to bear the envy of another nun who was hostile toward Mahākassapa too. The nun Thullanandā was learned in the Dhamma and a good preacher, but evidently she had more intelligence than gentleness of heart. She was self-willed and not prepared to change her conduct, as evidenced by several Vinaya texts. When Bhaddā, too, became a popular preacher of Dhamma, even preferred by some of Thullanandā's own pupils, Thullanandā became jealous. In order to annoy Bhaddā, once she and her pupil nuns walked up and down in front of Bhaddā's cell, reciting loudly. She was censured by the Buddha on that account.[6] Another time, at Bhaddā's request, she had arranged temporary living quarters for Bhaddā when the latter visited Sāvatthī. But then, in another fit of jealousy, she threw her out of those quarters.[7] Bhaddā, however, being an arahant, was no longer affected by such happenings and looked at them with detachment and compassion.

THE SAṀSĀRIC BACKGROUND

Mahākassapa and Bhaddā Kapilānī originally formed their aspirations to great discipleship under the Buddha Padumuttara, the fifteenth Buddha of antiquity, who arose a hundred thousand aeons in the past and had his main monastic seat in the Khema Deer Park near the city of Haṁsavatī.[8] At that time the future Kassapa was a wealthy landowner named Vedeha and Bhaddā was his wife. One day Vedeha went to the monastery and was seated in the assembly at the very moment that the Teacher declared an elder named Mahānisabha his third preeminent disciple, the foremost of the proponents of the ascetic practices (*etadaggaṁ dhutavādānaṁ*). The lay devotee Vedeha was pleased by this and invited the Teacher and his entire Sangha to his home for the next day's meal.

While the Buddha and the monks were in his house taking their meal, the lay devotee caught sight of the Elder Mahānisabha walking on his alms round down the street. He went outside and invited the elder to join the gathering, but the elder declined. Vedeha then took his bowl, filled it with food, and brought it back to him. When he returned to the house he asked the Buddha about the reason for the elder's strange refusal. The Teacher explained: "Lay devotee, we accept invitations to homes for meals, but that bhikkhu lives solely on food gained on alms round; we live in town monasteries, but he lives solely in the forest; we live with a roof over our head, but he lives out in the open air." When the lay devotee heard this he became even more pleased "like an oil lamp sprinkled with oil," and he reflected: "Why should I be satisfied simply with arahantship? I will make an aspiration to become the foremost disciple among the practitioners of the ascetic practices under a Buddha in the future."

Then he invited the Buddha and the community of monks to his home for alms for a week, made presentations of the triple robe to the entire Sangha, and prostrating himself at the Master's feet, he declared his aspiration. The Buddha Padumuttara looked into the future and saw that the aspiration would be fulfilled. He then gave Vedeha the prediction: "In the future, 100,000 aeons from now, a Buddha named Gotama will arise in the world. Under him you will be the third chief disciple named Mahākassapa." Bhaddā, on her part, had been inspired by the bhikkhunī pronounced the foremost among those who recollect their past lives and she formed the aspiration to attain this position under a future Buddha. She too was assured by the Lord Padumuttara that her wish would be fulfilled. For the rest of their lives the couple observed the precepts and did meritorious deeds, and after death they were reborn in heaven.

The next past life recorded for Mahākassapa and Bhaddā Kapilānī takes place much later, during the Dispensation of the Buddha Vipassī, the sixth predecessor of the Buddha Gotama. At this time they had been a poor brahmin couple. They were so extremely poor that they had only a single upper garment, and hence only one of them at a time could go out of their hut. In this story the brahmin was therefore called "he with one garment" (*ekasātaka*). Though it may not be easy for us to understand such extreme poverty, it will be still more difficult to understand that there have been many people for whom such utter poverty did not mean subjective deprivation. This was so with those two beings who later were to be Kassapa and Bhaddā. In their life as that poor brahmin couple, they had lived in such perfect harmony that their happiness was not diminished by their indigence.

One day, when the Buddha Vipassī was to give a special sermon, they both wished to attend, but as they had only a single upper garment between them they could not both go at the same time. The wife went during the day and her husband went at night. As the brahmin listened to the sermon, the value of giving and generosity became so deeply impressed on his mind that he wanted to offer his only upper garment to the Buddha. But after he had so resolved, scruples came to his mind: "This is our only upper garment, so perhaps I should first consult with my wife. How can we manage without an upper garment? How can we get a replacement?" But he resolutely pushed aside all such hesitation and placed the garment at the Blessed One's feet. Having done so, he clapped his hands and joyfully called out: "I have vanquished! I have vanquished!" When the king, who had listened to the sermon behind a curtain, heard that shout of victory and came to know the reason, he sent sets of garments to the brahmin and later made him his court chaplain. So the couple's plight had come to an end.

As a result of his selfless giving, the brahmin was reborn in a celestial world. After parting from there he became a king on earth, a great benefactor of his people who generously supported the ascetics living at that time. Bhaddā was then his chief queen.

As to Bhaddā, she was once the mother of a brahmin youth who was a pupil of the Bodhisatta (the future Buddha) and wanted to become an ascetic. Kassapa was her husband, Ānanda her son. Bhaddā had wanted her son to know the worldly life before she would permit him to become an ascetic. But that knowledge came to the young brahmin in a drastic and heart-rending way. His teacher's old mother fell passionately in love with him and was even ready to kill her son for his sake. This encounter with reckless passion caused in him a deep revulsion for worldly life, and after that experience his parents gave him permission to go forth as an ascetic (Jāt. 61).

Another time Kassapa and Bhaddā had been the brahmin parents of four sons who in the future were to be our Bodhisatta, Anuruddha, Sāriputta, and Mahāmoggallāna. All four wanted to become ascetics. At first the parents refused permission, but later they came to understand the fruits and benefits of the ascetic life and they themselves became ascetics (Jāt. 509).

In still another life, two village headmen who were friends decided that the children they were expecting should marry each other if they were of the opposite sex. And so it happened. But in their previous life both children had been deities of the Brahma-world. Hence they had no desire for sensual pleasures and, with their parents' permission, chose the ascetic life (Jāt. 540).

Bhaddā's only wrong act reported in the stories of her past lives was this: At a time between the appearance of two Buddhas, Bhaddā was the wife of a landowner. One day she had a quarrel with her sister-in-law. Just then a paccekabuddha drew near to their house on alms round.[9] When her sister-in-law offered him food, Bhaddā, seeking to spite her, took the paccekabuddha's bowl, threw away the food, and filled the bowl with mud. At once, however, she was stung by remorse. She took the bowl back, washed it with scent, and filled it with delicious, fragrant food. Then she offered it back to the paccekabuddha and apologized for her rudeness.

As a kammic consequence of this deed, a mixture of the dark and bright, in her next life Bhaddā possessed wealth and great beauty but her body exuded a loathsome odor. Her husband, the future Kassapa, could not bear the noxious smell and left her. As she was beautiful other suitors sought her hand, but all her later marriages had the same end. She was full of despair and felt there was no point continuing to live. To dispose of her property, she had her ornaments melted down and formed into a golden brick, which she brought to the monastery as a contribution to the stūpa being erected in honor of the Buddha Kassapa, who had just passed away. She offered the golden brick with great devotion, and as a consequence her body became fragrant again and her first husband, Kassapa, took her back.

Two lives before her present existence, Bhaddā was the queen of Benares and used to support several paccekabuddhas. Deeply moved by their sudden death, she renounced her worldly life as a queen and lived a meditative life in the Himalayas. By the power of her renunciation and her meditative attainments, she was reborn in a Brahma-world, and so was Kassapa. It was after that life in the Brahma-world that they were reborn in the human world as Pipphali Kassapa and Bhaddā Kapilānī.

From these accounts we gather that in their former existences both had lived a life of purity in the Brahma-world and that both had repeatedly been renunciants. Hence, in their final existence, it was not difficult for them to keep to a life of celibacy, to give up all possessions, and to follow the Buddha's Teaching to its culmination in arahantship.

HOW KASSAPA CAME TO THE BUDDHA

Continuing our story, we shall now return to Mahākassapa.[10] Where did he go after he had come to the crossroads? As mentioned above, when the two ascetics separated, the earth shook by the force of their act of renunciation. The Buddha perceived this trembling of the earth and knew that it meant an outstanding disciple was on the way to him. Without informing any of the monks, he set out on the road alone, walking the distance of five miles to meet his future pupil—an act of compassion which later was often praised (Jāt. 469, Introd.).

On the road between Rājagaha and Nālandā, the Master sat down under a banyan tree by the Bahuputtaka Shrine, waiting for his future disciple to arrive. He did not sit there like an ordinary ascetic but displayed all the sublime glory of a Buddha. He emitted rays of light for eighty meters all around, so that the entire thicket became a single mass of light, and he manifested all his thirty-two marks of a great man. When Kassapa reached the spot and saw the Buddha sitting there in the full splendor of an Enlightened One, he thought, "This must be my master for whose sake I have gone forth!" He approached the Buddha, fell at his feet, and exclaimed: "The Blessed One, Lord, is my teacher, and I am his disciple! The Blessed One, Lord, is my teacher, and I am his disciple!"

The Enlightened One said: "Kassapa, if anyone who does not know and see were to say to a disciple endowed with such sincerity as yourself, 'I know, I see,' his head would split. But, Kassapa, knowing, I say 'I know'; seeing, I say 'I see.'" He then gave Kassapa the following three exhortations as his first formal introduction to the Dhamma:

> You should train yourself thus, Kassapa: "A keen sense of shame and fear of wrongdoing (*hiri-ottappa*) shall be present in me towards seniors, novices, and those of middle status in the Order.
>
> "Whatever teaching I hear that is conducive to something wholesome, I shall listen with an attentive ear, examining it, reflecting on it, absorbing it with all my heart.
>
> "Mindfulness of the body linked with gladness shall not be neglected by me!" Thus should you train yourself.

According to the commentary, this triple exhortation constituted Kassapa's going forth (*pabbajjā*) and higher ordination (*upasampadā*) together. Then both Master and disciple walked toward Rājagaha. On the way, the Buddha wanted to rest and went off the road to the root of a tree. Mahākassapa then folded his double-robe in four and requested the Master to sit on it "as this will be for my benefit for a long time." The Buddha sat down on Kassapa's robe and said: "Soft is your robe of patched cloth, Kassapa." Hearing this, Kassapa replied: "May the Blessed One, O Lord, accept this robe of patched cloth out of compassion for me!"

"But, Kassapa, can you wear these hempen, wornout rag robes of mine?" Full of joy, Kassapa said: "Certainly, Lord, I can wear the Blessed One's rough and wornout rag robes."

This exchange of robes bestowed a great distinction on the Venerable Mahākassapa, an honor not shared by any other disciple. The commentary explains that the Buddha's intention in exchanging robes with Kassapa was to motivate him to observe the *dhutaṅga*, the austere practices, from the time of his very admission into the Bhikkhu Sangha. Although, after his Enlightenment, the Buddha condemned extreme self-mortification as a blind alley which is "painful, ignoble, and unbeneficial," he by no means rejected those ascetic practices that harmonized with the framework of the Middle Way. The true Middle Way is not a comfortable highway built out of easy compromises, but a lonely, steep ascent, which requires the renunciation of craving and the ability to endure hardship and discomfort. Hence the Buddha encouraged those monks who were truly keen on extricating from their hearts the subtlest roots of craving to adopt the *dhutaṅga*—special vows of austerity conducive to simplicity, contentment, renunciation, and energy—and he often applauded those monks who observed these vows. The ancient suttas repeatedly commend several austere practices: using only the triple set of robes (and refusing to use additional robes); wearing only rag robes (and refusing robes offered by householders); subsisting only on food collected on alms round (and refusing invitations to meals); living only in the forest (and refusing to live in town monasteries). In the commentaries the list of austere practices is expanded to thirteen, which are explained in detail in such works on the meditative life as the *Visuddhimagga*.[11]

The robe that the Buddha offered Kassapa was made from a shroud that he had picked up in a cremation ground, and in asking Kassapa whether he could wear that robe he was implicitly asking whether he would be able to make the full commitment to the austere practices that the use of such a robe would entail. When Kassapa affirmed that he could wear the robe, he was saying, "Yes, Lord, I can fulfill the ascetic practices you wish me to undertake." From that moment on Kassapa pledged himself to uphold a life of strict austerity, and even in old age he insisted on observing the same vows that he had undertaken in his youth. On a later occasion the Buddha declared Mahākassapa foremost among the bhikkhus who observed the austere practices (AN 1, chap. 14), thereby bringing to fulfillment Kassapa's original aspiration formed a hundred thousand aeons in the past.

It was only seven days after his ordination and the exchange of robes that Kassapa attained the goal he was striving for, arahantship, the mind's final liberation from defilements. Recounting this episode to Ānanda at a much later time, he declared: "For seven days, friend, I ate the almsfood of the country as a debtor, then on the eighth day the final knowledge of arahantship arose in me" (SN 16:11).

KASSAPA'S RELATIONSHIP TO THE BUDDHA

We have already seen that there was a deep inner relationship between the Venerable Mahākassapa and the Buddha. This relationship, according to our traditional sources, had its root in their past lives. According to the Jātaka stories, Kassapa was connected with the Bodhisatta in nineteen existences, frequently through a close family bond. No less than six times Kassapa had been the Bodhisatta's father (Jāt. 155, 432, 509, 513, 524, 540), twice his brother (488, 522), and often his friend or teacher. As it was thus not their first meeting, we can understand why such an immediate and strong devotion and wholehearted dedication toward the Master arose in Kassapa's heart at the first sight of him.

From Kassapa's final life, many conversations are reported between the Buddha and this great disciple. It happened on three occasions that the Master spoke to him: "Exhort the monks, Kassapa. Give them a discourse on the Dhamma, Kassapa. Either I, Kassapa, should exhort the monks, or you. Either I or you should give them a discourse on the Dhamma" (SN 16:6). These words imply a high recognition of Kassapa's ability, because not every arahant has the capacity to expound the Teaching well and effectively.

The commentary raises here the question why it was Mahākassapa who was placed by the Buddha on such a high footing in this respect, and not Sāriputta or Mahāmoggallāna. The Buddha did so, says the commentary, because he knew that Sāriputta and Moggallāna would not survive him, but Kassapa would, and he wanted to bolster Kassapa's stature before the other monks so they would consider him one whose advice is to be heeded.

On three occasions when the Buddha requested Kassapa to exhort the monks, he refused to comply. On the first of these occasions Kassapa said that it had now become difficult to speak to some of the monks: they were not amenable to advice, were untractable, and did not accept admonitions with respect. He had also heard that two monks had been boasting of their skill in preaching, saying: "Come, let us see who will preach more profusely, more beautifully, and at greater length!" When the Buddha was informed about this by Kassapa, he had these monks summoned and gave them a stern lecture, making them give up their childish conceit (SN 16:6). Hence we can see that Kassapa's negative report turned out to be of positive benefit to those monks. It was not done just for the sake of criticizing others.

On the second occasion, too, Kassapa did not wish to instruct the monks because they were not amenable to admonishment, lacked faith in the good, lacked a sense of shame and fear of wrongdoing, and were slack and devoid of wisdom. Kassapa compared such monks, in their state of decline, to the waning moon, which daily loses in beauty (confidence), in roundness (shame), in splendor (fear of wrongdoing), in height (energy), and in width (wisdom) (SN 16:7).

On still a third occasion the Buddha asked Kassapa to instruct the monks, and Kassapa again expressed his reluctance for the same reason as before. It seems that this time, too, the Buddha did not urge Kassapa to change his mind, but he himself spoke of the reasons for their conduct:

> Formerly, Kassapa, there were elders of the Order who were forest

> dwellers, living on almsfood, wearing rag robes, using only the set of three robes, having few wants and being contented, living secluded and aloof from society, energetic; and they praised and encouraged such a way of life. When such elders visited a monastery, they were gladly welcomed and honored as being dedicated to the practice of the Dhamma. Then the younger monks would also strive to emulate them in their way of life, and this would be of great benefit to them for a long time.
>
> But nowadays, Kassapa, those who are honored when visiting a monastery are not monks of austere and earnest life, but those who are well known and popular and are amply provided with the requisites of a monk. These are welcomed and honored, and the younger monks try to emulate them, which will bring them harm for a long time. Hence one will be right in saying that such monks are harmed and overpowered by what does harm to a monk's life. (Paraphrased from SN 16:8)

On another occasion, Kassapa asked the Buddha: "What is the reason that formerly there were fewer rules, but more monks were established in the knowledge of arahantship, while now there are more rules, but fewer monks are established in the knowledge of arahantship?" The Buddha replied:

> So it happens, Kassapa, when beings deteriorate and the true Dhamma vanishes: then there are more rules and fewer arahants. There will be, however, no vanishing of the true Dhamma until a sham Dhamma arises in the world. But when a sham Dhamma arises in the world, then the true Dhamma vanishes.
>
> But, Kassapa, it is not a cataclysm of the four elements—earth, water, fire, and air—that makes the true Dhamma disappear. Nor is the reason for its disappearance similar to the overloading of a ship that causes it to sink. It is rather the presence of five detrimental attitudes that causes the obscuration and disappearance of the true Dhamma.
>
> These are the five: it is the lack of respect and regard for the Buddha, the Dhamma, the Sangha, the training, and meditative concentration, on the part of monks and nuns, and male and female lay devotees. But so long as there is respect and regard for those five things, the true Dhamma will remain free of obscuration and will not disappear. (SN 16:13)

We should note that, according to this text, the male and female lay followers are also preservers of the Dhamma. From this we may conclude that even when the Dhamma has come to oblivion among the monks, it will still remain alive when honored and practiced by the laity.

Other discourses relating to Mahākassapa deal chiefly with his austere way of life, which was highly praised and commended by the Buddha. But on one occasion late in his ministry the Buddha reminded Kassapa that as he had now grown old he must find his coarse, worn-out rag robes irksome to use. Therefore, the Buddha suggested, he should now wear robes offered by householders, accept invitations for alms offerings, and live near him. But Kassapa replied: "For a long time I have been a forest dweller, going on alms round and wearing rag robes; and such a life I have commended to others. I have had few wants, lived contented, secluded, applying strenuous energy; and that too I have commended to others."

When the Buddha asked: "But for what reason do you live in this way?" Kassapa replied: "For two reasons: for my own pleasant abiding here and now, and out of compassion for later generations of monks who, when they hear about such a life, might think to emulate it." Then the Buddha said: "Well spoken, Kassapa, well spoken! You are living for the happiness of many, out of compassion for the world, for the benefit and welfare of gods and humans. You may then keep to your coarse rag robes, go out for alms, and live in the forest" (SN 16:5).

"This our Kassapa," said the Buddha, "is satisfied with whatever robes, almsfood, lodging, and medicine he obtains. For the sake of these he will not do anything that is unbefitting for a monk. If he does not obtain any of these requisites, he is not perturbed; and when he obtains them, he makes use of them without clinging or infatuation, not committing any fault, aware of (possible) dangers and knowing them as an escape (from bodily affliction). By the example of Kassapa, or by one who equals him, I will exhort you, monks. Thus admonished, you should practice in the same way" (SN 16:1).

The Buddha also mentioned that Mahākassapa was exemplary in his relation to the laity. When going among the families on his alms round or on invitation, he did not think wishfully, "May people give amply and give things of quality! May they give quickly and respectfully!" He had no such thoughts, but remained detached like the moon that sheds its mild light from a distance:

> When Kassapa goes among families, his mind is not attached, not caught up, not fettered. He rather thinks: "Let those who

> want gain acquire gain! Let those who want merit do merit!" He is pleased and glad at the gains of others, just as he is pleased and glad at his own gains. Such a monk is fit to go among families.
>
> When he preaches the doctrine, he will not do so for the sake of personal recognition and praise, but for letting them know the Teaching of the Exalted One, so that those who hear it may accept it and practice accordingly. He will preach because of the excellence of the Teaching and out of compassion and sympathy. (Paraphrased from SN 16:34)

But the strongest recognition of Mahākassapa's achievement, the highest praise given him by the Buddha, came when the Master said that Kassapa could attain at will, just as he himself could, the four fine-material and the four immaterial meditative absorptions, the cessation of perception and feeling, and could also attain the six supernormal knowledges (*abhiññā*), which include the supernormal powers and culminate in the attainment of Nibbāna (SN 16:9). Here his powerful meditative achievements, akin to those of the Buddha, appear as a characteristic trait of Mahākassapa's mind. It was because of that deep meditative calm that he could adapt himself, unperturbed, to all external situations and live as one of few wants, materially and socially.

In his verses preserved in the *Theragāthā*, Mahākassapa praises again and again the peace of the jhānas. He was one who went from abundance to abundance. In his lay life he had lived in the abundance of wealth and harmony. As a monk he dwelt in the abundance of jhānic experience, furthered by his former life in the Brahma-world. While in some of the texts he appears to be very severe, this should not lead us to believe that he was harsh by nature. When he occasionally rebuked others in stern words, he did so for pedagogical reasons, in order to help them. This we shall see especially when we deal with his relationship to Ānanda.

ENCOUNTERS WITH DEITIES

Our sources record two meetings of Mahākassapa with deities. They are related here because they illustrate his independence of spirit and his determination to keep to his austere way of living without accepting privileges even from beings of a higher order.

The first was with a young female deity named Lājā. She remembered that she had obtained her present celestial happiness because, in her previous human existence as a poor woman, she had offered parched rice to the Elder Mahākassapa with a believing heart, uttering the aspiration: "May I be a partaker of the truth you have seen!" On her way home, while reflecting on her offering, she was bitten by a snake and died, and was immediately reborn in the heaven of the Thirty-three in the midst of great splendor.

This the deity remembered, and in her gratitude she now wanted to serve the great elder. Descending to earth, she swept the elder's cell and filled the water vessels. After she had done so for three days, the elder saw her radiant figure in his cell, and after questioning her, asked her to leave; he did not wish monks of the future to criticize him for accepting the services of a deity. His entreaties were of no avail; the deity rose into the air, filled with great sadness. The Buddha, aware of what had happened, appeared to the deity and consoled her by speaking of the worth of meritorious deeds and their great reward. But he also said that it had been Kassapa's duty to practice restraint.[12]

In the other story it is told that Mahākassapa, while living at the Pipphali Cave, had entered a period of seven days' uninterrupted meditation. At the end of that period, after emerging from his absorption, he went to Rājagaha on alms round. At that time five hundred female deities of Sakka's retinue keenly desired to offer him alms. They approached the elder with the food they had prepared, asking him to bestow his favor upon them by accepting their offering. Kassapa, however, declined, for he wanted to bestow his favor on the poor so that they could earn merit. They entreated him several times, but finally left after he repeatedly refused to yield. When Sakka, king of the gods, heard about their vain effort, he too experienced a keen desire to offer alms to the elder. To avoid being refused, he assumed the guise of an old weaver, and when Mahākassapa approached he offered rice to him. At the moment the rice was accepted it turned exceedingly fragrant. Then Mahākassapa knew that this old weaver was not a human being but Sakka, and he reproached the deva king thus: "You have done a grievous wrong, Kosiya. By doing so, you have deprived poor people of the chance to acquire merit. Do not do such a thing again!" "We too need merit, revered Kassapa!" Sakka replied. "We too are in need of merit! But have I acquired merit or not by giving alms to you through deception?" "You have gained merit, friend." Now Sakka, while departing, gave voice to the following solemn utterance (*udāna*):[13]

> Oh, almsgiving! Highest almsgiving!
> Well bestowed on Kassapa!

RELATIONS WITH FELLOW MONKS

One as dedicated to the meditative life as the Venerable Mahākassapa was cannot be expected to have been eager to accept and train many pupils; and, in fact, the canonical texts mention only a few pupils of his.

One of Kassapa's few recorded discourses addressed to the monks deals with the subject of overestimating one's attainments: "There may be a monk who declares he has attained to the highest knowledge, that of arahantship. Then the Master, or a disciple capable of knowing the minds of others, examines and questions him. When they question him, that monk becomes embarrassed and confused. The questioner now understands that the monk has made this declaration through overrating himself out of conceit. Then, considering the reason for it, he sees that this monk has acquired much knowledge of the Teaching and proficiency in it, which made him declare his overestimation of himself to be the truth. Penetrating the mind of that monk, he sees that he is still obstructed by the five hindrances and has stopped halfway while there is still more to do" (AN 10:86).

Apart from the few instances where Mahākassapa is speaking to unnamed monks or a group of monks, the texts record only his relationship to Sāriputta and Ānanda. According to the Jātakas, in former lives Sāriputta was twice the son of Kassapa (Jāt. 509, 515) and twice his brother (326, 488); once too he was Kassapa's grandson (450) and his friend (525). In his verses, Kassapa tells that he once saw thousands of Brahmā gods descend from their heaven, pay homage to Sāriputta, and praise him (Thag. 1082–86).[14]

Two conversations between Mahākassapa and Sāriputta have been recorded in the Kassapa Saṁyutta. On both occasions it was in the evening, after meditation, that Sāriputta went to see Mahākassapa.

In the first text Sāriputta asked:

> "It has been said, friend Kassapa, that without ardor and without fear of wrongdoing, one is incapable of gaining enlightenment, incapable of attaining Nibbāna, incapable of attaining highest security, but that with ardor and with fear of wrongdoing, one is capable of such attainments. Now in how far is one incapable of such attainments and in how far is one capable of them?"
>
> "When, friend Sāriputta, a monk thinks: 'If bad and unwholesome states that have so far not arisen in me were to arise, this would bring me harm,' and if then he does not arouse ardor and

> fear of wrongdoing, then he is lacking ardor and fear of wrongdoing. When he thinks: 'If bad and unwholesome states that have now arisen in me are not abandoned, this would bring me harm,' or: 'If unarisen wholesome states were not to arise, this would bring me harm,' or: 'If arisen wholesome states were to vanish, this would bring me harm'—if on these occasions, too, a monk does not arouse ardor and fear of wrongdoing, then he is lacking these qualities, and lacking them, he is incapable of attaining enlightenment, incapable of attaining Nibbāna, incapable of attaining the highest security. But if a monk (on those four occasions for right effort) arouses ardor and fear of wrongdoing, he is capable of attaining enlightenment, capable of attaining Nibbāna, capable of attaining the highest security." (SN 16:2; condensed.)

On another occasion Sāriputta asked Mahākassapa whether the Tathāgata, the Perfect One, exists after death, or does not exist, or (in some sense) both exists and does not exist, or neither exists nor does not exist. In each case Mahākassapa replied:

> "This was not declared by the Blessed One. And why not? Because it is of no benefit and does not belong to the fundamentals of the holy life, because it does not lead to disenchantment, nor to dispassion, cessation, inner peace, direct knowledge, enlightenment, and Nibbāna."
>
> "But what, friend, did the Blessed One declare?"
>
> "This is suffering—so, friend, has the Blessed One declared. This is the origin of suffering...the cessation of suffering...the way to the cessation of suffering—so, friend, has the Blessed One declared. And why? Because it conduces to benefit and belongs to the fundamentals of the holy life, because it leads to turning away (from worldliness), to dispassion, cessation, inner peace, direct knowledge, enlightenment, and Nibbāna." (SN 16:12)

We have no explanation why Sāriputta posed these questions, which for an arahant should have been fully clear. It is, however, not impossible that this conversation took place immediately after Kassapa's ordination and before his attainment of arahantship, and that Sāriputta wanted to test his understanding; or perhaps the questions were asked for the sake of other monks who may have been present.

The *Mahāgosiṅga Sutta* (MN 32) records a group discussion led by the Venerable Sāriputta in which Mahākassapa along with several other eminent disciples once participated. At the time these elders were residing in the Gosiṅga forest along with the Buddha, and on a clear moonlit night they approached Sāriputta for a discussion on the Dhamma. Sāriputta declared: "Delightful is this Gosiṅga sāla-tree forest, it is a clear moonlit night, the sāla-trees are in full bloom, and it seems as if celestial scents are being wafted around." Then he asked each distinguished elder in the group—Ānanda, Revata, Anuruddha, Mahākassapa, and Mahāmoggallāna—what kind of monk could lend more luster to that forest. Mahākassapa, like the others, replied according to his own temperament:

> Here, friend Sāriputta, a monk is himself a forest dweller and he speaks in praise of forest dwelling; he is himself an almsfood collector and he speaks in praise of collecting almsfood; he is himself a rag-robe wearer and he speaks in praise of wearing rag robes; he is himself a triple-robe wearer and he speaks in praise of wearing the triple robe; he himself has few wishes, is content, secluded, and aloof from society, and he speaks in praise of each of these qualities; he himself has attained to virtue, to concentration, to wisdom, to liberation, and to knowledge and vision of liberation, and he speaks in praise of each of these attainments. This is the kind of monk who could lend more lustre to this Gosiṅga sāla-tree forest.

According to tradition, Mahākassapa also had close connections in former lives with the Venerable Ānanda. Ānanda had twice been his brother (Jāt. 488, 535), once his son (450), once even the murderer of his son (540), and in this life he was his pupil (Vin. 1:92). The Kassapa Saṁyutta likewise has two conversations between them. They concern practical questions, while those with Sāriputta referred to points of doctrine.

On the first occasion (related at SN 16:10) Ānanda asked Kassapa to accompany him to the nuns' quarters. Kassapa, however, refused and asked Ānanda to go alone. But Ānanda seemed to be intent on getting Kassapa to give a Dhamma talk to the nuns, and he repeated his request twice. Kassapa finally consented and went along. The result, however, turned out to be quite different from what Ānanda had expected. After the discourse one of the nuns, Thullatissā by name, raised her voice to make a rather offensive remark: "How could Master Kassapa presume to speak on the Dhamma in the presence of Master Ānanda, the learned sage? This is as if a needle peddler wanted to sell a needle to the needle maker." Obviously this nun preferred the gentle preaching of Ānanda to Kassapa's stern and sometimes critical approach, which may have touched on her own weaknesses.

When Kassapa heard the nun's remarks, he asked Ānanda: "How is it, friend Ānanda, am I the needle peddler and you the needle maker, or am I the needle maker and you the needle peddler?"

Ānanda replied: "Be indulgent, venerable sir. She is a foolish woman."

"Beware, friend Ānanda, or else the Sangha may further investigate you. How is it, friend Ānanda, was it you whom the Exalted One extolled in the presence of the Sangha, saying: 'I, O monks, can attain at will the four fine-material and immaterial meditative absorptions, the cessation of perception and feeling, the six supernormal knowledges; and Ānanda, too, can so attain'?"

"No, venerable sir."

"Or did he say: 'Kassapa, too, can so attain'?"

From the above account we see that the Venerable Mahākassapa did not think that Ānanda's conciliatory reply was adequate or did full justice to the situation. Thullatissā's remarks showed her personal attachment to Ānanda, who had always been a favorite with women, and who had also given his strong support to the founding of the Bhikkhunī Sangha. This emotional relation of Thullatissā's to Ānanda could not be put aside just by Ānanda's general remark. Hence Kassapa responded in a way which, at first glance, appears rather harsh: "Beware, friend Ānanda, or else the Sangha may further investigate you." With these words he wanted to warn Ānanda to avoid becoming too involved in ministering to the nuns, since they might become too fond of him and cause others to entertain doubts about him. Kassapa's reply has therefore to be seen as the earnest advice of a taint-free arahant to one who had not yet reached that state. When, immediately after, Kassapa stressed that it was his own meditative attainments that the Buddha had extolled, and not Ānanda's, this may be taken as pointing to the far different spiritual status of the two elders; and it may have served as a spur to Ānanda to strive for those attainments. The nun Thullatissā, however, left the Order.

Another conversation between the Venerable Mahākassapa and Ānanda arose on the following occasion (related at SN 16:11). Once the Venerable Ānanda went on a walking tour in the Southern Hills together with a large company of monks. This was at a time when thirty mostly young monks, pupils of Ānanda, had given up the robe and had returned to the lay life. After Ānanda had ended his tour, he came to Rājagaha and went to see the Venerable Mahākassapa. When he had saluted him and was seated, Kassapa said this:

> "What are the reasons, friend Ānanda, for the sake of which the Blessed One had said that no more than three monks should take their alms meal among families?"
>
> "There are three reasons, venerable sir: it is for restraining ill-behaved persons, for the well-being of good monks, and out of consideration for the lay families."
>
> "Then, friend Ānanda, why do you go on tour with those young new monks whose senses are unrestrained, who are not moderate in eating, not devoted to wakefulness? It seems you behave like one trampling the corn; it seems you destroy the faith of the families.[15] Your following is breaking up, your new starters are falling away. This youngster truly does not know his own measure!"
>
> "Grey hairs are now on my head, venerable sir, and still we cannot escape being called 'youngster' by the Venerable Mahākassapa."

But the Venerable Mahākassapa repeated the very same words he had spoken.

This could have ended the matter, as Ānanda did not deny that the reproach was justified. He objected only to the hurtful way in which Mahākassapa had expressed his censure. In response to the admonition, Ānanda would have tried to keep his pupils under stricter discipline. But, again, this matter was complicated by a nun, Thullanandā, who along with Thullatissā was one of the black sheep of the Bhikkhunī Sangha. She had heard that Ānanda had been called a "youngster" by the Venerable Mahākassapa, and full of indignation, she voiced her protest, saying that Kassapa had no right to criticize a wise monk like Ānanda, as Kassapa had formerly been an ascetic of another sect. In that way, Thullanandā diverted the matter of monastic discipline into personal detraction—personal detraction bordering on calumny; for, as our earlier account has shown, Kassapa had originally gone forth as an independent ascetic, not as a follower of another school. Thullanandā soon left the Order, just as the other wayward nun, Thullatissā, had done.

When the Venerable Mahākassapa heard Thullanandā's utterance, he said to Ānanda: "Rash and thoughtless are the words spoken by Thullanandā the nun. Since I left the home life, I have had no other teacher than the Blessed One, the Arahant, the Fully Enlightened One." Then he related the story of his first meeting with the Buddha (SN 16:11).

AFTER THE BUDDHA'S PARINIBBĀNA

What remains to be said about the Venerable Mahākassapa's relation to Ānanda is closely connected with his leading role in the Sangha after the Buddha's passing away. At the demise of the Buddha only two of the five most prominent disciples were present, Ānanda and Anuruddha. Sāriputta and Mahāmoggallāna had expired earlier that year, and Mahākassapa, with a large company of monks, was just then en route from Pāvā to Kusinārā. During that walk he happened to step aside from the road and sat down under a tree to rest. Just then a naked ascetic passed that way holding a coral-tree flower (*mandārava*), which is said to grow only in the world of the gods. When Mahākassapa saw this, he knew that something unusual must have happened for the flower to be found on earth. He asked the ascetic whether he had heard any news about his teacher, the Buddha, and the ascetic told him: "The recluse Gotama passed into Nibbāna a week ago. This coral-tree flower I picked up from the site of his demise."

Among the monks in Mahākassapa's company only the arahants remained calm and composed; those who were still unliberated from the passions fell to the ground, weeping and lamenting: "Too soon has the Blessed One passed into Nibbāna! Too soon has the Eye of the World vanished from our sight!" There was, however, one monk in the group named Subhadda, ordained in his old age, who addressed his comrades: "Enough, friends! Do not grieve, do not lament. We are well rid of the Great Ascetic. We were constantly troubled by his telling us: 'This is proper for you, that is improper.' Now we can do what we like, and we won't have to do what we don't like."

The Venerable Mahākassapa did not reply to those callous words at that time. Just then he may have wanted to avoid striking a discordant note by censuring the monk or having him disrobed as he deserved. But, as we shall see later, Mahākassapa referred to this very incident shortly after the Buddha's cremation when he spoke of the need to convene a council of elders to preserve the Dhamma and Vinaya for posterity. Now, however, he merely admonished his group of monks not to lament but to remember that all conditioned things are impermanent. He then continued his journey to Kusinārā together with his company.

Until then the village chieftains at Kusinārā had not been able to set the Buddha's funeral pyre alight. The Venerable Anuruddha explained that the deities, invisible but present, wanted to hold up the proceedings until the Venerable Mahākassapa came and paid his final homage to the Master's remains. When Mahākassapa arrived, he walked around the pyre three times, reverently, with clasped hands, and then with bowed head paid his homage at the feet of the Tathāgata. When his group of monks had done likewise, the pyre burst into flames by itself.

Hardly had the bodily remains of the Tathāgata been cremated when there arose a conflict about the distribution of the relics among the lay folk assembled and those who had sent messengers later. But the Venerable Mahākassapa remained aloof in that quarrel, as did the other monks like Anuruddha and Ānanda. It was a respected brahmin named Doṇa who finally divided the relics into eight portions and distributed them among the eight claimants. He himself took the vessel in which the relics had been collected.

The Venerable Mahākassapa himself brought to King Ajātasattu of Magadha his share of the relics. Having done so, he turned his thoughts to the preservation of the Master's spiritual heritage, the Dhamma and the Vinaya. The necessity for this was plainly demonstrated to him by Subhadda's challenge of the monastic discipline and his advocacy of moral laxity. Mahākassapa took this as a warning of what the future held in store unless clear strictures were established now. If Subhadda's attitude were to spread—and there were groups of monks who shared that attitude even while the Buddha was alive—it would rapidly lead to the decline and ruin of both the Sangha and the Teaching. To prevent this at the very start, Mahākassapa proposed holding a council of elders to rehearse the Dhamma and Vinaya and preserve them for posterity.[16]

With that suggestion, he turned to the monks gathered at Rājagaha. The monks agreed, and at their request Mahākassapa selected five hundred elders all but one of whom were arahants. The one exception was Ānanda, whose position was ambivalent. As he had not yet succeeded in reaching the final goal, he could not be admitted to the council; but as he excelled in remembering all the Buddha's discourses, his presence was essential. The only solution was to give him an ultimatum that he must reach arahantship before the council began, which he did on the very night before it opened. Thus Ānanda was admitted to complete the five hundred members of the First Council. All other monks were to leave Rājagaha for the duration of the meeting.

As the first item of the council's proceedings, the Vinaya, the code of monastic discipline, was recited by the Venerable Upāli, the leading Vinaya expert. The second item was the codification of the teachings laid down in the suttas. Here it was the Venerable Ānanda who, on being questioned by Mahākassapa, recited all those texts which were later collected into the five collections (*nikāya*) of the Sutta Piṭaka. Finally, some special matters concerning the Sangha were discussed. Among them, Ānanda mentioned that the Buddha, shortly before his death, had permitted the abolishment of the lesser and minor rules. When Ānanda was asked whether he had inquired from the Buddha what these minor rules were, he had to admit that he had neglected to do so. Now different monks expressed various opinions about this matter in the assembly. As there was no consensus, Mahākassapa asked the assembly to consider that if they were to abolish rules arbitrarily, the lay followers and the public in general would reproach them for being in a hurry to relax discipline so soon after the Master's death. Hence Mahākassapa suggested that the rules should be preserved intact without exception, and so it was decided.

After the holding of the First Council, the high regard in which the Venerable Mahākassapa was held grew still greater, and he was seen as the de facto head of the Sangha. His seniority would have contributed to this, as he was then one of the oldest living disciples.[17] Later on, Mahākassapa handed over the Buddha's alms bowl to Ānanda as a symbol of the faithful preservation of the Dhamma. Thus Mahākassapa, who had been generally recognized in the Order as the worthiest in succession, on his part chose Ānanda as being the worthiest after him.

There is no report in the Pāli literature about the time and circumstances of Mahākassapa's death, but a Sanskrit chronicle on "the Masters of the Law" offers us a curious account of the great elder's end according to the Northern Buddhist tradition.[18] According to this record, after the First Council Kassapa realized that he had fulfilled his mission and decided to attain final Nibbāna. He transmitted the Dhamma to Ānanda, paid his final respects to the holy places, and entered Rājagaha. He intended to inform King Ajātasattu of his impending demise, but the king was asleep and Kassapa did not wish to wake him up. Thus he climbed to the summit of Mount Kukkaṭapāda alone, sat down cross-legged in a cave, and made the determination that his body should remain intact until the coming of the future Buddha, Metteyya. It was to Metteyya that Kassapa was to hand over the robe of Gotama Buddha—the very same rag robe that the Blessed One had bestowed on him at their first meeting. Then Kassapa attained final Nibbāna, or, according to a variant, the meditative attainment of cessation (*nirodhasamāpatti*). The earth quaked, the devas strewed flowers over his body, and the mountain closed over him.

Soon afterwards King Ajātasattu and Ānanda went to Mount Kukkaṭapāda to see Mahākassapa. The mountain partly opened and Kassapa's body appeared before them. The king wanted to cremate it, but Ānanda informed him that Kassapa's body must remain intact until the coming of Metteyya. Then the mountain closed up again and Ajātasattu and Ānanda departed. Chinese Buddhist tradition locates Mount Kukkaṭapāda in Southwest China, and Chinese legend abounds in reports of pious monks who, on pilgrimage to the mountain, managed to gain a glimpse of Kassapa's corpse sitting in meditation posture awaiting the arrival of the next Buddha.

THE VERSES OF MAHĀKASSAPA

In the *Theragāthā,* forty verses (1051–90) are ascribed to the Venerable Mahākassapa. These stanzas mirror some of the great elder's characteristic qualities and virtues: his austere habits and his contentedness; his strictness toward himself and his brother monks; his independent spirit and his self-reliance; his love of solitude and aloofness from the crowds; his dedication to the practice of meditation and the peace of the jhānas. These verses also show what does not appear in the prose texts: his sensitivity to the beauty of nature that surrounded him.

Here only a selection of the stanzas is given, which may be read in full in the translations by C. A. F. Rhys Davids and K. R. Norman.[19] First, here is an exhortation to the monks to practice contentment with regard to the four basic requisites of a monk's life:[20]

Having come down from my mountain lodging,
I entered the city to collect my alms.
Courteously I came up to a man,
A leper who was eating a meal.

With his hand all leprous and diseased
He offered me a morsel of food.
As he placed the morsel in my bowl
A finger broke off and toppled in.

I sat down at the base of a wall
And ate the morsel he had given me.
While I was eating and after I had finished
I did not feel the least disgust.

Using left-over scraps as food,
Putrid urine as medicine,

The foot of a tree for one's lodging,
And a robe made from cast-off rags:
One who has gained mastery over these
Is truly a man everywhere at home.[21]

(Thag. 1054–57)

When Mahākassapa was asked why, at his advanced age, he still climbed daily up and down the rock, he replied:

While some grow weary as they climb
The steep slope of the rocky mountain,
Kassapa ascends, buoyed by psychic power—
The Buddha's heir, aware and mindful.

Having returned from his daily alms round,
Having climbed up the rocky mountain,
Kassapa meditates free from clinging,
With fear and trembling well abandoned.

Having returned from his daily alms round,
Having climbed up the rocky mountain,
Kassapa meditates free from clinging,
Quenched among those who burn with passion.

Having returned from his daily alms round,
Having climbed up the rocky mountain,
Kassapa meditates free from clinging,
His task done, his cankers gone.

(Thag. 1058–61)

People asked again why the Venerable Mahākassapa, at his age, wishes to live in forests and mountains. Does he not like monasteries such as the Bamboo Grove and others?

Spread over with *kareri* garlands,
These regions are delightful to my heart;
Resounding with elephants, so lovely,
Those rocky mountains give me delight.

The splendid hue of dark-blue clouds,
Where streams are flowing, cool and clear,

Covered with *indagopaka* insects:
Those rocky mountains give me delight.

Like towering peaks of dark-blue clouds,
Like lofty houses with gabled roofs,
Resounding with elephants, so lovely:
Those rocky mountains give me delight.

Their lovely surfaces lashed by rain,
The mountains are resorted to by seers.
Echoing with the cries of peacocks,
Those rocky mountains give me delight.

This is enough for me, desiring to meditate,
Enough for me, resolute and mindful;
This is enough for me, a bhikkhu,
Resolute, desirous of the goal.[22]

This is enough for me, desiring comfort,
A bhikkhu with a resolute mind.
This is enough for me, desiring exertion,
A stable one of resolute mind.

They are like the blue blossoms of flax,
Like the autumn sky covered with clouds,
With flocks of many kinds of birds:
Those rocky mountains give me delight.

No crowds of lay folk visit these hills,
But they are inhabited by herds of deer,
With flocks of many kinds of birds:
Those rocky mountains give me delight.

Wide gorges are there where clear water flows,
Haunted by monkeys and by deer,
Covered by wet carpets of moss:
Those rocky mountains give me delight.

The music of a five-piece ensemble
Can never give me so much delight

As I derive when with one-pointed mind
I gain proper insight into the Dhamma.

(Thag. 1062–1071)

In the following verses the Venerable Mahākassapa voices his own "lion's roar":

As far as the range of this Buddha-field extends,
Excepting the great sage himself,
I am the foremost in ascetic virtues:
One my equal cannot be found.[23]

The Teacher has been served by me,
The Buddha's Teaching has been done.
The heavy burden has been dropped,
The conduit to becoming has been uprooted.[24]

Gotama the immeasurable does not cling
To robe, to lodging, or to food.
He is untainted like a spotless lotus,
Bent on renunciation, beyond the three worlds.

The foundations of mindfulness are his neck;
The Great Sage has faith for his hands;
Above, his brow is perfect wisdom; nobly wise,
He ever wanders with all desire quenched.

(Thag. 1087–1090)

CHAPTER 4

ĀNANDA

GUARDIAN OF THE DHAMMA

Hellmuth Hecker

ĀNANDA'S PERSONAL PATH

AMONG ALL THE GREAT monks in the Buddha's retinue, the Venerabl Ānanda occupied a unique position, and this in many respects. Ānanda's unique position had already begun even before his birth. According to tradition, he came to earth, just as the Buddha did, from the Tusita heaven, and was born on the same day as the Buddha and in the same caste, the warrior caste of the royal family of the Sakyans. His father, Amitodana, was the brother of the Buddha's father, Suddhodana, so the two were cousins, and they grew up together in the Sakyans' capital city of Kapilavatthu. Amitodana was also the father of Anuruddha, another great disciple, but probably through a different wife.

When he was thirty-seven years old, Ānanda joined the Buddha's order of monks along with Anuruddha, Devadatta, and many other Sakyan nobles. The Venerable Belaṭṭhasīsa, an arahant, became his teacher and introduced him to the monk's discipline. Ānanda proved himself a willing and diligent pupil. During his first rains retreat he attained the fruit of stream-entry (Vin. 2:183). Later, he told his fellow monks that the Venerable Puṇṇa Mantāniputta, an outstanding exponent of the Dhamma, had been of great help to him during his training period. He had taught the Dhamma to the new monks and had given them a profound discourse on the relationship between the five aggregates and the idea "I am" (SN 22:83). As Ānanda listened to Puṇṇa's words he penetrated more and more deeply into the impermanence, suffering, and selfless nature of the five aggregates, and with the ripening of insight he made the breakthrough to the path and fruit of stream-entry.

Ānanda was always well contented with his life as a monk. He understood the blessings of renunciation and had entered upon the path to liberation, which is a joy to tread in the company of like-minded friends. During the first years of his life as a monk Ānanda was fully occupied with the purification of his own mind; he blended easily into the Sangha and slowly developed more and more resilience and mental strength.

When the Buddha and Ānanda were both fifty-five years of age, the Buddha called a meeting of the monks and declared: "In my twenty years as leader of the Sangha, I have had many different attendants, but none of them has really filled the post perfectly; again and again some wilfullness has become apparent. Now I am fifty-five years old and it is necessary for me to have a trustworthy and reliable attendant." At once all the noble disciples offered their services, but the Buddha did not accept them. Then the great monks looked at Ānanda, who had held back modestly, and asked him to volunteer.

Due to his impeccable behavior as a monk, Ānanda seemed predestined for the post. When he was asked why he was the only one who had not offered his services, he replied that the Buddha knew best who was suitable to be his attendant. He had so much confidence in the Blessed One that it did not occur to him to express his own wishes, even though he would have liked to become the Master's attendant. Then the Buddha declared that Ānanda would be pleasing to him and would be the best choice for the post. Ānanda was in no way proud that the Master had preferred him to the other disciples, but instead asked for eight favors.

The first four were negative in character: First, the Master should never pass a gift of robes on to him; second, he should never give him any almsfood which he himself had received; third, having received a dwelling place, he should never give it to him; fourth, he should never include him in any personal invitations (such as an occasion for teaching the Dhamma when a meal would be offered). The other four were positive: If he was invited to a meal, he asked for the right to transfer this invitation to the Buddha; if people came from outlying areas, he asked for the privilege to lead them to the Buddha; if he had any doubts or inquiries about the Dhamma, he asked for the right to have them cleared up at any time; and if the Buddha gave a discourse during his absence, he asked for the privilege to have it repeated to him privately. Ānanda explained that if he did not pose the first four conditions, then people could say that he had accepted the post of attendant only with an eye on the material gains he would enjoy by living so close to the Master. But if he did not express the other four conditions, then it could rightly be said that he fulfilled the duties of his post without being mindful of his own advancement on the noble path.

The Buddha granted him these very reasonable requests, which were quite in accordance with the Dhamma. From then on Ānanda was the constant companion, attendant, and helper of the Blessed One for twenty-five years. In those twenty-five years of service, he continued with the same incessant striving for purification as in the first eighteen years of his monkhood when he was an unknown disciple. He said of himself:

> Through the full twenty-five years
> That I have been in higher training,

No sensual perception has arisen in me:
See the excellence of the Dhamma!

Through the full twenty-five years,
That I have been in higher training,
No perception of hate has arisen in me:
See the excellence of the Dhamma!

(Thag. 1039–40)

The twenty-five years mentioned in this verse refer to the period during which he was the Buddha's attendant, and not to the whole of his life as a monk. During this period, though he was still a "learner,"[1] one in the higher training, no thoughts of lust or hate arose in him; the implication was that his close connection with the Buddha and his devotion to him gave no room for these. Only such a man could fill the post of a constant companion and attendant of the Awakened One.

ĀNANDA'S RENOWN

Ānanda's praise has been voiced on many occasions in the Pāli Canon. Once, for example, King Pasenadi of Kosala had met the Venerable Ānanda and had inquired from him about the criteria of proper conduct in body, speech, and mind. Ānanda answered the king's questions with his usual perspicacity, and the king was so delighted that he bestowed upon him a costly garment. Later Ānanda reported his meeting to the Blessed One, who then addressed the entire assembly of monks and said: "It is a gain for King Pasenadi of Kosala, monks, it is fortunate for King Pasenadi of Kosala, that he gained the opportunity to see Ānanda and to offer him service!" (MN 88).

Ānanda was so capable as a teacher of the Dhamma that the Buddha did not hesitate to ask him to take his place when he himself was not feeling fit. This happened among the Buddha's own relations, the Sakyans, at Kapilavatthu. When the Sakyans were about to open a new rest house, they invited the Buddha and his monks to spend the first night there in order to bestow their blessings upon the place. After the assembly had gathered, the Buddha spoke for much of the night, but then he turned to the Venerable Ānanda and said: "Speak to the Sakyans, Ānanda, about the disciple in higher training who is practicing the path. My back is aching and I need to stretch myself." Ānanda then proceeded to give a detailed sermon on the entire practice of the trainee, from the basic precepts of morality through to the final knowledge of arahantship. When he had finished the Buddha rose and said: "Excellent, Ānanda, excellent! You have given an excellent talk to the Sakyans on the disciple in higher training."

On several occasions the Buddha was not present when Ānanda spoke. It was his custom at times to utter a very brief, compressed statement on Dhamma to the monks, and then rise and enter his dwelling as though he were challenging the monks to tease out the meaning of his words on their own. On such occasions the monks would approach a learned elder to explain the Buddha's enigmatic utterance at length. Usually they would turn to the Venerable Mahākaccāna, the chief expositor of brief statements, but when he was not in residence they would turn to Ānanda, "for the Venerable Ānanda is praised by the Teacher and by his wise companions in the holy life." Ānanda would then give a full explanation of the Buddha's brief statement, after which the monks would report his words to the Buddha. Invariably the Buddha would declare: "Ānanda, monks, is wise, one of great understanding. If you had questioned me about this matter, I would have answered in the very same way that Ānanda has answered. That is the meaning, and so you should bear it in mind" (see SN 35:116, 117; AN 10:115).

So great was Ānanda's mastery of the Dhamma that the Buddha even spoke of him as a living embodiment of the Teaching. Once a lay disciple asked the Buddha how, after he had honored the Teacher and the Sangha, he could honor the Dhamma—and this in an age before the Dhamma was transcribed in books. The Buddha replied: "If you wish to honor the Dhamma, householder, go and honor Ānanda, the guardian of the Dhamma." Thereupon the lay disciple invited Ānanda to a meal and gave him a gift of valuable cloth. Ānanda offered this to Sāriputta, who in turn gave it to the Buddha, for he alone was the cause of all bliss (Jāt. 296). Another time, after Ānanda had answered a question of the Buddha and had left, the Buddha told the other monks: "Ānanda is still one on the path of higher training, yet it is not easy to find one who equals him fully in wisdom" (AN 3:78). And shortly before his Parinibbāna, the Master said: "Just as the multitude of nobles, brahmins, ordinary folk, and ascetics find joy in seeing a world monarch, equally joyful are the monks, nuns, male and female disciples about Ānanda. If a party of these goes to see Ānanda, his presence alone gives them joy. When he speaks on the Dhamma to them, there will be joy for them because of his words. And they are still not satisfied when Ānanda reverts to silence" (DN 16).

In view of this abundance of praise, honor, and recognition, mutterings of envy and resentment against Ānanda could have been expected, but this was not the case at all, for Ānanda was a man without enemies. This rare fortune had not come to him by chance but had been enjoyed by him in many previous existences as well. Ānanda had subordinated his life to the Dhamma so completely that fame could not touch him and make him proud. He knew that all that was good in him was due to the influence of the Teaching, and with such an attitude there was no scope in his mind for pride and complacency. One who is not proud has no enemies, and such a one does not meet with envy. If someone turns completely inward and shuns social contact, as Ānanda's half-brother Anuruddha did, then it is easy to be without enemies. But Ānanda, the intermediary between the Buddha and his many devotees, constantly exposed himself to the malice and resentment of the captious-minded. Thus the sheer fact that he lived without enemies, without rivals, without conflict and tension, borders on a miracle. This quality is truly a measure of Ānanda's uniqueness.

Although Ānanda did experience justified criticism and was occasionally admonished, that was something entirely different. A friendly reminder, a warning, or even a substantial reproach to change one's behavior are aids toward more intense purification. Such criticism, if taken to heart, leads to more inner clarity and higher esteem by others. But the instances in which Ānanda was admonished mostly referred to points of social behavior or to the minutia of the Vinaya, the monk's discipline. Hardly ever did they touch on matters of self-purification and never on his understanding of the Dhamma. The instances were as follows.

Once, when the Buddha was suffering from wind in his stomach, Ānanda cooked rice gruel for him, which had been beneficial when he had earlier suffered from this ailment. The Buddha admonished him: "It is not proper for ascetics to prepare meals in the house." After this incident it was decreed an offense for a monk to cook for himself (Vin. 1:210–11). Ānanda adhered to this rule from then on, with full insight into its necessity as part of true homelessness.

Once Ānanda went on alms round without his double robe. Fellow monks drew his attention to the rule established by the Buddha that a monk should always wear his three robes when going to the village. Ānanda agreed wholeheartedly and explained that he had simply forgotten it. Since this and the former case concerned a simple disciplinary rule, the matter was thereby settled (Vin. 1:298). That someone like Ānanda, who had a most extraordinary memory, could also forget something was due to the fact that even a stream-enterer is not yet perfect. The Buddha, however, required of the monks that they pay diligent attention to the small, everyday details of a monk's life, and that they base their higher spiritual exertions on the foundation of this discipline. This served to eliminate purely intellectual understanding and conceit.

A different kind of criticism was leveled at Ānanda in two instances by the Venerable Mahākassapa. Once Ānanda had asked Kassapa to accompany him to a nunnery in order to give a discourse to the nuns. After initial hesitation, Kassapa had agreed. When the discourse was over, a headstrong nun blamed Kassapa for doing all the talking without letting the wise Ānanda utter a single word. It was, she said, as if a needle peddler had tried to sell his wares in the presence of the needle maker. Ānanda begged Kassapa to forgive her, but Kassapa replied that Ānanda should show restraint, lest the Sangha should initiate an inquiry into his behavior (SN 16:10). Kassapa intended this reproach to be a reminder to Ānanda that in his zeal for teaching the nuns he had overlooked the danger of personal attachment. This criticism was no doubt of benefit to Ānanda in the future.

The second incident occurred soon after the Buddha's demise, when thirty disciples of Ānanda had left the Sangha. Kassapa reproached Ānanda for not guarding the young men sufficiently. He had gone on walking tours with them while they were still unrestrained in the senses, immoderate in eating, not devoted to wakefulness. Therefore he was a "trampler of the corn, a spoiler of families, whose followers are breaking away." Finally Kassapa said, "This youngster truly does not know his own measure."[2]

To this rather strong reproach, Ānanda only replied that gray hair had grown on his head and yet Kassapa still called him a "youngster." It may be that in this case Ānanda had overrated his own strength and underrated the worldliness of his pupils. Ānanda did not argue about the objective justification of the censure. After all, he was not yet an arahant and was still subject to some defilements. He only objected to the generalization implied in the criticism. One may, however, assume that an arahant like Kassapa would have known which form of criticism would be most helpful to Ānanda. In any case, Kassapa blamed Ānanda in both instances because of his love for him; there was always an excellent relationship between these two monks.

Another monk, Udāyī, once criticized Ānanda in the following way. Ānanda had asked the Blessed One how far his voice would reach in the universe. The Lord had answered that the Enlightened Ones were immeasurable and could reach farther than a thousandfold world system (with a thousand suns, a thousand heavens, and a thousand Brahma-worlds), even farther than a three-thousandfold world system. They could penetrate all those worlds with their shining splendor and reach all beings living there with their voice.

Ānanda was delighted with this description, so all-encompassing and transcending all horizons, and he exclaimed: "How fortunate I am, that I have such an almighty, powerful Master!" Udāyī objected: "What good does it do you, friend Ānanda, that your Master is almighty and powerful?" With these few words a strong reproach was uttered: that Ānanda always looked at the person of the Buddha only and thereby forgot his real benefit, his own enlightenment. The Buddha immediately took sides with Ānanda, saying: "Not so, Udāyī, not so, Udāyī! Should Ānanda die without being fully liberated, because of the purity of his heart he would be king of the gods seven times or king of the Indian subcontinent seven times. But, Udāyī, Ānanda will experience final liberation in this very life" (AN 3:80).

That the Buddha made this prophecy in Ānanda's presence showed his confidence in him. He knew that his wide knowledge of the Buddha's Word would not make Ānanda negligent in his practice. This utterance also indicated that the Buddha found it useful to shield Ānanda from reproach—self-inflicted and by others—by consoling him that his effort and striving would result in the highest attainment in this very lifetime. The Tathāgata could make such a declaration only in the case of one who tended to be extremely conscientious rather than too negligent.

The only time that the Buddha admonished Ānanda on his own accord was also the most important.[3] The Buddha had instructed Ānanda to oversee the distribution of cloth for robes to the monks, and Ānanda had accomplished this task very satisfactorily. The Buddha praised him for his circumspection and told the other monks that Ānanda was very skilled in sewing; he was able to make several different kinds of seams. For a good monk it was necessary that he hemmed his robes so that they did not fray at the edges, and one could not accuse him of carelessly handling and wasting the offerings of the laity (Vin. 1:287).

Later, when the Buddha was residing near his home town, he saw numerous seats prepared in a monastery and asked Ānanda whether many monks lived there. Ānanda confirmed this and added, "It is now time to prepare our robes, Lord." Ānanda referred here to the Buddha's instructions that a monk should care for his robes properly. However, Ānanda seemed to have arranged a sort of sewing circle, perhaps to teach his fellow monks the commended art of making seams. This was probably how it came to be a communal evening sewing hour. Ānanda had not considered that this would turn into a homelike conversational hour during which the monks would indulge in frivolous chatter. Therefore the Buddha gave this very emphatic injunction concerning the danger of mundane gregariousness for a monk: "A monk does not deserve praise who enjoys socializing, who finds joy in fellowship, finds contentment in it, enjoys togetherness, is pleased with it. That such a monk should attain at will the bliss of renunciation, the bliss of solitude, the bliss of tranquillity, the bliss of awakening, in their totality, that is impossible."

Whoever finds his whole happiness in togetherness has no access to the bliss that can only be won in seclusion. Even if such a person attains meditative absorption, that attainment will be fragile, easily shaken and lost. For a person who relishes companionship it will be still more difficult to attain final liberation. Therefore the Buddha ends his admonition with the statement that he cannot find any object of attachment that does not produce suffering because of its inherent impermanence. This is the universal aspect of the Dhamma.

Subsequently the Buddha expounded the path of practice, which he explained solely with reference to Ānanda. Because Ānanda had the faculty of deep meditation, the Buddha did not mention the first seven steps of the Noble Eightfold Path but started with the eighth step, right concentration. He expounded here the highest goal—total voidness of concepts, objects, and names—and stressed that this goal could be attained only by one who strives to master the mind in solitude. Furthermore, he appealed to Ānanda's love for him as the Master, and emphasized that this love could only be proven if Ānanda followed him into the highest attainment. One could say that he made use of both approaches, factual and personal, to help Ānanda cut off all remaining worldliness once and for all, and he concluded with this analogy: "Therefore, Ānanda, bear amity towards me, not hostility; long shall that be for your benefit and happiness. I shall not treat you, Ānanda, as the potter treats his unfired pots. Repeatedly admonishing, I shall speak to you, Ānanda, repeatedly testing. He who is sound will stand the test."

This analogy will be easier to understand if one takes a look at the *Gandhāra Jātaka* (Jāt. 406), which tells of a past life of Ānanda. He had been a king who abdicated his throne to become an ascetic, and the Bodhisatta too had done the same. One day it transpired that the first ascetic—the future Ānanda—had a small store of salt to flavor his food, which went against the ascetic rule of poverty. The Bodhisatta reprimanded him thus: "You have let go of all the riches of your kingdom, but now you have started to store provisions again." The ascetic became ill-humored because of that. He replied that one must not hurt the other person when reprimanding him; one must not be rough with one's reproach, as if cutting with a blunt knife. The Bodhisatta replied: "Among friends it isn't necessary to speak like a potter handling his unfired, i.e., very delicate, pots. A friend can also utter words of blame, because only through repeated exhortation and constant constructive criticism can one give a person the solidity of fired clay." Then the ascetic asked the Bodhisatta's pardon and requested that the Bodhisatta should, out of compassion, always guide him further.

The analogy of the clay pots—easily understandable in those days when pottery was a common trade—referred to sensitivity and touchiness. For a potter takes the raw, not quite dry, clay pot gently with both hands lest it should break. Then after firing he would repeatedly test it for flaws such as cracks or splits, and use it only if it is well baked. He would tap it again and again and only a sound one would stand the test. In the same way only a sound person, one with excellent qualities, would reach the path and fruit of arahantship.

In that past life the reproach of the Bodhisatta was fruitful and brought Ānanda—the ascetic—to the Brahma realms. So it was also fruitful this time, in their final existence, because Ānanda accepted the criticism happily, was content with it, took it to heart, and followed it until he attained to the total destruction of suffering.

THE BUDDHA'S ATTENDANT

One of the virtues of Ānanda that established his fame was his conduct as the Buddha's *upaṭṭhāka*, his personal attendant. The Buddha said of him that he was the best of all attendants, the foremost of all those monks who had ever filled this post (AN 1, chap. 14). The term "attendant" is actually not comprehensive enough to do full justice to the Venerable Ānanda's position. Such designations as "secretary" or "adjutant" fail to express the most intimate aspects of his attendance, extending to many little items of personal assistance given to the Master, while the term "servant" omits the organizational and directing aspects, implies too great a degree of subordination, and again leaves out the aspect of intimacy.

In three of his verses in the *Theragāthā* (1041–43), Ānanda sums up the way he served the Buddha through the last third of his life:

For twenty-five years I served the Blessed One,
I served him well with loving deeds
Like a shadow that does not depart.

For twenty-five years I served the Blessed One,
I served him well with loving speech
Like a shadow that does not depart.

For twenty-five years I served the Blessed One,
I served him well with loving thoughts
Like a shadow that does not depart.

If we look in the world's literature for examples of a great man's confidant who accompanied him constantly, nowhere would we find one comparable to Ānanda. His loving attention to the Master over such a long period consisted of the following services: Ānanda brought the Buddha water for washing his face and tooth-wood for cleaning his teeth; he arranged his seat, washed his feet, massaged his back, fanned him, swept his cell, and mended his robes. He slept nearby at night to be always on hand. He accompanied him on his rounds through the monastery (Vin. 1:294) and after meetings he checked to see whether any monk had left anything behind. He carried the Buddha's messages (Vin. 2:125) and called the monks together, even sometimes at midnight (Jāt. 148). When the Buddha was sick, he obtained medicine for him. Once when monks neglected a very sick fellow monk, the Buddha and Ānanda washed him and together carried him to a resting place (Vin. 1:301–2). In this way Ānanda performed the many daily tasks and cared for the physical well-being of his enlightened cousin like a good mother or a caring wife.

But above all, he also had the duties of a good secretary, facilitating the smooth communication between the thousands of monks and the Master. Together with Sāriputta and Moggallāna he tried to sort out, and attend to, the manifold problems of human relationships turning up in a community. In the case of the dispute of the monks of Kosambī (AN 4:241) and in the case of the schism in the Sangha through Devadatta (Ud. 5:8 and Vin. 2:199 ff.) Ānanda played the important role of clarifying doubts and keeping order. Often he was the go-between for the monks, arranging for them an audience with the Master, or he brought the Buddha's words to members of other sects. He refused no one and felt himself to be a bridge rather than a barrier.

On several occasions the monks made a great deal of noise, so that the Buddha asked Ānanda about the reason for this. Ānanda was always able to explain it fully and the Buddha then took the appropriate action (MN 67; Ud. 3:3; Vin. 4:129). The last of these three occasions is significant. On behalf of the Buddha, Ānanda called the large group of noisy monks together, reproached them for their behavior, and sent them away. Thereupon the group went into solitude and worked so diligently on the purification of their hearts that by the end of the rains retreat all of them had attained to the three true knowledges.[4] The Master then called them together once more. When they came into the presence of the Awakened One, he dwelt in imperturbable meditation.[5] The monks realized the depth of their master's meditation, sat down, and entered into the same absorption. After they had thus passed the first four hours of the night—truly the kind of "greeting" fit for holy ones—Ānanda got up and requested the Buddha to greet the monks who had arrived. Because all of them were in imperturbable meditation, no one could hear him. After a further four hours, Ānanda repeated his request. Again total silence answered him. And a third time, at dawn, Ānanda got up, prostrated before the Buddha, put his hands together, and requested a greeting for the monks. Thereupon the Buddha came out of his meditation and answered Ānanda: "If, Ānanda, you were able to understand our minds, then you would have known that all of us had entered into imperturbable absorption, where words cannot penetrate" (Ud. 3:3).

This account serves to show the unerring patience Ānanda possessed, as well as his limitations. Such an occurrence may have contributed to Ānanda's determination to practice meditation again and again, despite his many duties. The traditional texts speak of two occasions when he asked the Buddha for a meditation subject that he could practice in solitude. The Master told him on one occasion to concentrate on the five aggregates (SN 22:158), on the other to contemplate the six sense spheres (SN 35:86).

Among the many things which Ānanda requested from the Buddha for others, the following may be mentioned: When the monks Girimānanda and Phagguna were sick, Ānanda asked the Exalted One to visit them and strengthen them with talk on the Dhamma (AN 10:60, 6:58). It was also Ānanda who asked the Buddha—on Anāthapiṇḍika's suggestion—to have a shrine erected in the Jetavana monastery (Jāt. 479).

In these and many other ways Ānanda showed himself to be a solicitous monk who combined maternal and paternal qualities. His ability for organization, negotiation, and arrangements had already been manifested earlier, when—in a past life—he fulfilled a similar function for the king of the devas, Sakka. In the few instances when Ānanda's past lives in the deva- and Brahma-worlds are mentioned, it always related to those lives in which he held the position of a main helper and adjutant of Sakka; particularly as the heavenly charioteer Mātali (in four cases, Jāt. 31, 469, 535, 541), or as a deva such as the heavenly architect Vissakamma (489), or the rain god Pajjunna (75), or the five-crested celestial musician Pañcasikha (450).

Especially worth mentioning is Ānanda's willingness to sacrifice himself. When Devadatta let loose a wild elephant to kill the Buddha, Ānanda threw himself in front of the Buddha, ready to die himself rather than let the Blessed One be killed or injured. Three times the Buddha asked him to step back, but he did not comply. Only when the Master moved him gently from the spot through supernatural powers could he be dissuaded from his intention to sacrifice himself (Jāt. 533). This action of Ānanda spread his fame even further. The Buddha told the other monks that already in four former lives Ānanda had shown himself equally willing to sacrifice himself. Even in the distant past as an animal—as a swan (502, 533, 534) or a gazelle (501)—he had stayed with the Bodhisatta when he had been caught in a trap. In another case the Bodhisatta first sacrificed himself for his monkey mother, then Ānanda (222). And in three other recorded cases, Ānanda—in his former rebirths—saved the life of the Buddha-to-be through his care and skill. These stories amplify the virtues of Ānanda and his age-old association with the Buddha.

THE GUARDIAN OF THE DHAMMA

Among the disciples whom the Buddha declared preeminent, the Venerable Ānanda had the unique distinction of being pronounced preeminent in *five* qualities. All the other leading disciples excelled in only one category—or, in the case of two monks, in two—but Ānanda was declared the bhikkhu disciple who was foremost in five categories:

1. of those who had "heard much," i.e., who had learned much of the Buddha's discourses (*bahussutānaṁ*);
2. of those who had a good memory (*satimantānaṁ*);
3. of those who had mastery over the sequential structure of the teachings (*gatimantānaṁ*);
4. of those who were steadfast in study, etc. (*dhitimantānaṁ*); and
5. of the Buddha's attendants (*upaṭṭhakānaṁ*).

On examination one can see that these five qualities all stem from mindfulness (*sati*). Mindfulness is power of the mind and power of memory, mastery over recollections and ideas. It is the faculty of using the mind at any time, as one wishes, as its master. In short, mindfulness is circumspection and orderliness, self-restraint, control, and self-discipline. In a narrower sense, *sati* is the ability to remember. Ānanda had this ability to a phenomenal degree. He could immediately remember everything, even if he had heard it only once. He could repeat discourses of the Buddha flawlessly up to sixty thousand words, without leaving out a single syllable. He was able to recite fifteen thousand four-line stanzas of the Buddha.

It may sound incredible to us that anyone could accomplish such a feat. But the reason our own memories are so limited is because we encumber our minds with a hundred thousand useless things which hinder us from becoming master over our memory. The Buddha once said that the only reason why one forgets anything is the presence of one or all of the five hindrances: sensual desire, ill will, lethargy and drowsiness, restlessness and worry, and skeptical doubt (AN 5:193). Because Ānanda was one in the higher training, he was able to let go of these hindrances at will and so could concentrate completely on what he heard. Because he did not want anything for himself, he absorbed the discourses without resistance or distortion, arranged them properly, knew what belonged together, recognized within different expressions the common denominator, and like a faithful and skilled registrar could find his way around in the dark corridors of memory.[6]

All these factors enter into the quality of "having heard much." He who has heard much in this sense has discarded willfulness and has become a vessel of truth. He has heard much truth, and that means that he has erased all untruth in himself. Such a one is "born from the mouth" of the Teacher, is truly trained, because he let himself be shaped by the Teaching of the Enlightened One. Hence he who has heard much is the one who is most humble and a most sincere champion of truth. Everything good which he carries in his mind and upon which he acts, he does not ascribe to his own ability but to the Dhamma, which he has heard from his teacher. Such a person is truly humble.

This quality of listening well and training the mind is named as the first of the five specific abilities of Ānanda, and it is recorded that all his disciples, too, were devoted to learning (SN 14:15). But the Buddha said it would not be easy to find one who equaled Ānanda in this respect (AN 3:78). When Ānanda was asked by Sāriputta as to which monk could lend radiance to the Gosiṅga sāla-tree forest,[7] he answered thus:

> The monk is one who has heard much, who remembers what he has heard, who treasures what he has heard. As to those teachings that are good in the beginning, good in the middle, and good at the end, and transmit word by word and in the right way the completely purified life of holiness: all this he has heard much of, bears in mind, has familiarized himself with by verbal recitation, has examined with his mind, and penetrated thoroughly by view. He speaks on the Dhamma to the four kinds of listeners, in whole and in part and in the right context to bring them to the final eradication of the underlying defilements. (MN 32)

The second quality, *sati* or mindfulness, in this context means the retention in mind of the discourses heard and their application to one's own self-inquiry. For the third quality, *gati*, widely differing renderings have been proposed by translators, but according to the ancient commentary it refers to the capacity to perceive in the mind the internal connection and coherence of a discourse. This Ānanda was able to do because he understood well the meaning and significance of the teaching concerned, with all its implications. Hence, even when his recitation was interrupted by a question, he was able to resume the recital exactly at the point where he had broken off. The fourth quality was his steadfastness (*dhiti*), his energy and unflagging dedication to the tasks of studying, memorizing, and reciting the Buddha's words and of personally attending on the Master. The fifth and last quality was that of a perfect attendant, which was described earlier.

These five qualities in unison qualified Ānanda for his special role within the Buddha's Dispensation, that of the Guardian of the Dhamma (*dhammabhaṇḍāgārika*). Within a political state the *bhaṇḍāgārika* is the treasurer, the one responsible for storing, preserving, protecting, and dispensing the national wealth. If the treasurer is inept and irresponsible, the state's revenue will decline and the nation will plunge into bankruptcy and disaster. If the treasurer is astute, the national wealth will be wisely utilized and the nation will enjoy prosperity and peace. In the Buddha's Dispensation the wealth is the teachings, and the health and longevity of the Dispensation, especially after the Buddha's Parinibbāna, required that these teachings be carefully preserved and faithfully transmitted to posterity. The post of treasurer of the Dhamma therefore was of immense importance, so much so that the one who held it, by maintaining intact the Buddha's Teaching within the world, could rightly call himself "the eye of the entire world":

If one wishes to understand the Dhamma,
One should resort to such a one,
Who is of great learning, a bearer of Dhamma,
A wise disciple of the Buddha.

Of great learning, bearer of the Dhamma,
The guardian of the Great Seer's treasure,
He is the eye of the entire world,
Deserving worship, of great learning.

(Thag. 1030–31)

In selecting Ānanda as the treasurer or guardian of his Dispensation, the Buddha had chosen one whose personal qualities coincided perfectly with the demands of the post. By virtue of his devotion to learning, Ānanda was ideally suited to receive the manifold teachings delivered over a forty-five year period; by virtue of his phenomenal memory, he could retain them in mind exactly as spoken by the Master; by virtue of his sense of order, he could be relied on to preserve them in the correct sequence and to explain them in such a way that the structure of ideas accorded with the Buddha's intention; and by virtue of his steadfastness, he would so endeavor that the pupils under his charge would receive the teachings fully and be properly trained so that they in turn could pass them on to their own pupils.

Buddhist tradition specifies the number of recitation units (*dhammakkhandha*, lit. "aggregates of Dhamma") in the Buddha's Teaching as eighty-four thousand, and in one verse Ānanda claims to have received them all:

I received from the Buddha 82,000,
And from the bhikkhus 2,000 more.
Thus there are 84,000 units,
Teachings that are set in motion.

(Thag. 1024)

Because of his key position among the Buddha's entourage of monks, Ānanda was naturally the focus of much attention, and he had to deal with a great number of people. To all those who came into contact with him, he was a model in his blameless conduct, in his untiring solicitude for the Master and for the community of monks, in his unperturbable friendliness, his patience, and his readiness to help. Some potential conflicts did not even arise in his presence, and those that did arise were mitigated and resolved through his influence. Ānanda, as a man without enemies, made a strong and deep impact upon others through his exemplary conduct as well as through his instructions. His image, as the Buddha's faithful companion, left particularly strong traces in the minds of his contemporaries.

Ānanda was always master of a situation, and like a king he had a sovereign comprehension of affairs. Therefore, thanks to his circumspection, he could handle and organize whatever occurred in the daily life of the Buddha and the Sangha. Through the extraordinary power of his memory, he was able to learn from his experiences and never repeat the same mistakes, as most people are liable to do again and again due to their weak memory. Hence he could remember people well, though he may have met them only once, and he could therefore deal with them suitably, without leaving the impression that he manipulated them. His circumspection accorded with the facts of a situation so naturally that all reasonable people could only agree with him.

ĀNANDA'S ATTITUDE TOWARD WOMEN

Because of his natural kindliness and compassionate concern, Ānanda was especially solicitous for the welfare of all four classes of disciples, not only monks and laymen, but also nuns and laywomen. Without Ānanda, in fact, there might have been only three kinds of disciples, for he was the one who was instrumental in the founding of the Bhikkhunī Sangha, the order of nuns, as reported in the Vinaya Piṭaka (Vin. 2:253 ff.; also AN 8:51).

When many nobles of the Sakyan clan had left the household life for the homeless state under their illustrious kinsman, their wives, sisters, and daughters also expressed the desire to live a life of renunciation under the Enlightened One. A number of Sakyan women, under the guidance of the Buddha's stepmother Mahāpajāpatī Gotamī, approached the Buddha and appealed to him to establish a Bhikkhunī Sangha. Three times Mahāpajāpatī voiced her request, but three times the Buddha replied: "Do not be eager, Gotamī, to obtain the going forth of women from home into homelessness in the Dhamma and Discipline proclaimed by the Tathāgata."

When he had finished his stay in Kapilavatthu, accompanied by the bhikkhus, the Buddha left for Vesālī, a distance of several hundred miles. Mahāpajāpatī, along with several other Sakyan women, followed close behind. On arrival she stood outside the gate of the monastery "her feet swollen, her limbs covered with dust, with tearful face and crying." When Ānanda saw her in this condition and asked about the reason for her sorrow, she replied that the Master had three times rejected her request for the establishment of an order of nuns.[8]

Out of compassion Ānanda decided to intercede. He went to the Master and repeated her request three times, but each time the Buddha discouraged him: "Do not be eager, Ānanda, to obtain the going forth of women from home into homelessness in the Dhamma and Discipline proclaimed by the Tathāgata." Then Ānanda decided to use an indirect method. He asked the Master: "Is a woman able to gain the fruit of stream-entry, or of once-returning, or of non-returning, or of arahantship, if she leaves the household life and enters into homelessness in the Dhamma and Discipline of the Tathāgata?"

The Buddha affirmed this. Thereupon Ānanda rephrased his request: "If a woman is able to do this, Lord—and moreover Mahāpajāpatī Gotamī has rendered great service to the Blessed One: she is his aunt, his governess, and nurse, nourished him with her own milk after his mother died—therefore it would be good if the Blessed One would allow women to leave home for the homeless life in the Dhamma and Discipline of the Tathāgata."

Ānanda here brought forth two arguments. First, he appealed to the fact that a woman in the Order could gain the highest fruit and become an arahant, a goal that can be attained only very rarely in the household life. Second, he brought up the very personal element of the meritorious services that Mahāpajāpatī had rendered the Buddha in his childhood, which would be a good reason for him to help his stepmother now to gain final liberation. In response to these arguments the Buddha agreed to the establishment of an order of nuns, provided certain precautions and rules were followed.

One might gain the impression from this account that it needed Ānanda's clever arguments and keen tenacity to change the Buddha's mind. But an Awakened One's mind cannot be changed, because he is always in touch with absolute reality. What happened here was solely the same event which all Buddhas encounter, because all of them have established an order of nuns. The whole incident was not meant to prevent the founding of the female branch of the Order, but only to strengthen by that hesitation the message that this brought great dangers with it. For this reason, the Buddha stipulated eight conditions, which were so selected that only the best women would agree to abide by them. They also served to bring about a separation of the sexes in the Order in the most prudent manner possible. In spite of this, the Exalted One declared that because of the founding of the order of nuns the Dispensation would last only five hundred years instead of a full thousand years.[9]

Following the Buddha's proclamation of the rules and regulations for nuns, Ānanda asked him about the qualities a monk should have to be a teacher of nuns. The Buddha did not reply that he had to be an arahant, but indicated eight practical and concrete qualities, which someone like Ānanda, who was not yet an arahant, could also possess. These eight qualities were, first, the teacher of nuns must be virtuous; second, he must have comprehensive knowledge of the Dhamma; third, he must be well acquainted with the Vinaya, especially the rules for nuns; fourth, he must be a good speaker with a pleasant and fluent delivery, faultless in pronunciation and intelligibly conveying the meaning; fifth, he should be able to teach Dhamma to the nuns in an elevating, stimulating, and encouraging way; sixth, he must always be welcome to the nuns and liked by them—that is, they must be able to respect and esteem him not only when he praises them but especially when there is an occasion for reproach; seventh, he must never have committed sexual misconduct with a nun; eighth, he must have been a fully ordained Buddhist monk for at least twenty years (AN 8:52).

Since Ānanda had been instrumental in the founding of the order of nuns, he now also wanted to help them to advance on the noble path. This brought about some difficulties for him. There were two occasions in which nuns stood up for him without justification against the Venerable Mahākassapa.[10] Both nuns left the Order; they showed thereby that they were no longer able to sustain the necessary impersonal and purely spiritual relationship with their teacher, Ānanda.

Even more extreme was the case of a nun in Kosambī, whose name is not recorded. She sent a messenger to Ānanda, asking him to visit her, as she was sick. In reality she had fallen in love with Ānanda and wanted to seduce him. Ānanda mastered the situation with complete aplomb. In his sermon to her he explained that this body had arisen because of nutrition, craving, and pride. But, he said, one could use these three as means for purification. Supported by nutrition, one could transcend nutrition. Supported by craving, one could transcend craving. Supported by pride, one could transcend pride. The monk consumed such nutriment as would enable him to lead the holy life. He sublimated his craving and was supported by his longing for holiness. And pride spurred him on to reach what others had already attained, namely, the destruction of all defilements. In this way he could, in due course, transcend nutrition, craving, and pride. But there was a fourth cause for the arising of the body—sexual intercourse—which was an entirely different matter. This had been called the destruction of the bridge to Nibbāna by the Blessed One. In no way could its sublimation be used as a path to holiness.

Thereupon the nun got up from her bed, prostrated before Ānanda, confessed her offense, and asked for forgiveness. Ānanda accepted the confession and declared that in the Order it was an advantage to confess one's faults and to restrain oneself thereafter (AN 4:159). This incident is an excellent example of Ānanda's great skill in giving a suitable Dhamma discourse on the spur of the moment, in finding the right word at the right time.

Another incident happened with regard to the wives of King Pasenadi. Despite their keen desire to learn the Dhamma, they could not go to the monastery to hear the Buddha preach. As the king's women they were confined to the harem like birds in a cage, and that was really a disaster for them. They went to the king and asked him to request the Buddha to send a monk to the palace to teach them the Dhamma. The king, having promised, asked his wives which monk they would prefer. They discussed the issue among themselves and unanimously requested the king to ask Ānanda, the Guardian of the Dhamma, to come and teach them. The Blessed One complied with the request presented to him by the king and from then on Ānanda regularly went to teach the Dhamma to the women (Vin. 4:157–58).

One day during this period one of the crown jewels was stolen. Everything was searched and the women felt very troubled by the situation. Because of this they were not as attentive and eager to learn as usual. Ānanda asked them the reason and when he heard it, out of compassion he went to the king and advised him to summon all the suspects and give them an opportunity to return the jewel unobtrusively. He should have a tent erected in the courtyard of the palace, put a large pot of water inside, and have everyone enter alone. So it was done, and the jewel thief, alone in the tent, let the jewel drop into the pot. Thereby the king regained his property, the thief went unpunished, and peace reigned once again in the palace. This incident increased Ānanda's popularity even more and thereby the popularity of the Sakyan monks. The monks also praised Ānanda, as he had restored peace through gentle means (Jāt. 92).

Shortly before the Buddha passed away, Ānanda asked him a question concerning women:

> "How shall we relate to women, Lord?"
> "Do not look at them."
> "But if we see one, Lord?"
> "Do not address her."
> "But if one talks to us?"
> "Keep to mindfulness and self-control." (DN 16)

This question was posed by Ānanda in view of the imminent demise of the Master, just prior to the preparations for the funeral. This problem must therefore have been an important one for him. He himself did not need an admonition to practice self-control, for he had overcome sensual desire for twenty-five years. But again and again he had seen how the problem of the relationship between the sexes stirred up tumultuous emotions, and he must have known too, from his discussions with the younger monks, how difficult it was to lead the perfectly pure and stainless holy life aimed at the transcendence of sensuality. He may also have had in mind the Buddha's warning that the Dispensation was endangered through the foundation of the nun's order and he may have wanted to give his contemporaries—and successors—a last word of the Buddha on this topic.

ĀNANDA AND HIS FELLOW MONKS

Of all the monks, the Venerable Sāriputta was Ānanda's closest friend. There does not seem to have been a close relationship between Ānanda and his half-brother Anuruddha, because the latter preferred solitude while Ānanda was fond of people. Sāriputta was the disciple who most resembled the Master, and with whom he could talk in the same way as with the Buddha. It is remarkable that of all the monks only Sāriputta and Ānanda received honorary titles from the Buddha: Sāriputta was called the marshal of the Dhamma (dhammasenāpati) and Ānanda its guardian or treasurer (dhammabhaṇḍāgārika). One can see their complementary roles in this. Sāriputta, the lion, was the active teacher, Ānanda more the preserver and treasurer. In certain respects, Ānanda's methods resembled more those of Mahāmoggallāna, whose inclinations were also motherly and preserving.

Ānanda and Sāriputta often worked together as a team. They went twice to visit the sick lay supporter Anāthapiṇḍika (MN 143; SN 55:26) and dealt with the dispute of the monks of Kosambī (AN 4:221). They also had many Dhamma discussions with each other. So close was their friendship that when Sāriputta attained final Nibbāna, Ānanda, even despite all his training in meditation, felt almost as if he had fallen into an abyss:

> All the quarters have become dim,
> The teachings are not clear to me;
> Indeed my noble friend has gone
> And everything is cast in darkness.
>
> (Thag. 1034)

His body felt drained of strength and even the sustenance of the Dhamma seemed to have deserted him at that moment—such was the impact of the death message. Then the Buddha consoled him. He asked Ānanda to reflect whether Sāriputta had taken from him his own virtue, meditation, wisdom, liberation, or the knowledge of liberation. Ānanda had to agree that these, the only important aspects, had not changed. But, he added, Sāriputta had been such a helpful companion and friend for him and others. Again the Buddha directed the conversation to a higher level by reminding Ānanda of what he, the Buddha, had always taught: that nothing that has arisen can remain forever. The death of Sāriputta was, for the other disciples, like cutting off the main branch of a large tree. But that should only be another reason for relying on oneself, on no one else, and for being one's own island and refuge (SN 47:13).

Many discussions that Ānanda had with other monks are also recorded. Only a few can be related here.

One day the Venerable Vaṅgīsa accompanied Ānanda to the king's palace, where Ānanda was to teach the Dhamma to the women of the harem. Vaṅgīsa, it seems, had a strong streak of sensuality in his character, and when he saw the beautiful palace women dressed up in all their finery his heart was flooded with sensual desire. Suddenly he felt the celibate life of a monk, to which he had taken so readily, as oppressive as a lead weight, and thoughts of disrobing and indulging in sensual pleasures played havoc with his mind. As soon as they could speak in private, Vaṅgīsa explained his plight to Ānanda and appealed for his help and guidance. As he was the foremost poet in the Sangha he spoke in verse, addressing Ānanda by his clan name, Gotama:

I am burning with sensual lust,
My mind is all engulfed by fire.
Please tell me how to extinguish it,
Out of compassion, O Gotama.

And Ānanda replied in verse:

It is due to an inversion of perception
That your mind is engulfed by fire.
Turn away from the sign of beauty,
The aspect linked to sensual lust.

See constructions as alien,
See them as suffering, not as self.
Extinguish the mighty fire of lust;
Do not burn up again and again.

Develop meditation on the foul,
With mind one-pointed, well concentrated;
Let your mindfulness dwell upon the body,
Be engrossed in disenchantment.

Develop the signless meditation,
Discard the tendency to conceit.
Then, by breaking through conceit,
You will fare with heart at peace.

(SN 8:4; see also Thag. 1223–26)

Ānanda showed Vaṅgīsa that he constantly refueled sensual desire because his perception fastened upon the superficial appearance of feminine charm. The fascination with beauty gave rise to a feeling of deprivation, which manifested as weariness of mind and as a kind of aversion toward the ascetic life. Therefore Vaṅgīsa had to contemplate soberly those things that seemed beautiful and desirable. With the scalpel of meditative insight he had to dissect the body and probe beneath its charming exterior in order to see the wretchedness and misery lying within. In this way his lust would fade away and he would be able to stand up, strong and invincible, amid the enticements of worldly enjoyment.

The monk Channa was plagued with doubts about the Dhamma. During the Buddha's lifetime he had been an obdurate bhikkhu, self-willed and difficult to train, but after the Master's Parinibbāna he was filled with a compelling sense of urgency. Though he humbly sought instructions from the other monks, he could not make satisfactory progress. He could understand that the five aggregates are impermanent, but when he tried to contemplate the principle of nonself he came to a standstill, stricken with the fearful thought that Nibbāna would be the destruction of his precious ego. So he came for advice to Ānanda. Ānanda first expressed his joy that Channa had relinquished his obstinacy and was earnestly intent on understanding the Dhamma. Channa was delighted and listened with undivided attention to Ānanda's exposition of the Buddha's discourse to Kaccānagotta (SN 12:15) on transcending the extremes of being and nonbeing. By the end of Ānanda's explanation,

Channa had arrived at the path and fruit of stream-entry. Thereupon he exclaimed how wonderful it was to have such wise friends as teachers. He had at last become securely established in the Dhamma (SN 22:90).

CONVERSATIONS WITH THE BUDDHA

If one also considers as conversations the silent, inner rapport with a Dhamma discourse, then the whole Sutta Piṭaka actually consists of Ānanda's conversations with the Buddha. He was almost always present when the Buddha gave a discourse, and those few talks that the Blessed One gave when Ānanda was absent he repeated for him afterwards.[11]

The Buddha often addressed the Venerable Ānanda with questions on the teachings, which were either meant for Ānanda's spiritual growth or gave the occasion for a discourse to all the monks present. It is always more stimulating for the listeners when two experts discuss a subject with each other, rather than when only one speaks. In this way many of the conversations between the Buddha and Ānanda are discourses for the instruction of others.

Several times the Buddha created the special occasion for a discourse by smiling when he came to a certain locality. Ānanda knew that a Fully Enlightened One does not smile without cause, and he understood immediately that there was reason for a question. So he asked the Awakened One why he had smiled. Thereupon the Master gave a detailed explanation of an incident in the past, a Jātaka story, which had taken place at that locality.[12]

The conversations in which the Venerable Ānanda took the initiative by asking a question are far more numerous than the ones the Buddha initiated. For instance, Ānanda asked whether there was a fragrance which went against the wind, different from that of flowers and blossoms. The answer was: the fragrance of one who has taken the Triple Refuge and who is virtuous and generous (AN 3:79).

Another time Ānanda asked how one could live happily in the Order. The answer was: if one is virtuous oneself but does not blame others for lack of virtue; if one watches oneself but not others; if one does not worry about lack of fame; if one can obtain the four meditative absorptions without difficulty; and finally if one becomes an arahant. So here the first step on the path to holiness is mentioned as not criticizing or watching others, but only making demands on oneself (AN 5:106).

Ānanda asked, "What is the purpose and blessing of virtue?" And the Buddha answered, "To be free of self-reproach and feelings of guilt and to enjoy a clear conscience." But Ānanda asked further, "What is the purpose and blessing of a clear conscience?" The Buddha replied: "It brings joy in wholesome thoughts and actions, happiness with the progress made, and gives an incentive for further striving." "And what results from that?" "One experiences exultation in one's heart, is drawn towards the good and perfect bliss, and from that results deep calm and insight" (AN 10:1). In this way Ānanda inquired about many aspects of the Dhamma.

Sometimes Ānanda reported certain views of his to the Buddha so that the Master could either accept them or correct them. For instance, one time he approached the Buddha and said, "It seems to me, Lord, that good friendship is half of the holy life." Unexpectedly the Buddha disagreed: "Do not speak thus, Ānanda! Noble friendship is more than half the holy life. It is the entire holy life!" For what would the holy life be like if they had not all come to the Buddha, as their best friend, to be shown the right way? (SN 45:2).

The best-known remark of Ānanda must surely be the assertion with which he opens the *Mahānidāna Suttanta* (Great Discourse on Causation; DN 15): "Dependent origination (*paṭicca-samuppāda*), Lord, is very profound, but to me it seems as clear as clear can be." Again the Buddha disagreed: "Not so, Ānanda, not so! This dependent origination is profound and appears profound; it is truly very difficult to penetrate. Because they have not understood and penetrated this one principle, beings are caught on the wheel of birth and death and cannot find the means to freedom." And then the Buddha explained to Ānanda dependent origination in its manifold aspects.

Once Ānanda saw an archer perform extraordinary feats. He told the Buddha how much this had impressed him—and coming from the warrior caste, Ānanda must have been temperamentally disposed to appreciate such displays of martial skill. The Buddha used this statement to draw an analogy. He said it was more difficult to understand and penetrate the Four Noble Truths than to hit and penetrate with an arrow a hair split seven times (SN 56:45).

Another report says that Ānanda once saw the famous brahmin Jāṇussoṇi, a disciple of the Buddha, driving along in his glorious white chariot. He heard the people exclaim that the brahmin's chariot was the most beautiful of all. Ānanda reported this to the Buddha and asked him how one could describe the best chariot according to the Dhamma. The Buddha explained the vehicle to Nibbāna by means of a detailed simile:

Faith and wisdom are the draught-animals, moral shame the

brake, intellect the reins, mindfulness the charioteer, virtue the accessories, meditation the axle, energy the wheels, equanimity the balance, renunciation the chassis; the weapons are love, harmlessness, and solitude, and patience is its armour (SN 45:4).

ĀNANDA'S FORMER LIVES

Ānanda's original aspiration to great discipleship was formed under the Buddha Padumuttara, one hundred thousand aeons in the past.[13] The Buddha Padumuttara was the son of King Nanda, who dwelt in the royal city of Haṁsavatī. His younger brother was the Crown Prince Sumanakumāra, who reigned over a fiefdom given to him by his father. Once, while the Buddha was dwelling at the capital with a retinue of one hundred thousand monks, Sumanakumāra went at his father's behest to suppress a rebellion in the border region. When he returned to the capital his father offered him a boon, and the prince choose to conduct the Buddha and his Sangha to his own city and attend on them for the three months of the rains retreat.

The prince had been extremely impressed by the Buddha's personal attendant, a monk named Sumana, and observed him closely during the rainy season. At the end of the three-month period, during which he had provided the Buddha and the Sangha with all their requirements and attended on them with great devotion, he prostrated himself at the Master's feet and dedicated his merits to the future attainment of the post of personal attendant under a Fully Enlightened One. The Buddha looked into the future and told him that his aspiration would come to fulfillment during the Dispensation of the Buddha Gotama, one hundred thousand aeons in the future. From that day on, it is said, Sumanakumāra felt as if he were already walking behind the Buddha Gotama carrying his bowl and extra robe.

In the Jātaka stories we often find prominent characters identified as earlier incarnations of Ānanda. What is most striking in these tales is Ānanda's extremely intimate connection with the Bodhisatta, the future Buddha Gotama. Often he is the Bodhisatta's brother, son, father, assistant, colleague, and friend. The three examples of former lives given here stress his own exertions to perfect his virtue. A complete survey of his former lives would show that he was only seldom a deva or an animal; most often he was a human being. In this respect he contrasts with Anuruddha, who almost always appears as a deva, and with Devadatta, who appears most often as an animal.

JĀTAKA 498

Ānanda and the Bodhisatta were born as cousins among the outcasts or *caṇḍālas.* Their job was the fumigation of malodorous places. In order to escape the contempt they were held in, they disguised themselves as young brahmins and went to the university at Takkasilā to study. Their deceit was discovered and they were beaten up by their fellow students. A wise and kindly man ordered the students to stop and advised the two caṇḍālas to become ascetics. They followed this advice, in due course died, and as punishment for their deceit, were reborn as animals, as offspring of a doe. They were inseparable and died together by the arrow of a hunter. In the next life they were sea hawks and again died together because of a hunter.

With this, their existences below the human level came to an end. Ānanda was born as the son of a king and the Bodhisatta as the son of the royal chaplain. While Ānanda held the higher position in a worldly sense, the Bodhisatta had more innate abilities; for one thing, he could remember all the above three lives, while Ānanda could only remember his life as a caṇḍāla. At the age of sixteen, the Bodhisatta became a sincerely striving ascetic while Ānanda became king. Later the Bodhisatta visited the king. He praised the happiness of asceticism and explained the unsatisfactoriness of the world of the senses. Ānanda admitted that he realized this but could not let go of his desires, to which he was held fast like an elephant in a swamp.

Thereupon the Bodhisatta advised him that even as a king he could practice virtue, for instance, by not levying unjust taxes and by supporting ascetics and priests. But when hot passions arose in him, he should remember his mother: how he had been completely helpless as a baby, and how without his mother's care he would never have become king. Thereupon Ānanda resolved to become an ascetic, and both attained to the Brahma-world.

JĀTAKA 421

The Bodhisatta had been born as a poor laborer and endeavored to keep the Uposatha.[14] As the fruit of this he was reborn as a king. Ānanda lived in his kingdom as a poor water-carrier. His whole fortune consisted of a coin which he had hidden under a stone in a certain place. When the people in the city held a festival, the water-carrier's wife urged him to enjoy himself too and asked him whether he had any money. He said he had one coin but it was twelve miles away. She told him to get it and said she had saved up the same amount. They could buy garlands, incense, and drinks with that. Ānanda set out in spite of the midday heat, happy in the expectation of enjoying the festival. When he passed through the courtyard of the king's palace he sang a song. The king saw him and asked the reason for his joyfulness. He answered that he did not notice the heat, as he was being driven by hot desire, and told his story.

The king asked how much his treasure amounted to: maybe one hundred thousand pieces? When he finally heard that it was only one coin, he exclaimed that Ānanda should not walk through the heat but that he would give him a similar coin. Ānanda replied that he was very grateful because then he would have two coins. The king then offered him two coins but Ānanda said he would fetch his own coin nevertheless. The king now became excited and raised his offer to millions, to the post of viceroy, but Ānanda would not let go of his coin. Only when the king offered him half his kingdom did he agree. The kingdom was divided up, and Ānanda was called King One-Coin.

One day the two kings went hunting. When they became tired, the Bodhisatta put his head in the lap of his friend and fell asleep. Then the thought came to Ānanda to kill the king and rule the whole kingdom by himself. He was drawing his sword when he remembered how grateful he—a poor yokel—should be to the king, and how wicked it was of him to allow such a wish to arise. He put his sword back in its sheath, but even a second and a third time he was overcome by the same desire. Feeling that this thought might rise in him again and again and could lead him on to very evil deeds, he threw away his sword, woke the king, prostrated before him, and asked his forgiveness. The Bodhisatta forgave him and said he could have the whole kingdom; he himself would be satisfied to serve as viceroy under him. But Ānanda replied that he was finished with his lust for power: he wanted to become an ascetic. He had seen the cause of desire and how it grew, and now he wanted to pull it out by the roots. He went to the Himalayas and practiced meditation. The Bodhisatta remained in the world.

Jātaka 282

The Bodhisatta was a righteous king of Benares who practiced the royal virtues: he gave alms, followed the precepts, and observed the Uposatha days. Now one of his ministers carried on an intrigue in his harem. When he was caught, the gentle king waived the death penalty, only banishing him and allowing him to take his family and fortune along. The minister then went to live at a neighboring king's court. He became the king's confidant and told him he could easily occupy Benares, because its king was much too gentle. But the neighboring king, Ānanda, was suspicious, because he knew well the strength and power of Benares. The minister advised him to experiment. He should destroy one village of Benares. If any of his men were caught, the king would probably even reward the prisoners. True enough, when the marauders were brought before the Bodhisatta and lamented that they had plundered out of hunger, he gave them money.

This served to convince Ānanda of the truth of the treacherous minister's words, and he marched into Benares. The commander-in-chief of the Bodhisatta's army wanted to defend the kingdom, but the Bodhisatta said that he did not want to be the cause of harm for others. If the other king wanted his kingdom, he should have it. He let Ānanda capture him and put him into prison. There he practiced loving-kindness meditation toward the rapacious King Ānanda, who was struck down by a fever and plagued by a guilty conscience. Ānanda asked the Bodhisatta's pardon, returned his kingdom to him, and swore to be his ally forever. The Bodhisatta returned to his throne and spoke to his ministers about the virtues and rewards of harmlessness, saying that because he had made peace with the invaders, hundreds were spared death on the battlefield. Then he renounced his throne, became an ascetic, and attained to the Brahma-world. Ānanda, however, remained king.

THE LAST DAYS OF THE BUDDHA

The single most important sutta highlighting Ānanda's relationship to the Buddha is the *Mahāparinibbāna Sutta* (DN 16), the chronicle of the Buddha's last days and ultimate entrance into Nibbāna.[15] These records convey a special mood, the mood of parting, which was especially painful for Ānanda. It is also the first small beginning of the decline of the Dhamma, which will gradually disappear with increased distance from the Buddha's lifetime until a new Buddha arises. This entire text gives, as it were, voice to the admonition to practice the Dhamma while there is still a chance. It reflects once more Ānanda's whole character, and therefore we will follow its course, emphasizing those passages in which the spotlight falls on Ānanda.

The first section of the sutta starts at Rājagaha, the capital of the state of Magadha. Devadatta's attempt to create a schism in the Sangha had failed seven years earlier. King Ajātasattu still reigned in Magadha. King Pasenadi of Kosala had just been overthrown and the Sakyan clan had come to its tragic end in which many of Ānanda's close relatives were killed. At that time, three famous warrior clans lived north of the river Ganges, near the Himalayas. They were the Koliyas, the Mallas, and the Vajjians, all of whom had retained relative independence from King Ajātasattu. He had the intention of destroying the Vajjians and incorporating their land into his growing empire.

While the Buddha could not prevent the ruin of those Sakyans who had not entered the Order, as they had to pay a kammic debt, he did help the Vajjians and later indirectly also the Mallas. This is the external "political" background of the last years of the Buddha's life. In detail, this incident happened as follows.

King Ajātasattu gave orders to his minister, Vassakāra, to go to the Buddha and announce his intention to enter into battle against the Vajjians. While Vassakāra delivered his message, the Venerable Ānanda was standing behind the Buddha fanning him. The Enlightened One turned to Ānanda and put seven questions to him about the lifestyle and conditions of the Vajjians. In reply to these questions Ānanda declared that the Vajjians often had council meetings and deliberated harmoniously, did not repeal their old laws, followed the advice of their elders, did not rape women, honored their temples and shrines and did not revoke gifts to religious places, and gave protection and hospitality to all true priests and ascetics. With these seven qualities, said the Buddha, one could expect prosperity for the Vajjians, not decline. Sometime earlier the Buddha had given them these seven rules. The king's minister replied that even one of these qualities would be enough to ensure their continued existence as a clan. As long as the Vajjians kept to these seven rules, it would be impossible for the king to conquer them, except through inner dissension or treachery.

Vassakāra left with this conviction in mind and reported to the king that it would be useless to start a war against the Vajjians. Indians in those days had so much confidence in the spiritual strength of a people that the hint of moral superiority was sufficient to prevent a war. Only much later, after the demise of the Buddha, was it possible for the king to overrun the Vajjians, and this only because they had meanwhile forsaken their moral integrity.

This highly political discussion was used by the Buddha as an occasion to request Ānanda to call all the monks of the area together. He would give them an exhortation about seven things that would enable the Sangha to flourish: "The bhikkhus should assemble frequently, and should conduct their affairs amicably; they should not make new rules but obey the old ones; they should honor the elders of the Sangha and give heed to their advice; they should resist craving, enjoy solitude, and practice mindfulness at all times, so that like-minded persons would be attracted and those who were already living the holy life would be happy."

After the Buddha had addressed the monks in this way, he gave them the following terse summary of the Teaching, which recurs many times throughout this narrative: "Such is virtue, such is concentration, such is wisdom. Concentration fortified with virtue brings great benefits and great fruits. Wisdom fortified with concentration brings great benefits and great fruits. The mind fortified with wisdom is liberated from all cankers, namely, from the canker of sensual desire, the canker of desire for becoming, and the canker of ignorance."

After this exhortation, the Buddha commenced his last journey. He always went to places where there were people ready to understand the Dhamma, or where misunderstandings needed to be sorted out, or where brute force could be prevented. On this last journey he went first in the direction of the Ganges River to Nālandā, which later became a famous Buddhist educational center. This town was near Sāriputta's birthplace, and here Sāriputta took leave of the Buddha: he wanted to stay behind and teach the Dhamma to his mother before he attained final Nibbāna.[16] When saying farewell, this great disciple voiced once more the Buddha's praise: "It is clear to me, Lord, that there is no one more distinguished in wisdom than yourself."

Then the Awakened One went with a large company of monks to Vesālī. This town was the capital of the Vajjians, whose virtue he had praised, and from whom he had averted the threat of King Ajātasattu's attack. At Vesālī he fell ill with a deadly disease, which he suppressed by sheer willpower, as he did not want to die without having assembled the disciples once more. That a Buddha can become ill is due to the imperfection of the body, but that he can master the illness at will is due to his spiritual perfection.

Ānanda had been despondent over the Buddha's illness, so dejected that he could not think properly. He told the Buddha that he had found consolation in the fact that surely the Awakened One would not attain final Nibbāna without having given some regulations about the Order to the monks. But the Buddha rejected this: "What more does the Sangha expect from me, Ānanda? I have taught the Dhamma without making any distinction of esoteric and exoteric doctrine. There is nothing that the Tathāgata holds back with the closed fist of a teacher. Whoever thinks that it is he who should lead the Sangha of bhikkhus, or that the Sangha of bhikkhus depends upon him, such a one would have to give last instructions. But the Tathāgata has no such idea, so what instructions should he have to give to the Sangha of bhikkhus?" The Buddha continued: "Now I am almost eighty, Ānanda. I have come to the end of my life, and I can maintain the body only with difficulty, just as one maintains a dilapidated old cart. My body is at ease only when I enter upon and dwell in the signless deliverance of the mind."[17] But the Master immediately gave Ānanda an antidote for the sadness caused by these words: "So, Ānanda, each of you should be an island unto yourself, dwell with yourself as a refuge and with no other as your refuge; each of you should make the Dhamma your island, dwell with the Dhamma as your refuge and with no other as your refuge."

The third section of the sutta is located at Vesālī, where the Buddha stayed for the rains retreat. One day, after the rains, he requested Ānanda to take a sitting mat and accompany him to the Cāpāla Shrine in order to pass the day there in meditation. When they were seated the Blessed One looked at the peaceful landscape before him and reminded Ānanda of the many beautiful spots in the vicinity. The reason for this seemingly unmotivated description of the countryside becomes clear later.

The Buddha then said: "Anyone who has developed the four roads to psychic power,[18] made them his vehicle and his foundation, could, if he wished, live out the aeon (kappa) or the remainder of the aeon.[19] The Tathāgata has done all that, and he could, if requested, live to the end of this aeon." But although Ānanda was given such a plain and broad hint, which certainly coincided with his own longing, he did not beg the Buddha to stay alive out of compassion for all beings. Not only once, but a second and third time the Buddha addressed Ānanda in the same way. But each time Ānanda failed to catch the hint; in his confusion his mind had been ensnared by Māra, the Evil One, who still had some degree of power over him.

At this moment Ānanda, who usually was so circumspect, had lost his mindfulness, which previously had happened only in negligible matters. Otherwise our whole aeon would have taken quite a different turn. Could it be that at just that moment Ānanda was so absorbed in the pleasure of being in close companionship with the Buddha that the Master's hint failed to register on his mind? Was it, perhaps, just his very attachment to the Buddha's company, reinforced by the enchanting evening hour and the peaceful forest, that prevented him from responding in the way proper to such deep attachment—a response that would have accorded with his deepest wishes for a longer life for the Blessed One? If Māra had not intervened, Ānanda would have asked the Buddha to accept the burden of a prolonged life, and the Buddha would have consented, out of compassion for the world. But Māra, afraid that innumerable beings would have thereby escaped his clutch, hastened to prevent this, and the course of history was sealed. This scene, so poignant and suggestive, belongs to the mysteries of the Pāli Canon, and one could puzzle about it endlessly.

But let us continue the account: The Buddha dismissed Ānanda, who seated himself under a nearby tree and started meditating. Then Māra appeared before the Buddha and reminded him of a promise made forty-five years before, immediately after his Enlightenment. Māra had then requested the Buddha to enter final Nibbāna and not to teach, but the Buddha had replied that he would not die until he had thoroughly trained and instructed the monks, nuns, laymen, and laywomen and the holy life was well established. Now, however, all that had been accomplished, and Māra had come to remind him that it was time to fulfill his promise. The Buddha replied: "Do not trouble yourself, Evil One. Before long the Parinibbāna of the Tathāgata will come about. Three months from now the Tathāgata will pass utterly away." Then the Blessed One, with mindfulness and clear comprehension, relinquished his will to live on. And just as he did so the earth quaked and trembled, and thunder resounded in the heavens; such was the powerful effect on the natural elements when he renounced them as a basis for life.

When Ānanda became aware of the earthquake and thunder, he asked the Buddha for their cause. The Buddha replied that there were eight reasons for earthquakes. The first is an occasion when great forces move; the second is when a monk or brahmin possessing supernormal power reaches a certain kind of meditation; the last six are at the conception, birth, Enlightenment, the first teaching of the Dhamma, the relinquishing of the will to live, and the final Nibbāna of a Buddha. One can see from this how deep is the connection between a Buddha—the highest of all beings—and the whole cosmos.

The expositions that follow on the eight kinds of assemblies, the eight fields of mastery, and the eight liberations seem to be a digression. It appears to be one of those occasions for a spontaneously arisen discourse. Scholars speak about insertions into the text because at first there were eight reasons for earthquakes, then three other "eights" were brought in. In reality there is a deeper connection, designed to bring Ānanda from the superficial to the profound and to let him know the quickly approaching death of the Buddha in such a way that it would not disturb him.

After the Buddha had helped to direct Ānanda on the path toward enlightenment, he related how he had told Māra forty-five years ago that he would not attain final Nibbāna until the Dhamma was well established.

Now Māra had appeared before him and he had told Māra he would live for only another three months. Therefore he had now relinquished the will to live, and that had been the reason for the earthquake.

Now, without a moment's hesitation, Ānanda begged the Awakened One three times to remain for the whole aeon. But the Buddha replied that the appropriate time for this had lapsed. When Ānanda asked for the third time, the Buddha inquired: "Do you have faith, Ānanda, in the Enlightenment of the Tathāgata?" When Ānanda affirmed this, he asked, "Why then, Ānanda, do you persist against the Tathāgata up to the third time?"

Then the Buddha made it clear to Ānanda that he had let the opportunity slip by: "The fault is yours, Ānanda. Here you have failed, inasmuch as you were unable to grasp the plain suggestion given by the Tathāgata and you did not ask him to remain. For if you had done so, Ānanda, twice the Tathāgata might have declined, but the third time he would have consented." He also reminded Ānanda that not only now, but already fifteen times previously he had told him that he could remain for a whole aeon, but each time Ānanda had remained silent.

Finally the Buddha added his admonition on impermanence: "Have I not taught from the very beginning that with all that is dear and beloved there must be change, separation, and severance? Of that which is arisen, come into being, conditioned, and subject to decay, one cannot bring it about that it will not come to dissolution. Further, it is impossible for a Tathāgata to go back on his word: in three months' time he shall attain final Nibbāna." Thereupon he requested Ānanda to assemble the monks of the area. He addressed the assembly with the exhortation to learn and practice the path to enlightenment which he had so clearly taught throughout his ministry, so "that this holy life may endure long, for the welfare and happiness of many, out of compassion for the world, for the good, welfare, and happiness of devas and humans." At the end of the discourse he announced that "three months from now the Tathāgata's Parinibbāna will take place," and he gave the monks some stanzas for contemplation:

> My years are now full ripe, the life span left is short.
> Departing, I shall leave you, relying on myself alone.
> Be earnest then, monks, mindful and pure in virtue!
> With firm resolve guard your own mind!
>
> One who in this Dhamma and Discipline
> Dwells in constant heedfulness

Shall abandon the wandering on in birth
And make an end to suffering.

The fourth section of the sutta tells of the Buddha resuming his journey after the rains retreat and declaring that he would not return to Vesālī. On the way he spoke to the monks on the same topics he had expounded earlier. He declared that they had to travel through this long round of rebirths because they had not penetrated four things: a noble one's virtue, a noble one's concentration, a noble one's wisdom, and a noble one's deliverance. And again, as so often on this last journey, he emphasized concentration fortified by virtue and wisdom fortified by concentration.

At the next resting place he explained to the monks how they should act if someone purported to quote his words. One should remember these sentences and look for verification in the Vinaya or confirmation in the suttas. If one could not find them there, then one would have to come to the conclusion that it had been wrongly learned by that person, and one should reject it. This admonition was extremely important for the faithful transmission of his words and has been the reason why even to this day one can distinguish between the Buddha's own words and postcanonical or inauthentic texts.

After this, the Buddha journeyed to the province of the Mallas, the warrior clan nearest to the Himalayas. It is possible that in the meantime he had also been in Sāvatthī, because it was there that the news of Sāriputta's death reached him. In the land of the Mallas, the neighbors of the Sakyans, the goldsmith Cunda invited him and the monks for a meal. The chief food item was a dish called *sūkara-maddava.*[20] The Buddha asked the goldsmith to serve this dish only to him and to offer the other items to the monks. Then he asked that the remainder of the food be buried, "for I do not see in all this world anyone who could eat it and entirely digest it except the Tathāgata alone." After the meal the Buddha became ill with a severe attack of dysentery, but he bore this illness with equanimity and was not deterred from continuing on his journey. Along the way he told Ānanda to spread his robe as he was exhausted and wished to rest. He then asked Ānanda to bring him some water from the nearby stream, but Ānanda said he would prefer to bring water from the river, because the stream had been churned up by many carts. After the Buddha had repeated his request three times, however, the obedient Ānanda went to the stream and saw that in the meantime, through a miracle, the water had become clear.

On the way, the Buddha met Pukkusa, a Malla who was a disciple of

Āḷāra Kālāma. The Buddha won Pukkusa's confidence with an account of his own meditative powers, and Pukkusa took refuge and became a lay disciple, the last one in the Buddha's lifetime. Then he presented two sets of golden-hued robes to the Buddha. The Buddha told him to give one to himself and the other to Ānanda. On this occasion Ānanda did not reject the gift. He remarked that the golden hue of the robe appeared almost dull compared to the bright radiance of the Buddha's skin. The Blessed One then said that there are two occasions when the complexion of the Tathāgata becomes exceptionally clear and bright: on the day of his Enlightenment and on the day of his final Nibbāna. In the last hours of the following night he would attain final Nibbāna.

After bathing, the Buddha told Ānanda that no one should reproach the goldsmith Cunda because the Buddha had died after taking a meal from him. There were two offerings in the world that were best: the almsfood after which the Bodhisatta becomes enlightened and the almsfood after which the Buddha attains final Nibbāna. Cunda would gain much merit from his gift: long life, good health, much influence, fame, and a heavenly rebirth.

The fifth chapter starts with the Buddha's request to Ānanda to accompany him to the region of Kusinārā, to the sāla-tree grove of the Mallas. When they arrived, Ānanda arranged a couch for him, with the head to the north, between two large sāla trees. Although it was not the right season, the trees flowered and sprinkled their blossoms over the body of the Blessed One. And blossoms of the heavenly coral tree fell from the sky, together with heavenly scents, and there was music of the spheres. The Awakened One then said: "It is not thus, Ānanda, that the Tathāgata is venerated and honored in the highest degree. But whatever bhikkhu or bhikkhunī, layman or laywoman, abides by the Dhamma, lives uprightly in the Dhamma, walks in the way of the Dhamma, it is such a one that venerates and honors the Tathāgata in the highest degree."

Just then, the Venerable Upavāṇa was fanning the Blessed One. When the Buddha requested Upavāṇa to stand aside, Ānanda wanted to know why he was so summarily dismissed. The Buddha explained that innumerable deities had come from all directions of the world to have a last glance at a Fully Enlightened One, who so seldom can be seen. But since Upavāṇa, an eminent monk, was standing in front of him, they could not see him. Upavāṇa's spiritual radiance must have been more powerful than the penetrative ability of the gods.

Ānanda inquired further into details about the gods and learned that those who were not free from passion were weeping and wailing, but those free from passion were resigned and calm. The Buddha gave Ānanda another directive: "There are four places in the world worthy of veneration, which would inspire a faithful follower—the birthplace of the Buddha (Lumbinī), the place of Enlightenment (Buddha Gayā), the place where he taught the Dhamma for the first time (Sarnath), and the place of his Parinibbāna (Kusinārā). Anyone who passes away with confident heart while on pilgrimage to these shrines will attain a heavenly rebirth."

Seemingly out of context, Ānanda asked the question, already narrated, how one should act toward women. Then he asked how to deal with the body of the Blessed One. Sharp came the reply: "Do not hinder yourselves, Ānanda, in honoring the body of the Tathāgata. Rather, you should strive for your own good. There are wise householders who will render honor to the body of the Tathāgata." Then Ānanda wanted to know how the laypeople should carry out the funeral ceremony. The Buddha gave detailed instructions about the cremation and the erection of a stūpa.[21] There were four beings worthy of a stūpa: a supreme Buddha, a paccekabuddha, an arahant disciple, and a world monarch.[22] One who worships there would also attain much merit.

Then Ānanda, overpowered by grief, went aside, clasped the door jamb, and wept. He knew he still had to fight and conquer, and the Master, who had so much compassion for him, would soon be no more. What remained as the fruit of his twenty-five years of service? This famous scene is often depicted in Buddhist art and is reminiscent of the weeping Christians beneath the cross.

When the Buddha did not see Ānanda and inquired where he was, he had him summoned and said to him: "Do not sorrow, Ānanda. Have I not told you many times that everything changes and vanishes? How could something that has come into being not be destroyed? For a long time, Ānanda, you have attended on the Tathāgata, gladly, sensitively, sincerely, and without reserve, with deeds, speech, and thoughts of loving-kindness. You have made great merit, Ānanda; keep on striving and soon you will be free from all cankers!" He then told of an incident long ago, in a past life, in which Ānanda had served him and made much worldly merit (Jāt. 307).

After the Awakened One had foretold a second time that Ānanda would soon attain arahantship, he turned to the monks and once more proclaimed praise of Ānanda: "All the Buddhas of the past had had such excellent attendants, and all Buddhas of the future will have them too. His skill in dealing with people is admirable. If a company of bhikkhus goes to see Ānanda, they become joyful on seeing him; and if he speaks to them on the Dhamma, they are made joyful by his discourse; and when he becomes silent, they are disappointed. And so it is also with the bhikkhunīs, the laymen, and the laywomen: each assembly taught by Ānanda is always overjoyed and everyone wants to listen to him further. Ānanda has such remarkable, extraordinary popularity, as one otherwise finds only in a world monarch." Here too, as so often in the texts, we can find the two complementary ways the Buddha addressed Ānanda: on the one hand, great praise for him and a summons to the monks to appreciate his greatness; on the other, always the reminder to overcome the last defilements.

After this praise, Ānanda turned the conversation to another topic. He suggested that it might be better if the Buddha did not die here in the backwoods, but in one of the great capitals, such as Sāvatthī, Rājagaha, Kosambī, or Benares. It is noteworthy that he did not propose the Buddha's home town of Kapilavatthu, which had just recently been ransacked and almost destroyed by the son of King Pasenadi. So Ānanda did not mention it, just as he did not mention Vesālī, because the Buddha had said that he would not return there. Ānanda thought that the funeral ceremony could be performed better in one of the large cities by the lay followers living there. But the Buddha, lying on his deathbed, explained to him in great detail why Kusinārā was not an unimportant place at all. The Buddha had lived there a long time ago as the world monarch Mahā Sudassana, and he had left his body there no less than six times as a world monarch; this was the seventh and last time. The splendor and magnificence of that kingdom had been destroyed, had disappeared, and vanished. This, indeed, was enough to make one weary of all conditioned things.

The Buddha's discourse about Mahā Sudassana was the last great teaching he gave. Subsequently he let Ānanda summon the Mallas of Kusinārā, so that they could bid farewell to him. At that time, a wanderer named Subhadda was in Kusinārā and heard about the forthcoming Parinibbāna of the Buddha. Reflecting on how rare it was for a Buddha to appear in the world, he wished to have a doubt resolved by him before it was too late. He begged Ānanda to let him approach the Buddha, but Ānanda refused, saying that the Master should not be troubled on his deathbed. Ānanda refused permission three times, out of love for his Master. But the Buddha, who overheard the conversation, told Ānanda to let the wanderer approach: "He wants to inquire about the Dhamma for the sake of knowledge and not to cause trouble." Subhadda then posed a question "All the present-day teachers claim to be enlightened, yet their teachings contradict one another. Which ones are truly enlightened?" The Buddha dismissed the question and said: "Wherever one finds the Noble Eightfold Path, there one can find the true holy life, and there the four fruits of the homeless life can be found. If monks live in the right way, then the world will never be devoid of arahants, of true saints. Over fifty years I have been a monk and have expounded the Dhamma—and apart from adherence to the Dhamma there can be no holy life."

This short discourse was sufficient for Subhadda to realize the Dhamma in its manifold aspects and to go for refuge to the Buddha. When Subhadda asked for admission into the Order, the Buddha told him about the rule according to which wanderers of other sects had to live on probation for four months. Subhadda agreed readily even if he had to wait on probation for four years. Thereupon the Buddha accepted him immediately, making a last exception, and within minutes this very last monk disciple of the Buddha became an arahant.

The sixth section of the sutta begins with the last instructions of the Buddha. First, he advised the monks never to think, after his death, that they no longer had a teacher, "for the Dhamma and Vinaya will be your teacher after I am gone." Even to this day, the word of the Buddha laid down in the texts is decisive for his followers. Second, after his death the monks should no longer address each other indiscriminately as "friend" (*āvuso*). The senior monks could address the junior ones as "friend" or by their names, while the junior ones should use "venerable sir" (*bhante*). This rule affirmed reverence according to seniority in the Order independently of the personal qualities that monks or nuns may have. The third rule gave the monks permission to abolish the lesser and minor rules and all they entailed, according to their own judgment. The fourth and last instruction was to impose the "higher penalty" (*brahmadaṇḍa*) on the monk Channa. Ānanda asked how that was to be understood, and the Buddha explained that Channa was not to be spoken to or advised or instructed unless he repented.

After these primarily external directions which Ānanda was to fulfill, the Buddha once more turned to the whole assembly of monks and asked them whether they had any doubt or problem concerning the Enlightened One, the content and meaning of the Dhamma, the order of monks, and above all about the path or way of practice. They should express their doubts so that they would not regret it later when the voice of the Teacher had been silenced. But upon being asked three times, the group did not respond. Thereupon Ānanda said it was amazing that not even one monk had any doubts. The Buddha corrected him once again, because Ānanda could not know for sure that really no one had any doubts. It was possible that a monk did not want to voice his doubt or that he was not conscious of it in this last hour. Only with such total knowledge could one speak in this manner. But in reality it was exactly as Ānanda had said. The Buddha showed in this way the difference between Ānanda's confidence and his own, the Perfect One's, insight. The least of the five hundred monks present was a stream-enterer, because the absence of doubt is one of the signs of this attainment.

And once more the Master turned to the assembly of monks to give them his final words of farewell: "Now, monks, I declare this to you: It is the nature of all conditioned things to vanish. Strive for the goal with diligence!"

After the Exalted One had spoken these last words, he entered into the four jhānas and the formless spheres of meditative absorption, until he attained the stage of cessation of perception and feeling. While the Master was in cessation Ānanda said to Anuruddha: "The Blessed One has attained final Nibbāna, venerable sir." He no longer addressed him as "friend," but as a senior monk, although both had been ordained on the same day. Anuruddha, however, had the divine eye and corrected him: "The Buddha is in the state of cessation, but has not yet passed away." To recognize this last subtle difference of a state of mind was only possible for an arahant like Anuruddha, who was skilled in clairvoyance. Subsequently the Buddha entered the nine stages of concentration in reverse order, back to the first jhāna. Then he rose again through the four jhānas, and during his absorption in the fourth jhāna he passed away.

At the moment his life ended the earth quaked and thunder roared, just as he had predicted. The Brahmā Sahampati, who had induced the Buddha to teach and who himself was a non-returner, spoke a stanza which pointed to the impermanence of even a Buddha's body. The king of the devas, Sakka, a stream-enterer, spoke a stanza which repeated the famous lines that the Buddha had proclaimed during his own discourse: "Conditions truly are transient." Anuruddha gave voice to two serene verses. But Ānanda lamented:

> Then there was terror, and the hair stood up, when he,
> The all-accomplished one, the Buddha, passed away.

And all those of the five hundred monks who had not yet attained full liberation from passions lamented like Ānanda. The Venerable Anuruddha, however, consoled them all. He pointed to the immutable law of impermanence and turned their attention to the presence of invisible deities, amongst whom there were also those who lamented and those who were free of passions.

Anuruddha passed the rest of the night talking to Ānanda about the Dhamma. In the forty-three years of their lives as homeless ones, not a single conversation about the Dhamma seems to have taken place between these two very dissimilar siblings. But now Anuruddha devoted himself to his younger half-brother, who was so much in need of consolation. Towards morning Anuruddha, who naturally assumed the role of director among the close disciples, asked Ānanda to inform the Mallas of the Buddha's final Nibbāna.

When Ānanda delivered his message, the Mallas gathered all the requisites for a great funeral ceremony, such as flowers and incense, and went in a procession to the sāla-tree grove. There they paid homage to the body of the Buddha with festive dance, singing, and music, with banners and flags, with flowers and incense, until the seventh day. One may wonder why they thought of festivities at such a time. But why should they grieve? That would have changed nothing. With their dancing and singing they showed respect and veneration for the Master: they exulted that a Buddha had appeared in the world, that they had heard his Dhamma, that he had wandered through India for such a long time teaching the multitudes, and that he had founded the Sangha to preserve the Dhamma.

On the seventh day they erected a pyre for the cremation. When the Mallas wanted to light the funeral pyre, they were unable to do so. Anuruddha explained that the deities were preventing them, because they wanted to wait for the arrival of the Venerable Mahākassapa, who had not been present during the Buddha's last days and was now on his way to Kusinārā with a group of monks. When Kassapa arrived, together with his company of monks he circumambulated the corpse three times as a last mark of respect toward the Blessed One. Then the funeral pyre ignited by itself, and the corpse burned until only the bones remained; no ashes were to be seen.

When the neighboring clans heard the news of the Master's death, they all sent messengers to ask for relics, so that they could erect stūpas for them. However, the Mallas requested the relics for themselves, for the Buddha had died on their land. Only when a brahmin urged them not to dispute over the relics of the greatest peacemaker, and suggested that they divide everything into eight parts, did they relent. So it came about that the bones of the Buddha were divided into eight parts. The brahmin asked for the urn, and another clan received the ashes of the coals. In this way ten stūpas were erected as memorials.

AFTER THE BUDDHA'S PARINIBBĀNA

In verse Ānanda expressed his situation after the Master's passing:

My companion has passed away,
The Master, too, is gone.
There is no friendship now that equals this:
Mindfulness directed to the body.

The old ones now have passed away,
The new ones do not please me much,[23]
Today I meditate all alone
Like a bird gone to its nest.

(Thag. 1035–36)

After the funeral ceremonies were over, Ānanda saw only one duty left for himself, namely, to attain total liberation as prophesied to him by the Buddha. Kassapa advised him to live in the forest in the province of Kosala, which was near the Mallas and the Sakyans. But when it became known that the Buddha's attendant was living in solitude in the forest nearby, he was inundated with visitors. The lay disciples wanted to be consoled about the death of the Buddha and also about the deaths of Sāriputta and Moggallāna, and of their just and beloved King Pasenadi. All four had died within the year. Day and night, in the village and in the forest, Ānanda had to console the lay disciples and was never alone. Thereupon a deity who lived in the forest, concerned about Ānanda's spiritual progress, appeared to him and advised him as follows:

Having entered the thicket at the foot of a tree,
Having placed Nibbāna in your heart,
Meditate, Gotama, and be not negligent!
What will this hullabaloo do for you?

(SN 9:5)

Exhorted by the deity, Ānanda was stirred to a fresh sense of urgency.

In the meantime the Venerable Mahākassapa had decided to call a council of monks to strengthen the Dhamma and the Vinaya.[24] Because of unsafe conditions in the country of Kosala, the council was to take place in Rājagaha under the protection of King Ajātasattu. Five hundred monks were to participate, among whom Ānanda was the only one who was not an arahant. Ānanda knew most of the discourses of the Buddha and therefore was indispensable to the council.

When the date set for the council came closer, the Venerable Anuruddha suggested that Ānanda should only be admitted if he could overcome the last cankers and attain arahantship. Anuruddha knew the power of such an incentive, and it had the intended effect. When Ānanda heard this stern stipulation, he decided to apply every bit of strength he had to realize Nibbāna. He practiced the four foundations of mindfulness throughout the night—sitting and walking, sitting and walking, sitting and walking. In the early hours of the morning, as he was preparing to lie down after a full night of striving, just when he had raised his legs off the ground but had not yet laid his head on the pillow, his mind was released from all cankers. That day the council was to begin, and in the hope that he would succeed a place had been reserved for him. Soon after all the other monks were seated Ānanda arrived through the air by psychic power and sat down in his seat. When Anuruddha and Kassapa saw this, they knew he had reached his goal and expressed their brotherly joy with him. Then they declared the council open.

During the council, Kassapa questioned the Keeper of the Discipline, Upāli, about each rule and its origin, so that the Vinaya was laid down first. The next item on the agenda was the doctrine. Kassapa asked Ānanda first about the longest discourses, which became the Dīgha Nikāya, then about the middle-length ones, which became the Majjhima Nikāya, and then about the other collections.[25]

After the recitation of the Dhamma and the Vinaya, Ānanda mentioned those matters that the Buddha had left as a legacy with him to settle. He told the assembly that the Master had allowed the minor and lesser rules to be abolished. The senior monks could not agree what was meant by "the minor and lesser rules." Thereupon Kassapa spoke up: "If now the Sangha starts abolishing rules, laypeople will say that so soon after the passing of the Blessed One we have become lax. Since it is not known which rules were meant, it would be best not to abolish any of them. In that case we shall be sure that we are not acting contrary to the Master's wishes." And so it was done.

The elder monks present said it had been a breach of discipline for Ānanda not to ask what was meant by the minor rules, and he should confess this as a wrongdoing. Second, he was accused of having sewn a robe for the Blessed One after having stepped on the cloth. He replied that nothing had been further from his mind than disrespect for the Blessed One. Nevertheless if the venerable ones considered it a wrongdoing, he would acknowledge it as such. Third, he was criticized for allowing the women to salute the remains of the Blessed One first. He replied that at the time of the funeral he had thought this would enable the women to return home before dark and therefore he had allowed them to pay their homage first; but here too he would accept the verdict of his elders. The fourth accusation that the monks leveled at Ānanda referred to his failure to beg the Blessed One to remain for an aeon. Ānanda defended himself by saying he had been possessed by Māra at the time, and therefore was not responsible for his actions—how could he have otherwise failed to make this request? Ānanda's behavior in the face of these accusations was exemplary: he submitted to the judgment of the other elders, although he himself could not see any wrongdoing, a fact that he did not fail to mention.

Subsequently Ānanda reported the second instruction that the Buddha had given immediately before his death, namely, imposing the higher penalty on the monk Channa. The assembly requested Ānanda himself to present this decision to Channa. Ānanda objected that Channa was a violent and unruly person. The assembly advised him to take a number of monks along. Leading a large group he journeyed to Kosambī where Channa was living, and he informed him of the last will of the Buddha, that he had been declared "dead in the Order."

This penalty had been explained by the Buddha to the horse trainer Kesi.[26] He would use it against monks who could not be persuaded to reform their behavior either through admonition or discipline. Whoever could not be trained in this way would be considered as dead in the Order: he would not be spoken to, whatever he did. When Channa heard this, he became so horrified that he fainted. When he regained his senses, he was deeply ashamed that the Master had proclaimed this penalty against him as his last instruction to the Order. This gave him the impetus to put forth his most strenuous effort and within a short time he became an arahant. So this penalty showed itself to be the Buddha's last act of compassion for the benefit and happiness of the monk Channa, being effective even after the Buddha's death. When Channa had become a holy one, he went to Ānanda and begged him for a repeal of the penalty. Ānanda replied that as soon as he had attained release from the cankers the penalty had ceased to be operative.

After the Parinibbāna of the Buddha, the Venerable Mahākassapa, as the most respected disciple, had taken over the guidance of the Order. His status, however, was not that of a "refuge" as the Buddha had been, nor was it that of a patriarch. He was simply the most authoritative and most highly revered of the monks, and he thus functioned, so to say, as the symbol for the observance of the Dhamma and the Discipline.

Everyone turned to him for his decisions on all questions regarding the Order. In this way he became the chief elder of the Sangha. After him Ānanda became the second leading elder, the second most venerated holy one, who was designated to look after the Order. After he had already been a monk for over forty years, he survived the Buddha by another forty years. And after having been the personal attendant of the Buddha for twenty-five years, he became the foremost of the arahants for a similar length of time. At the time of the Second Council, 100 years after the Buddha's Parinibbāna, a personal disciple of Ānanda's was still alive. He was a very old monk named Sabbakāmī, who, it was said, had been in the Order for 120 years (Vin. 2:303).

When Ānanda was 120 years old, he felt that his end was near. He went from Rājagaha on a journey to Vesālī, just as his Master had done. When the king of Magadha and the princes of Vesālī heard that Ānanda would soon attain final Nibbāna, they hurried to him from both directions to bid him farewell. In order to do justice to both sides, Ānanda chose a way to die in keeping with his gentle nature: he raised himself into the air through his supernormal powers and let his body be consumed by the fire element. The relics were divided and stūpas erected.

After his passing the elders who compiled the subsequent recension of the canon added three verses to his collection in the *Theragāthā*:

> Of great learning, bearer of the Dhamma,
> The guardian of the Great Seer's treasure,
> Ānanda, the eye of the entire world,
> Has attained final Nibbāna.
>
> Of great learning, bearer of the Dhamma,
> The guardian of the Great Seer's treasure,
> Ānanda, the eye of the entire world,
> Was a dispeller of gloom in the darkness.
>
> The seer who was so retentive,
> Of keen memory and resolute,
> The elder sustaining the true Dhamma,
> Ānanda was a mine of gems.
>
> (Thag. 1047–49)

CHAPTER 5

ANURUDDHA

Master of the Divine Eye

Hellmuth Hecker

EARLY LIFE AND ORDINATION

LIKE ĀNANDA, ANURUDDHA was a noble of the Sakyan clan and a cousin of the Buddha. He and Ānanda were begotten by the same father, the Sakyan prince Amitodana, though their mothers must have been different as the texts do not refer to the two as brothers and imply that they grew up in different households. Anuruddha's full brother was Mahānāma the Sakyan, and he also had a sister named Rohiṇī.

As a youth from an aristocratic clan Anuruddha was raised in luxury. The texts describe his early years in the same terms they use to describe the Bodhisatta's upbringing: "Anuruddha the Sakyan was delicately nurtured. He had three palaces, one for the cold season, one for the hot season, and one for the rainy season. Being waited on in his palace for the four months of the rains by female musicians, he did not come down from that palace" (Vin. 2:180). A charming story recorded in the Dhammapada Commentary reveals to us the blissful oblivion and innocence in which Anuruddha grew up.[1] It is said that in his youth he lived in such luxury that he had never even heard the phrase "there isn't any" (*natthi*)—for whatever he might want, his desire would immediately be fulfilled. One day Anuruddha was playing at marbles with five other Sakyan youths, and he had bet cakes on the result. The first three times he lost and sent home to his mother for cakes, and three times his mother promptly supplied them. When he lost the fourth time, however, and again sent for cakes, his mother replied, "There isn't any cake to send" (*natthi pūvaṁ*). Since Anuruddha had never before heard the expression "there isn't any," he assumed this *natthi pūvaṁ* must be a kind of cake, so he sent a man to his mother with the message, "Send me some there-isn't-any cakes." To teach him a lesson his mother sent him an empty platter, but even then fortune was still on his side. Owing to his past merits from an earlier life, the gods were determined that Anuruddha should not be disappointed, and thus they filled the empty platter with delicious celestial cakes. When Anuruddha tasted them he was so delighted that he repeatedly sent back to his mother for more platters of there-isn't-any cakes, and by the time each platter arrived it had been filled with the heavenly delicacies.

Thus Anuruddha passed his early years in the joyful pursuit of fleeting pleasures, giving little thought to the meaning and purpose of existence. The turning point in his life came shortly after his illustrious cousin, the

Buddha, visited Kapilavatthu.[2] By his example and his teaching the Buddha had inspired many of his relatives to go forth into the homeless life as monks. One day Anuruddha's brother Mahānāma reflected on the fact that while many distinguished Sakyans had gone forth, no one from their own family had done so. He then approached Anuruddha and told him what he had been thinking, concluding with an ultimatum: "Well now, either you go forth or I will go forth."

For Anuruddha such a command must have come as a shock and he demurred: "But I have been delicately nurtured; I am not able to go forth from home into homelessness. You go forth."

Mahānāma then vividly described to him the burdens of a householder's life that he would have to shoulder: "First the fields have to be ploughed, then they must be sown, then water must be led into them, then the water must be led away, then the weeds must be dug up, then the crop must be reaped, then it must be harvested, then it must be made into stooks, then you must have them threshed, then you must have the straw winnowed, then you must have the chaff winnowed, then you must have the chaff sifted, then you must have it brought in. And the same must be done the next year and the year after that."

Anuruddha inquired: "When will the work stop? When will an end to the work be discerned? When will we be able to amuse ourselves unconcerned, supplied and furnished with the five cords of sensual pleasure?"

His brother replied sharply: "There is no stop to the work, my dear Anuruddha. No end to the work is ever to be discerned. Even when our fathers and grandfathers passed away the work was not to be stopped."

By the time he finished speaking Anuruddha had already made up his mind: "You look after what belongs to the household life, brother. I will go forth from home into homelessness." The thought of the endless cycle of strife and toil, and the even more vicious cycle of rebirth, had awakened in him a sense of urgency. He saw himself bound to struggle again and again through every moment of his life, then to die and take birth elsewhere, over and over in an endless round. When he saw this, his present life appeared to him insipid and meaningless, and the one hopeful alternative, which now seemed increasingly attractive, was to follow his cousin into homelessness and struggle to break through the cycle of repeated becoming.

Immediately he went to his mother and asked her for permission to become a monk. She, however, refused, unwilling to be separated from even one of her sons. But when Anuruddha insisted, she told him that if his friend, Prince Bhaddiya, the Sakyan chieftain, would be willing to enter the Order, then she would give him her permission. She must have been convinced that Bhaddiya would never give up the privileges of rulership and that Anuruddha would then choose to remain in the household life with his friend.

Anuruddha next went to Bhaddiya and told him: "My ordination depends on yours. Let us go forth together into homelessness." Bhaddiya replied: "Whether it depends on me or not, there should be ordination. I with you..." Here he stopped in the middle of the sentence. He had wanted to say, "I shall come with you," but broke off because of feelings of regret. Overcome by attachment to worldly power and pleasure, he could only say: "Go and be ordained, according to your wish." But Anuruddha pleaded with him again and again: "Come, friend, let both of us go forth." When Bhaddiya saw how earnest his friend was, he softened and said: "Wait, friend, for seven years. After seven years we will both go forth from home into homelessness." But Anuruddha replied: "Seven years is too long, friend. I cannot wait for seven years." By his repeated entreaties Anuruddha forced Bhaddiya step by step to reduce the delay to seven days, the time he would need to settle his worldly affairs and install his successor. He was true to his word, and so Anuruddha was free to go with him.

Anuruddha's example induced other Sakyan princes, too, to follow their great kinsman, the Buddha, and join his fraternity of monks. Thus, when the appointed day arrived, six Sakyan princes together with Upāli, the court barber, and an armed escort, set out from their homes. They were the Sakyans Bhaddiya, Anuruddha, Ānanda, Bhagu (Thag. 271–74), Kimbila (Thag. 118, 155–56), and Devadatta. To avoid arousing suspicion over the purpose of their departure, they left as if they were going to the pleasure gardens for an outing. Having gone a long distance, they then sent the escort back and entered the neighboring principality. There they took off their ornaments, tied them into a bundle, and gave them to Upāli, saying, "This will be enough for your livelihood. Now return home." But the barber Upāli, while already on his way back, stopped and thought: "The Sakyans are a fierce people. They will think that I have murdered the youths, and they might kill me." He hung the bundle on a tree and hurried back to join the princes. He told them of his fears and said, "If you, O princes, are going forth into the homeless life, why shouldn't I do the same?"

The young Sakyans, too, thought Upāli was right in not going back and allowed him to join them on their way to see the Blessed One. Having come into the Master's presence, they asked him for ordination, adding: "We Sakyans are a proud people, Lord. This Upāli the barber has attended on us for a long time. Please, Lord, give him ordination first. Since he will then be our senior, we shall have to salute him and do the duties proper to his seniority. Thus our Sakyan pride will be humbled." The Buddha did as requested, and thus these seven received ordination with Upāli as the first (Vin. 2:182–83).

Within one year most of them had achieved some spiritual attainment. Bhaddiya was the first to attain arahantship, as one endowed with the three true knowledges.[3] Anuruddha acquired the divine eye, Ānanda the fruit of stream-entry, and Devadatta ordinary (i.e., mundane) supernormal powers. Bhagu, Kimbila, and Upāli became arahants later, as did Ānanda and Anuruddha. But Devadatta's reckless ambition and misdeeds led him to hell.

THE STRUGGLE FOR ARAHANTSHIP

The divine eye is the ability to see beyond the range of the physical eye, extending in Anuruddha's case to a thousandfold world system. This faculty, which we will discuss more fully below, is of a mundane (*lokiya*) character, one whose acquisition does not necessarily entail that its possessor has gained realization of the Dhamma. Anuruddha attained the divine eye before he became an arahant, and to reach the heights he still had to overcome many inner obstacles. Three reports in the canon tell of his struggles.

Once, when the Venerable Anuruddha was living in the Eastern Bamboo Park with two friends, his cousin Nandiya and the Sakyan noble Kimbila, the Buddha visited them and inquired about their progress.[4] Anuruddha then told him about a difficulty he had experienced in a very sublime meditation he had been practicing. He had perceived an inner light and radiance and had a vision of sublime forms.[5] But that light and vision of forms disappeared very soon, and he could not understand the reason.

The Buddha declared that when he was still striving for enlightenment he too had met the same difficulty but had discovered how to master it. He explained that to experience these subtle states in full and obtain a steady perception of them one should free oneself from eleven imperfections (*upakkilesa*). The first is *uncertainty* about the reality of these phenomena and the significance of the inner light, which might easily be taken for a sensory illusion. The second is *inattention*: one no longer directs one's full attention to the inner light but disregards it, evaluating it as unremarkable or inessential. The third imperfection is *lethargy and drowsiness*; the fourth, *anxiety and fright*, which occurs when threatening images or thoughts arise from the subconscious. When these imperfections have been mastered, *elation* may arise, which excites body and mind. Such exultation is often a habitual reaction to any kind of success. When that elation has exhausted itself, one may feel emotionally drained and fall into *inertia*, a heavy passivity of mind. To overcome it, one makes a very strong effort, which may result in an *excess of energy*. On becoming aware of this excess, one relaxes and falls again into *sluggish energy*. In such a condition, when mindfulness is weak, *strong longing* may arise for desirable objects of the celestial or the human world, according to the focusing of the inner light which had been widened in its range. This longing will reach out to a great variety of objects and thus lead to another imperfection, a large *diversity of perceptions*, be it on the celestial or human plane. Having become dissatisfied with this great diversity of forms, one chooses to contemplate one of them, be it of a desirable or undesirable nature. Concentrating intensely on the chosen object will lead to the eleventh imperfection, the *excessive meditating* on these forms.

Addressing Anuruddha and his two companions the Buddha thus described vividly, from his own experience, the eleven imperfections that may arise in the meditative perception of pure forms, and he explained how to overcome them (MN 128).

When Anuruddha had perfected himself more and more in the jhānas and in those refined meditative perceptions, he one day went to see the Venerable Sāriputta and said: "Friend Sāriputta, with the divine eye that is purified, transcending human sight, I can see the thousandfold world system. Firm is my energy, unremitting; my mindfulness is alert and unconfused; the body is tranquil and unperturbed; my mind is concentrated and one-pointed. And yet my mind is not freed from the cankers, not freed from clinging."

Thereupon Sāriputta replied: "Friend Anuruddha, that you think thus of your divine eye: this is conceit in you. That you think thus of your firm energy, your alert mindfulness, your unperturbed body, and your concentrated mind: this is restlessness in you. That you think of your mind not being freed from the cankers: this is worrying in you. It would be good, indeed, if you would abandon these three states of mind and, paying no attention to them, direct your mind to the deathless element, Nibbāna."

Having heard Sāriputta's advice, Anuruddha again resorted to solitude and earnestly applied himself to the removal of those three obstructions within his mind (AN 3:128).

Sometime later Anuruddha was living in the country of the Cetiya people, in the Eastern Bamboo Grove. There, in his contemplations, it occurred to him that there were seven thoughts that should be cherished by a truly great man (*mahāpurisavitakka*):

> This Dhamma is for one with few wishes, not for one with many wishes; this Dhamma is for one who is content, not for one who is discontent; this Dhamma is for one bent on seclusion, not for one who is gregarious; this Dhamma is for one who is energetic, not for one who is lazy; this Dhamma is for one who is mindful, not for one who is confused; this Dhamma is for one who is concentrated, not for one who is unconcentrated; this Dhamma is for one who is wise, not for one who is dull-witted.

When the Buddha perceived in his own mind the thoughts that had arisen in Anuruddha's mind, he appeared before him in a mind-made body (*manomaya-kāya*) and applauded him: "Good, Anuruddha, good! You have well considered seven thoughts of a great man. You may now also consider this eighth thought of a great man: 'This Dhamma is for one who inclines to the non-diffuse, who delights in the non-diffuse; not for one who inclines to worldly diffuseness and delights in it.'"[6]

The Buddha then said that when Anuruddha contemplates these eight thoughts, he will be able to attain at will the four meditative absorptions. He would then no longer be affected by worldly conditions but would regard the four simple requisites of a monk's life—robes, almsfood, shelter, and medicines—in the same way as a layperson would enjoy luxuries. Such simple living would make his mind joyous and unperturbed and thus be helpful to his attainment of Nibbāna.

In parting, the Buddha advised Anuruddha to stay on at the Eastern Bamboo Grove. Anuruddha did so, and during that same rainy season he attained the consummation of his striving: arahantship, the undefiled liberation of the mind (AN 8:30). At the hour of his attainment the Venerable Anuruddha uttered the following verses, in which he expresses his gratitude to the Master for helping him bring his spiritual work to completion:

> Having understood my mind's intention,
> The unsurpassed Teacher in the world
> Came to me by psychic power
> In the vehicle of a mind-made body.

When the intention arose in me,
Then he gave me a further teaching.
The Buddha who delights in the non-diffuse
Gave me instructions on the non-diffuse.

Having understood his Dhamma,
I dwelt delighting in his Teaching.
The three knowledges have been attained,
The Buddha's Teaching has been done.

(AN 8:30; Thag. 901–3)

ANURUDDHA'S SPIRITUAL PATH

The Venerable Anuruddha's spiritual path is marked by two prominent features: first, his mastery of the divine eye and other supernormal faculties; and second, his cultivation of the four foundations of mindfulness (*satipaṭṭhāna*). We will discuss each of these in turn.

The divine eye (*dibbacakkhu*) is so called because it is similar to the vision of the devas, which is capable of seeing objects at remote distances, behind barriers, and in different dimensions of existence.[7] The divine eye is developed by meditative power. It is not a distinct sense organ but a type of knowledge, yet a knowledge that exercises an ocular function. This faculty is aroused on the basis of the fourth jhāna, and specifically through one of the meditative supports called the light kasiṇa or the fire kasiṇa, a visualized circle of light or fire. After mastering the four jhānas through either of these kasiṇa, the meditator descends to a lower level of concentration called "access concentration" (*upacāra-samādhi*) and extends light to the immediately surrounding area, thereby bringing into view forms that are ordinarily imperceptible. As the meditator becomes progressively more adept in this ability to radiate light, he can then suffuse increasingly larger areas with light and project the radiance outwardly to distant world systems and to planes of existence above and below the human plane. This will reveal many dimensions of being that are inaccessible to the ordinary fleshly eye.

The characteristic function of the divine eye, according to the texts, is the knowledge of the passing away and rebirth of beings (*cutūpapāta-ñāṇa*). This knowledge was achieved by the Buddha on the night of his own Enlightenment and was always included by him in the complete step-by-step gradual training, where it appears as the second of the three true knowledges (*tevijjā*; see, for example, MN 27) and the fourth of the six superknowledges (*chaḷabhiññā*; see MN 6). By means of this faculty the meditator is able to see beings as they pass away from one form of existence and take rebirth elsewhere. But it is not only the actual passage from life to life that the divine eye reveals. With the appropriate determination it can also be used to discover the particular kamma that brought about rebirth into the new form of existence. In this application it is called the knowledge of faring on in accordance with one's kamma (*kammūpaga-ñāṇa*). At its maximum efficiency the divine eye can illuminate the entire panorama of sentient existence—spread out over thousands of world systems and extending from the highest heavens to the lowest hells—revealing too the kammic laws that govern the process of rebirth. While only a supreme Buddha will have absolute mastery over this knowledge, disciples who have perfected the divine eye can perceive regions of the sentient universe that elude our most powerful telescopes.

The Venerable Anuruddha was designated by the Buddha as the foremost bhikkhu disciple endowed with the divine eye (*etadaggaṁ dibbacakkhukānaṁ*; AN 1; chap. 14). Once, when a number of eminent monks living together in the Gosiṅga sāla-tree forest exchanged views on the kind of monk that could beautify that forest, Anuruddha characteristically replied that it was one who, with the divine eye, could survey a thousand world systems, just as a man standing on a high tower could see a thousand farmsteads (MN 32). Anuruddha also helped his own pupils to acquire the divine eye (SN 14:15) and in his verses celebrates his skill in this faculty:

Absorbed in five-factored concentration,
Peaceful, with a unified mind,
I had gained tranquillity
And my divine eye was purified.

Standing on the five-factored jhāna
I know the passing and rebirth of beings;
I know their coming and their going,
Their life in this world and beyond.

(Thag. 916–17)

The other major facet of Anuruddha's spiritual path was the arduous practice of *satipaṭṭhāna*, the four foundations of mindfulness: "Here a bhikkhu dwells contemplating the body in the body...feelings in feelings...mind in mind...mental phenomena in mental phenomena, ardent, clearly comprehending and mindful, having removed covetousness and grief in regard to the world."[8] The practice of *satipaṭṭhāna* is sometimes taken to be a quick, "dry" path to enlightenment which bypasses the jhānas and superknowledges, but from Anuruddha's words it is clear that for him, as well as for those trained under him, this method of meditation could be used as a vehicle for the acquisition of psychic powers and superknowledges along with the final fruit of liberation. Whenever the Venerable Anuruddha was asked how he had gained proficiency in the "great superknowledges" (*mahābhiññatā*), which include the five mundane superknowledges and arahantship as the sixth, he always replied that it was through the development and cultivation of the four foundations of mindfulness (SN 47:28, 52:3, 6, 11). It was through this practice, he says, that he could recollect a thousand past aeons, exercise the supernormal powers, and directly perceive a thousandfold world system (SN 52:11, 12, 6).

Anuruddha also said that *satipaṭṭhāna* enabled him to gain that perfect control of emotive reactions called the "power of the noble ones" (*ariya-iddhi*), by which one can regard the repulsive as nonrepulsive, the nonrepulsive as repulsive, and view both with equanimity (SN 52:1).[9] He further stresses the importance of this practice by saying that whoever neglects the four foundations of mindfulness has neglected the noble path leading to the extinction of suffering while whoever undertakes it has undertaken the noble path leading to the extinction of suffering (SN 52:2); he also declares that this fourfold mindfulness leads to the destruction of craving (SN 52:7). Just as the river Ganges would not deviate from its course to the ocean, in the same way a monk who practices the four foundations of mindfulness could not be deflected from the life of renunciation and made to return to the worldly life (SN 52:8).

Once, when Anuruddha was ill, he surprised the monks by his equanimity in bearing pain. They asked him how he was able to bear up as he did, and he replied that his composure was due to his practice of the fourfold mindfulness (SN 52:10). Another time Sāriputta came to see Anuruddha in the evening and asked him what he now regularly practiced so that his face always radiated happiness and serenity. Anuruddha again said that he spent the time in the regular practice of the four foundations of mindfulness, and that this was the way in which arahants live and practice. Sāriputta thereupon expressed his joy at Anuruddha's words (SN 52:9). Once, when questioned by Sāriputta and Mahāmoggallāna about the difference between those who are still "in training" (*sekha*)[10] and an arahant who is "beyond training" (*asekha*), he said that they differ in the practice of the fourfold mindfulness: while the former accomplishes it only partly, the latter does so completely and perfectly (SN 52:4–5).

Anuruddha also claimed to possess, through his practice of right mindfulness, ten lofty qualities elsewhere called "the ten powers of a Tathāgata" (*dasatathāgatabala*; see MN 12). These are: the knowledge of what is possible and impossible; the knowledge of the result of the acquisition of kamma by way of stage and cause; the knowledge of the paths leading to the different destinations of rebirth; the knowledge of the world with its many diverse elements; the knowledge of the different dispositions of beings; the knowledge of the degree of maturity in the faculties of other beings; the knowledge of the jhānas and other advanced meditative states; and finally the three true knowledges (SN 52:15–24). The commentary says that Anuruddha possessed these knowledges only in part, as in their completeness they are unique to a Fully Enlightened One.

LIFE IN THE SANGHA

From the Pāli Canon it appears that Anuruddha, in contrast to such monks as Sāriputta, Mahāmoggallāna, and Ānanda, preferred a life of quiet seclusion to one of active involvement in the affairs of the Sangha. Thus he does not appear as frequently as the above-named elders in the events connected with the Buddha's ministry. His verses in the *Theragāthā* also suggest that he was strongly inclined to the ascetic practices, like the Venerable Mahākassapa, who was their most distinguished exponent:

When he has returned from his alms round
The sage dwells alone without companion;
Anuruddha who is free of the cankers
Seeks discarded rags to make a robe.

Anuruddha, the sage, the thinker,
One who is free from the cankers,
Sifted, took, washed, and dyed,
And then wore a robe of rags.

When one is greedy and discontent,
Fond of company, easily excited,
Then there arise in one's mind
Qualities that are evil and defiled.

But when one is mindful, with few wishes,
Content and free from disturbance,
Fond of seclusion and joyful,
With energy constantly aroused,

Then there occur in one's mind
Wholesome qualities leading to awakening.
Thus one is freed from the cankers—
This has been said by the Great Sage.

For fifty-five years I have been one
Who observes the sitter's practice.
It has been twenty-five years
Since torpor has been uprooted.

(Thag. 896–900, 904)

In these verses Anuruddha refers to three of the ascetic practices—the going on alms round, the use of robes made from discarded rags, and the sitter's practice. The last is the vow not to lie down but to sleep while sitting in the meditation posture. In his last verse Anuruddha implies that for twenty-five years he had not slept at all. Perhaps through the power of meditative absorption he was able to refresh his mind so fully that sleep had become unnecessary. But the commentary indicates that in the later part of his life Anuruddha allowed himself a short period of sleep to dispel physical fatigue.

Although the Venerable Anuruddha preferred solitude to company, he was not a complete recluse. In one sutta the Buddha states that Anuruddha had a number of pupils whom he trained in the development of the divine eye (SN 14:15), while the commentaries speak of him as traveling about with an entourage of five hundred pupils—probably an inflated figure. He also engaged in discussions on the Dhamma with other monks and with knowledgeable lay followers, and fortunately for us several of these have been preserved in the Pāli Canon. Once, for example, the court carpenter of Sāvatthī, Pañcakaṅga, invited Anuruddha and some other monks for a meal. From other texts we know that Pañcakaṅga was a person well versed in the Dhamma and devoted to its practice. So, after the meal, he asked a rather subtle question from Anuruddha. He said that some monks had advised him to practice the "measureless liberation of mind," and others recommended the "exalted liberation of mind," and he wanted to know whether these two are different or the same.

Anuruddha replied that these two meditations are different. The measureless liberation of mind (*appamāṇā cetovimutti*) is the cultivation of the four divine abodes (*brahmavihāra*)—boundless loving-kindness, compassion, altruistic joy, and equanimity. But the exalted liberation of mind (*mahaggatā cetovimutti*) proceeds by widening the inner perception from a limited extent to a vast, oceanlike extent; it is obtained by expanding the reflex image (*paṭibhāga-nimitta*) of the kasiṇa, which arises by concentration on a limited surface of earth, water, colored disks, etc. Anuruddha went on to speak of a class of deities called the radiant gods.[11] He said that although they all belong to the same order, there are differences among them in their radiance, which may be limited or measureless, pure or tainted, in accordance with the different quality of the meditation that had caused their rebirth in that world. On being questioned by a monk, Anuruddha confirmed that he spoke about these deities from his own experience, as he had previously lived in their midst and conversed with them (MN 127).

On another occasion the Buddha was sitting in the open, surrounded by many monks, to whom he was giving a discourse. He then turned to Anuruddha and asked whether they were all contented in leading the ascetic life. When Anuruddha confirmed this, the Buddha praised such contentment and said:

> Those who have left the home life while still young, becoming monks in the prime of their life, did not do so fearing punishment by kings, nor being motivated by loss of property, by debts, worries or poverty. Rather, they took to the ascetic life out of their faith in the Dhamma and inspired by the goal of liberation. What should such a one do? If he has not yet gained the peace and happiness of the meditative absorptions or something higher, then he should strive to get rid of the five mental hindrances and other defilements of the mind so that he may achieve the bliss of meditation or a peace that is still higher.

In concluding his discourse, the Buddha said that when he declares the attainment and future destiny of disciples who have died, he does so to inspire others to emulate their example. These words of the Blessed One gave Anuruddha much contentment and joy (MN 68).

Once one of the Brahmā gods conceived the idea that no ascetic would be able to penetrate to the heights of the Brahma-world. When the Buddha perceived in his mind the thoughts of that deity, he appeared before him in a blaze of light. Just then four of his great disciples—the Venerables Mahāmoggallāna, Mahākassapa, Mahākappina, and Anuruddha—considered where the Blessed One might be dwelling, and with their divine eyes they saw him seated in the Brahma-world. Then, by their supernormal power, they too transported themselves to that heavenly world and sat down at a respectful distance from the Buddha. Seeing this, the deity was cured of his pride and acknowledged the superior power of the Buddha and his disciples (SN 6:5).

Another time the Venerable Anuruddha had woken up in the middle of the night and recited verses of the Dhamma until dawn arrived. A female spirit with her small son was listening devoutly to the recitation, and she told her son to keep quiet: "It may be, if we understand the holy words and live accordingly, this will lead to our welfare and may free us from rebirth in the lower spirit worlds" (SN 10:6).

When the quarrel erupted between two groups of monks at Kosambī, the Venerable Ānanda went to see the Buddha, who asked him whether the quarrel had been settled. Ānanda had to tell him that the quarrel still continued: a pupil of Anuruddha's insisted on creating disharmony in the Sangha, and Anuruddha did not reproach him. This happened at a time when Anuruddha, together with Nandiya and Kimbila, had gone to the Gosiṅga forest to devote themselves to a strictly meditative life, and Ānanda was insinuating that it was wrong of Anuruddha to dwell in seclusion when his own pupil was instigating trouble.

The Buddha, however, came to Anuruddha's defense. He said that there was no need for Anuruddha to concern himself with such matters, as there were others like Sāriputta and Moggallāna, and Ānanda himself, who were quite capable of resolving disputes. Besides, he added, there are incorrigible monks who are quite pleased when others quarrel as this would divert attention from their own bad conduct and thus they could avoid being sent away (AN 4:241). An example of this is the pair of conceited monks who tried to compete with each other in regard to their learning. One was a pupil under Ānanda, who carefully concerned himself with all the affairs of the Sangha; the other was a pupil under Anuruddha, who, as we saw above, had a more detached attitude. Those two vainglorious monks just acted according to their character though they had different teachers to guide them (SN 16:6).

The best known account of Anuruddha's friendships is that found in the *Cūlagosiṅga Sutta* (MN 31). One time, while Anuruddha was dwelling in the Gosiṅga forest together with his friends Nandiya and Kimbila, the Buddha came to visit him. After they had paid respects to the Master, the Buddha asked Anuruddha whether he and his companions were living in harmony. Anuruddha replied: "Surely, Lord, we are living in concord, with mutual appreciation, without disputing, blending like milk and water, viewing each other with kindly eyes."

Then the Buddha asked how they managed to maintain such total harmony. Anuruddha's reply is a perfect lesson in the most vexatious art of interpersonal relations: "I do so by thinking, 'How blessed and fortunate I am to be living with such companions in the holy life!' I maintain towards my companions loving-kindness in bodily action, speech, and thought, and I consider, 'Let me set aside what I wish to do and do what these venerable ones wish to do.' In this way, though we are different in body, we are one in mind."

The Buddha, after expressing his approval, next inquired from them whether they had attained "any superhuman states, any distinction in knowledge and vision worthy of the noble ones." Anuruddha's answered that they had all attained the four jhānas, the four formless attainments, and the cessation of perception and feeling, and moreover they had all reached arahantship, the destruction of the cankers. After the Buddha left, the other two monks inquired from Anuruddha how he could speak so confidently about their own meditative attainments when they had never informed him about them. Anuruddha answered that while they had never reported to him that they had attained those states, "by encompassing your minds with my own mind, I know that you have obtained those abidings and attainments, and deities have also reported this to me."

Meanwhile a spirit named Dīgha Parajana came to the Buddha and spoke in praise of the three monks, Anuruddha, Nandiya, and Kimbila. The Buddha responded by first applauding the spirit's utterance and then adding a glowing eulogy of his own:

> So it is, Dīgha, so it is! If the clan from which those three young men went forth from the home life into homelessness should remember them with confident heart, that would lead to the welfare and happiness of that clan for a long time. If the village...the town...the city...the country from which they went forth should remember them with confident heart, that would lead to the welfare and happiness of that country for a long time. If all nobles...all brahmins...all merchants...all menials remember them. If all the world with its devas, its Māras, and its Brahmās, this generation with its recluses and brahmins, its princes and its people, should remember these three young men

with confident heart, that would lead to the welfare and happiness of the whole world for a long time. See, Dīgha, how those three young men are practicing for the welfare and happiness of the many, out of compassion for the world, for the good, welfare, and happiness of devas and humans.

ANURUDDHA AND WOMEN

An unusually large number of texts in which Anuruddha appears are concerned with women. It seems that despite his own inner purity of heart and complete detachment from sensuality, Anuruddha, endowed by birth with the physical bearing of a noble warrior, emanated a personal charisma that made him attractive to women, not only of the human world but of the celestial worlds as well. Some of these encounters also no doubt stemmed from kammic relationships formed in earlier lives, which still affected the female members even though Anuruddha himself had transcended them.

For example, on one occasion, when Anuruddha was dwelling alone in a forest resort, a female deity named Jālinī came from the realm of the Thirty-three gods and appeared before him (SN 9:6). In Anuruddha's previous existence, when he was Sakka, the ruler of the heaven of the Thirty-three, she had been his wife and chief queen. Out of her old attachment to him, she longed to be reunited with him and wanted them to resume their relationship as heavenly king and queen. With this intention she urged him to aspire for rebirth into that world:

Direct your mind there to that realm
Where you had lived in the past
Among the devas of the Thirty-three
Amply endowed with all sense pleasures.
You will shine forth highly honored,
Surrounded by celestial maidens.

But Anuruddha replied:

Miserable are celestial maidens,
Established in personality,
And miserable too are those beings
Who remain attached to celestial maidens.

Jālinī had no understanding of such words, and thus she tried to lure him by describing the splendor of the deva-world:

> They do not know happiness
> Who have not seen Nandana,
> The abode of the glorious devas
> Belonging to the host of Thirty.

Anuruddha, however, remained firm in his decision, which sprang from his deep insight into the impermanence of all conditioned things:

> Do you not know, you fool,
> That pithy maxim of the arahants?
> Impermanent are all formations,
> Subject to arising and vanishing.
> Having arisen, they then cease:
> Blissful is the appeasement of them.
>
> Now I will never again dwell
> Among the deva host, O Jālinī!
> The wandering on in birth is ended:
> For me there is no more re-becoming.

On another occasion, many female deities called "the graceful ones" (*manāpakāyikā devatā*) appeared before Anuruddha and told him all the marvelous things they could do. They could instantly assume any color they wanted, produce any sound or voice at will, and obtain instantly any pleasure. To test them, Anuruddha mentally wished that they would become blue; and so, as they could read his thoughts, they became blue, with blue clothes and blue ornaments. When he wished them to change into other colors, they did so—yellow, red, and white, with matching clothes and ornaments. Now these female deities thought that Anuruddha was pleased with their presence, and they started to sing and dance very beautifully. But Anuruddha turned his senses away from them. When the deities noticed that Anuruddha did not find pleasure in their performance, they instantly left (AN 8:46).

If we remember how the Venerable Anuruddha had spent his youth as a prince, enchanted by the arts and music, we may understand better how this scene could materialize around him. If he had not trodden the Buddha's path to liberation, he quite possibly might have taken rebirth among these deities, who were superior in rank to the Thirty-three gods. Anuruddha must have thought this experience worth telling, for when he saw the Buddha in the evening he recounted it to him. He then raised the question: "What attributes should a woman have to be reborn in the realm of those graceful spirits?" His thirst for knowledge must have made him wish to know the moral level of these deities.

The Buddha replied willingly and said that eight qualities were needed in order to be reborn in that realm: the wife has to be kindly and sympathetic toward her husband; she should be courteous and hospitable toward people her husband holds dear, such as his parents and certain ascetics and priests; she should do her housework carefully and with diligence; she was to care for and guide the servants and domestic workers in a purposeful manner; she should not squander her husband's possessions, but should guard them well; as a lay follower she should take refuge in the Triple Gem; she should observe the Five Precepts;[12] and lastly, she should find joy in sharing and in giving, showing concern for those in need (AN 8:46).

While on both these occasions female deities appeared before Anuruddha, at other times Anuruddha used his divine eye to understand how women are born in heaven or in hell. Once he asked the Buddha which qualities led a woman to rebirth in hell, and the Teacher replied that there were five major vices that were responsible for such a rebirth: lack of faith, lack of a sense of shame, moral recklessness, anger, and stupidity; further, such qualities as revengefulness, jealousy, avarice, immorality, sloth, and unmindfulness would also lead to rebirth in hell. Only those with the opposite qualities would be reborn in a heavenly world (SN 37:5–24).

Another time Anuruddha reported to the Buddha that he had often seen how a woman after her death was reborn in a lower world, even in hell. The Buddha replied that there are three harmful qualities which will lead a woman to hell: if in the morning she is full of avarice, at noon full of envy, and in the evening full of sensual desire (AN 3:127).

Reports of Anuruddha's past lives also refer to his relationships with women. There is only one instance that mentions his rebirth as an animal. Once, when he was reborn as a wood pigeon, his mate was seized by a hawk. Tormented by passion and grief, he decided to fast until he had overcome his love for her and the grief of separation:

> Once I was in love with a female pigeon,
> In this very spot we flew about in sport.
> Then a hawk pounced on her and fled;
> Against my will she was taken from me.

Since we have been parted and separated
I experience pain constantly in my heart.
Hence I observe the vows of the holy day,
That lust may never again cross my path.

(Jāt. 490)

Other rebirth stories tell us the following: Once when Anuruddha was born as a king he saw a lovely fairy woman in the forest, fell in love with her, and shot at her husband in order to take possession of her. Full of the pain of sorrow, she cried out and denounced the king for his cruelty. Hearing her accusations, the king came to his senses and went his way. At that time when Anuruddha was the jealous king, Yasodharā was the fairy woman, and her husband was the Bodhisatta, who was now Anuruddha's Master and whom in that past life he had almost killed out of lust for a woman (Jāt. 485).

In a divine form of existence, as Sakka, king of the devas, he helped the Bodhisatta to regain his reputation when he was the famous musician Guttila. As a test, three times he made appear on earth three hundred celestial maidens who danced when Guttila played on his lute. Then Sakka invited Guttila into his heavenly world at the request of the heavenly nymphs who wanted to hear his music. After he had played to them, he asked them to tell him which good deeds had brought them to this heavenly world. They told him that in the past they had given small gifts to monks, heard their discourses, shared what they had with others, and were without anger and pride. Hearing this, the Bodhisatta rejoiced in the benefit he had thus gained in his visit to Sakka's heaven (Jāt. 243).

In his last life Anuruddha helped his sister Rohiṇī to gain access to the Dhamma. Once, together with five hundred of his pupils, he visited his home city Kapilavatthu. When his relatives heard that he had arrived they all went to the monastery to pay respects to him—all, that is, except Rohiṇī. The elder inquired why his sister was absent, and they informed him that she was suffering from a skin eruption and was too ashamed to show herself in public. The elder asked that she be sent to him immediately.

Rohiṇī came, her face covered by a cloth, and the elder instructed her to sponsor the construction of an assembly hall. Rohiṇī sold her jewels to raise money for the project. Anuruddha supervised the arrangements and the young men of the Sakyan clan did the work. As soon as the construction of the hall was completed her skin eruption subsided. She then invited the Buddha and his monks to attend the opening ceremony for the assembly hall. In his discourse the Buddha explained the kammic cause for her skin ailment. In a previous life, he said, when she was the chief consort of the king of Benares, she became jealous of one of the king's dancing girls and, to torment her, had sprinkled dried scabs over her body and her bed. The skin ailment from which she had suffered was the fruit of that evil deed. At the end of the Buddha's discourse Rohiṇī was established in the fruit of stream-entry. After her death she was reborn among the gods of the Thirty-three and became the beloved consort of Sakka.[13]

In Anuruddha's life as a monk, there was one incident which led to the promulgation of a disciplinary rule by the Buddha. Once Anuruddha was wandering through the kingdom of Kosala toward Sāvatthī. In the evening he reached a village but could not find any special accommodation reserved for wandering ascetics and monks. He went to the village inn and asked for a night's lodging, which was granted. Meanwhile more travelers began to arrive at the inn for the night and the dormitory where Anuruddha was to stay became crowded. The inn hostess, seeing this, told Anuruddha that she could prepare his bedding in an inside room where he could spend the night peacefully. Silently Anuruddha agreed. The hostess, however, had made this suggestion only because she had fallen in love with him. She now perfumed herself, put on her jewelry, and approached Anuruddha, saying: "You, respected sir, are handsome, graceful, and good-looking, and so am I. It will be good if the respected sir will take me as his wife."

Anuruddha, however, remained silent. Then the inn hostess offered him all her riches. Anuruddha still remained silent. Then she took off her upper garment and danced in front of him, then she sat down, and then she lay down in front of him. But Anuruddha had his senses well under control and paid no attention to her. Seeing that none of her allurements moved him, she exclaimed: "It is astonishing, dear sir, it is extraordinary! So many men have offered me hundreds and thousands to win my hand, but this ascetic whom I myself have asked does not desire me or my wealth."

The woman then put on her upper garment again, fell at Anuruddha's feet, and asked him to forgive her for her audacity. Now for the first time he opened his mouth to pardon her, exhorting her to guard herself in the future. She then left. The next morning she brought him his breakfast as if nothing had happened. Anuruddha then proceeded to give her a talk on the Dhamma which so touched her that she became a devout lay follower of the Buddha.

Anuruddha, however, continued his journey, and when he reached the monastery at Sāvatthī he told the monks about his adventure. The Buddha called him and reproached him for having spent the night in a woman's quarters. He then proclaimed a rule which prohibited this (Pācittiya 6).

This story shows well how the Venerable Anuruddha's self-restraint had saved him from becoming a slave to sensual desire. His strength of character had made such a deep impression on that woman that she repented, listened to him, and took refuge in the Buddha. Thus Anuruddha's self-control was not only for his own good but also brought benefit to the woman. But when the Buddha reprimanded him, he did so because weaker characters could well succumb to temptation in such situations. Hence, out of compassion for them, the Buddha prescribed the rule that a monk should not expose himself to such dangers. Frequently we can observe that the Buddha wanted to prevent weaker characters from overrating their strength and trying to emulate an ideal too high for them.

This story closely parallels a similar experience which befell St. Bernard of Clairvaux, who resembles Anuruddha in his strength of will. One day, as a young monk, Bernard came to an inn and asked for lodgings for the night. He was offered a bench in the public room, as there was no other place available. The innkeeper's daughter had fallen in love with the handsome young Cistercian monk and went to him during the night. He, however, turned to the wall, drew his cape up, and said to her, "If you are looking for a place to sleep, there is room enough!" This total disinterest in her person sobered her and she slinked away ashamed. Like Anuruddha, he too had mastered the situation, not through arguments, but simply through the strength of his purity.

ANURUDDHA'S EARLIER LIVES

Like many other prominent disciples, the Venerable Anuruddha had formed his original aspiration for great discipleship one hundred thousand aeons in the past during the Dispensation of the Buddha Padumuttara.[14] At that time he was a wealthy householder. When he saw the Buddha appoint a bhikkhu to the post of "foremost among those who have the divine eye," he aspired to this station himself, made abundant offerings to the Blessed One and the Sangha, and then received from the Master the prediction of his future success. After that Buddha's Parinibbāna he approached the bhikkhus and asked about the preliminary practice for gaining the divine eye. They told him that offerings of lamps would be particularly appropriate. Thus the householder offered many thousands of lamps at the golden shrine constructed to hold the Buddha's bodily relics. Again, in a subsequent life during the time of the Buddha Kassapa, after the Buddha's Parinibbāna he placed bowls filled with cream of ghee all around the Buddha's shrine and lit them; he himself circumambulated the shrine all night bearing a lighted bowl on his head.

The *Apadāna* mentions a similar incident that took place during the time of a previous Buddha named Sumedha. Anuruddha had seen this Buddha meditating alone at the foot of a tree, set up lights all around him, and replenished them with fuel for seven days. As a kammic result he became the king of the devas for thirty aeons and a human king twenty-eight times, with a faculty of vision that could see for a *yojana* (about six miles) all around (Ap.i, 3:4, vv. 421–33).

The longest account of any of Anuruddha's previous lives tells of the time between the arising of two Buddhas when he was reborn into a poor family in Benares.[15] His name was Annabhāra (Food Carrier), and he earned his living in the service of a wealthy merchant named Sumana. One day the paccekabuddha Upariṭṭha emerged from the attainment of cessation and entered the city on alms round. Annabhāra saw him, proposed to give him alms, and conducted him to his home, where he and his wife each gave him the portions of food they had prepared for themselves.

The wealthy merchant Sumana, having learned of his employee's noble deed, wanted to purchase his merits from him, but Annabhāra would not sell them even for a lavish amount of wealth. When Sumana pressured him, Annabhāra consulted with the paccekabuddha, who told him that the merit could be shared simply by inviting Sumana to rejoice in the offering. Just as a flame is not diminished when other lamps are lit from it, so, he explained, merit increases and does not diminish when others are invited to rejoice in one's meritorious deeds. Sumana appreciated this opportunity, gave Annabhāra a generous reward, and brought him to the king. The king, too, on hearing the report, gave Annabhāra a bonus and had a site appointed to build a new home for him. On that site, wherever the workmen dug the ground in order to start building, they uncovered pots of treasure. These had materialized through the merit of Annabhāra's offering to the paccekabuddha, and Annabhāra was consequently appointed the king's treasurer. As a kammic fruit of his offering to the paccekabuddha, it is said, in his youth Anuruddha was never to hear the words "there isn't any."

After he attained arahantship, one day the Venerable Anuruddha thought, "Where has my old friend, the merchant Sumana, been reborn?" With the divine eye he then saw that he was a child of seven years named Culla Sumana, living in a market town not far away. Anuruddha proceeded there and spent the rainy season of three months living with the support of Culla Sumana's family. After the rains, he gave Culla Sumana the novice ordination, and as soon as he shaved his head the boy attained arahantship.[16]

In his verses of the *Theragāthā* Anuruddha says of himself:

> I know well my past abodes,
> Where it is that I lived before.
> I dwelt among the Thirty-three devas
> Occupying the rank of Sakka.
>
> Seven times I was a human king
> And there I exercised rulership.
> Lord of Jambusaṇḍa, a conqueror,
> I ruled over the entire continent.
> Without force, without weapons,
> I exercised command by Dhamma.
>
> From here seven, and another seven,
> Thus fourteen turns in the round of births,
> I recall my previous abodes:
> I then dwelt in the deva-world.
>
> (Thag. 913–15)

In the Jātaka tales, there are no less than twenty-three accounts telling us of Anuruddha's earlier lives. In most cases he was Sakka, king of the gods (Jāt. 194, 243, 347, 429, 430, 480, 494, 499, 537, 540, 541, 545, 547). Once he was Sakka's messenger, a deity called Pañcasikha, who was a celestial musician. In the seven earthly lives that are mentioned, he was most often an ascetic (423, 488, 509, 522), and twice a brother of the Bodhisatta. In three other human rebirths he was a king (485), a court priest (515), and a court charioteer (276). Only once is his rebirth as an animal reported, namely, as that amorous wood pigeon mentioned above (490). Thus in all the Jātakas record that he was fifteen times a deity, seven times a human being, and once an animal.

The fact that he was so often a king, celestial or human, indicates the power and strength in his nature. But he was quite a different god-king than Zeus with his amorous liaisons, and different also from Jehovah, who often inflicted harsh punishment on people. As Sakka, king of the Thirty-three gods, he was rather one who always protected and helped others. When the Bodhisatta was in need of help, he came to his succor. He protected him from being executed when he was defamed. On that occasion the

Bodhisatta's wife had raised her voice to high heaven over this injustice, and Sakka—the future Anuruddha—was so moved by her impassioned entreaty that he took action and saved the Bodhisatta (Jāt. 194).

On another occasion the Bodhisatta, a king, had forbidden animal sacrifices in his kingdom. A bloodthirsty demon resented this and wanted to kill the king, but Sakka appeared and protected the Bodhisatta once again (347).

On other occasions Sakka wanted to put the Bodhisatta to a test in order to strengthen his virtue. So in the last of the Jātaka tales, the *Vessantara Jātaka*, Sakka, in the guise of an old brahmin, asked the Bodhisatta for his wife in order to test his joyful generosity (547). On another occasion Sakka also wanted to test whether the Bodhisatta was firm in his vow of generosity and asked him for his eyes (499). When the Bodhisatta was leading the life of an ascetic, Sakka wanted to test his patience and forbearance and blamed him for his physical ugliness. The Bodhisatta told him of his ugly deeds that had made him so ugly, and he praised the goodness and purity for which he was now striving. Then Sakka said that he would grant him a wish. What the Bodhisatta asked for was freedom from malice, hate, greed, and lust; further he wished that he might never hurt anyone. All that, Sakka explained, was not in his own power to grant, but had to come from one's own moral effort (440). Sakka also tested the Bodhisatta's frugality (429, 430).

In a third group of accounts, Sakka—once again the future Anuruddha—invited the Bodhisatta to his heaven and showed him the mysteries of the celestial and the hell worlds. This was told in the story of the musician Guttila, which we have already recounted (Jāt. 243). In the stories of King Nimi (541) and of the charitable King Sādhīna (494), Sakka also invited them to his heaven.

From his lives as a human being we may note two revealing episodes. In one birth, when Anuruddha was a court brahmin and counselor, the king asked him how advantageous actions and justice could be united by one who was a ruler. Without intellectual pride, the brahmin admitted that he could not answer that question. Instead, he went assiduously in search of one who knew, and he found him in the Bodhisatta (Jāt. 515). When he was a royal charioteer, he once wanted to avoid a heavy downpour which was threatening. To speed up the horses, he hit them with the goad. From that time on, whenever the horses came to that particular spot on the road, they would start to gallop as if aware of a danger lurking just there. Seeing this, the charioteer regretted deeply that he had frightened and hurt those noble steeds, and he admitted that by having done so he did not fully observe the traditional Kuru virtues (276).

All these diverse and colorful stories have a common feature. They show several characteristic qualities of Anuruddha: his strong active striving for virtue, his strength of character, and his concern for the welfare of others. They also show that his skill in meditation and his mastery of supernormal faculties had their roots in his experiences during many lives as Sakka, ruler of the gods.

THE BUDDHA'S PARINIBBĀNA AND AFTERWARD

The Venerable Anuruddha was present at the Buddha's decease, recounted in the *Mahāparinibbāna Sutta* (DN 16; see also SN 6:15), and he played a major role in the affairs of the newly orphaned Sangha. When the Master knew that death was close, he entered into the full sequence of the meditative absorptions and then attained the cessation of perception and feeling. At that moment Ānanda turned to Anuruddha and said: "Venerable Anuruddha, the Blessed One has passed away." But Anuruddha, an arahant endowed with the divine eye, had been able to gauge the level of meditation into which the Buddha had entered, and he corrected the younger monk: "Not so, friend Ānanda, the Blessed One has not passed away. He has entered the cessation of perception and feeling."

The Buddha, however, rising from the attainment of cessation, turned his mind back to the stages of absorption in their reverse order until he reached the first jhāna, then rose up again to the fourth jhāna, and rising from it he instantly passed away into the Nibbāna-element without any residue.

When the Enlightened One had finally passed away, both Brahmā, the high divinity, and Sakka, king of the Thirty-three gods, honored the Buddha in verses evoking the law of impermanence. The third to speak was Anuruddha, who uttered these verses:

> There was no more in-and-out breathing
> In the Stable One of steady mind
> When unstirred, bent on peace,
> The One with Vision attained final Nibbāna.
>
> With unshrinking mind
> He endured the painful feeling;
> The deliverance of the mind
> Was like the quenching of a lamp.

Many of the monks attending the Buddha's last hours grieved and lamented over the Master's death. But Anuruddha exhorted them with a reminder of impermanence: "Enough, friends! Do not grieve, do not lament! For has not the Blessed One declared that with all that is dear and beloved there must be change, separation, and severance? Of that which is arisen, come into being, compounded, and subject to decay, how can one say: 'May it not come to dissolution!'" He also informed the monks that the deities, too, were lamenting: "There are deities who are earthly-minded and with dishevelled hair they weep, with uplifted arms they weep; flinging themselves on the ground, they roll from side to side lamenting: 'Too soon has the Blessed One attained Parinibbāna! Too soon has the Sublime One attained Parinibbāna! Too soon has the Eye of the World vanished from our sight!'" But, he added, those deities who were free of passion, mindful and clearly comprehending, simply reflected: "Impermanent are all compounded things. How could this be otherwise?"

Anuruddha and Ānanda spent the rest of the night near the deceased Master. In the morning, Anuruddha asked Ānanda to announce the passing away of the Blessed One to the householders living in the next village, Kusinārā. At once they gathered and prepared the funeral pyre. When, however, eight strong men tried to lift the body up to the pyre they could not do so. They then went to the Venerable Anuruddha and asked why the body could not be moved. Anuruddha told them that the deities wanted a different ceremony and explained their intentions, whereupon all happened just as the deities wished. With regard to the procedure of burning the body, the householders turned to the Venerable Ānanda for advice. This shows the different competence of the two half-brothers: Anuruddha was master of otherworldly affairs, while Ānanda was well versed in practical matters.

After the Buddha's demise, the guidance of the Order did not go to his next of kin, as for instance the arahant Anuruddha. The Buddha had not nominated any formal successor, but the natural veneration of the monks and laypeople concentrated on the Venerable Mahākassapa. He was the one who initiated the First Council at which five hundred arahant monks rehearsed and codified the Buddha's teachings. Before the council opened, the Venerable Ānanda had not yet attained to arahantship and this would have excluded him from participating. The elder monks, headed by Anuruddha, therefore urged him to make a determined effort to break through the last fetters and realize final liberation. Within a short time Ānanda succeeded and so could join the other elders in the council as an arahant. During its sessions, he recited the numerous teachings, which he of all monks had best retained in his memory.

In this manner Anuruddha had helped his half-brother to attain the goal of liberation, for the good of the Sangha and for the good of all who seek a path to deliverance; and this has remained a blessing for us even today. According to the commentary to the Dīgha Nikāya, Anuruddha himself was entrusted at the council with the preservation of the Aṅguttara Nikāya.

About the Venerable Anuruddha's death nothing else is known except the serene final stanza of his twenty verses in the *Theragāthā*:

> In the Veḷuva village of the Vajjians,
> Below a thicket of bamboo trees,
> Cankerless, I shall pass into Nibbāna
> When my life force is spent.

(Thag. 919)

CHAPTER 6

MAHĀKACCĀNA

Master of Doctrinal Exposition

Bhikkhu Bodhi

INTRODUCTION

As a skilled and versatile teacher, the Buddha adopted different styles of discourse to communicate the Dhamma to his disciples. Often he would explain a teaching in detail (*vitthārena*). Having introduced his topic with a short statement or synopsis (*uddesa*), he would then explain it at length (*niddesa*), analyzing it, drawing out its implications, and sometimes attaching a simile (*upamā*) to reinforce his point. Finally, he would restate the introductory declaration as a conclusion (*niggamana*), now supported by the entire weight of the foregoing analysis. On other occasions, however, the Buddha would not teach in detail. Instead, he would present the Dhamma briefly (*saṅkhittena*), offering only a short, sometimes even cryptic, statement charged with a profound but highly concentrated meaning.

The Buddha did not teach the doctrine in this way in order to conceal an esoteric message. He used this technique because it sometimes proved more effective than a detailed elaboration in shaking and transforming the minds of his listeners. Although direct explanation of the meaning may have transmitted information more efficiently, the purpose of the teaching is not to convey information but to lead on—to insight, higher wisdom, and deliverance. By requiring the disciples to reflect upon the meaning and to draw out the implications by sustained inquiry and mutual discussion, the Buddha ensured that his utterance would serve this purpose.

While such brief teachings would escape the understanding of the great majority of the monks, those disciples with sharp faculties of wisdom could readily fathom their meaning. Under such circumstances the ordinary monks, reluctant to trouble their Master with requests for an explanation, would turn for clarification to the senior disciples whose comprehension of the Dhamma had already been confirmed by the Blessed One. So important did this function become in the early Sangha that the Buddha himself established a separate category of eminent disciples called "the foremost of those who analyze in detail the meaning of what was stated (by me) in brief" (*aggaṁ saṅkhittena bhāsitassa vitthārena atthaṁ vibhajantānaṁ*). The bhikkhu whom the Master assigned to this post was the Venerable Mahākaccāna—Kaccāna the Great, so called to distinguish him from others who bore the common brahmanical clan name of Kaccāyana (shortened to Kaccāna).[1]

After his ordination as a monk Mahākaccāna usually resided in his homeland of Avantī, a remote region to the southwest of the Middle Country where the Buddha dwelt. For this reason he did not spend as much time in the Blessed One's presence as some of the other great disciples did, and we do not find him figuring as prominently in Sangha affairs as the closer disciples like Sāriputta, Mahāmoggallāna, and Ānanda. Nevertheless, on account of the astuteness of his intellect, the profundity of his insight into the Dhamma, and his skill as a speaker, whenever Mahākaccāna did join the Buddha's company the other monks frequently turned to him for help in illuminating the brief statements of the Buddha that had been causing them bafflement. We thus find in the Pāli Canon a sheaf of discourses spoken by Mahākaccāna that occupy a place of primary importance. These texts, always methodically refined and analytically precise, demonstrate with astounding lucidity the far-ranging implications and practical bearings of several brief statements of the Buddha that would otherwise, without his explanations, escape our understanding.

THE SAṀSĀRIC BACKGROUND

As in the case of all the Buddha's chief disciples, the Venerable Mahākaccāna's elevation to a position of preeminence in the Sangha was the flowering of a seed that had been planted long ago in the rolling cycles of saṁsāra, the round of rebirths, and had been brought to gradual maturity over countless lives. The biographical sketch of Mahākaccāna relates that his original aspiration to a leading role in the Sangha was formed a hundred thousand aeons in the past, during the Dispensation of the Buddha Padumuttara.[2] At that time Kaccāna had been reborn into a wealthy householder family. One day, when he went to the monastery, he saw the Buddha appoint a certain bhikkhu the foremost of those who can analyze in detail what had been stated by him in brief. The young householder was deeply impressed by the monk on whom this honor was bestowed, and the thought occurred to him: "Great indeed is that bhikkhu, in that the Teacher praises him so. I ought to attain such a position in the Dispensation of some future Buddha."

To obtain the merit needed to support such a lofty aspiration the young householder invited the Teacher to receive alms at his home, and for a full week he bestowed lavish offerings on the Buddha and his Sangha. At the week's end he prostrated himself at the Blessed One's feet and voiced his heart's desire. Then the Buddha, looking into the future with his unimpeded knowledge, saw that the youth's aspiration would be fulfilled. He told him: "Young man, in the future, after a hundred thousand aeons have elapsed, a Buddha named Gotama will arise. In his Dispensation you will be the foremost of those who can analyze in detail the meaning of what the Buddha has stated in brief."

The *Apadāna* relates that in this same past life, Kaccāna had built for the Buddha Padumuttara a stūpa with a stone seat, which he had covered with gold; he had the stūpa embellished with a jeweled parasol and an ornamental fan.[3] According to the above text, it was after he made this offering that Padumuttara predicted his future attainment to the position of a great disciple in the Dispensation of the Buddha Gotama. In this prediction the Blessed One also makes other prophecies concerning Kaccāna's future, which from our temporal perspective would now constitute his past history. The Buddha foretold that as the fruit of his meritorious gifts, the householder would become a lord of the devas for thirty aeons. Having returned to the human world, he would become a world monarch named Pabhassara, whose body would emit rays of light all around. He would spend his next to last existence in the Tusita heaven, and passing away from there he would be reborn in a brahmin family with the clan name Kaccāna. In that life he would attain arahantship and be appointed a great disciple by the Buddha.

A later section of the *Apadāna* gives a somewhat different account of Mahākaccāna's original aspiration to great discipleship.[4] In this version, at the time of the Buddha Padumuttara, the future disciple was an ascetic living in seclusion in the Himalayas. One day, while traveling through the sky by supernormal power, he passed over a populated area and saw the Victorious One down below. He descended, approached the Master to listen to the Dhamma, and heard him praise a certain bhikkhu (whose name was also Kaccāna) as the chief among those who can elaborate on brief statements. Thereupon the ascetic went to the Himalayas, collected a bouquet of flowers, and, quickly returning to the assembly, presented them to the Lord. At that point he formed the aspiration to become the chief expositor of the Dhamma, and the Blessed One prophesied that his aspiration would be fulfilled under the Buddha Gotama.

In this same series of verses Mahākaccāna states that as a result of his offering to the Buddha he never took rebirth in the nether world—in the hells, the animal realm, or the sphere of ghosts—but was always reborn either in the world of the devas or in the human realm. Also, when he took rebirth as a human being, he was always reborn into the upper two social classes—among nobles or brahmins—and never into low-class families.

At the time of the Buddha Kassapa, Kaccāna had taken rebirth in a family of Benares. After the Lord Kassapa's Parinibbāna he offered a precious golden brick for the construction of a golden stūpa for the Buddha. On presenting it he made the wish: "Whenever I am reborn, may my body always have a golden hue." As a result, when he was reborn during the time of our Buddha, his body was endowed with a beautiful golden hue, which deeply impressed those who beheld it.[5] In one case, which we will discuss below, this physical attribute of the elder led to a bizarre series of events.

KACCĀNA'S CONVERSION TO THE DHAMMA

In his last existence, when the Buddha Gotama appeared in the world, Kaccāna was born as the son of the chaplain (*purohita*) in the city of Ujjeni, the capital of Avantī, to the southwest of the Middle Country.[6] His father's personal name was Tiriṭivaccha, his mother's Candimā,[7] and they were of the Kaccāyana clan, one of the oldest and most highly respected lines of brahmins. Since he was born with a golden-colored body, his parents exclaimed that he had brought his name along with him at birth, and they named him Kañcana, which means "golden." As a brahmin and the son of the court chaplain, when Kañcana grew up he studied the Three Vedas, the traditional sacred scriptures of the brahmins, and after his father's death he succeeded him in the position of court chaplain.

The king of Avantī at the time that Kaccāna became chaplain was Caṇḍappajjota, Pajjota the Violent. He was called thus because of his explosive and unpredictable temper. When King Caṇḍappajjota heard that the Buddha had arisen in the world, he assembled his ministers and asked them to go and invite the Blessed One to visit Ujjeni. The ministers all agreed that the only one who could handle this assignment was the chaplain Kaccāna. Kaccāna, however, would go on this mission only under one condition: that he would be permitted to become a monk after meeting the Enlightened One. The king, ready to accept any condition in exchange for a meeting with the Tathāgata, gave his consent.

Kaccāna set out accompanied by seven other courtiers. When they met the Master he taught them the Dhamma, and at the end of the discourse Kaccāna and his seven companions all attained arahantship together with the four analytical knowledges (*paṭisambhidā-ñāṇa*). The Buddha granted them ordination simply by raising his hand and welcoming them into the Sangha with the words, "Come, bhikkhus."[8]

The new bhikkhu, now the Venerable Mahākaccāna, then began to praise the splendors of Ujjeni to the Buddha. The Master realized that his new disciple wanted him to travel to his native land, but he replied that it would be sufficient for Kaccāna to go himself, as he was already capable of teaching the Dhamma and of inspiring confidence in King Caṇḍappajjota.

In the course of their return journey the party of monks arrived at a town named Telapanāḷi, where they stopped to gather alms. In that town lived two maidens, merchants' daughters of different families. One girl was beautiful, with lovely long hair, but both her parents had died and she lived in poverty, looked after by her governess. The other girl was wealthy but was afflicted with an illness that had caused her to lose her hair. Repeatedly she had tried to persuade the poor girl to sell her hair to her so she could make a wig, but the poor girl had consistently refused.

Now, when the poor girl saw Kaccāna and his fellow monks walking for alms, their bowls empty, she felt a sudden surge of faith and devotion arise in her toward the elder and decided to offer them alms. However, as she had no wealth, the only way she could obtain money to buy provisions was to sell her hair to the rich girl. This time, as the hair came to the rich girl already cut, she paid only eight coins for it. With these eight coins the poor girl had almsfood prepared for the eight monks, using one coin for each portion. After she had presented the alms, as an immediate fruit of the meritorious deed her full head of hair instantly grew back to its original length.

When Mahākaccāna arrived back in Ujjeni, he reported this incident to King Caṇḍappajjota. The king had the girl conveyed to his palace and at once appointed her his chief queen. From that time onward the king greatly honored Mahākaccāna. Many people of Ujjeni who heard the elder preach gained faith in the Dhamma and went forth under him as monks. Thus the entire city became (in the words of the commentary) "a single blaze of saffron robes, a blowing back and forth of the banner of sages." The queen, who was exceedingly devoted to the elder, built for him a dwelling in the Golden Grove Park.

So says the Aṅguttara Commentary, but the Pāli Canon itself suggests that the Sangha was not as well established in Avantī as the commentator would lead us to believe. The evidence for this is a story reported in the *Mahāvagga* of the Vinaya Piṭaka.[9] When this story opens, Mahākaccāna was dwelling in Avantī at his favorite residence, the Osprey's Haunt on Precipice Mountain. A lay disciple of his named Soṇa Kuṭikaṇṇa came to him and expressed the wish to go forth under him as a monk. But Kaccāna, seeing perhaps that the householder was not yet ready to take such a big step, discouraged him with the words: "Difficult, Soṇa, is it to sleep alone, to eat one meal a day, and to observe celibacy for as long as life lasts. While remaining a householder you should apply yourself to the Buddha's Teaching, and at the proper times you may sleep alone, eat one meal a day, and observe celibacy."

With these words Soṇa's enthusiasm for ordination subsided. Some time later, however, the urge was rekindled, and he approached the elder with the same request. A second time Kaccāna discouraged him, and a second time Soṇa's desire for ordination abated. When Soṇa approached for the third time, Mahākaccāna gave him the "going forth" (*pabbajjā*), the initial ordination as a novice (*sāmaṇera*).

During the Buddha's time it seems to have been customary to grant both ordinations in immediate succession to mature men who were already endowed with faith in the Dhamma and well acquainted with the teachings. The novice ordination would be given first and then, right afterwards, the higher ordination (*upasampadā*), making the postulant a bhikkhu, a full member of the Sangha. But at the time the above incident took place Avantī was short of monks, being a region quite far from the Buddha's own missionary rounds and from the other centers of Buddhist activity. According to the disciplinary regulations that were still in effect, the higher ordination had to be performed by a chapter of at least ten bhikkhus (*dasavagga-bhikkhusaṅgha*). But such was the situation in Avantī that the Venerable Mahākaccāna could not easily find even nine other bhikkhus to confer the higher ordination on Soṇa. It was only three years later that the elder could, "with trouble and difficulty," convene an assembly of ten bhikkhus from different places in the region to give Soṇa the higher ordination.

When Soṇa had completed his first rains retreat as a bhikkhu, a keen desire arose in him to pay a visit to the Buddha. He had heard many times the highest praise of the Blessed One, his lord and refuge, yet he had never seen the Master face to face, and now the desire to pay homage to him in person had become irresistible. He went to his preceptor to ask for his permission to make the long journey to Sāvatthī, where the Buddha was residing. Not only did Mahākaccāna applaud his disciple's request, but he asked Soṇa to convey to the Lord an appeal that certain monastic regulations be relaxed to suit the different social and geographical conditions that prevailed in Avantī and in other border regions.

When Soṇa came to the Buddha and explained his preceptor's petition, the Master readily agreed. First, to determine what districts should count as border regions, the Buddha defined the boundaries of the Middle Country, wherein the original regulations were to remain binding. Then he announced the revised versions of the rules that would apply in the border regions, though not in the Middle Country. These revised rules are the following: the higher ordination would not require ten bhikkhus but could now be given by a chapter of five, one of whom must be an expert in the Vinaya, the monastic discipline; monks are allowed to use sandals with thick linings, as the ground in those regions is rough and hard on the feet; monks are permitted to bathe frequently, as the people of Avantī attach great importance to bathing; sheepskins, goatskins, etc., could be used as coverlets; robes could be accepted on behalf of a monk who has left the district, and the ten days' period during which (under the rule) an extra robe could be kept would begin only when the robe actually reaches his hands.

VARIOUS INCIDENTS

Neither the suttas nor the commentaries offer us very much biographical information about the Venerable Mahākaccāna's life in the Sangha. They focus, rather, on his role as teacher, especially on his detailed expositions of the Buddha's brief statements. From the settings (*nidāna*) to the suttas in which Mahākaccāna appears we can infer that after his ordination he spent most of his time in Avantī. Usually, it seems, he dwelt quietly in seclusion, though when occasion arose he gave instruction to others. Periodically he would go to visit the Buddha at his main places of residence, and it seems likely that he also sometimes accompanied him on his preaching tours. The three suttas of the Majjhima Nikāya in which Mahākaccāna appears in the role of expositor open at three different locales—in Kapilavatthu, Rājagaha, and Sāvatthī. As these cities were, relative to the geographical extent of the Ganges Valley, widely separated, and as all were far from Avantī, this suggests either that Kaccāna spent long periods accompanying the Buddha on his journeys or that he would travel to the different monastic centers where the Buddha resided when he heard that the Master intended to stay there for some time.

We do not find in the texts indications that Mahākaccāna entered into close friendships with the other leading monks, as for instance Sāriputta, Mahāmoggallāna, and Ānanda did with one another. He seems to be one who generally lived aloof, though he did not place a strict emphasis on seclusion in the manner of one like Mahākassapa, nor did he seem especially stern in his asceticism.[10] He was ready to assume teaching duties on request, as we shall see, but we find that he always appears in the suttas in the role of expositor and elucidator of the Dhamma to others. We do not see him engage in person-to-person dialogues with other monks, as we see in the case of all the above-mentioned elders; neither do we see him address inquiries to the Buddha, as even the wisest of the bhikkhus, the Venerable Sāriputta, often did. His absence is conspicuous in the *Mahāgosiṅga Sutta* (MN 32), wherein the other outstanding disciples gather on a full-moon night to discuss the ideal bhikkhu who could illuminate the forest. Surely, however, if Mahākaccāna was present on that occasion he would have described such a monk as one skilled in the detailed exposition of brief sayings.

Mahākaccāna did grant ordination, as we saw above in the case of Soṇa, though his pupils, despite the words of the Aṅguttara Commentary, were probably not very numerous. One was the bhikkhu Isidatta, who even while very young had impressed many of the older monks with his incisive replies to difficult questions on the Dhamma.[11] There can be little doubt that Isidatta's skill in tackling subtle points of doctrine reflects the rigorous training he must have received from Mahākaccāna.

On one occasion when Mahākaccāna visited the Buddha he received special homage from Sakka, the king of the gods.[12] This occurred when the Buddha was dwelling at the Eastern Park at Sāvatthī, in the Mansion of Migāra's Mother. The Lord was sitting surrounded by a company of great disciples on the occasion of the *pavāraṇā*, the ceremony of mutual criticism among the monks that terminates the annual rains retreat. Because Mahākaccāna regularly used to visit the Buddha in order to hear the Dhamma, coming even from a long distance, the other elders would always reserve a seat for him in case he should unexpectedly turn up.

On this occasion Sakka, along with his celestial retinue, drew near to the holy assembly and prostrated himself before the Blessed One. Since he did not see Mahākaccāna, he thought to himself: "It would be good indeed if the noble elder would arrive." Just at that moment Kaccāna approached and took his seat. When Sakka beheld him, he grasped him firmly by the ankles, expressed his joy over the elder's arrival, and honored him with gifts of scents and flowers. Some of the younger monks were upset and complained that Sakka was being partial in his display of reverence, but the Buddha reproved them with the words: "Monks, those monks who, like my son Mahākaccāna, guard the doors of the senses are beloved both among devas and humans." He then pronounced the following stanza of the *Dhammapada*:

Even the devas hold him dear,
Whose senses are subdued
Like horses trained well by a charioteer,

Whose pride is destroyed,
And who is free from corruptions.

(Dhp. 94)

That Kaccāna was actually one who devoted close attention to the mastery of the sense faculties is borne out by his discourses, which (as we shall see below) often emphasize the need for guarding "the doors of the senses."

The commentaries record two curious series of events, both of which stemmed from the impression that the elder's physical form made on the minds of others. One of these, reported in the Dhammapada Commentary,[13] involved a young man named Soreyya, who was the son of the treasurer in the city of the same name. One day the youth Soreyya was driving out of the city in a carriage, en route to a bathing spot together with an intimate friend and a merry band of companions. Just as they were leaving the city the Venerable Mahākaccāna was standing at the city gate, putting on his outer robe before entering to walk on alms round. When the youth Soreyya beheld the golden-hued body of the elder, he thought to himself: "Oh, that this elder might become my wife! Or may the hue of my wife's body become like the hue of his body!"

At the very moment this wanton thought passed through his mind, Soreyya was instantly transformed from a man into a woman. Startled by this inexplicable change of sex, he jumped out of the carriage and fled before the others could notice what had occurred. Gradually he made his way to the city of Takkasilā. His companions searched for him in vain and reported his strange disappearance to his parents. When all attempts to trace him proved futile, his parents concluded that he had died and they had the funeral rites performed.

Meanwhile the woman Soreyyā, on reaching Takkasilā, met the son of the city's treasurer, who fell in love with her and took her as his wife. In the first years of their marriage she gave birth to two sons. Previously, while a man, Soreyya had fathered two sons through his wife in his native city. Thus he was the parent of four children, two as a father and two as a mother.

One day the former intimate friend of Soreyya came to Takkasilā on some personal business. Lady Soreyyā saw him in the street and called him into her house, revealing to him the secret of her mysterious metamorphosis from a man into a woman. The friend proposed that Soreyyā should offer alms to Mahākaccāna, who was living close by, and then beg pardon from him for having given rise to such a lewd thought.

The friend then went to the elder and invited him to come to the lady's house for alms on the following day. When the Venerable

Mahākaccāna arrived, the friend brought Lady Soreyyā into his presence, informed him of what had happened long ago, and asked him to pardon her for that transgression. As soon as the elder uttered the words "I pardon you," Lady Soreyyā was transformed back into a man. Shaken out of all worldly complacency by this double metamorphosis, Soreyya determined that he could never again lead the household life. He took ordination as a bhikkhu under Mahākaccāna, and after a short time attained arahantship together with the supernormal powers.

Vassakāra, the chief minister of Magadha under King Ajātasattu, was less fortunate, though his misfortune sprang entirely from his own pride and obstinacy and not from some force outside his control. The commentary to the Majjhima Nikāya reports that one day, when Vassakāra saw the Venerable Mahākaccāna coming down from Vulture's Peak, he exclaimed: "He looks just like a monkey!"[14] Such an exclamation seems strange, particularly as Mahākaccāna is described in the texts as being especially handsome and graceful; but whatever the reason for the remark, news of the incident spread and eventually reached the Buddha. The Blessed One said that if Vassakāra would go to the elder and beg his pardon, all would be well; but if he did not ask pardon he would be reborn as a monkey in the Bamboo Grove in Rājagaha. This was reported back to Vassakāra. As the chief minister of the kingdom, Vassakāra must have been too proud to beg forgiveness from a mendicant monk. Thus, reflecting that whatever the Buddha says must be true, he resigned himself to his future fate and made preparations for his next existence by planting trees in the Bamboo Grove and setting up a guard to protect the wildlife there. It is said that some time after his death a monkey was born in the Bamboo Grove who would draw near when people called out "Vassakāra."

The circumstances of the Venerable Mahākaccāna's death are not recorded in the texts, but at the end of the *Madhura Sutta* (discussed below) Mahākaccāna declares that the Buddha has attained Parinibbāna, so it is evident that he himself outlived his Master.

THE ELABORATOR OF BRIEF STATEMENTS

The Buddha honored the Venerable Mahākaccāna by naming him his foremost disciple in the ability to provide detailed expositions of his own brief statements. Mahākaccāna earned this distinguished title principally because of eight suttas found in the Nikāyas: three in the Majjhima, three in the Saṁyutta, and two in the Aṅguttara. Besides these, we find in the

Nikāyas several other discourses of Mahākaccāna's that are not based on a brief utterance of the Buddha. Taken together, all these discourses have a uniform and distinctive flavor that reveal the qualities of the mind from which they sprang. They are thorough, balanced, careful and cautious, substantial in content, meticulous in expression, incisive, well conceived, and well rounded. They are also, admittedly, a little dry—unemotional and unsentimental—and bare of the rhetorical devices utilized by other renowned exponents of the Dhamma. We find in them no similes, parables, or stories; their language is plain but impeccably precise. In this respect his sermons contrast with those of the Buddha, Sāriputta, and Ānanda, all of whom were skilled in devising striking similes that impress the formal message of the discourse indelibly on the auditor's mind. Mahākaccāna's discourses, it seems, owe their effectiveness entirely to their content rather than to literary embellishment, but with no wastage of words they never fail to lead straight to the heart of the Dhamma.

As an analyst of the Dhamma, Mahākaccāna most closely approximates to the Venerable Sāriputta, and indeed the discourses of both exhibit similar traits. The difference between them is principally a matter of emphasis rather than of substance. Sāriputta's Dhamma talks, as seen for example in the *Sammādiṭṭhi Sutta* and the *Mahāhatthipadopama Sutta*,[15] begin with a specified topic, which they develop analytically by dissecting that topic into its components and exploring each component in turn (often with still finer subdivisions). Within his own specialized sphere Mahākaccāna generally starts not with a general topic but with a short utterance of the Buddha, often one that is intuitive, poetic, or exhortatory in character. His exposition then unfolds by reformulating the gnomic or inspirational phrasing of the Buddha's statement in ways that link it up with more familiar frameworks of established doctrine, often the six spheres of sense and the practice of sense restraint. Yet, despite their differences in emphasis, both these great disciples share a predilection for systematic analysis and both display the same concern for razor-sharp precision in their thinking.

For this reason, no doubt, within the Theravāda tradition each elder has come to be regarded as the father of a particular methodology for interpreting the Dhamma that rose to prominence in the early centuries of Buddhist literary history. Sāriputta is, of course, viewed as the original systematizer of the Abhidhamma, which (according to tradition) he elaborated based on the outlines that the Buddha taught him during his periodic visits to the human realm while expounding the Abhidhamma to the devas in the Tāvatiṁsa heaven.[16] Mahākaccāna is regarded as the author of an exegetical system embedded in two postcanonical works that exerted an important influence on the early Buddhist commentators. About these two works—the *Peṭakopadesa* and the *Nettippakaraṇa*—we shall have more to say below.

THE MAJJHIMA NIKĀYA

The first sutta in the Majjhima Nikāya in which the Venerable Mahākaccāna plays a prominent role is the *Madhupiṇḍika Sutta* (MN 18), the Honeyball Discourse, a title assigned to it by the Buddha himself—perhaps a unique instance of the Master conferring a title upon a sutta spoken by a disciple.

The sutta opens on an occasion when the Blessed One is dwelling at the city of Kapilavatthu in his native land, the Sakyan republic. One day, while he is sitting in meditation in Nigrodha's Park, an arrogant Sakyan named Daṇḍapāṇi approaches him and asks, in a deliberately discourteous manner: "What does the recluse assert, what does he proclaim?" The Buddha replies with an answer intended to underscore his own refusal to be dragged into the type of conflict that his questioner wants to instigate: "Friend, I assert and proclaim such (a teaching) that one does not quarrel with anyone in the world, with its gods, its Māras and its Brahmās, in this generation with its recluses and brahmins, its princes and its people; such (a teaching) that perceptions no more underlie that brahmin who abides detached from sensual pleasures, without perplexity, shorn of worry, free from craving for any kind of being."

The reply is utterly incomprehensible to Daṇḍapāṇi, who raises his eyebrows in bewilderment and departs. Later, in the evening, the Buddha informs the bhikkhus what had transpired. One monk inquires: "What exactly is the teaching that the Blessed One proclaims whereby one can avoid all quarrels and, at the same time, be free from the pernicious influence of craving?" The Buddha answers with the following pithy statement: "Bhikkhus, as to the source through which perceptions and notions tinged by mental proliferation beset a person: if nothing is found there to delight in, welcome, and hold to, this is the end of the underlying tendencies to lust, aversion, views, doubt, conceit, the desire for being, and ignorance; this is the end of reliance on rods and weapons, of quarrels, brawls, disputes, recrimination, malice, and false speech; here these evil unwholesome states cease without remainder." Having said this, before the monks even have time to ask for an explanation, the Lord rises from his seat and enters his dwelling.

After the Buddha has retired, the bhikkhus ponder his statement, and realizing that they cannot understand it on their own, they consider: "The Venerable Mahākaccāna is praised by the Teacher and esteemed by his wise companions in the holy life. He is capable of expounding the detailed meaning. Suppose we went to him and asked him the meaning of this."

When they approach Mahākaccāna and make their request, he first chides them for coming to him rather than asking the Buddha to clarify it. To come to him when the Blessed One is present, he says, is like seeking heartwood among the branches and leaves of a great tree after passing over the trunk. The Blessed One is the one who knows and sees; he is vision, he is knowledge, he has become the Dhamma, become the holy one; he is the sayer, the proclaimer, the elucidator of meaning, the giver of the Deathless, the Lord of the Dhamma, the Tathāgata.

The bhikkhus, however, while admitting that the elder's reproach is warranted, still insist that he himself is well qualified to explain the meaning. Finally the elder consents. He then gives the following explanation of the Buddha's brief statement: "Dependent on the eye and forms, eye-consciousness arises. The meeting of the three is contact. With contact as condition there is feeling. What one feels, that one perceives. What one perceives, that one thinks about. What one thinks about, that one mentally proliferates. With what one has mentally proliferated as the source, perceptions and notions tinged by mental proliferation beset a person with respect to past, future, and present forms cognizable through the eye." The same pattern is repeated for each of the other sense bases. The elder then connects the entire exposition with the principle of conditionality, showing how each term in the series arises in dependence on the preceding term and ceases with the cessation of its predecessor.

This passage, rich in implications, offers a penetrative account of the process by which the deluded mind becomes overwhelmed by its own imaginary creations—its distorted perceptions and mental constructs. The sequence begins as a straightforward description of the conditioned genesis of cognition: each type of consciousness arises in dependence on its respective sense faculty and object. The process unfolds in the natural order through contact, feeling, and perception as far as the stage of thinking. But in the unenlightened worldling, who lacks correct insight into the true nature of things, at the stage of thinking, cognition is vitiated by the influence of *papañca*, a difficult Pāli word best rendered as "conceptual proliferation."[17] Instead of correctly comprehending the objects of perception, the deluded mind, infiltrated by *papañca*, spins out a complex mental commentary that embellishes things with the erroneous notions of "mine," "I," and "my self." Thereby the person is overrun by "perceptions and notions tinged by mental proliferation" (*papañcasaññāsaṅkhā*).

The underlying springs of this conceptual proliferation are three defilements: craving (*taṇhā*), conceit (*māna*), and wrong view (*diṭṭhi*). When these three gain control of the thought process, cognition runs wild, spilling out a host of delusive ideas, obsessions, and passions that overpower the subject and reduce him to their hapless victim. This process of sense perception, as Mahākaccāna shows, is "the source through which perceptions and notions tinged by mental proliferation beset a person," referred to by the Buddha in his brief statement. When there is no delighting in the process of perception by way of craving, which elaborates upon experience in terms of the notion "mine"; when there is no welcoming it by way of conceit, which introduces the notion "I am"; when there is no holding to it by way of wrong view, which proliferates in notions of a self, then all the underlying tendencies to the defilements will be uprooted, and one can dwell in the world as a liberated sage, holy and wise, without quarrels, conflicts, and disputes.

Such was the explanation of the Buddha's words that Mahākaccāna offered to the monks. Afterwards the monks approached the Blessed One and told him what Mahākaccāna had said. The Buddha replied with words of the highest praise for his disciple: "Mahākaccāna is wise, bhikkhus, Mahākaccāna has great wisdom. If you had asked me the meaning of this, I would have explained it to you in the same way that Mahākaccāna has explained it. Such is the meaning of this, and so you should remember it."

Just then the Venerable Ānanda, standing nearby, added a memorable simile to highlight the beauty of Mahākaccāna's exposition: "Just as if a man exhausted by hunger and weakness came upon a honeyball, in the course of eating it he would find a sweet delectable flavour; so too, venerable sir, any able bhikkhu, in the course of scrutinizing with wisdom the meaning of this discourse on the Dhamma, would find satisfaction and confidence of mind." On the basis of this simile the Buddha named the discourse the *Madhupiṇḍika Sutta*, "The Honeyball Discourse."

The other two Majjhima Nikāya suttas featuring Mahākaccāna, and one in the Aṅguttara Nikāya, conform to this same stereotyped pattern: the Buddha makes a brief statement, gets up, and enters his dwelling; the monks approach the elder to ask for an explanation of the meaning; he reprimands them for coming to him rather than asking the Lord himself, but finally he complies with their request and elucidates the Buddha's utterance; the monks return to the Buddha and repeat his analysis, which the Master applauds with words of praise.

The *Mahākaccāna Bhaddekaratta Sutta* (MN 133) centers around the famous Bhaddekaratta poem, a set of verses spoken by the Buddha that had been circulating within the Sangha. The poem stresses the need to abandon longing for the past and anticipation of the future, calling instead for urgent effort to marshal all one's energies for penetrating with insight the present reality itself. Many of the Buddha's disciples had learned the poem by heart, along with the Buddha's own exegesis of it, and had been using it as an inspiration for their meditation practice and as a theme for sermons.[18]

One bhikkhu named Samiddhi, however, did not know even the poem, let alone its exegesis. One day a benevolent deity, taking compassion on him, came to him in the early morning and urged him to learn the Bhaddekaratta poem and exposition. Samiddhi went to the Buddha and asked him to teach these to him. The Buddha recited the poem:

Let not a person revive the past
Or on the future build his hopes,
For the past has been left behind
And the future has not been reached.

Instead with insight let him see
Each presently arisen state;
Let him know that and be sure of it,
Invincibly, unshakably.

Today the effort must be made;
Tomorrow Death may come, who knows?
No bargain with Mortality
Can keep him and his hoards away.

But one who dwells thus ardently,
Relentlessly, by day, by night—
It is he, the Peaceful Sage has said,
Who has had one excellent night.

Then the Blessed One rose from his seat and entered his dwelling.

Samiddhi, and the other monks present at the time, went to the Venerable Mahākaccāna in search of an explanation. As in the prelude to the *Madhupiṇḍika Sutta*, Mahākaccāna at first remonstrates with them but then agrees to share his understanding of the poem. Taking up the first two lines as the theme of his exposition, he explicates each by way of the six sense bases.

One "revives the past" when one recollects the eye and forms seen in the past, dwelling upon them with desire and lust; so too with the other five sense faculties and their objects. One "builds up hope upon the future" when one sets one's heart on experiencing in the future sense objects one has not yet encountered. One who does not bind himself by desire and lust to memories of past sensory experience and yearnings for future sensory experience is one who "does not revive the past or build up hope upon the future." Similarly, one whose mind is shackled by lust to the present sense faculties and their objects is called "one vanquished in regard to presently arisen states," while one whose mind is not bound to them by lust is called "one invincible in regard to presently arisen states."

Again, the monks return to the Buddha, who says, "If you had asked me the meaning of this, I would have explained it to you in the same way that Mahākaccāna has done."

The third Majjhima sutta, the *Uddesavibhaṅga Sutta* (MN 138), opens with the Buddha announcing to the monks that he will teach them a summary (*uddesa*) and an exposition (*vibhaṅga*). He recites the summary thus: "Bhikkhus, a bhikkhu should examine things in such a way that while he is examining them, his consciousness is not distracted and scattered externally nor stuck internally, and by not clinging he does not become agitated. If his consciousness is not distracted and scattered externally nor stuck internally, and if by not clinging he does not become agitated, then for him there is no origination of suffering—of birth, aging, and death in the future." Then, as on prior occasions, he rises from his seat and retires, without giving the exposition—a strange omission, as he had announced that he would teach it! But the monks do not feel lost, for the Venerable Mahākaccāna is in their midst, and his explanation would certainly win the approbation of the Master.

After his usual protest, Kaccāna begins his analysis by taking up each phrase in the Buddha's summary and dissecting it in minute detail. How is consciousness "distracted and scattered externally"? When a monk has seen a form with the eye (or has experienced some other sense object with its corresponding faculty), "if his consciousness follows after the sign of form, is tied and shackled by gratification in the sign of form, is fettered by the fetter of gratification in the sign of form, then his consciousness is called 'distracted and scattered externally.'" But if, on seeing a form with the eye, etc., the monk does not follow after the sign of form, does not become tied and shackled to the sign of form, then his consciousness is called "not distracted and scattered externally."

His mind is "stuck internally" if he attains any of the four jhānas, the meditative absorptions, and his mind becomes "tied and shackled" by gratification in the superior rapture, bliss, peace, and equanimity of the jhāna. If he can attain the jhānas without becoming attached to them, his mind is "not stuck internally."

There is "agitation due to clinging" (*upādāya paritassanā*) in the "uninstructed worldling" (*assutavā puthujjana*), who regards his five aggregates as self. When his form, or feeling, or perception, or volitional formations, or consciousness undergoes change and deterioration, his mind becomes preoccupied with the change, and he becomes anxious, distressed, and concerned. Thus there is agitation due to clinging. But the instructed noble disciple does not regard the five aggregates as his self. Therefore, when the aggregates undergo change and transformation, his mind is not preoccupied with the change and he dwells free from anxiety, agitation, and concern.

This, the elder states, is how he understands in detail the summary stated in brief by the Blessed One, and when the monks report to the Master, he endorses his disciple's explanation.

THE SAṀYUTTA NIKĀYA

The Saṁyutta Nikāya contains three suttas in which the Venerable Mahākaccāna displays his ingenuity in elaborating upon brief utterances of the Buddha: SN 22:3, SN 22:4, and SN 35:130. These suttas are different in both setting and character from the three analytical discourses of the Majjhima Nikāya. In all three the elder is not dwelling in the company of the Buddha, but in Avantī, at the Osprey's Haunt on Precipice Mountain, presumably a remote place difficult of access. A lay devotee named Hāliddikāni, evidently quite learned in the Dhamma, visits him and asks him to explain in detail a short discourse of the Buddha's. Mahākaccāna's reply is addressed to the householder Hāliddikāni alone, not to a group of monks, and there is no subsequent confirmation of his exposition by the Buddha at the end of the discourse. It seems impossible to determine whether these exchanges took place during the Buddha's life or afterwards, but obviously, to have been incorporated into the Pāli Canon, reports of the discussions must have reached the main centers of the Buddhist community.

In SN 22:3, Hāliddikāni asks the elder to explain in detail the meaning of a verse from "The Questions of Māgandiya," included in the Aṭṭhakavagga of the *Suttanipāta*:

Having left home to roam without abode,
In the village the sage is intimate with none;
Rid of sense pleasures, without preference,
He would not engage people in dispute.

(Snp. 844)

In responding to the lay devotee's request, the Venerable Mahākaccāna introduces a methodology that is strikingly different from his approach to interpretation in the three suttas of the Majjhima Nikāya. Here he does not simply elaborate upon the literal meaning of the Buddha's statement as he did on those occasions. Instead he transposes the key expressions of the verse to a different level of discourse, treating them not merely as obscure terms in need of clarification but as metaphors or figures of speech that to be properly understood must be redefined in terms of their nonfigurative meanings. He does this, as we shall see just below, by first eliciting from the selected figurative terms their implicit literal meanings and then mapping those meanings on to other, more systematic schemes of doctrine. This technique was to become characteristic of the Pāli commentaries in later centuries, and we might even regard Mahākaccāna's style of exegesis here as being, in certain respects at least, the original prototype of the commentarial method.

Taking up first the expression "having left home" (*okaṁ pahāya*), Mahākaccāna treats the word "home" not as meaning simply a place where people live but as an elliptical reference to the "home of consciousness" (*viññāṇassa oko*). He explains that the "home of consciousness" is the other four aggregates—material form, feeling, perception, and volitional formations—which are here referred to as elements (*dhātu*); elsewhere these are described as the four "stations of consciousness" (*viññāṇa-ṭhiti*).[19] If consciousness is bound by lust to these four elements, one is said to move about in a home. If one has abandoned all desire, lust, delight, and craving for these four homes of consciousness, one is said to "roam about homeless" (*anokasārī*). It should be noted that this last term does not actually occur in the verse, but Mahākaccāna has introduced it to fill out his exposition.

Next the elder explicates the phrase "to roam without abode" (*aniketasārī*). He first defines the counterpart, "roaming about in an abode" (*niketasārī*), which also does not appear in the verse. As before, Mahākaccāna treats this expression as a metaphor to be reformulated in terms of systematic doctrine. In this instance, rather than using the five aggregates as his scaffold, he draws in the six external sense bases. By being shackled to the sign of forms (sounds, odors, etc.), by moving about in the abode of forms, etc., one is called "one who roams about in an abode." When one has abandoned all bondage to the sign of forms, etc., cut them off at the root, then one is said to "roam without abode."

The remaining sections of the exposition proceed more literally and simply offer straightforward definitions of the phrases used in the verse, always in terms of contrasting pairs. One who is "intimate with none in the village" is defined as a bhikkhu who keeps aloof from laypeople and their worldly concerns. One "rid of sense pleasures" is one devoid of lust and craving for sensual pleasures. One "without preferences" (*apurakkharāno*) is one who does not yearn for the future. And one who "would not engage people in dispute" is one who does not become embroiled in quarrels and disputes over the interpretation of the Dhamma.

In the next sutta (SN 22:4) Hāliddikāni asks how one should understand in detail the following brief statement of the Buddha's, found in "The Questions of Sakka":[20] "Those recluses and brahmins who are liberated by the full destruction of craving are those who have reached the ultimate end, the ultimate security from bondage, the ultimate holy life, the ultimate goal, and are best among devas and humans." Mahākaccāna explains:

> Householder, through the destruction, fading away, cessation, giving up, and relinquishment of the desire, lust, delight, craving, engagement and clinging, mental standpoints, adherences, and underlying tendencies regarding the material-form element, the mind is called well liberated. So too in regard to the feeling element, the perception element, the volitional-formations element, the consciousness element.
>
> Thus, householder, it is in such a way that the meaning of what was stated in brief by the Blessed One should be understood in detail.

In a third sutta (SN 35:130) Hāliddikāni begins a query with a quotation from the Buddha, but this time he does not ask: "How should the meaning of this brief statement be understood in detail?" Rather, he simply requests the elder to explain the following excerpt from the Dhātu Saṁyutta (SN 14:4): "Bhikkhus, it is in dependence on the diversity of elements that there arises the diversity of contacts; in dependence on the diversity of contacts that there arises the diversity of feelings."

The Buddha himself had explained this assertion by showing how the different kinds of elements condition their corresponding kinds of contact and feeling: "In dependence on the eye element there arises eye-contact; in dependence on eye-contact there arises feeling born of eye-contact." And so for the other sense faculties. Mahākaccāna, however, does not merely parrot the Buddha's analysis but carries the divisions down to a finer level:

> Here, householder, having seen a form with the eye, a bhikkhu understands an agreeable form thus: "Such it is. In dependence on eye-consciousness and a contact to be experienced as pleasant, there arises a pleasant feeling." Then, having seen a form with the eye, a bhikkhu understands a disagreeable form thus: "Such it is. In dependence on eye-consciousness and a contact to be experienced as painful, there arises a painful feeling." Then, having seen a form with the eye, a bhikkhu understands a form that is a basis for equanimity thus: "Such it is. In dependence on eye-consciousness and a contact to be experienced as neither-painful-nor-pleasant, there arises a neither-painful-nor-pleasant feeling."

The same analysis is applied to each of the other sense faculties. Thus, while the Buddha merely differentiates the contact and feeling by way of the sense faculty, Mahākaccāna distinguishes within each sense sphere three qualities of the object—agreeable, disagreeable, and indifferent; three qualities of the contact—to be felt as pleasant, to be felt as painful, and to be felt as neither; and three qualities of the feeling—pleasant, painful, and neither-painful-nor-pleasant. These triads are then collated and shown to originate in a conditional relationship: the quality of the object conditions the quality of the contact; the quality of the contact conditions the quality of the feeling. As the entire process is said to be contemplated by a bhikkhu endowed with understanding, this also implies that he has the capacity for overcoming the bondage to feelings by insight into their conditioned origination.

THE AṄGUTTARA NIKĀYA

The Aṅguttara Nikāya offers two further examples of Mahākaccāna's exegetical skills. In one short sutta in this collection (AN 10:26) the elder interprets a verse, the meaning of which seems completely explicit as it stands, by transposing it into a figurative mode and then extracting the implicit meaning by mapping it on to a frame of systematic doctrine. Here a woman lay disciple named Kālī comes to the elder and asks him to explain in detail a verse from "The Maiden's Questions." The reference is to the story of the Buddha's encounter with Māra's daughters when they tried to seduce him in the first year after his Enlightenment (SN 4:25). The daughter Taṇha (Craving) had asked him why, instead of forming intimate relationships in the village, he squanders his time meditating alone in the woods. To this the Buddha replied:

> Having conquered the army of the pleasant and agreeable,
> Meditating alone I discovered bliss—
> The attainment of the goal, the peace of the heart.
> Therefore I do not make friends with people,
> Nor does intimacy with anyone flourish for me.

It is this verse that Kālī asks the Venerable Mahākaccāna to elucidate. The elder explicates the verse in a way that does not appear to be derivable from the words themselves. His interpretation contrasts the Buddha's attitude to the kasiṇa—the meditations on special devices for inducing concentration[21]—with that of other recluses and brahmins. He explains that some recluses and brahmins regard the attainment of the earth *k*asiṇa as the supreme goal and thereby generate this attainment. Others may take one of the other kasiṇa as supreme—the water kasiṇa, the fire kasiṇa, etc.—and reach the corresponding meditative state. But for each kasiṇa, the Blessed One has directly understood to what extent it is supreme, and having understood this, he saw its origin, danger, and the escape, and he saw the knowledge and vision of the true path and the false. Having seen all this, he understood the attainment of the goal and the peace of the heart. It is in this way, the elder concludes, that the meaning of the above verse should be understood in detail.

Interpreted by way of its apparent meaning, the verse seems to be extolling the bliss of secluded meditation above the pleasures of sensual and social contact—the very enjoyments with which Māra's daughters have been trying to tempt the Enlightened One. But Mahākaccāna gives a different twist to the meaning. For him, the contrast is not merely between sensual pleasure and meditative bliss but between two different attitudes to advanced stages of meditative absorption. The ordinary recluses and brahmins take the jhānas and other extraordinary states of consciousness attainable through the kasiṇa meditations to be the final goal of spiritual endeavor. By doing so, they fall into the trap of craving for becoming and fail to find the way to final deliverance. Because they become attached to the exalted bliss and quiet serenity of the jhānas, they cannot see that these states too are conditioned and transient and thus they cannot relinquish their attachment to them. They therefore remain caught within

Māra's domain, vanquished by his army of "agreeable and pleasant forms," however sublime such may be. But the Buddha has seen the origin (*ādi*)[22] of these attainments, i.e., craving as the origin of suffering; he has seen the danger (*ādīnava*), i.e., that they are impermanent, unsatisfactory, and subject to change; he has seen the escape (*nissaraṇa*) from them, i.e., Nibbāna; and he has obtained the knowledge and vision by which he can distinguish the true path from the false, i.e., the Noble Eightfold Path from the wrong eightfold path. By means of this fourfold knowledge, which in effect is knowledge of the Four Noble Truths, he has attained the goal, Nibbāna, experienced as the peace of heart that can arise only when all defilements have been extinguished without residue.

Finally, toward the end of the massive Aṅguttara Nikāya, we find one more sutta constructed on the same pattern as the three Majjhima Nikāya suttas. This sutta (AN 10:172) opens with a short statement of the Buddha's: "Bhikkhus, non-Dhamma should be understood, and so too Dhamma should be understood. Harm should be understood, and benefit should be understood. Having understood all this, one should practice in accordance with Dhamma, in accordance with benefit." Having said this, the Blessed One rose from his seat and entered his dwelling.

The monks then approach the Venerable Mahākaccāna to request an explanation. Following the stock formulas of protest and insistence, Mahākaccāna interprets the Buddha's injunction by way of the ten unwholesome and ten wholesome courses of kamma: taking life is non-Dhamma, abstaining from taking life is Dhamma; the numerous evil unwholesome states that arise on account of taking life—this is harm; the numerous wholesome states that arise conditioned by abstinence from taking life and that go to fulfillment by development—this is benefit. The same pattern is applied to stealing, sexual misconduct, lying, slander, harsh speech, and gossip. Finally, covetousness, ill will, and wrong view are non-Dhamma, and the evil states that arise from them are harm; non-covetousness, goodwill, and right view are Dhamma, and the wholesome states conditioned by them that go to fulfillment by development are benefit.

OTHER TEACHINGS OF MAHĀKACCĀNA

Not all the discourses spoken by Mahākaccāna take the form of commentaries on brief statements by the Buddha. He also delivered Dhamma talks that unfold along independent lines, and he was skilled in resolving the doubts of inquirers and fellow monks with his own original insights into the Teaching.

The Majjhima Nikāya contains a full-length dialogue between the great elder and King Avantiputta of Madhurā, who was (according to the commentary) the grandson of King Caṇḍappajjota of Avantī. Once, when the Venerable Mahākaccāna was dwelling at Madhurā, the king heard the favorable report that was circulating about him: "He is wise, discerning, sagacious, learned, articulate, and perspicacious; he is aged and he is an arahant." Desiring to converse with such a worthy monk, the king drove out to his hermitage to meet him, and the conversation that resulted has been recorded as the *Madhurā Sutta* (MN 84).

The question with which the king opened this dialogue did not concern a profound problem about the nature of reality or the deeper realizations of insight meditation. It revolved around a practical issue that must have been weighing heavily on the minds of many of the noble-caste rulers of the time: the attempts of the brahmins to establish their own hegemony over the entire Indian social system. The brahmins tried to justify this drive for power by appealing to their divinely ordained status. King Avantiputta relates to Mahākaccāna the claim that they had been advancing: "The brahmins are the highest caste, those of any other caste are inferior; brahmins are the fairest caste, those of any other caste are dark; only brahmins are purified, not non-brahmins; brahmins alone are the sons of Brahmā, the offspring of Brahmā, born of his mouth, born of Brahmā, created by Brahmā, heirs of Brahmā."

The Venerable Mahākaccāna, though of pedigree brahmin stock himself, was well aware of the presumption and arrogance that lay behind this proclamation. He replied that the claim of the brahmins is "just a saying in the world," one with no divine sanction at all to support it. To prove his point Mahākaccāna brought forth a powerful array of arguments in its favor: one of any social class who gains wealth can command the labor of those in the other castes; even a menial could enroll a brahmin in his service. One of any caste who violates the principles of morality would be reborn in hell, while one of any caste who observes the moral precepts would be reborn in a happy realm. One of any caste who breaks the law would be punished. One of any caste who renounces the world and becomes an ascetic would receive homage and respect. As each argument draws to a close, the king proclaims: "These four castes are all the same; there is no difference between them at all."

At the end of the discussion, after expressing his appreciation of Mahākaccāna's replies, King Avantiputta declares: "I go to Master

Kaccāna for refuge and to the Dhamma and to the Sangha of bhikkhus." But the elder corrects him: "Do not go to me for refuge, great king. Go for refuge to that same Blessed One to whom I have gone for refuge"—the Fully Enlightened Buddha. When the king asks where the Blessed One is now living, the elder explains that he has attained Parinibbāna. This reply indicates that Mahākaccāna's own death must have taken place after that of the Buddha.

The Saṁyutta Nikāya includes a sutta (SN 35:132) that shows how the Venerable Mahākaccāna's skill in handling a group of rowdy young brahmin boys helped to transform the attitude of a learned old brahmin and his entourage of pupils. On one occasion the elder was living in Avantī in a forest hut. Then a number of young brahmin boys, pupils of the renowned brahmin teacher Lohicca, drew near to the hut while collecting firewood. As the brahmins of that period often harbored hostile feelings toward the renunciant Buddhist monks, these boys, behaving as boys typically do when on a group outing, trampled around the hut, deliberately making a racket to disturb the meditating monk. They also shouted the words which the brahmins used to taunt the non-brahmin ascetics: "These bald-pated ascetic rascals, menials, swarthy offspring of the Lord's feet, are honored, respected, esteemed, worshipped, and venerated by their servile devotees."

The Venerable Mahākaccāna came out from the hut and addressed the boys with verses in which he reminded them of the ancient brahmanical ideals, so badly neglected by the brahmins of that day:

> Those men of old who excelled in virtue,
> Those brahmins who recalled the ancient rules,
> Their sense doors guarded, well protected,
> Dwelt having vanquished wrath within.
> They took delight in Dhamma and meditation,
> Those brahmins who recalled the ancient rules.
>
> But these have fallen, claiming "We recite"
> While puffed up on account of their descent.
> They conduct themselves in unrighteous ways;
> Overcome by anger, armed with various weapons,
> They transgress against both frail and firm.
>
> For one who does not guard the sense doors
> (All the vows he undertakes) are vain

Just like the wealth a man gains in a dream:
Fasting and sleeping on the ground,
Bathing at dawn, (study of) the Triple Veda,
Rough hides, matted locks, and dirt;
Hymns, rules and vows, austerities,
Hypocrisy, crookedness, rinsing the mouth:
These are the emblems of the brahmins
Performed to increase their worldly gains.

A mind that is well concentrated,
Purified and free from blemish,
Tender towards all sentient beings—
That is the path for reaching Brahmā.

When they heard this the brahmin boys were angry and displeased. On returning to their teacher, the brahmin Lohicca, they reported that the recluse Mahākaccāna was "denigrating and scorning the sacred brahmin hymns." After his first flush of anger had subsided, Lohicca, being a man of sense, realized that he should not rush to conclusions merely on the basis of hearsay reported by youngsters, but should first inquire from the monk himself whether there was any truth in their accusation. When Lohicca went to Mahākaccāna and asked him about the conversation he had with the boys, the elder reported everything as it occurred, repeating the poem. Lohicca was deeply impressed by the poem, and even more so by the ensuing discourse on how to guard the senses. At the end of the discussion not only did the brahmin go for refuge to the Triple Gem, but he invited the elder to visit his household, assuring him that "the brahmin boys and maidens there will pay homage to Master Kaccāna; they will stand up for him out of respect; they will offer him a seat and water; and that will lead to their welfare and happiness for a long time."

The Venerable Mahākaccāna seems to have had a particularly deep insight into the causal basis of human quarrels and disputes. We have already seen how he traced the causal roots of conflict in his exposition in the *Madhupiṇḍika Sutta* and his skill in transforming Lohicca's retinue of disciples. On another occasion (AN 2:4:6) a brahmin named Ārāmadaṇḍa came to him and asked: "Why is society rent by such bitter conflicts—conflicts that pit nobles against nobles, brahmins against brahmins, householders against householders?" To this the elder replied: "It is because of sensual lust, attachment, greed, and obsession with sensual pleasures that nobles fight with nobles, brahmins with brahmins, householders with householders." Next Ārāmadaṇḍa asked: "Why is it that ascetics fight with ascetics?" And Mahākaccāna replied: "It is because of lust for views, attachment, greed, and obsession with views that ascetics fight with ascetics." Finally the brahmin asked whether there was anyone in the world who had transcended both sensual lust and lust for views. Although Mahākaccāna, as an arahant, could have put himself forth as an example of such a one, with characteristic modesty and self-effacement he named instead the Blessed One, who was dwelling at Sāvatthī at the time. When this was said, the brahmin Ārāmadaṇḍa knelt down on the ground, held out his hands in reverential salutation, and exclaimed three times: "Homage to the Blessed One, the Arahant, the Fully Enlightened One."

In the next sutta (AN 2:4:7) a brahmin named Kaṇḍarāyana reproached Mahākaccāna for not showing proper respect toward aged brahmins. The elder defended himself by distinguishing the conventional usage of the words "aged" and "young" from their proper meaning within the discipline of the Noble One. On this latter criterion, even if a person is eighty, ninety, or a hundred years from birth, if he is still addicted to sensual pleasures he is reckoned as a child, not an elder. But even if a person is young, with jet black hair, endowed with the blessing of youth, if he has broken free from sensual desires, he is then reckoned as an elder.

Once the Venerable Mahākaccāna gave the monks a discourse on the six recollections (*cha anussati*)—the contemplations of the Buddha, the Dhamma, the Sangha, virtue, generosity, and the devas (AN 6:26). He declared that it is wonderful and marvellous how the Blessed One has discovered these six recollections as the way to freedom for those still trapped in the confines of the world. He describes the six recollections in exactly the same terms that the Buddha himself has used to describe the four foundations of mindfulness. They are the means "for the purification of beings, for the overcoming of sorrow and lamentation, for the passing away of pain and grief, for the arrival at the right method, and for the realization of Nibbāna."

On another occasion (AN 6:28) some elder bhikkhus were holding a discussion about the right time to approach "a monk worthy of esteem" (*manobhāvanīyo bhikkhu*). One said he should be approached after he has finished his meal, another said he should be approached in the evening, while still another contended that the early morning was the most fitting time to speak with him. Unable to reach accord, they came to Mahākaccāna with their problem. The elder replied that there were six proper times for approaching a worthy monk. The first five are when the mind is overcome and obsessed by the five mental hindrances—sensual desire, ill will, sloth and torpor, restlessness and remorse, and doubt—and one cannot find an outlet from them on one's own. The sixth occasion to approach is when one does not know a suitable object to attend to in order to reach the destruction of the cankers (*āsavakkhaya*).

It was not always with words that the Venerable Mahākaccāna taught, but also by silent example. On one such occasion the Buddha was moved to extol him in an *udāna*—an inspired utterance—preserved for us in the canonical collection of that name (Ud. 7:8). One evening the Buddha was seated in his cottage at Jeta's Grove in Sāvatthī when he saw Mahākaccāna nearby "sitting cross-legged, holding his body erect, having mindfulness with regard to the body set up and well established within him." On realizing the significance of this, the Blessed One uttered this inspired utterance:

> He who always has mindfulness
> Continually established on the body thus:
> "If there had not been, there would not be for me;
> There will not be, so there will not be for me,"
> If he dwells on this in graded steps
> In time he will pass beyond attachment.

The Udāna Commentary, in its explanation of this sutta, helps shed light on the approach that Mahākaccāna adopted to reach arahantship. Although this explanation conflicts with the account of his "instantaneous enlightenment" found in the biographical sketch of the Aṅguttara Commentary (see above, p. 216), it appears more realistic. The Udāna Commentary explains that in his endeavor to attain arahantship, Kaccāna first developed jhāna using mindfulness of the body (*kāyagatā sati*) as his subject of meditation. Taking that jhāna as his foundation, he then redirected mindfulness of the body onto the track of insight meditation (*vipassanā*), using the wisdom of insight that arose from this contemplation to realize the supramundane paths and fruits. Passing through each stage in succession, he brought his work to its consummation in the fruit of arahantship. Thereafter he would regularly adopt the same approach in order to enter the fruition attainment of arahantship (*arahattaphala-samāpatti*), the special meditative absorption, exclusive to the arahant, in which the bliss of Nibbāna is experienced even in this very life.

It was just on such an occasion, when the elder was sitting absorbed in fruition attainment, that the Buddha caught sight of him and extolled him in this inspirational verse. The couplet by which the Buddha expresses the theme of contemplation is taken, by the commentary, to signify "four-cornered emptiness" (*catukoṭi-suññatā*): the absence of "I" and "mine" in the past and present ("If there had not been, there would not be for me"), and the absence of "I" and "mine" in the future ("There will not be, so there will not be for me"). By applauding the Venerable Mahākaccāna with this inspired utterance, the Buddha has held him up as a model for later generations to emulate in the quest to overcome attachment to the world.

THE *THERAGĀTHĀ* VERSES

The *Theragāthā*, the verses of the ancient elders, includes eight verses ascribed to Mahākaccāna (494–501). These verses are in no way exceptional and merely express, in verse form, injunctions to proper discipline for monks and practical advice for householders. Although Kaccāna's verses addressed to the brahmin Lohicca did serve effectively as a didactic tool, he does not seem to have been as amply endowed with the gift of poetic expression as several of the other great disciples, such as Mahākassapa, Sāriputta, and Vaṅgīsa. His sphere of excellence was analysis and exegesis, not inspirational eloquence or artistic creativity.

The first two verses, according to the commentary, were spoken as an exhortation to the bhikkhus. One day the elder had noticed that a number of monks had laid aside their meditation practice in order to delight in work and in company. They were also growing too fond of the delicious food provided by their devoted lay supporters. He therefore admonished them thus:

> One should not do much work
> One should avoid people,
> One should not bustle (to obtain gifts).
> One who is eager and greedy for flavours
> Misses the goal that brings happiness.
>
> They knew as a bog this homage and veneration
> Obtained among devoted families.
> A subtle dart, difficult to extract,
> Honor is hard for a vile man to discard.
>
> (Thag. 494–95)

The other six verses, again according to the commentary, were spoken as exhortations to King Caṇḍappajjota. The king, it is said, placed faith in the brahmins and performed animal sacrifices at their behest; he also would impose penalties and confer favors arbitrarily, presumably on account of that impulsive temperament of his that earned him the title "the Violent." Therefore, to dissuade the king from such reckless behavior, the elder recited the next four verses:

It is not on account of another
That a mortal's kamma is evil.
On one's own accord one should not resort to evil,
For mortals have kamma as their kinsmen.

One is not a thief by another's word,
One is not a sage by another's word;
It is as one knows oneself
That the devas also know one.

Others do not understand
That we all come to an end here.
But those wise ones who understand this
Thereby settle their quarrels.[23]

The wise man lives indeed
Even despite the loss of his wealth.
But if one does not obtain wisdom,
Then even though rich one is not alive.

(Thag. 496–99)

The last two stanzas were spoken by the elder when the king came to him one day and informed him of a disturbing dream he had seen the previous night:

One hears all with the ear,
One sees all with the eye,
The wise man should not reject
Everything that is seen and heard.

One with eyes should be as if blind,
One with ears as if deaf,
One with wisdom as if mute,

One with strength as if feeble.
Then, when the goal has been attained,
One may lie upon one's death bed.

(Thag. 500–501)

The commentary explains the purport of the verses thus: A wise person should not reject everything, but should first investigate virtues and faults and then should reject whatever should be rejected and accept whatever is acceptable. Therefore, in regard to what should be rejected, though one possesses vision one should be as if blind, and though able to hear, one should be as if deaf. When tempted to speak what is unfit to be uttered, one who is intelligent and a good speaker should be as if dumb; and in regard to what should not be done, one who is strong should be as if feeble.

The last line is ambiguous, in the Pāli as well, and the commentary interprets it in two different ways: When a task that should be done has arisen, one should investigate it and not neglect it even if one is lying on one's death bed. Alternatively, if a task that one should not do has arisen, one should prefer to die—to lie down on one's death bed—rather than do it. Neither explanation sounds convincing, and the sense consonant with the spirit of the *Theragāthā* as a whole would seem to be: One should die as one who has attained the goal, i.e., as an arahant.

THE EXEGETICAL TREATISES

Before concluding this survey of the Venerable Mahākaccāna's contribution to the Buddha's Dispensation, we should briefly take note that the Theravāda tradition ascribes to him two exegetical treatises—the *Peṭakopadesa* and the *Nettippakaraṇa*—and an influential grammar of the Pāli language called the *Kaccāyana-Vyākaraṇa.* The two treatises are not included in the Pāli Canon (except in Burma, where they were lately incorporated into the Sutta Piṭaka), but they have exerted a major influence on the evolution of Theravādin exegetical method.

Bhikkhu Ñāṇamoli, who translated both works into English, holds that the *Nettippakaraṇa* is a later, more refined version of the *Peṭakopadesa.*[24] Both deal with essentially the same method of exegesis, which in the *Nettippakaraṇa* is clearer and more streamlined. The method is designed to elicit from the Buddha's discourses the unifying principles that underlie the variegated expressions of the Dhamma. It is founded on the assumption that beneath the many diverse utterances of the Master, spoken in accordance with the temperament and situation of the auditors, there runs a single consistent system, which with the right exegetical techniques can be extracted from the particular statement under investigation and displayed in its unadorned essence. The *Nettippakaraṇa* is intended to define that system.

The *Netti*, as Ven. Ñāṇamoli has explained, is not itself a commentary but a guide for commentators. It explicates not so much the teachings themselves (except by way of exemplification) as the tools that are to be used to elicit the structural elements that underlie and shape the expression of the teachings. Its methodology is set up under two main headings, the phrasing (*byañjana*) and the meaning (*attha*). The phrasing is handled by sixteen "modes of conveyance" (*hāra*), techniques of verbal and logical analysis that can be applied to any specified passage in order to extract the principles that lie behind the verbal formulation and logical organization of its content. The meaning is handled by three methods or "guidelines" (*naya*). These take the meaning to be the aim or goal of the doctrine (the Pāli word *attha* signifies both "meaning" and "goal"), which is the attainment of Nibbāna, and then disclose how the teaching in question "signifies" the attainment of that goal. Two additional methods are then proposed for correlating the sutta's terminology with the methods for explicating the meaning.[25] The method is applied by the subcommentaries to the first sutta of each of the four Nikāyas in special supplements to the main portion of the subcommentary.[26] A commentary on the *Netti*, attributed to Ācariya Dhammapāla, also exists.

The colophons of both exegetical treatises—the *Peṭakopadesa* and the *Nettippakaraṇa*—attribute them to the Buddha's disciple Mahākaccāna. The *Netti* colophon states further that it was approved by the Blessed One and recited at the original Buddhist Council. Western scholars have been inclined to dismiss the ascription of authorship to Mahākaccāna as fanciful. Ven. Ñāṇamoli, however, in the introduction to his translation of the *Netti*, offers an explanation that preserves at least a grain of credibility in the traditional Buddhist view without falling into the opposite extreme of credulity.[27]

Ven. Ñāṇamoli proposes that we distinguish between the authorship of the *exegetical method* on the one hand, and the authorship of the *treatises* on the other. He suggests as a hypothesis—possible though neither provable nor refutable—that the Elder Mahākaccāna and his lineage of pupils in Avantī may have formulated a compendious method for interpreting the Buddha's discourses, and that this method—or at least its elements—may have been discussed at the early Councils and transmitted orally in skeletal form. At a later date, the method could have given birth to a treatise intended to coordinate its elements and to illustrate their application to specific texts. This treatise eventually became the *Peṭakopadesa.* Some time later, perhaps even centuries later, a more polished and perspicuous version of the same work was made, this being the *Nettippakaraṇa.* As the original methodology embedded in these treatises was derived from the Venerable Mahākaccāna, or at any rate was believed to have been derived from him, out of reverence for its architect—and also perhaps to boost the prestige of the treatises—their compilers billed him as the author. G. P. Malalasekera offers a parallel hypothesis to explain the imputed authorship of the Pāli grammar, the *Kaccāyana-Vyākaraṇa,* to the Buddha's great disciple.[28]

While such propositions must remain conjectural, as both Ven. Ñāṇamoli and Malalasekera themselves acknowledge, the type of detailed analysis of textual statements found in the *Nettippakaraṇa* is consonant with the approach that the historical Mahākaccāna brought to bear on the interpretation of the Buddha's brief utterances. Thus it would seem that even if no direct connection actually exists between the great elder and the ancient Pāli treatises ascribed to him, the fact remains that they embody the spirit that he represented. This spirit, so evident in the suttas that record his elucidations of the Buddha's Word, couples acuity of insight with terseness of expression, precision of formulation with profundity of meaning. It was on the basis of such skills that the Enlightened One named him the foremost master of doctrinal exposition, and it is this that constitutes his outstanding contribution to the Buddha's Dispensation.

CHAPTER 7

GREAT WOMEN DISCIPLES OF THE BUDDHA

Hellmuth Hecker

VISĀKHĀ: THE BUDDHA'S CHIEF PATRONESS

IN THE CITY OF BHADDIYA in the country of Aṅga there lived a rich man named Meṇḍaka. In an earlier life, in a time of famine, he had given the last provisions belonging to him and his family to a paccekabuddha, a privately enlightened one. For this sacrifice, this self-conquest, he obtained supernatural merit in his present life: the provisions in his house were never exhausted, however much he consumed them or gave them away, and his fields carried a rich harvest without interruption.

It was not Meṇḍaka alone who possessed supernatural merit. His wife, his son and daughter-in-law, and his slave had all shared in the same past deed of self-abnegation in that earlier life, and as a result they had all acquired miraculous powers in their present life. Their shared participation in that noble deed had become a bond uniting them in successive existences as they transmigrated through the round of rebirths. The son Dhanañjaya and his wife Sumanādevī had a young daughter named Visākhā, who was also a repository of past merits. In a previous life, one hundred thousand aeons earlier, she had formed the aspiration at the feet of the Buddha Padumuttara to become the chief patroness of a Buddha and his Sangha. To fulfill this goal she had performed virtuous deeds under many previous Buddhas, accumulating the spiritual perfections required of a great disciple. Now that merit had matured and was about to yield its fruit.[1]

One day, when Visākhā was seven years of age, the Buddha arrived in the city of Bhaddiya accompanied by a great retinue of monks. When Meṇḍaka heard that the Awakened One had come, he sent for his beloved granddaughter and said to her: "Dear girl, this is a happy day for us, for the Teacher has arrived in our own city. Summon all your maid-servants and go out to meet him."

Visākhā did as she was told. She approached the Blessed One, paid homage to him, and stood to one side. The Buddha then taught the Dhamma to her and her entourage, and at the end of the discourse Visākhā and all her five hundred maid-servants were established in the fruit of stream-entry. Meṇḍaka too listened to the Dhamma—along with his wife, his son and daughter in-law, and his slave—and all attained to stream-entry.

At that time the country of Aṅga belonged to the kingdom of Magadha, which was ruled by the devout King Bimbisāra. When King Pasenadi of Kosala heard that five people of supernatural merit were living in the neighboring kingdom, he requested King Bimbisāra, his friend and brother-in-law, to send one of these people to his own country, the state of Kosala, so that his subjects would have the opportunity to witness a shining example of virtue. Thus Meṇḍaka's son Dhanañjaya, along with his family, moved to the country of Kosala and built a beautiful city named Sāketa near the capital Sāvatthī. There Visākhā grew up in the midst of this saintly family where the Blessed One was highly venerated and his monks were frequently invited to receive alms and to preach the noble Dhamma.

In Sāvatthī, the capital of Kosala, there lived a wealthy householder named Migāra, who had a son named Puṇṇavaddhana. When the son reached manhood his parents urged him to marry, but Puṇṇavaddhana insisted that he would take as wife only a girl who possessed the "five beauties"—beauty of hair, beauty of flesh, beauty of teeth, beauty of skin, and beauty of youth. His parents employed a team of brahmins to explore the entire country looking for a girl who could meet their son's stringent requirements. The brahmins traveled to all the great towns and cities, searching diligently, but they could not find a single maiden endowed with all five kinds of beauty. On their return journey, when they reached Sāketa, they saw Visākhā, who at that time was fifteen or sixteen years of age. They were struck immediately by her beautiful features, which measured up to four of their young lord's expectations; the one feature they could not see was her teeth. To obtain a glimpse of this, they decided to engage her in conversation.

When they spotted her, Visākhā and her companions were on their way to the river to bathe. Just then a thunderstorm burst. The other girls ran away hastily to avoid getting wet, but Visākhā continued to walk with great dignity and poise. The brahmins approached her and asked why she did not run for shelter like the others. She answered: "Just as it is unbecoming for a king to run from the rain like an ordinary man, so it is unbecoming for a young girl of good family to run from the rain. Besides, as an unmarried girl I have to take care of myself, as if tending merchandise offered for sale, so that I may not suffer damage and become useless."[2] The brahmins were so impressed by their conversation with this girl that they went to her father and asked for her hand in marriage for their lord's son. Dhanañjaya agreed to the proposal, and soon afterwards the householder Migāra with his son Puṇṇavaddhana and his whole family went to fetch the bride. When King Pasenadi of Kosala heard of it, he joined the group together with his entire court.

All these people were entertained joyfully and lavishly in Sāketa by the bride's father. Meanwhile goldsmiths were manufacturing the jewelry for the bride. After three months the jewelry was not yet completed, but the firewood was used up cooking meals for so many guests. For two weeks old houses were demolished and the wood used for cooking. The jewelry was still not complete. The people of Sāketa then took clothes out of their wardrobes, soaked them with oil, and used them to kindle the cooking fires. After another two weeks the jewelry was complete, and the whole splendid assembly began the return journey.

Dhanañjaya gave to his daughter as dowry many hundreds of carts laden with silk, gold, silver, and servant girls. He also gave her a herd of cattle so large that all the roads in the city were choked. When these cattle left the stables, the remaining cows also tore their ropes and joined the traveling herd. People from fourteen villages belonging to Dhanañjaya wanted to follow Visākhā to her new home, so much was she liked everywhere. Such abundant wealth and such a large retinue Visākhā had obtained through acts of merit in many earlier lives, since she had already served the Buddha Padumuttara countless aeons ago.

When Visākhā took leave of her father, he gave her ten maxims of advice in metaphorical form and admonished her always to keep the virtue of generosity in high regard. He also appointed eight confidential advisers to examine carefully any complaint that might be raised against his daughter. The ten maxims her father gave her are as follows: (1) do not carry outside the indoor fire, (2) do not take inside the outdoor fire, (3) give only to those that give, (4) do not give to those that do not give, (5) give both to those that give and do not give, (6) sit happily, (7) eat happily, (8) sleep happily, (9) tend the fire, and (10) honor the household divinities.

Their implied meaning is as follows: (1) the wife should not speak ill of her husband and parents-in-law to others; neither should their shortcomings or household quarrels be reported elsewhere; (2) a wife should not listen to the reports and stories of other households; (3) things should be lent only to those who return them; (4) no article should be lent to those who do not return them; (5) poor relatives and friends should be helped even if they do not repay; (6) a wife should sit in a becoming way; on seeing her parents-in-law or her husband, she should keep standing and not sit; (7) before partaking of her meals, a wife should first see that her parents-in-law and husband are served, and should also see that her servants are well cared for; (8) before going to bed at night, a wife should see that all doors are closed, that the furniture is safe, that the servants have performed their duties, and that her parents-in-law have retired; as a rule a wife should rise early in the morning and, unless unwell, she should not sleep during the day; (9) parents-in-law and husband should be regarded as fire; and one should deal carefully with them as one would with fire; and (10) parents-in-law and husband should be regarded as divinities.

On the day she arrived in Sāvatthī, the city of her husband, Visākhā was showered with various presents sent from people of all ranks according to their status and ability. But so kind and generous was she that she distributed them among the donors themselves with a kind message and treated all the residents of the city as her own kinsfolk. By this noble gesture she endeared herself to all the people of the city on the very first day that she came to her husband's home.

There is an incident in her life which reveals her dutiful kindness even toward animals. Hearing that her well-bred mare had given birth to a foal in the middle of the night, immediately Visākhā rushed to the stable with her female attendants bearing torches in their hands, and attended to all the mare's needs with the greatest care and attention.

Her father-in-law Migāra, being a staunch follower of an order of naked ascetics, never invited the Buddha to his house for alms, even though the Master frequently dwelt at a nearby monastery. Shortly after the wedding, to obtain merit, he invited a large company of naked ascetics for alms, whom he treated with deep respect and presented with fine foods. On their arrival he told his new daughter-in-law, "Come, dear, and render homage to the arahants." Visākhā was delighted to hear the word "arahants" and hurried to the hall, expecting to see Buddhist monks. But she saw only naked ascetics devoid of all modesty, a sight that was unbearable for such a refined lady. She reproached her father-in-law and retired to her quarters without entertaining them. The naked ascetics took offense and reproached the millionaire for having brought a female follower of the ascetic Gotama to his house. They asked him to expel her from the house immediately, but Migāra, with much effort, managed to pacify them.

One day, while Migāra was eating rich rice porridge mixed with honey in a golden bowl, a Buddhist monk came to the house in quest of alms. Visākhā was fanning her father-in-law. She stepped to the side so that Migāra could see the monk and give him alms; but though the monk was in full view, Migāra pretended not to notice him and continued with his meal. So Visākhā told the monk, "Pass on, venerable sir. My father-in-law is eating stale food."[3] Migāra was furious at this remark and wanted to throw his daughter-in-law out of the house, but the servants—who had been brought to the house by Visākhā herself—refused to carry out his orders. The eight advisors, to whom Migāra's complaint against Visākhā was put, concluded on examination of the matter that Visākhā was blameless.

After this incident Visākhā informed her husband's family that she would be returning to her parents. Migāra asked her forgiveness, and Visākhā consented to stay, on the condition that she would be permitted to invite the Buddha and the order of monks to the house. Reluctantly he gave his consent, but following the advice of the naked ascetics he did not serve the monks personally. Just to be polite, he appeared shortly after the meal and then concealed himself behind a curtain while listening to the Buddha's sermon. However, the Buddha's words moved him so deeply that, while sitting there hidden from view, he penetrated the ultimate truth about the nature of existence and attained to stream-entry. Filled with overwhelming gratitude he told Visākhā that from now onwards he would respect her like his own mother, and accordingly he called her Migāra-mātā, which means "Mother of Migāra." He then went up to the Blessed One, prostrated at his feet, and declared his allegiance to the Triple Gem. Visākhā invited the Buddha for the next day's meal, and on that occasion her mother-in-law too attained stream-entry. From that time on the entire family became staunch supporters of the Enlightened One and his community of monks and nuns.

In course of time Visākhā gave birth to no less than ten sons and ten daughters, and all of them had the same number of descendants down to the fourth generation. Visākhā herself lived to the remarkably high age of 120, but (according to the commentaries) all her life she retained the appearance of a sixteen-year-old girl. This was the result of her merit and her enjoyment of the Dhamma, which filled her completely throughout the day. It is also said that she was as strong as an elephant and could work untiringly looking after her large family. She found time to feed the monks every day, to visit the monasteries, and to ensure that none of the monks and nuns lacked food, clothing, shelter, bedding, and medicines. Above all she still found time to listen to the Teaching of the Blessed One again and again. Therefore the Blessed One said about her: "Visākhā stands foremost among my women lay supporters who serve as supporters of the Order" (AN 1, chap. 14).

One illustration of this is specifically mentioned in the Vinaya Piṭaka. One day Visākhā left her valuable bridal jewelry in the hall after listening to the Dhamma, and it was taken into custody by Ānanda (Vin. 4:161). She interpreted this lapse as an invitation to do good and decided not to wear this jewelry again, but to sell it and to give alms to the Order from the money obtained. But in the whole city of Sāvatthī there was no one who could buy this very precious jewelry. So she bought it herself out of her other property, and with the proceeds of the sale she built a large monastic establishment in the Eastern Park (Pubbārāma) before the city gate of Sāvatthī. It was called the Mansion of Migāra's Mother (Migāramātu-pāsāda). It is often mentioned in the introduction to many Buddhist suttas, for the Blessed One frequently stayed there during the last twenty years of his life, just as he did in the Jetavana monastery built by his other great patron, Anāthapiṇḍika.

In the Pāli Canon several episodes from the life of Visākhā are reported. Once some noble disciples requested her to take their wives to see the Blessed One. She did so, but some of the women were drunk and behaved improperly. She asked the Blessed One how the evil of intoxicating drink originated, and he told her the *Kumbha Jātaka* (Jāt. 512): In the forest a man had found the juice of fermented fruits in the hollow of a tree, tasted it, and felt wonderfully elated. Again and again he provided himself with this enjoyment, so that he soon became a drunkard; he also enticed many of his friends and relatives to drinking, and they in turn spread the bad habit to others. The whole of India would soon have become addicted to liquor if Sakka, king of the devas, had not interceded. He appeared to the humans and explained to them the evil consequences of intoxicating drink.

On another occasion, when Visākhā sent some valuable gifts to her relatives in the country of Aṅga, the guards at the border wanted to levy a very high custom's duty on them. She reported this to the king, but he left the matter unattended to, being occupied with affairs of state. Visākhā went to the Blessed One and asked his advice. The Buddha spoke only a few short verses which relieved her of her worry and anger:

> Painful is all subjection;
> Blissful is complete control;
> People are troubled in common concerns,
> Hard to escape are the bonds.
>
> (Ud. 2:9)

Again, another time she went to see the Blessed One in the middle of the day, in spite of the hot sun: her favorite grandchild Dattā, who had always helped her to distribute alms, had suddenly passed away. When she told the Blessed One of her sorrow, he asked whether she wanted to have as many children and grandchildren as there were people in the city of Sāvatthī. She joyfully agreed. "But how many people die in Sāvatthī every day?" asked the Blessed One. She considered and said: "O Lord, in Sāvatthī ten or nine people, five or three, or two people, but at least one person is dying every day. Sāvatthī is never free from dying." Being asked whether in this case she would ever be without sorrow, she had to admit that she would feel sorrow every single day. The Blessed One said: "Those who have one hundred loved ones have one hundred sorrows, those who have ninety...five...four...three...two...one loved one have one sorrow, but those who have no loved ones have no sorrow. These alone, I say, are without sorrow, without suffering, without desperation" (Ud. 8:8).

In three suttas in the Aṅguttara Nikāya the Blessed One answers questions put by Visākhā. On a full-moon day she came to her monastery and greeted the Buddha. Asked why she had come, she said she was keeping the Uposatha day, the day devoted entirely to learning and practicing the Dhamma. On this unspoken request for instruction the Blessed One gave a lengthy discourse (AN 3:70) on the two wrong ways and one right way to keep the Uposatha. The Uposatha of cowherds and ordinary householders consists of thinking about the enjoyments of tomorrow while observing ascetic rules today. The Uposatha of the Jains consists of showing loving-kindness to some people, while at the same time boasting of one's own freedom from sense enjoyments. The true Uposatha day of the noble ones consists of observance of the Eight Precepts and reflection on the greatness of the Blessed One, the Dhamma, and the Sangha, and on the devas and one's own virtues.[4] The Buddha went on to describe the happy and carefree life of the gods up to the Brahma-world, concluding: "Miserable is the glory of humans compared to such heavenly bliss."

Another question of Visākhā concerned the qualities in a woman that lead to her rebirth in the company of "the graceful gods" (*manāpakāyikā devā*). In answer the Blessed One stated eight conditions (AN 8:47): (1) she is always an agreeable and pleasant companion to her husband, irrespective of his own conduct; (2) she honors and looks after the people who are dear to her husband—his parents and the wise men worshipped by him; (3) in her housework she is industrious and careful; (4) she supervises the servants well and cares for them properly, considers their health and their food; (5) she guards her husband's property and does not dissipate his wealth; (6) she takes refuge in the Blessed One, the Dhamma, and the Sangha; (7) she observes the Five Precepts; and (8) she delights in generosity and renunciation.

A third question was: Which qualities in a woman would enable her to conquer this world and the next? The Blessed One answered: She conquers this world by industry, care for her servants, love for her husband, and guarding his property; the other world, by faith, virtue, generosity, and wisdom (AN 8:49).

The promulgation of a number of rules for the Sangha is connected with Visākhā. Thus, for instance, one of her nephews had decided to join the Order as a monk. But when he requested acceptance into the Order in Sāvatthī the monks there told him that they had agreed among themselves not to ordain novices during the three months' rains retreat, and therefore he should wait until the rains retreat was over. But when the rainy season had passed he had given up the idea of becoming a monk. When Visākhā came to know of this, she went to the Blessed One and said: "The Dhamma is timeless, there is no time when the Dhamma cannot be followed." The Blessed One prescribed that ordination should not be refused during the rainy season (Vin. 1:153).

Once when the Blessed One and his monks were guests of Visākhā she requested him to grant her eight boons (Vin. 1:290–94). He replied that the Perfect One had gone beyond the fulfilling of boons. She said that she did not wish for something blameworthy but for allowable things. The Blessed One let her mention her wishes. She requested to give gifts to the Order in eight ways: (1) robes for the rains, (2) food for arriving monks, (3) food for monks setting out on a journey, (4) medicine for sick monks, (5) food for sick monks, (6) food for monks tending the sick, (7) regular distribution of rice gruel, and (8) bathing robes for nuns to bathe in the river.

The Blessed One then asked her for which special reasons she made these requests. She explained in detail: (1) some monks had been forced to walk half-naked in the streaming rain to preserve their robes and thus were mistaken for naked ascetics; therefore she wanted to give rains' robes; (2) newly arrived monks in Sāvatthī, who did not know the town yet, had difficulty obtaining food, and had to walk for alms despite their weariness from their journey. Therefore all arriving monks should be sent to her to receive food; (3) in the same way she would like to give a good meal to monks setting out on a journey; (4) and (5) sick monks have to suffer much, and may even die, if they lack suitable food and medicine; therefore she would like to cook food for the sick; (6) a monk tending the sick had to go on alms round for himself as well as for the sick monk; he could easily be late, and both would not be able to eat after noon because the meal time had already passed; therefore she wanted to provide food for monks tending the sick; (7) she had also heard how many benefits were connected with rice gruel in the early morning, so she would like to provide gruel to the Order; and (8) it was unsuitable for nuns to bathe without clothes, as had happened recently; therefore she would like to provide them with a suitable covering.

After Visākhā had thus explained in detail the external benefits of her wishes, the Blessed One asked her what inner benefits she expected. Her answer shows how subtly and profoundly she had grasped the distinction between outward acts of virtue and inner mental training. She replied:

> As to that, Lord, bhikkhus who have spent the rains in different regions will come to Sāvatthī to see the Blessed One. They will approach the Blessed One and question him thus: "Lord, the bhikkhu named so-and-so has died. What is his destination? What is his rebirth?" The Blessed One will tell how such a one had reached the fruit of stream-entry, or of once-returning, or of non-returning, or of arahantship. I shall approach the bhikkhus and ask: "Lords, did that bhikkhu ever come to Sāvatthī?" If they answer that he did, I shall conclude that surely a rains cloth will have been used by that bhikkhu or visitors' food or food for one going on a journey or food for the sick or food for a sick-nurse or medicine for the sick or the morning rice-gruel. When I remember it, I shall be glad. When I am glad, I shall be happy. When my mind is happy, my body will be tranquil. When my body is tranquil, I shall feel pleasure. When I feel pleasure, my mind will become concentrated. That will bring the development of the spiritual faculties in me and also the development of the spiritual powers and the enlightenment factors.[5] This, Lord, is the benefit I foresee for myself in asking the eight boons of the Perfect One.

"Good, good, Visākhā!" the Enlightened One replied. "It is good that you have asked the Perfect One for the eight boons foreseeing these benefits. I grant you the eight boons."

So lived Visākhā, "Migāra's Mother," a model female lay devotee, endowed with unwavering confidence in the Triple Gem, securely settled in the fruit of stream-entry, bound for a happy rebirth and, in the end, for final deliverance from suffering.

MALLIKĀ: THE FLOWER-GIRL QUEEN

At the time of the Buddha, a daughter was born to the foreman of the guild of garland-makers in Sāvatthī. She was beautiful, clever, and well behaved and a source of joy to her father. Her name was Mallikā.

One day, when she had just turned sixteen, she went to the public flower gardens with her girlfriends, taking three portions of fermented rice along in her basket for her meal.[6] When she was just leaving by the city gate, a group of ascetics came into town to obtain alms. Their leader stood out: one whose grandeur and sublime beauty impressed her so much that she impulsively offered him all the food in her basket.

That great ascetic was the Buddha, the Awakened One. He let her put her offering into his bowl. After Mallikā—without knowing to whom she had given the food—had prostrated at his feet, she walked on full of joy. The Buddha smiled. Ānanda, who knew that the Enlightened One does not smile without a reason, asked why. The Buddha replied that this girl would reap the benefits of her gift this very same day by becoming the queen of Kosala.

This sounded unbelievable. How could the king of Kosala elevate a woman of low caste to the rank of queen? In the India of those days, with its very strict caste system, this seemed quite impossible.

The ruler over the united kingdom of Benares and Kosala in the Ganges Valley was King Pasenadi, the mightiest monarch of his day. At that time he was at war with his neighbor, Ajātasattu, the parricide king of Magadha. The latter had won a battle and King Pasenadi had been forced to retreat. As he was returning to his capital on his horse, just before he entered the city he heard a girl sing in the flower gardens. It was Mallikā, who was singing melodiously because of her joy in meeting the illustrious sage. The king was enchanted by the song and rode into the gardens. Mallikā did not run away from the strange warrior, but came nearer, took the horse by its reins, and looked straight into the king's eyes. He asked her whether she was already married and she replied in the negative. Thereupon he dismounted, lay down with his head in her lap, and let her console him about his ill luck in battle.

After he had recovered, he let her mount his horse behind him and took her back to the house of her parents. In the evening he sent an entourage with much pomp to fetch her and made her his principal wife and queen.

From then on she was dearly beloved to the king. She was given many loyal servants and in her beauty she resembled a goddess. It became known throughout the whole kingdom that because of her simple gift she had been elevated to the highest position in the state and this induced her subjects to be kind and generous toward their fellow men. Wherever she went, people would joyously proclaim: "That is Queen Mallikā, who gave alms to the Buddha."

After she had become queen, she soon went to visit the Enlightened One to ask him something that was puzzling her: how it came about that one woman could be beautiful, wealthy, and of great power; another beautiful but poor and powerless; yet another ugly, rich, and very powerful; and finally, another ugly, poor, and powerless. These differences can constantly be observed in daily life. But while the ordinary person is satisfied with such commonplace explanations as fate, heredity, and chance, Queen Mallikā wanted to probe deeper, for she was convinced that nothing happens without a cause.

The Buddha explained to her in great detail that the qualities and living conditions of people everywhere reflect the moral nature of their deeds in earlier lives. Beauty was caused by patience and gentleness, prosperity by generosity, and power by never envying others but rather by rejoicing in their success. Whichever of these three virtues a person had cultivated would show up as their "destiny," usually in some mixture of the three. Only rarely would a person be favorably endowed with all three attributes. After Mallikā had listened to this discourse, she resolved in her heart to be always gentle toward her subjects and never to scold them; to give alms to all monks, brahmins, and the poor; and never to envy anyone who was happy. At the end of the Buddha's talk she took refuge in the Triple Gem and remained a faithful disciple for the rest of her life (AN 4:197).

Mallikā showed her great generosity not only by giving regular alms but also by building a large, ebony-lined hall for the Sangha, which was used for religious discussions (MN 78; DN 9). She exhibited her gentleness by serving her husband with the five qualities of a perfect wife: by always rising before him, by going to bed after him, by always obeying his commands, by always being polite, and by using only kind words. Even the monks praised her gentleness in their discussions about virtue.

Soon she was to prove that she was also free of jealousy. The king had decided to marry another wife and brought a cousin of the Buddha home as his second chief queen. Although it is said that it is in the nature of a woman not to allow a rival into her home, Mallikā related to the other wife without the slightest malice (AN 6:52). Both women lived in peace and harmony at the court. Even when the second wife gave birth to a son, the crown prince, and Mallikā had only a daughter, she was not envious. When the king voiced disappointment about the birth of that daughter, the Buddha said to him that if a woman was clever, virtuous, well behaved and faithful, she was superior to a man. Then she might become the wife of a great king and give birth to a mighty ruler (SN 3:16). When the daughter, Princess Vajirā, grew up, she in fact became queen of Magadha.

After Mallikā had become a faithful lay devotee of the Buddha, she also won her husband over to the Dhamma. That happened as follows: One night the king had a succession of sixteen disturbing dreams during which he heard gruesome, unfathomable sounds from four voices, which uttered: "*Du, Sa, Na, So.*" He woke up in the middle of the night, gripped by terror, and sitting upright, trembling, he awaited the sunrise. The next day, when his brahmin priests asked him whether he had slept well, he related the terror of the night and asked them what he should do to counteract such a menace. The brahmins declared that he would have to offer a great sacrifice to pacify the evil spirits, and out of fear the king agreed to this suggestion.

The brahmins rejoiced, thinking of the gifts they would surely reap for conducting the sacrifice, and they busily began to make preparations. They had a sacrificial altar built and many animals tied to posts as victims for the offering. For greater efficacy, they demanded the sacrifice of four human beings as well, and these also awaited their death, tied to posts.

When Mallikā became aware of all this activity, she went to the king and asked him why the brahmins were running about so busily full of joyous expectation. The king replied that she did not pay enough attention to him and did not know his sorrows. Thereupon he told her of his dreams. Mallikā asked the king whether he had also consulted the first and best of brahmins about the meaning of the dreams: the Buddha, the foremost in the world of gods and humans, the best of all brahmins. King Pasenadi decided to ask the Awakened One's advice and went to the Jetavana monastery.

He related his dreams to the Buddha and asked him what would happen to him. "Nothing," the Awakened One replied, and explained the meaning to him. The sixteen dreams, he said, were prophecies showing that living conditions on earth would deteriorate steadily due to the increasing moral laxity of the kings. In a meditative moment, King Pasenadi had been able to see future occurrences within his sphere of interest because he was a monarch concerned with the well-being of his subjects.

The four voices which he had heard belonged to four men who had lived in Sāvatthī and had been seducers of married women. Because of that they were reborn in hell and for thirty thousand years they drowned in red-hot cauldrons, coming nearer and nearer to the fire, which intensified their unbearable suffering. During another thirty thousand years they slowly rose up in those iron cauldrons and had now come to the rim, where they could once again at least breathe the air of the human realm.

Each one wanted to speak a verse, but because of the gravity of the deed, could not get past the first syllable. Not even in sighs could they voice their suffering, because they had long lost the gift of speech. The four verses, which start in Pāli with *du, sa, na,* and *so,* were recognized by the Buddha as follows:

Du: Dung-like life we lived,
No willingness to give.
Although we could have given much,
We did not make our refuge thus.

Sa: Say, the end is near?
Already 60,000 years have gone;
Without respite the torture is
In this realm of hell.

Na: Naught, no end near. Oh, would it end!
No end in sight for us.
Who once did misdeeds here
For me, for you, for both of us.

So: So, could I only leave this place
And raise myself to the human realm,
I would be kind and moral too,
And do good deeds abundantly.

After the king had heard these explanations, he became responsive to the request of the compassionate queen. He granted freedom to the imprisoned men and animals and ordered the sacrificial altar to be destroyed (Jāt. 77, 314).

The king, who had become a devoted lay disciple of the Buddha, visited him one day again and met a wise and well-learned layman there. The king asked him whether he could give some daily Dhamma teaching to his two queens and the other ladies of the palace. The layman replied that the teaching came from the Enlightened One and only one of his ordained disciples could pass it on to the women. The king understood this and requested the Buddha to give permission to one of his monks to teach. The Buddha appointed the Venerable Ānanda for this task. Queen Mallikā learned easily in spite of her uneducated background, but Queen Vasabhakhattiyā, cousin of the Buddha and mother of the crown-prince, was unconcentrated and learned with difficulty (Vin. 4:158).

One day the royal couple looked down upon the river from the palace and saw a group of the Buddha's monks playing about in the water. The king said to Queen Mallikā reproachfully: "Those playing about in the water are supposed to be arahants." Such was the reputation of this group of the so-called seventeen monks, who were quite young and of good moral conduct. Mallikā replied that she could only explain it thus, that either the Buddha had not made any rules with regard to bathing or that the monks were not acquainted with them, because they were not among the rules which were recited regularly.

Both agreed that it would not make a good impression on laypeople and on those monks not yet secure if those in higher training played about in the water and enjoyed themselves in the way of untrained worldly people. But King Pasenadi wanted to avoid blackening those monks' characters and just wanted to give the Buddha a hint, so that he could lay down a firm rule. He conceived the idea to send a special gift to the Buddha to be taken by those monks. They brought the gift and the Buddha asked them on what occasion they had met the king. Then they told him what they had done, and the Buddha laid down a corresponding rule (Vin. 4:112).

One day when the king was standing on the parapet of the palace with the queen and was looking down upon the land, he asked her whether there was anyone in the world that she loved more than herself. He expected her to name *him,* since he flattered himself to have been the one who had raised her to fame and fortune. But although she loved him, she remained truthful and replied that she knew of no one dearer to her than herself. Then she wanted to know how it was with him: Did he love anyone—possibly her—more than himself? Thereupon the king also had to admit that in his case too self-love was predominant. But he went to the Buddha and recounted the conversation to find out how a sage would consider this.

The Buddha confirmed their statements, but drew from them a lesson in compassion and nonviolence:

> Having traversed all quarters with the mind,
> One finds none anywhere dearer than oneself.
> For others too each holds himself most dear;
> Hence one who loves himself should not harm others.
>
> (SN 3:8; Ud. 5:1)

One day a man came to the Buddha utterly distraught over the death of his only child. He could not eat, could not work; he had become depressed, and spent all his time in the charnel ground, crying out, "Where are you, my only child? Where are you, my only child?" The Buddha taught him a tough lesson: "Those who are dear bring sorrow, lamentation, pain, grief, and despair"—the suffering that results from attachment. Though his own experience bore out the Buddha's words, the man resented this maxim and left in an angry mood. The conversation was reported to the king, and he asked his wife whether it was really true that sorrow could result from love. "If the Awakened One has said so, O king, then it is so," she replied devotedly.

The king demurred that she accepted every word of the Buddha's like a disciple from a guru. Thereupon she sent a messenger to the Buddha to ask if the report were true and to obtain more details. The Buddha confirmed it and gave a fuller explanation. But Mallikā did not pass the Buddha's reply on directly to the king. Instead she used an indirect approach. She asked him whether he loved his daughter, his second wife, the crown prince, herself, and his kingdom. Naturally he confirmed this: these five were dear to him and deeply loved. But if something happened to these five, Mallikā inquired, would he not feel sorrow, lamentation, pain, grief, and despair, which comes from such love? Then the king understood and realized how wisely the Buddha could penetrate all existence: "Very well then, Mallikā, continue to venerate him." And the king rose, uncovered his shoulder, prostrated deferentially in the direction where the Blessed One was residing, and saluted him three times: "Homage to the Blessed One, the Arahant, the Fully Awakened One!" (MN 87).

But their lives together did not remain altogether free of conflict. One day an argument arose between the couple about the duties of the queen. For some reason the king had become angry at her and was treating her as if she had disappeared into thin air. When the Buddha arrived at the palace the next day for his meal, he asked about the queen, who had always been present earlier. Pasenadi scowled and said: "What about her? She has gone mad because of her fame." The Buddha replied that he himself had raised her up to that position and should therefore be reconciled with her. Somewhat reluctantly the king had her called. The Buddha then praised the blessing of amity and their rift was forgotten as if it had never occurred (Jāt. 306).

Later, however, a new round of friction set in between the couple, and again the king would not look at Mallikā and pretended she did not exist. When the Buddha became aware of this he asked about her, and Pasenadi again said that her good fortune had gone to her head. Immediately the Awakened One related an incident from a former life when both were heavenly beings, a deva couple, who loved each other dearly. One night they were separated from each other because of the flooding of a stream. They both regretted this irretrievable night, which could never be replaced during their life span of a thousand years. And for the rest of their lives they never parted from each other's company and always remembered to use this separation as a warning so that their happiness would endure until the end of their days. The king was moved by this story and became reconciled to the queen. Mallikā then spoke this verse to the Buddha:

> With joy I heard your varied words,
> Which were spoken for our welfare;
> With your talk you dispelled my sorrow,
> May you live long, my ascetic, bringer of joy!
>
> (Jāt. 504)

A third time the Buddha told of a former life of the royal couple when Pasenadi was a crown prince and Mallikā his wife. When the crown prince became afflicted with leprosy and had to relinquish his claim to the throne, he resolved to withdraw into the forest by himself so as not to become a burden to anyone. His wife, however, refused to desert him but accompanied him and looked after him with touching attention. Rather than lead a carefree life in pomp and splendor, she chose to remain faithful to her repulsive husband. Through the power of her virtue she was able to effect his recovery. But when the king ascended to the throne and she became his queen, he promptly forgot her and enjoyed himself with the dancing girls. Only when the king was reminded of his queen's good deeds did he change his ways. He asked her forgiveness and lived together with her in harmony and virtue (Jāt. 519).

Queen Mallikā committed only one deed in this life which had evil results and which led her to the worst rebirth. Once, when she was drying herself after a bath, her pet dog approached her from behind and mounted her. Instead of driving the dog away, she allowed it to continue. The king had caught a glimpse of this bizarre incident through an open window and later scolded Mallikā for her transgression. However, rather than admit her guilt, the queen insisted on her innocence and convinced the king that his eyes had played a trick on him.[7]

When Mallikā died her twofold transgression—her sexual contact with the dog and her mendacious attempt to free herself from blame—caught up with her and brought about a rebirth in hell. This evil, however, lasted for only seven days, after which it was overpowered by Mallikā's great merits. At the time of her death King Pasenadi was listening to the Buddha give a Dhamma talk. When the news reached him he was deeply shaken, to such an extent that his grief could not be assuaged even by the Buddha's reminder that there was nothing in the world that could escape decay and death (AN 5:49).

His attachment—"from love comes sorrow"—was so strong that he went to the Buddha every day to find out about the future destiny of his wife. If he had to get along without her on earth, at least he wanted to know about her rebirth. But for seven days the Buddha distracted him from his question through fascinating and moving Dhamma discourses, so that he remembered his question only when he arrived home again. Only on the seventh day would the Buddha answer his question and said that Mallikā had been reborn in the Tusita heaven, "the heaven of the blissful devas." So as not to add to the king's sorrow, he did not mention the seven days she had spent in hell. Although it was a very short-termed sojourn there, one can see that Mallikā had not yet attained stream-entry during her life on earth, since a stream-enterer cannot take rebirth below the human level. However, this experience of infernal suffering together with her knowledge of the Dhamma must have quickened Mallikā's ripening for the attainment of stream-entry.

KHEMĀ OF GREAT WISDOM

Just as the Buddha has appointed two chief disciples in the order of monks, Sāriputta and Moggallāna, he likewise named two women his foremost disciples in the Bhikkhunī Sangha, the order of nuns. These two were the bhikkhunīs Uppalavaṇṇā and Khemā, the former excelling in psychic power, the latter in wisdom (AN 1, chap. 14). The Buddha has held up these two as the models and examples for all the nuns to emulate, the standard against which other nuns could evaluate themselves (SN 17:24).

The name "Khemā" means security and is a synonym for Nibbāna. The nun Khemā belonged to a royal family from the land of Magadha. She was extremely beautiful and fair to behold, and when she reached marriageable age she became one of the chief consorts of King Bimbisāra. This king was a stream-enterer and a generous benefactor of the Blessed One. He has donated his own Bamboo Grove to the Sangha and constantly looked after the monks with great solicitude. But although Khemā often heard about the Buddha from the king, she resisted going to see him, fearful that he would find fault with her beauty of form and preach to her about the vanity of sensual pleasures, to which she was tightly attached. The king, however, found a way to induce her to listen to the Teaching.[8] He hired a troop of singers to sing songs to her in praise of the harmony, peacefulness, and beauty of the Bamboo Grove monastery, and because Khemā loved the beauties of nature she decided to visit there.

Decked out in royal splendor with silk and sandalwood, she went to the monastery and was gradually drawn to the hall where the Buddha was preaching. The Buddha, who read her thoughts, created by his psychic powers a beautiful young woman standing beside him fanning him. Khemā was enthralled by this lovely woman and thought to herself: "Never before have I seen such a woman. I myself do not come within even a fraction of her beauty. Surely those who say the ascetic Gotama disparages beauty of form must be misrepresenting him." The Buddha then made this created image gradually change from youth to middle age, and then to old age, with broken teeth, gray hair, and wrinkled skin, until it finally fell to the ground lifeless. Only then did she realize the vanity of external beauty and the fleeting nature of life. She thought, "Has such a body come to be wrecked like that? Then my body too must share that fate."

The Buddha read her mind and said:

> Khemā, behold this mass of elements,
> Diseased, impure, decaying;
> Trickling all over and oozing,
> It is desired only by fools.

At the conclusion of the stanza Khemā was established in the fruit of stream-entry. But the Buddha continued to teach her, concluding his sermon with another verse:

> Those enslaved by lust drift down the stream
> As a spider glides on its self-spun web.
> Having cut off even this, the wise wander
> Indifferent to the pleasures they've renounced.
>
> (Dhp. 347)

Khemā penetrated the sermon fully, and right on the spot, while still dressed in her royal attire, she attained arahantship together with the analytical knowledges. Thereafter, having received her husband's permission, she joined the order of nuns.

An ordinary person, hearing Khemā's story, sees only the wonder of the present happening. A Buddha, however, can see beyond this and knows that this woman did not come to full liberation by chance or good fortune. Such an attainment, almost like lightning, is only possible for one whose seed of wisdom has long been ripening and whose virtue is fully matured. In past aeons, Khemā had planted the roots of merit under many former Buddhas. Due to her innate attraction toward the highest truth, she always came to birth wherever a Buddha, a Bearer of Truth, lived. It is said that already one hundred thousand aeons ago she had sold her beautiful hair to give alms to the Buddha Padumuttara. During the time of the Buddha Vipassī, ninety-one aeons ago, she had been a bhikkhunī and a teacher of the Dhamma. Further, it is told that during the Dispensations of the three Buddhas of our happy aeon, the predecessors of our Buddha Gotama, she was a lay disciple and gained happiness through building monasteries for the Sangha.

While most beings drift around in heavenly or infernal realms during the lifetime of a Buddha, Khemā always tried to be near the source of wisdom. When no Buddha appeared in the world she would be reborn at the time of paccekabuddhas or in proximity to the Bodhisatta, the future Buddha Gotama. In one birth (Jāt. 354) she was the wife of the Bodhisatta, who always exhorted his peaceful family thus:

According to what you have, give alms;
Observe the Uposatha, keep the precepts pure;
Dwell upon the thought of death, mindful of your mortal state.
For in the case of beings like us,
Death is certain, life uncertain;
All existing things must pass, subject to decay.
Therefore be heedful day and night.

One day Khemā's only son in this life was suddenly killed by the bite of a poisonous snake, yet she was able to keep total equanimity:

Uncalled he hither came, unbidden soon to go;
Even as he came, he went. What cause is here for woe?
No friend's lament can touch the ashes of the dead:
Why should I grieve? He fares the way he had to tread.
Though I should fast and weep, how would it profit me?
My kith and kin, alas! would more unhappy be.
No friend's lament can touch the ashes of the dead:
Why should I grieve? He fares the way he had to tread.[9]

Another time she was the daughter-in-law of the Bodhisatta (Jāt. 397), many times a great empress who dreamed about receiving teachings from the Bodhisatta and then actually received such teachings (Jāt. 501, 502, 534). It is further recounted that as a queen her husband the king was the future Sāriputta. This husband in former lives was a righteous king who upheld the ten royal virtues: generosity, morality, renunciation, truthfulness, gentleness, patience, amity, harmlessness, humility, and justice. Because of these virtues the king lived in happiness and bliss. Khemā, too, lived in accordance with these precepts (Jāt. 534). It was only because Khemā had already purified her heart in many past lives that she was mature enough, on her first meeting with the Buddha, to realize the ultimate truth in the twinkling of an eye.

Khemā's transformed attitude to sensuality is starkly revealed to us by a dialogue in verse, recorded in the *Therīgāthā*, in which she fends off the advances of a charming seducer. According to the commentary, the seducer is actually Māra, the Tempter, who had approached intending to divert her from her quest for liberation—vainly, as she was already an arahant:

"You are so young and beautiful,
And I myself am in the bloom of youth.
Come, noble lady, let us rejoice
In the music of a fivefold ensemble."

"I am repelled and humiliated
By this putrid fleshly body,
Afflicted by illness, so very fragile;
I have uprooted sensual craving.

Sensual pleasures are now like sword stakes,
The aggregates are their chopping block.
That which you call sensual delight
Has become for me no delight at all.

Everywhere delight has been destroyed,
The mass of darkness has been shattered.
Know this, O Evil One—
You are defeated, Exterminator."

(Thig. 139–42)

The Buddha praised Khemā as the nun foremost in wisdom (*etadaggaṁ mahāpaññānaṁ*). A dialogue that has come down in the Saṁyutta Nikāya (44:1) confirms this, illustrating how her wisdom made a deep impact on King Pasenadi. The king was traveling through the countryside of Kosala and arrived one evening at a small township. Wishing to have a conversation about spiritual matters, he ordered a servant to find out whether there was a wise ascetic or brahmin in the town. The servant inquired everywhere. He could not find any ascetic or brahmin for his master to converse with, but he learned that a bhikkhunī, an ordained disciple of the Buddha, was dwelling in the town. It was the saintly Khemā, who was famed everywhere for her wisdom, deep insight, great learning, and perspicacity in discussion.

When the king received this report he went to her, greeted her with respect, and questioned her about the after-death condition of a Tathāgata, a liberated sage:

> "Does a Tathāgata—a Perfect One—exist after death?"
> "The Exalted One has not declared that a Tathāgata exists after death."
> "Then a Tathāgata does not exist after death?"
> "That, too, the Exalted One has not declared."
> "Then a Tathāgata both exists and does not exist after death?"
> "Even that, the Exalted One has not declared."
> "Then does a Tathāgata neither exist nor not exist after death?"
> "That, too, the Exalted One has not declared."

Thereupon the king wanted to know why the Buddha had rejected these four questions. To understand the reason we must first understand what these four views imply. The views concern a Tathāgata, which here means not only a supreme Buddha but any liberated sage. The four views, however, conceive the Tathāgata in terms of the category of selfhood; assuming that the liberated being is a substantial self, they formulate contradictory theses on the fate of that self. The first view, which is conditioned by the craving for existence, maintains that those who have reached the highest goal continue on after death in some metaphysical dimension, either as distinct individuals or as absorbed into some transpersonal spiritual essence. This answer is the one given by most religions, including several later interpretations of Buddhism.

The second answer—that a Tathāgata does not exist after death—reflects the craving for nonexistence, for annihilation. The theorist regards the Perfect One as a truly existent self whose fate at death is complete annihilation. From this perspective deliverance is nothing more than the absolute dissolution of a real self.

The third answer seeks a compromise: everything impermanent in a Tathāgata would be annihilated at death, but the permanent essence, his soul, would remain. The fourth answer tries to escape the predicament by formulating a "neither-nor" solution—a skeptical approach that still implicitly accepts the validity of the Tathāgata as a real self.

All four formulas have been rejected by the Buddha as wrong views. They all presuppose that there is an "I" distinct from the world—an "I" which is either raised to eternal life or annihilated in the abyss of nothingness—while in reality "I" and "world" are mere abstractions posited on the basis of the five aggregates that constitute the process of experience. Only the Enlightened Ones and their wise disciples can actually see this as it is. Those who do not share this insight assume one of the four speculative views. They suppose either that an "I," an essentially permanent "self," is wandering through saṁsāra, the round of birth and death, gradually ascending higher and higher until it is liberated into the divine essence; or they conclude that liberation is simply the destruction of a real self; or they attempt to formulate a syncretic position; or they fall into skepticism.

The Buddha, however, teaches that there is no real "I" or "self" to be either projected into eternity or utterly destroyed; such a substantial self has never existed and thus has never wandered through saṁsāra. What we call "I" and what we call "world" are in reality a constantly changing process, always in flux. This process throws up the illusions of "I" and "world," which then become objects of speculation regarding their past origin and future destiny. The way to liberation requires that we stop speculating about the "I," abandon our habitual views and formulas, and directly examine the phenomena on the basis of which views of self are formulated: the concrete processes of mind and body.

Liberation is to be won, not by fashioning metaphysical hypotheses, but by observing with mindfulness the arising and passing away of the five aggregates: form, feeling, perception, volitional formations, and consciousness. All these phenomena have arisen due to causes; therefore they are impermanent and subject to dissolution. But whatever is impermanent and subject to decay cannot be a self. Since the five aggregates are subject to destruction—since they become sick, disintegrate, and pass away—they are not "my" self, they are not "mine"; they are merely empty phenomena occurring through conditions.

Because all views of self are only mental constructions, products of speculative thought, any designation of the Enlightened One after death is an illusion born from a compulsive urge for conceptual certainty. Whoever has followed the Buddha's Teaching, as Khemā did, is greatly relieved to see that the Buddha did not teach the destruction of an existing entity, the annihilation of a self. We live in a world of perpetual destruction and uncontrollable transiency, in the realm of death, and whatever we look upon as "I" and "mine" is constantly vanishing. It is only by renouncing these things that we can reach a refuge of true peace and security. Thus the Blessed One proclaimed: "Open are the doors to the Deathless. Let those with ears send forth faith."

In her discussion with King Pasenadi, Khemā illustrated her point with a simile. She asked the king whether he had a skillful mathematician or statistician who could calculate for him how many grains of sand are contained in the river Ganges. The king replied that this was not possible, for the grains of sand in the Ganges were innumerable and incalculable. The nun then asked him whether he knew of anyone who could figure out how many gallons of water are contained in the great ocean. That, too, the king considered impossible, for the ocean is deep, immeasurable, hard to fathom. Just so, said Khemā, is the Tathāgata. Whoever wishes to define the Perfect One can only do so through the five aggregates, yet those who have reached awakening no longer hold to any of them as their personal identity: "The Tathāgata is released from reckoning by form, feeling, perception, volitional formations, and consciousness; he is deep, immeasurable, hard to fathom like the great ocean." Therefore it is not appropriate to say that after death the Tathāgata exists or does not exist, or that he both exists and does not exist, or that he neither exists nor does not exist. None of these designations can define the undefinable.

The king rejoiced in the penetrating explanation of the nun Khemā. Later he met the Buddha and asked him the same four questions, and the Master replied exactly as Khemā had done, using the very same words. The king was amazed and recounted his conversation with the holy nun Khemā, the woman disciple who excelled in wisdom.

BHADDĀ KUṆḌALAKESĀ: THE DEBATING ASCETIC

In Rājagaha, the capital of the kingdom of Magadha, there lived a girl of good family named Bhaddā, the only daughter of a rich merchant.[10] Her parents kept her confined to the top floor of a seven-storied mansion, for she had a passionate nature and they were afraid that her awakening sexuality would lead her into trouble. One day Bhaddā heard a commotion down below in the street, and when she looked out the window she saw a criminal being led to the place of execution. He was a young man of station who had become a thief and was caught committing a robbery. As soon as Bhaddā set eyes upon him love arose in her heart, and she lay down on her bed, refusing to eat unless she could have him for her husband. Her parents tried to dissuade her from such folly, but she would see no alternative. Thus her rich father sent a generous bribe to the guard and asked him to bring the man to his mansion.

The guard did as he was instructed, substituting a local derelict for the robber. The merchant gave the robber to his daughter in marriage, hopeful that his character might alter through this sudden change of fortune. Soon after the wedding, however, the bridegroom became obsessed with a desire to take possession of his wife's jewelry. Thus he told her that while he was being led to the execution block he had vowed that if he could escape death he would make an offering to a certain mountain deity. He urged Bhaddā to put on all her finest ornaments and accompany him to this deity's haunt, a cliff off the top of a steep mountain. When they came to the cliff, called Robbers' Precipice because it was here that the king would have criminals thrown to their death, her husband demanded that Bhaddā hand over all her jewelry to him. Bhaddā saw only one way to escape this predicament. She asked her husband permission to pay final obeisance to him, and as she embraced him she threw him over the cliff, to be dashed to pieces down below.

Burdened by the enormity of her deed, Bhaddā had no desire to return to lay life, for sensual pleasures and possessions no longer had any meaning for her. Therefore she decided to become a wandering ascetic. First she entered the order of the Jains, and as a special penance her hair was torn out by the roots when she ordained. But it grew again and became very curly, for which reason she was called Kuṇḍalakesā, which means "Curly-hair."

The teaching of the Jain sect did not satisfy her, so she became a solitary wanderer. Traveling through India, she visited many spiritual teachers, learned their doctrines, and thereby obtained an excellent knowledge of religious texts and philosophies. She became especially skilled in the art of debate and in a short time became one of the most famous debaters in India. Whenever she entered a town, she would make a sandpile and stick a rose-apple branch into it, announcing that whoever would engage in debate with her should notify her by trampling upon the sandpile.

One day she came to Sāvatthī and again erected her little monument. At that time the Venerable Sāriputta was staying at the Jetavana monastery. He heard of the arrival of Bhaddā and, as a sign of his willingness for debate, he told several children to go and trample on the sandpile. Thereupon Bhaddā went to Jetavana, confident of victory, accompanied by a large number of people.

She put a number of questions to Sāriputta, and he answered them all until she had nothing more to ask. Then Sāriputta questioned her. Already the first question affected Bhaddā profoundly, namely, "What is the one?" She remained silent, unable to determine what the elder could have intended. Surely, she pondered, he did not mean "God," or "Brahman," or "the Infinite." But what was it then? The answer should have been "nutriment," because all beings are sustained by food. Admitting defeat, Bhaddā asked Sāriputta for the answer, but he said that he would tell her only if she entered the Buddhist Order. The elder then sent her to the bhikkhunīs and had her ordained, and after a few days she attained arahantship.

Such is the version of Bhaddā's meeting with the Dhamma that has been recorded in the Dhammapada Commentary, but Bhaddā's verses in the *Therīgāthā* present a different picture:

> Formerly I traveled in a single cloth
> With plucked hair, covered with mud,
> Imagining flaws in the flawless
> And seeing no flaws in what is flawed.
>
> Having come out from my daytime dwelling,
> On the mountain Vulture's Peak
> I saw the spotless Enlightened One
> Accompanied by the Bhikkhu Sangha.
>
> Then I humbly bowed down on my knees
> And in his presence saluted him.
> "Come, Bhaddā," he said to me—
> And that was my ordination.
>
> (Thig. 107–9)

In this version the meeting between Bhaddā and the Buddha takes place, not at Sāvatthī, but at Vulture's Peak near Rājagaha, and Bhaddā receives ordination, not by the established procedure of a formal ceremony, but simply by the Buddha's invitation to her to become a bhikkhunī. The discussion that took place between them is not recorded in the verses themselves, but Bhaddā must have attained realization very quickly; for the Buddha later declared her to be the foremost of the bhikkhunīs with respect to quickness of understanding (*khippābhiññā*). The Therīgāthā Commentary, in commenting on the verses, attempts to reconcile the verses and the old commentarial tradition. According to this version, after Bhaddā admitted defeat to Sāriputta, she paid homage to him and he brought her into the presence of the Buddha. Then the Teacher, aware that her wisdom was ripe, spoke to her a verse of the *Dhammapada*:

> Though one hears a thousand verses
> Made of lines devoid of meaning,
> Better is a single meaningful line
> By hearing which one is set at peace.
>
> (Dhp. 101)

At the conclusion of the verse she attained arahantship together with the analytical knowledges (*paṭisambhidā-ñāṇa*). Thereupon she requested the going forth. The Buddha consented to this and sent her to the order of nuns, where she received formal ordination.

The *Apadāna* offers still another perspective on Bhaddā's awakening. After Bhaddā had gone forth as a Jain nun she studied their philosophical system. One day, while she was sitting alone reflecting on their doctrine, a dog approached her with a mutilated human hand in its mouth, which it deposited right in front of her. When Bhaddā saw this, and noticed that the hand was crawling with worms, she received a deep spiritual shock. In a state of excitement she asked who could explain to her the significance of that incident. Her inquiries led her to the Buddhist monks, who brought her to the Master:

> He then taught me the Dhamma,
> The aggregates, sense bases, and elements,[11]
> The Leader told me about foulness,
> Impermanence, suffering, and nonself.
>
> Having heard the Dhamma from him,
> I purified the vision of the Dhamma.
> When I had understood true Dhamma,
> (I asked for) the going forth and ordination.
>
> Requested, the Leader then said to me,
> "Come, O Bhaddā!"
> Then, having been fully ordained,
> I observed a little streamlet of water.

Through that stream of foot-washing water
I knew the process of rise and fall.
Then I reflected that all formations
Are exactly the same in nature.

Right on the spot my mind was released,
Totally freed by the end of clinging.
The Victor then appointed me the chief
Of those with quick understanding.

(Ap.ii, 3:1, vv. 38–46)

The last couplet refers to the occasion when the Buddha declared Bhaddā the nun foremost in quickness of understanding (AN 1: chap. 14). This was a quality she shared with the monk Bāhiya, who reached arahantship in an instant when the Buddha told him: "In the seen there should be for you only the seen, in the heard only the heard, in the sensed only the sensed, in the cognized only the cognized" (Ud. 1:10). Both had grasped the highest truth so quickly, and had penetrated it so deeply, that in a split-second they ascended from the stage of a worldling to arahantship.

Bhaddā's later life was spent in traveling over the North Indian countryside, preaching the Dhamma and guiding others to the same goal of deliverance that she herself had reached:

Free from defilements, for fifty years
I traveled in Aṅga and Magadha.
Among the Vajjis, in Kāsī and Kosala,
I ate the almsfood of the land.

That lay-supporter—wise man indeed—
Who gave a robe to Bhaddā,
Has generated abundant merit,
For she is one free of all ties.

(Thig. 110–11)

KISĀGOTAMĪ: THE MOTHER WITH THE DEAD CHILD

There lived in Sāvatthī a girl named Gotamī, in poor circumstances, the daughter of an impoverished family. Because she was very thin and haggard (*kisa*), everyone called her Kisāgotamī, Haggard Gotamī.[12] When one saw her walking around, tall and thin, one could not fathom her inner riches. One might truly say of her:

> Her beauty was an inner one,
> One could not see its spark outside.

Due to her poverty and unattractiveness Kisāgotamī was unable to find a husband, and for her this was a cause of deep dejection. But one day it suddenly happened that a rich merchant chose her as his wife, for he appreciated her inner wealth and considered it more important than her family background or outer appearance. However, the other members of her husband's family despised her and treated her contemptuously. This animosity caused her great unhappiness, especially because of her beloved husband, who found himself caught between love for his parents and love for his wife.

But when Kisāgotamī gave birth to a baby boy, the husband's whole clan finally accepted her as the mother of the son and heir. Her relief was immense and she felt that a great burden had fallen from her back. Now she was totally happy and contented. Beyond the usual love of a mother for her child, she was especially attached to this infant because he was the guarantee of her marital bliss and peace of mind.

Soon, however, her happiness showed itself to be built on an illusion, for one day her little son suddenly fell ill and died. The tragedy was too much for her. She worried that her husband's family would again despise her, saying she was kammically unable to have a son, and other people in the town would say, "Kisāgotamī must have done some very despicable deeds to merit such a fate." Even her husband, she feared, might now reject her and seek another wife from a more favorable background. All such imaginings revolved in her mind and a dark cloud descended upon her. Refusing to accept the fact that the child was dead, she convinced herself that he was only sick and would recover if she could find the right medicine for him.

With the dead child in her arms, she ran away from her home and went from house to house asking for medicine for her little son. At every door she begged: "Please give me some medicine for my child." And always people replied that medicine was useless, for the child was dead. She, however, refused to accept this, and passed on to the next house, still convinced that the child was only ill. While many scorned her and others mocked her, at last she met, among the many selfish and unsympathetic people, a wise and kind man who recognized that she had become mentally deranged because of her grief. He advised her to visit the best physician, the Buddha, who would surely know the right remedy.

She immediately followed his advice and hurried to Jetavana, Anāthapiṇḍika's monastery, where the Buddha was staying. Arriving in renewed hope, with the child's corpse in her arms, she ran up to the Buddha and said to him, "Master, give me medicine for my son." The Awakened One replied kindly that he knew of a medicine, but she would have to procure it herself. Eagerly, she asked what it could be.

"Mustard seeds," he replied, astounding everyone present.

Kisāgotamī inquired where she should go to obtain them and what kind to get. The Buddha replied that she need bring only a very small quantity from any house where no one had ever died. She trusted the Blessed One's words and went to the town. At the first house she asked whether any mustard seeds were available. "Certainly," was the reply. "Could I have a few seeds?" she inquired. "Of course," she was told, and some seeds were brought to her. But then she asked the second question, which she had not deemed quite as important: "Has anyone ever died in this house?" "But of course," the people told her. And so it was everywhere. In one house someone had died recently, in another house a year or two ago; in one house a father had died, in another a mother or a son or a daughter. She could not find any house where no one had ever died. "The dead," she was told, "are more numerous than the living."

Towards evening she finally realized that she was not alone in being stricken by the death of a loved one: this was the common human fate. What no words had been able to convey to her, her own experience of going from door to door had made clear. She understood the law of existence, the law of impermanence and death within the ever recurring round of becoming. In this way, the Buddha was able to heal her obsession and bring her to an acceptance of reality. Kisāgotamī no longer refused to believe that her child was dead: she understood that death is the destiny of all beings.

Such were the means by which the Buddha could heal grief-stricken people and bring them out of their overpowering delusion, in which they perceived the whole world from the narrow perspective of their own personal loss. Once, when someone was lamenting the death of his father, the Buddha asked him which father he meant: the father of this life, or of the last life, or of the life before that. For if one wanted to grieve, then it would be just as well to grieve for the other fathers too (Pv. 8; Jāt. 352). Another time a grief-stricken person came to his senses when the Buddha pointed out to him that his son would be reborn and that he was only lamenting for an empty shell (Pv. 12; Jāt. 354).

After Kisāgotamī had emerged from her delusion, she took the child's lifeless body to the cemetery, buried it, and then returned to the Enlightened One. When she came to him he asked her whether she had gotten the mustard seeds. "Done, venerable sir, is the business of the mustard seeds," she replied, "only grant me a refuge." Thereupon the Master spoke the following verse to her:

When a person's mind is deeply attached,
Infatuated with sons and cattle,
Death grabs him and carries him away
As a flood does a sleeping village.

(Dhp. 287)

As her mind had matured in the course of her ordeal, on hearing this one verse she won insight into reality and became a stream-enterer. Thereupon she asked for admission into the order of nuns. The Buddha gave his consent and sent her to the nuns' quarters, where she received the going forth and the higher ordination as a bhikkhunī.

After her ordination Kisāgotamī passed her time practicing and studying the Dhamma. One evening, as she watched her oil lamp sputter, it occurred to her that the restlessly hissing flames were like the ups and downs of life and death. The Blessed One, aware that she was ripe for full attainment, came to her and again spoke a short verse:

Though one should live a hundred years
Not seeing the deathless state,
Yet better is it to live for a single day,
Seeing the deathless state.

(Dhp. 114)

When she heard these lines, she was able to shed all fetters and became one of the arahants, the liberated ones.

In her stanzas in the *Therīgāthā*, Kisāgotamī describes the great joy the Buddha imparted to her. Therefore she praises friendship with the noble and holy ones:

To the world the Sage has praised
The value of noble friendship.
By resorting to noble friends
Even a fool becomes wise.

One should resort to worthy people,
For thus one's wisdom ever grows.
By resorting to worthy people
One is freed from all suffering.

One should know the Four Noble Truths:
Suffering and its origination,
Then the cessation of suffering
And the Noble Eightfold Path.

(Thig. 213–15)

Kisāgotamī knew the value of noble friendship from her own firsthand experience, for the compassionate Buddha, the most noble friend of all, had saved her from all the suffering encountered in the terrible round of rebirths. In her verses of liberation, recorded in the *Therīgāthā*, Kisāgotamī describes the various sufferings that are peculiar to women. Only when one penetrates a woman's suffering as thus described can one realize the full extent of her gratitude toward the Buddha, who showed her the way to freedom:

The woman's state is declared as painful
By the trainer of persons to be tamed.
The trainer of persons to be tamed
Has declared as painful the life of a woman.
Painful too is the state of a co-wife.

Some, having borne a child once,
In desperation cut their throats;
The delicate ones take poison.
When the baby obstructs the birth,
Both come to disaster—mother and child.

(Thig. 216–17)

The final note of Kisāgotamī's verses is not a lament but a cry of triumph, expressing her joy in finding liberation and release from all suffering:

Developed by me is the noble path,
The eightfold path leading to the Deathless.
I looked into the mirror of the Dhamma
And thereby I realized Nibbāna.

With dart drawn out, the burden dropped,
I have done what had to be done.
The elder nun Kisāgotamī has recited this,
One with a mind well released.

(Thig. 222–23)

A set of verses spoken by Kisāgotamī is also found in the Saṁyutta Nikāya, embedded in a dialogue with Māra. One day, when Māra came to distract her from her meditation—a favorite pastime of his, regardless of his victim's gender—he taunted her with a verse:

Why now when you've lost your son
Do you sit alone with a tearful face?
Having entered the woods all alone,
Are you on the lookout for a man?

Then Kisāgotamī thought to herself: "Now who has recited this verse—a human being or a nonhuman being?" Then it occurred to her: "This is Māra the Evil One, who has recited the verse desiring to arouse fear, trepidation, and terror in me, desiring to make me fall away from concentration." She then replied:

I have gotten past the death of sons;
With this the search for men has ended.
I do not sorrow, I do not weep,
Nor do I fear you, friend.

Delight everywhere has been destroyed,
The mass of darkness has been sundered.
Having conquered the mighty army of Death,
I dwell without defiling taints.

(SN 5:3)

By addressing Māra as "friend" she shows her lack of fear and her equanimity, and Māra, once recognized for who he really is, has no choice but to disappear. The nun Kisāgotamī, having risen from personal tragedy to the highest sanctity, was praised by the Buddha as the foremost nun among those who wore coarse garments, one of the ascetic practices (AN 1, chap. 14).

SOṆĀ WITH MANY CHILDREN

There was a housewife in Sāvatthī who had ten children. She was always occupied with giving birth, with nursing and raising her children, with educating them, and with arranging marriages for them. Her whole life centered upon her children, and she was therefore known as "Soṇā with many children."[13] We may find such an abundance of offspring in one family somewhat strange, but in the past this was not at all uncommon in Asia and is not unusual even today.

Soṇā's husband was a lay follower of the Buddha. After having scrupulously observed the precepts for several years as a householder, he decided to devote himself fully to the holy life, and so he took ordination as a monk. It was not easy for Soṇā to accept this decision, yet she did not waste her time with regrets and sorrow but decided to live a more devout life herself. She called her ten children together, turned her considerable wealth over to them, and asked them to provide her only with her bare necessities.

For a while all went well with this arrangement: she had sufficient support and could spend her time in religious activities. But before long the old woman became a burden to her children and their spouses. They had never really accepted their father's decision to enter the Order, and even less did they sympathize with their mother's religious devotion. Indeed, they thought their parents to be fools for forsaking the pleasures that their wealth could purchase. In their eyes their parents were mentally unstable religious fanatics, and thus their attitude toward their mother quickly changed from respect to contempt.

They no longer gave thought to how deeply they were indebted to their mother for all their wealth and for the many years of care and attention she had lavished on them. Looking only to their own convenience, they considered the old woman a nuisance and a burden. The words of the Buddha, that a grateful person is as rare in the world as a saint, again proved true in this case (AN 3:112, 5:143, 195).

The disdainful treatment from her children was even more painful for Soṇā than separation from her husband. She became aware that waves of bitterness arose in her, that reproaches and accusations toward her children intermingled in her mind. She realized that what she had taken to be selfless love, pure mother's love, was in reality self-love coupled with expectations of requital. She had been relying on her children completely and had been convinced that she would be supported by them in her old age as a tribute to her long years of solicitude for them; she had assumed that gratitude, appreciation, and participation in their affairs would be her reward. Hadn't she, then, really looked at her children as an investment, as insurance against the fear and loneliness of old age? In this manner, she investigated her motives and found the truth of the Enlightened One's words in herself: that it was a woman's way not to rely on possessions, power, and abilities, but solely on her children, while it was the way of the ascetic to rely on virtue alone (AN 6:53).

Her reflections brought her to the decision to enter the order of nuns so that she could develop the qualities of selfless love and virtue. Why should she remain in her home, where she was accepted only grudgingly? She looked upon the household life as gray and oppressive, and she pictured the life of a nun as bright and beautiful. Thus, following her husband's path, she went forth into homelessness and became a nun in the Blessed One's Bhikkhunī Sangha.

But after a while Soṇā came to realize that she had simply taken her self-love along with her into her new life. Having entered the Sangha as an old woman, she had dozens of habits and peculiarities that were obstacles in this new environment. She was used to doing things in a certain way, while the other nuns did them differently, and therefore she made herself the target of criticism and correction by those much younger than herself.

Soṇā soon discovered that it was not so easy to reach noble attainments, and that the order of nuns was not the paradise she had envisioned. Just as she had not found security with her children, so ordination as a nun did not bring immediate peace of heart. She also understood that she was still held fast by her womanly limitations. It was not enough that her weaknesses were abhorrent to her and that she was longing for more masculine traits. She also had to know what to do to effect the change. She accepted the fact that she would have to make tremendous efforts, not only because she was already advanced in years but also because until now she had only cultivated female virtues. The masculine characteristics that she was lacking were energy and circumspection. Soṇā did not become discouraged, nor thought of the path as too difficult.

It became clear to Soṇā that she had to fight hard to win victory over her willfulness and credulity. She realized that it was necessary to practice mindfulness and self-observation, and to implant into her memory those teachings that could be at her disposal when needed to counteract her emotions. What use would be all her knowledge and vows if she were carried away by her emotions and if her memory failed her when it was most needed? These were the thoughts that ran through her mind, strengthening her determination to submit her self-will fully to the training.

Because Soṇā had entered the Order in old age she applied herself to the practice with a compelling sense of urgency. She would even pass entire nights in sitting and walking meditation, taking only minimal sleep. So as to avoid calling attention to herself she practiced walking meditation during the night, in the darkness of the lower hall. She guided her steps by grabbing hold of the pillars, thereby ensuring that she would not stumble or bump into unseen objects. In this way her energy quickly gathered momentum.

Soṇā's attainment of arahantship took place without any special circumstances to herald it, on an occasion when she had been left behind in the convent while the other nuns went out. She describes it in her own words in her verses in the Apadāna:

Then the other bhikkhunīs
Left me alone in the convent.
They had given me instructions
To boil a cauldron of water.

Having fetched the water,
I poured it into the cauldron;
I put the cauldron on the stove and sat—
Then my mind became composed.

I saw the aggregates as impermanent,
I saw them as suffering and nonself.
Having expelled all the cankers from my heart,
Right there I attained to arahantship.

(Ap.ii, 3:6, vv. 234–36)

When the other nuns returned they asked for the hot water, which Soṇā still had not boiled. Using the supernormal power of the fire element, Soṇā quickly heated the water and offered it to the nuns. They reported this to the Buddha, who rejoiced and recited a verse in praise of her attainment:

Though one should live a hundred years
As a lazy, sluggish person,
Better it is to live a single day
Firmly arousing one's energy.

(Dhp. 112)[14]

In the *Therīgāthā* Soṇā describes her life in five verses:

I bore ten children in this body,
In this physical frame of mine.
Then when I was old and frail
I went up to a bhikkhunī.

She gave me a discourse on the Teaching—
On the aggregates, sense bases, elements.
Having heard the Dhamma discourse from her,
I shaved my hair and then went forth.

While still a probationer
I purified the divine eye;
Now I know my past abodes,
Where it is that I lived before.

With one-pointed mind, well composed,
I developed the signless state.[15]
Immediately I was released,
Quenched with the end of clinging.

The five aggregates are fully understood,
They stand cut off at the root.
Fie on you, O wretched aging:
Now there is no more re-becoming.

(Thig. 102–6)

NANDĀ: THE BUDDHA'S HALF-SISTER

When she was born, Nandā was lovingly welcomed by her parents—the father of the Buddha and his second wife, Mahāpajāpatī Gotamī.[16] Her name means joy, contentment, pleasure, and this name was given when parents were especially joyful about the arrival of a baby. Nandā was extremely well bred, graceful, and beautiful. To distinguish her from others by the same name, she was later called Rūpā-Nandā or sometimes Sundarī-Nandā, both meaning "beautiful Nandā."

In due course many members of her family—the royal house of the Sakyans—left the household for the homeless life, influenced by the amazing fact that one of their clan had become the fully enlightened Buddha. Among them was her brother Nanda, her cousins, and finally her mother, together with many other Sakyan ladies. Thereupon Nandā too took this step. She did not do so, however, out of confidence in the Teacher and the Teaching, but out of love for her relatives and from a wish to conform to them.

One can easily imagine the love and respect accorded the graceful half-sister of the Buddha, and how touched the people were by the sight of the lovely royal daughter, so near in family ties to the Blessed One, wandering among them in the garb of a nun. But it soon became obvious that this was not a proper basis for a nun's life. Nandā's thoughts were mainly directed toward her own beauty and her popularity with the people, traits which were resultants of former good kamma. These resultants now became dangers to her, since she forgot to reinforce them with sincere efforts at self-purification. She felt that she was not living up to the high ideals the people envisioned for her, and that she was far from the goal for which so many noble-born men and women had gone forth into the homeless life. Certain that the Blessed One would censure her, for a long time, instead of correcting her ways, she made every effort to evade him.

One day the Buddha requested all the nuns to come to him, one by one, to receive instructions. Nandā, however, did not comply. The Master had her called specially, and then she appeared before him, showing by her demeanor that she was ashamed and anxious. The Buddha addressed her and appealed to all her positive qualities so that she listened to him willingly and took delight in his words. Although the Blessed One knew that the talk had uplifted her, had made her joyful and ready to accept his teachings, he did not immediately explain to her the Four Noble Truths, as he often did on other such occasions. He knew that she was not yet ripe enough to penetrate the four truths, and thus he resorted to an expedient device to hasten her maturation.

Because Nandā was so enthralled with her own physical beauty, the Buddha used his psychic powers to conjure up the vision of an even more beautiful woman, who then aged visibly and relentlessly before her very eyes. Thereby Nandā could see, compressed within a few moments, what otherwise one can only notice in people through decades—and what often, because of proximity and habit, one does not even fully comprehend: the fading away of youth and beauty, the advance of decay, the proximity of death. The vision affected Nandā deeply; she was shaken to the center of her being.

After having given her this graphic lesson in impermanence, the Buddha could explain the Dhamma to her in such a way that she penetrated the four truths completely, and thereby attained the knowledge of future liberation—stream-entry. As a meditation subject the Buddha assigned to her the contemplation of the impermanence and foulness of the body. She persevered for a long time with this practice, "unwearying by day and night," as she exhorts herself in her verses:

Nandā, behold this body,
Ailing, impure, and putrid,
Develop the meditation on the foul,[17]
Make the mind unified, well composed:

"As is this, so was that,
As is that, so this will be,
Putrid, exhaling a foul odor,
A thing in which fools find delight."

Inspecting it as it is,
Unwearying by day and night,
With my own wisdom I pierced right through
And then I saw for myself.

As I dwelt ever heedful
Dissecting it with methodical thought,
I saw this body as it really is
Both inside and outside too.

Then I become disenchanted with the body,
My inward attachment faded away.
Being diligent and detached at heart,
I live at peace, fully quenched.

(Thig. 82–86)

Because Nandā had been so infatuated with her physical beauty, it was necessary for her to apply the austere meditation on bodily unattractiveness as a countermeasure before she could find equanimity—the balance between opposites. Having overcome her attachment to the body, Nandā had touched the true beauty of the Deathless, and nothing could ever again disturb the cool peace of her heart.

Later the Buddha praised his half-sister as the foremost among nuns who practiced meditation. This meant that she had not only followed the analytical way of insight, but had also experienced the jhānas, the attainments of tranquillity. Enjoying this pure felicity, she no longer needed any lower enjoyments and soon found indestructible peace. Although she had gone into homelessness because of attachment to her relatives, she became totally free, a true spiritual heir of the Master she venerated.

QUEEN SĀMĀVATĪ: EMBODIMENT OF LOVING-KINDNESS

In the days when India was the fortunate home of an Awakened One, a husband and wife lived within its borders with their only daughter named Sāmāvatī, who was exceedingly beautiful. Their family life was a happy and harmonious one. But then one day disaster struck: pestilence broke out in their hometown, and the couple, along with their grown-up daughter, fled from the area.[18]

They headed for Kosambī, the capital of the kingdom of Vaṁsa in the Ganges Valley, intending to seek support from her father's old friend Ghosaka, a finance minister of the king. Within the city the municipality had erected a public alms hall for the refugees. There the daughter, Sāmāvatī, went to obtain food. The first day she took three portions, the second day two portions, and on the third day only one portion. Mitta, the man who was distributing the food, could not resist asking her, somewhat ironically, whether she had finally realized the capacity of her stomach. Sāmāvatī replied quite calmly: "On the first day there were three of us, my parents and myself. That day my father succumbed to the plague, and so on the second day I needed food for only two people; after the meal my mother died, and so today I now need food for myself alone." The official felt ashamed of his sarcastic remark and wholeheartedly begged her forgiveness. A long conversation ensued, and when he found out that she was now all alone in the world, he proposed to adopt her as his foster child. She was happy to accept.

Sāmāvatī immediately began helping her foster father with the distribution of the food and the care of the refugees. Thanks to her efficiency and circumspection, the former chaos became channeled into orderly activity. Nobody tried to get ahead of others anymore, nobody quarreled, and everyone was content.

Soon Ghosaka, the king's finance minister, became aware that the public food distribution was taking place without noise and tumult. When he expressed his praise and appreciation to the food distributor, the official replied modestly that his foster daughter was mainly responsible for this.

In this way Ghosaka met Sāmāvatī, the orphaned daughter of his late friend, and he was so impressed with her noble bearing that he decided to adopt her as his own daughter. His manager consented, even if somewhat woefully, because he did not want to stand in the way of Sāmāvatī's fortune. So Ghosaka took her into his house. Thereby she became heiress of a vast estate and mixed with the most exalted circles of the land.

The king, who was living in Kosambī at that time, was named Udena. He had two chief consorts. One was Vāsuladattā, whom he had married both for political reasons and because she was very beautiful. The second was Māgandiyā, who was beautiful and clever but cold and self-centred. Neither could offer the king the warmth of loving affection and emotional contentment that he craved.

One day King Udena met the charming adopted daughter of his finance minister and fell in love with her at first sight. He felt magically attracted by her loving and generous nature. Sāmāvatī had exactly what was missing in both his other wives. King Udena sent a messenger to Ghosaka asking him to give Sāmāvatī to him in marriage. Ghosaka was thrown into an emotional upheaval. On the one hand, he loved Sāmāvatī above all else, and she had become indispensable to him. She was the delight of his life. On the other, he knew his king's temperament and was afraid to deny him his request. But in the end his attachment to Sāmāvatī won and he thought: "Better to die than to live without her."

As usual, King Udena lost his temper. In his fury he dismissed Ghosaka from his post as finance minister, banned him from his kingdom, and did not allow Sāmāvatī to accompany him. He took over his minister's property and locked up his magnificent mansion. Sāmāvatī was desolate that Ghosaka had to suffer so much on her account and had lost not only her but also his home and belongings. Out of compassion for her adopted father, to whom she was devoted with great gratitude, she decided to make an end to this dispute by voluntarily becoming the king's wife. She went to the palace and informed the king of her decision. The king was immediately appeased and restored Ghosaka to his former position, also rescinding all other measures against him.

Because Sāmāvatī had great love for everyone, she had so much inner strength that this decision was not a difficult one for her. It was not important to her where she lived: whether in the house of the finance minister as his favorite daughter, or in the palace as the favorite wife of the king, or in obscurity as when she was in the house of her parents, or as a poor refugee—she always found peace in her own heart and was happy regardless of outer circumstances.

Sāmāvatī's life at the royal court fell into a harmonious pattern. Among her servants there was one, named Khujjuttarā, who was outwardly ugly and ill formed but otherwise very capable. Every day the queen gave her eight gold coins to buy flowers for the women's quarters of the palace. But Khujjuttarā always bought only four coins' worth of flowers and used the remaining four coins for herself. One day, when she went to buy flowers for her mistress, the florist informed her that this day he had invited the Buddha and his order of monks for a meal, and he urged Khujjuttarā to participate. Following the meal the Buddha gave a discourse to his hosts, and as he spoke his words went directly to Khujjuttarā's heart. Listening with total attention, tranquil and uplifted, she took in every word as though it was intended just for her, and by the time the Buddha concluded his talk she had attained the path and fruit of stream-entry. Without quite knowing what had happened to her, she had become a totally changed person, one endowed with unwavering faith in the Triple Gem and incapable of violating the basic laws of morality. The whole world, which had always seemed so obvious and real to her, now appeared as a dream.

The first thing she did after this spectacular inner transformation was to buy flowers for all of the eight coins, deeply regretting her former dishonesty. When the queen asked her why there were suddenly so many flowers, Khujjuttarā fell at the queen's feet and confessed her theft. After Sāmāvatī forgave her magnanimously, Khujjuttarā told her what was closest to her heart, namely, that she had heard a discourse by the Buddha which had changed her life. She could not be specific about the contents of the Teaching, but Sāmāvatī could see for herself what a wholesome and healing impact it had made on her servant. She appointed Khujjuttarā her personal attendant and told her to visit the monastery every day to listen to the Dhamma and then repeat it to her and the other women of the palace. Khujjuttarā had an outstanding memory, and what she had heard only once she could repeat verbatim. Each day, when she returned from the monastery, the high-bred women of the palace would place her on a high seat, as if she were the Buddha himself, and sitting down below they would listen devotedly to the discourse. Later on Khujjuttarā made a collection of the short discourses she had heard from the Buddha, which became the book of the Pāli Canon now called the *Itivuttaka* (The Buddha's Sayings), composed of 112 suttas in mixed prose and verse.[19]

When King Udena once again told his beloved Sāmāvatī that she could wish for anything and he would fulfill it, she wished that the Buddha would come to the palace daily to have his food there and propound his doctrine. The king's courier took the message of this perpetual invitation to the Buddha, but he declined and instead sent Ānanda. From then on the Venerable Ānanda went to the palace daily for his meal and afterwards gave a Dhamma discourse. The queen had already been well prepared by Khujjuttarā's reports, and within a short time she understood the meaning and attained to stream-entry, just as her maid-servant had done.

Now, through their common understanding of the Dhamma, the queen and the maid became equals. Within a short time, the Teaching spread through the whole of the women's quarters and there was hardly anyone who did not become a disciple of the Awakened One. Even Sāmāvatī's step-father, the finance minister Ghosaka, was deeply touched by the Teaching. He donated a large monastery in Kosambī to the Sangha, so that the monks would have a secure and satisfying shelter when they came to the city. Every time the Buddha visited Kosambī he stayed in this monastery, named Ghositārāma, and other monks and holy people also found shelter there.

Through the influence of the Dhamma, Sāmāvatī became determined to develop her abilities more intensively. Her most important asset was the way she could feel sympathy for all beings and could suffuse everyone with loving-kindness and compassion. She was able to develop this faculty so strongly that the Buddha called her the woman lay disciple most skilled in spreading *mettā*, "loving-kindness" (AN 1, chap. 14).

This all-pervading love was soon to be tested severely in her relationship with the second main consort of the king, Māgandiyā. This woman was imbued with virulent hatred against everything Buddhist. Some years earlier her father had met the Buddha, and it had seemed to him that the handsome ascetic was the most worthy candidate to marry his daughter. In his naive ignorance of the rules of monks, he offered his daughter to the Buddha as his wife.

Māgandiyā was very beautiful and her hand had already been sought by many suitors, but the Buddha declined the offer with a single verse about the unattractiveness of the body (Snp. v. 835). This verse wounded Māgandiyā's vanity, but it had such a profound impact on her parents that right on the spot they realized the fruit of non-returning. Māgandiyā took the Buddha's rejection of her as a personal insult and came to harbor a bitter hatred against him, a hatred she could never overcome. Later her parents brought her to King Udena, who fell in love with her at first sight and took her as his wife. When he took a third wife, she could willingly accept this, as it was customary for the kings of the period to maintain several wives. But that Sāmāvatī had become a disciple of the Buddha and had converted the other women in the palace to the Dhamma—this she could not tolerate. Her hatred against everything connected with the Buddha now turned against Sāmāvatī as his representative.

Māgandiyā thought up one mean deed after another, and her sharp intelligence served only to conjure up new misdeeds. First she told the king that Sāmāvatī was trying to take his life. But the king was well aware of Sāmāvatī's great love for all beings, so that he did not even consider this accusation seriously, barely listened to it, and forgot it almost immediately. Next, Māgandiyā ordered one of her maid-servants to spread rumors about the Buddha and his monks in Kosambī, so that Sāmāvatī would also be maligned. With this she was more successful. A wave of aversion struck the whole Order to such an extent that Ānanda suggested to the Buddha that they leave town. The Buddha smiled and said that the purity of the monks would silence all rumors within a week. Hardly had King Udena heard the gossip leveled against the Order than it had already subsided. Māgandiyā's second attempt against Sāmāvatī had failed.

Some time later Māgandiyā had eight specially selected chickens sent to the king and suggested that Sāmāvatī should kill them and prepare them for a meal. Sāmāvatī refused to do this, as she would not kill any living beings. Since the king knew of her all-embracing love, he did not lose his temper, but accepted her decision. Māgandiyā then tried for a fourth time to harm Sāmāvatī. Just prior to the week which King Udena was to spend with Sāmāvatī, Māgandiyā hid a poisonous snake in Sāmāvatī's chambers, but the poison sacs had been removed. When King Udena discovered the snake, all evidence pointed towards Sāmāvatī. His passionate fury made him lose all control. He reached for his bow and arrow and shot at Sāmāvatī, but through the power of her loving-kindness the arrow rebounded from her without doing any harm. His hatred could not influence her loving concern for him, which protected her life like an invisible shield.

When King Udena regained his equilibrium and saw the miracle—that his arrow could not harm Sāmāvatī—he was deeply shaken. He begged her forgiveness and was even more convinced of her nobility and faithfulness. He became interested in the teaching that had given such strength to his wife. Just about this time a famous monk named Piṇḍola Bhāradvāja came to stay at the Ghosita Monastery. The king visited him and discussed the Teaching with him. He inquired how the young monks could live the celibate life joyously, and Piṇḍola explained that according to the Buddha's advice they did so by regarding women as their mothers, sisters, and daughters. At the end of the discourse, the king was so impressed that he took refuge in the Buddha and became a lay disciple (SN 35:127).

Sāmāvatī had been thinking about the wonders of the Dhamma and the intricacies of kammic influences. One thing had led to another: she had come to Kosambī as a poor refugee; then the food distributor had given her shelter; the finance minister had adopted her as his daughter; then she became the king's wife; her maid-servant had brought the Teaching to her; and she became a disciple and a stream-enterer. Subsequently she spread the Dhamma to all the women in the palace, then to Ghosaka, and now lastly also to the king. How convincing truth was! Having reflected in this way, she permeated all beings with loving-kindness, wishing them happiness and peace.

The king now tried more determinedly to control his passionate nature and to subdue greed and hate. His talks with Sāmāvatī were very helpful to him in this respect. Slowly this development culminated in his losing all sexual craving when he was in Sāmāvatī's company. He had become aware of her deep spirituality and related to her as a sister and friend rather than as a lover. While he was not free of sexual desire toward his other wives, he was willing to let Sāmāvatī continue unhindered on her path to emancipation. Soon she attained to the stage of once-returner and drew nearer and nearer to that of non-returner, an attainment which many laypeople could achieve in those days.

Māgandiyā had suspended her attacks for some time, but she continued to ponder how to take vengeance against Sāmāvatī. After much brooding, she hatched a plan with some of her relatives, whom she had won to her point of view by cunning and calumny. She proposed to kill Sāmāvatī by setting the whole women's palace on fire in such a way that it would appear to be an accident. The plan was worked out in all details. Māgandiyā left town some time beforehand, so that no suspicion could fall on her.

This arson resulted in sky-high flames which demolished the wooden palace totally. All the women residing in it were killed, including Sāmāvatī. The news of this disaster spread around town very quickly, and no other topic of conversation could be heard. Several monks, who had not been ordained very long, were also affected by the agitation, and after their alms round they went to the Buddha and inquired what would be the future rebirth of these women lay disciples with Sāmāvatī as their leader.

The Awakened One calmed their excited hearts and diverted their curiosity by answering very briefly: "Among these women, monks, some were stream-enterers, some were once-returners, and some were non-returners. None of these lay disciples had died destitute of the noble fruits" (Ud. 7:10).

The Buddha mentioned here the first three fruits of the Dhamma:

stream-entry, once-returner, and non-returner. All these disciples were safe from rebirth below the human realm, and each one was securely bound for the final goal of total liberation. This was the most important aspect of their lives and deaths and the Buddha would not go into detail.

At a later time, when the monks were discussing how unjust it was that these faithful disciples should die such a terrible death, the Buddha explained to them that the women experienced this because of a joint deed they had committed many lifetimes ago. Once, when Sāmāvatī had been queen of Benares, she had gone with her ladies-in-waiting to bathe, and feeling cold, she had asked that a bush be burned to give some warmth. Only too late she saw that a paccekabuddha was sitting immobile within the bush. Although he was not harmed, the women did not know this and feared that they would be blamed for having made a fire without due caution. Thereupon Sāmāvatī had the deluded idea to pour oil over this ascetic who was sitting in total absorption, so that burning him would obliterate their mistake. This plan could not succeed, but the evil intention and attempted murder had to bear fruit, and it was in this lifetime that the result had ripened.

The Buddha declared that one of the favorable results of the practice of loving-kindness is that fire, poison, and weapons cannot harm the practitioner. This has to be understood to mean that during the actual emanation of loving-kindness the one who radiates this quality cannot be hurt, as Sāmāvatī proved when the king's arrow did not penetrate her. But at other times the practitioner is vulnerable. Sāmāvatī had become a non-returner and was therefore free of all sensual desire and hate and of all identification with her body. It was only her body that was burnt by the fire, not her inner being. Her soft, radiant heart, imbued with love and compassion, was unassailable and untouched by the fire. It is rare for one of the saintly disciples to be murdered[20] or for a Buddha to be threatened with murder, and equally rare is it for one perfected in *mettā* and a non-returner to die a violent death. All three types of persons, however, have in common that their hearts can no longer be swayed by such violence.

Sāmāvatī's last words were: "It would not be an easy matter, even with the knowledge of a Buddha, to determine exactly the number of times our bodies have thus been burnt with fire as we have passed from birth to birth in the beginningless round of existence. Therefore, be heedful!" Stirred by these words, the ladies of the court meditated on painful feeling and thereby gained the noble paths and fruits.

Referring to the tragedy at Kosambī, the Buddha spoke the following inspirational verse to the monks:

The world is held in bondage by delusion
And only appears to be capable.
To a fool, held in bondage by his acquisitions,
Enveloped in a mass of darkness,
It appears as if it were eternal;
But for one who sees there is nothing.

(Ud. 7:10)

King Udena was overwhelmed with grief at Sāmāvatī's death and kept brooding about who could be the perpetrator of this ghastly deed. He came to the conclusion that it must have been Māgandiyā. He did not want to question her directly because he knew that she would deny it. So he thought of a ruse. He said to his ministers: "Until now I have always been apprehensive, because Sāmāvatī was forever seeking an occasion to slay me. But now I shall be able to sleep in peace." The ministers asked the king who it could have been that had done this deed. "Only someone who really loves me," the king replied. Māgandiyā had been standing nearby and when she heard that, she came forward and proudly admitted that she alone was responsible for the fire and the death of the women and Sāmāvatī. The king said that he would grant her and all her relatives a boon for this.

When all the relatives were assembled, the king had them burnt publicly and then had the earth plowed under so that all traces of the ashes were destroyed. He had Māgandiyā executed as a mass-murderess, which was his duty and responsibility, but his fury knew no bounds and he still looked for revenge. He had her killed with utmost cruelty. She died an excruciating death, which was only a foretaste of the tortures awaiting her in the nether world, after which she would have to roam in saṁsāra for a long, long time to come.

Soon King Udena regretted his cruel, revengeful deed. Again and again he saw Sāmāvatī's face in front of him, full of love for all beings, even for her enemies. He felt that by his violent fury he had removed himself from her even further than her death had done. He began to control his temper more and more and to follow the Buddha's teachings ardently.

Meanwhile Sāmāvatī had been reborn in the Pure Abodes, where she would be able to reach Nibbāna without ever returning from that world. The different results of love and hate could be seen with exemplary clarity in the lives and deaths of these two queens. When one day the monks were discussing who was alive and who dead, the Buddha said that Māgandiyā while living was dead already, while Sāmāvatī, though dead, was truly alive. Then he spoke these verses:

Heedfulness is the path to the Deathless,
Heedlessness is the path to death.
The heedful ones do not die;
The heedless are likened to the dead.

The wise then, recognizing this
As the distinction of heedfulness,
In heedfulness rejoice, delighting
In the realm of the noble ones.

The steadfast meditate persistently,
Constantly they firmly strive,
Aspiring to reach Nibbāna,
The unexcelled security from bonds.

(Dhp. 21–23)

The Buddha declared Sāmāvatī to be foremost among those female lay disciples who dwell in loving-kindness (*mettā*).

PAṬĀCĀRĀ: PRESERVER OF THE VINAYA

Paṭācārā was the beautiful daughter of a very wealthy merchant of Sāvatthī.[21] When she was sixteen years of age her parents had her confined to the top floor of a seven-story high mansion, where she was surrounded by guards to prevent her from keeping company with young men. In spite of this precaution, she became involved in a love affair with a servant in her parents' house.

When her parents arranged a marriage for her with a young man of equal social standing, she decided to elope with her lover. Having escaped from the tower by disguising herself as a servant girl, she met her lover in town, and the couple went to live in a village far from Sāvatthī. There the husband earned his living by farming a small plot of land, and the young wife had to do all the menial chores, which formerly had been performed by her parents' servants. Thus she reaped the results of her deed.

When she became pregnant she begged her husband to take her back to her parents' house to give birth there; for, she said, one's mother and father always have a soft spot in their hearts for their child and can forgive any wrongdoing. Her husband refused, however, afraid that her parents would have him arrested or even killed. When she realized that he would not yield to her entreaties, she decided to go by herself. So one day, while her husband was away at work, she slipped out the door and set out down the road toward Sāvatthī. When her husband learned from the neighbors what had happened, he followed her and soon caught up with her. Though he tried to persuade her to return, she would not listen to him but insisted on continuing. Before they could reach Sāvatthī the birth-pains started and she soon gave birth to a baby son. As she had no more reason to go to her parents' house, they turned back.

Sometime later Paṭācārā became pregnant a second time. Again she requested her husband to take her home to her parents, again he refused, and again she took matters into her own hands and started off, carrying her son. When her husband followed her and pleaded with her to return with him, she refused to listen. After they had traveled about half way to Sāvatthī a fearful storm arose quite out of season, with thunder and lightning and incessant rain. Just then her birth-pains started.

She asked her husband to find her some shelter. The husband went off to search for material to build a shed. As he was chopping down some saplings a poisonous snake, hidden in an anthill, came out and bit him. Its poison was like molten lava and instantly he fell down dead. Paṭācārā waited and waited for him, but in vain. Then she gave birth to a second son. Throughout the night both children, terrified by the buffeting of the storm, screamed at the top of their lungs, but the only protection their mother could offer them was her body, lean and haggard from her tribulations.

In the morning she placed the newborn baby on her hip, gave a finger to the older child, and set out upon the path her husband had taken, saying: "Come, dear child, your father has left us." As she turned the bend in the road she found her husband lying dead, his body stiff as a board. She wailed and lamented, blaming herself for his death, and continued on her journey.

After some time they came to the river Aciravati. On account of the rain the river had swollen and was waist-high, with a violent current. Feeling too weak to wade across with both children, Paṭācārā left the older boy on the near bank and carried the baby across to the other side. Then she returned to take the first-born across. When she was in mid-stream, a hawk in search of prey saw the newborn baby. Mistaking it for a piece of meat, the hawk came swooping down, pounced on the child, and flew off with the baby in its talons, while Paṭācārā could only look on helplessly and scream. The older boy saw his mother stop in mid-stream and heard her shouts. He thought she was calling him and started out after her, but as soon as he stepped into the river he was swept off by the turbulent current.

Wailing and lamenting, Paṭācārā went on her way, half-crazed by the triple tragedy that had befallen her: the loss of her husband and both her sons in a single day. But more misfortune lay ahead. As she approached Sāvatthī she met a traveler who was coming out from the city, and she asked him about her family. "Ask me about any other family in town but that one," he told her. "Please don't ask me about that family." She insisted, however, and thus he had to speak: "Last night, during the terrible storm, their house collapsed, killing both the elderly couple and their son. All three were cremated together just a short while ago. There," he said, pointing to a wisp of pale blue smoke swirling up in the distance, "if you look where I'm pointing you can see the smoke from their funeral pyre."

When she saw the smoke, instantly Paṭācārā went mad. She tore off her clothing and ran about naked, weeping and wailing, "Both my sons are dead, my husband on the road lies dead, my mother and father and brother burn on one funeral pyre!" Those who saw her called her a crazy fool, threw rubbish at her, and pelted her with clods of earth, but she continued on until she reached the outskirts of Sāvatthī.

At this time the Buddha was residing at the Jetavana monastery surrounded by a multitude of disciples. When he saw Paṭācārā at the entrance to the monastery he recognized her as one who was ripe for his message of deliverance. The lay disciples cried out, "Don't let that crazy woman come here!" But the Master said, "Do not hinder her; let her come to me." When she had drawn near, he told her, "Sister, regain your mindfulness!" Instantly, she regained her mindfulness. A kindly man threw her his outer cloak. She put it on, and approaching the Enlightened One, she prostrated herself at his feet and told him her tragic story.

The Teacher listened to her patiently, with deep compassion, and then replied, "Paṭācārā, do not be troubled any more. You have come to one who is able to be your shelter and refuge. It is not only today that you have met with calamity and disaster, but throughout this beginningless round of existence, weeping over the loss of sons and others dear to you, you have shed more tears than the waters of the four oceans." As he went on speaking about the perils of saṁsāra, her grief subsided. The Buddha then concluded his instructions with the following verses:

> The four oceans contain but a little water
> Compared to all the tears that we have shed,
> Smitten by sorrow, bewildered by pain.
> Why, O woman, are you still heedless?
>
> (Dhp. Comy. 2:268; BL 2:255)

No sons are there for shelter,
Nor father, nor related folk;
For one seized by the Ender
Kinsmen provide no shelter.

Having well understood this fact,
The wise man well restrained by virtues
Quickly indeed should clear
The path going to Nibbāna.

(Dhp. 288–89)

This exposition of the Enlightened One penetrated her mind so deeply that she could completely grasp the impermanence of all conditioned things and the universality of suffering. By the time the Buddha had finished his discourse, it was not a lamenting madwoman that sat at his feet but a stream-enterer, a knower of the Dhamma, one assured of final liberation.

Immediately after attaining stream-entry Paṭācārā requested the going forth and the higher ordination, and the Buddha sent her to the bhikkhunīs. After entering the Bhikkhunī Sangha, the order of nuns, Paṭācārā practiced the Dhamma with great diligence. Her efforts soon bore fruit and she attained her goal. She describes her development in her verses in the *Therīgāthā*:

Ploughing the field with their ploughs,
Sowing seeds upon the ground,
Maintaining their wives and children,
Young men acquire wealth.

Then why, when I am pure in virtue,
Practicing the Master's Teaching,
Have I not attained Nibbāna—
For I am not lazy, nor puffed up?

Having washed my feet,
I reflected upon the waters.
When I saw the foot water flow
From the high ground down the slope,
My mind became concentrated
Like an excellent thoroughbred steed.

Having taken a lamp, I entered my cell.
I inspected the bed and sat down on the couch.
Then, having taken a needle,
I pulled down the wick.
The liberation of the mind
Was like the quenching of the lamp.

(Thig. 112–16)

As Paṭācārā observed the water trickling down the slope, she noticed that some streams sank quickly into the ground, others flowed down a little farther, while others flowed all the way to the bottom of the slope. This, she recognized, was a perfect metaphor for the nature of sentient existence: some beings live for a very short time only, like her children; others live into their adult years, like her husband; still others live into old age, like her parents. But just as all the streams of water eventually had to disappear into the soil, so Death, the End-maker, lays his hand upon all living beings, and none can escape his grasp.

When this realization dawned upon Paṭācārā her mind immediately became composed. With steady concentration she contemplated conditioned phenomena as impermanent, suffering, and nonself. But still, in spite of her efforts, she could not make the breakthrough to final liberation. Fatigued, she decided to retire for the night. When she entered her dwelling and sat down on the bed, just as she extinguished the oil lamp all the momentum she had built up through her previous practice bore fruit. In a fraction of a second, simultaneously with the quenching of the lamp, supreme knowledge arose. She had reached her goal, Nibbāna, the permanent quenching of the fires of greed, hatred, and delusion.

During her career as a bhikkhunī, Paṭācārā achieved the distinction of being designated by the Buddha as the foremost among the bhikkhunīs who are experts in the Vinaya (*etadaggaṁ bhikkhunīnaṁ vinayadharānaṁ*). She was thus the female counterpart of the Elder Upāli, the chief Vinaya specialist among the bhikkhus. This appointment was the fruition of an ancient aspiration. We are told that in the Dispensation of the Buddha Padumuttara Paṭācārā had seen the Teacher assign to an elder nun the position of preeminence among nuns versed in the Vinaya, and it seemed to her as if he were taking that nun by the arm and admitting her to the Garden of Delight. So she formed her resolve and made this aspiration: "Under a Buddha like you may I become preeminent among nuns versed in the Vinaya." The Lord Padumuttara, extending his mind into the future, perceived that her aspiration would be fulfilled and gave her the prediction.

It is perhaps natural that Paṭācārā should have been particularly concerned with discipline, since in her earlier years she had experienced so keenly the bitter fruit of reckless behavior. In the order of nuns she had learned that intensive training in discipline is indispensable for achieving peace and serenity. Through her own experience, moreover, she had acquired a deep understanding of the ways of the human heart and was thus able to help other nuns in their training. Many of the nuns turned to her for guidance and found great consolation in her advice.

One example is Sister Candā, who expresses her gratitude to Paṭācārā in a verse of the *Therīgāthā*:

Because she had compassion for me,
Paṭācārā gave me the going forth;
Then she gave me an exhortation,
And enjoined me in the ultimate goal.

Having heard her word,
I followed her instruction;
The lady's exhortation was not vain.
I am canker-free with the triple knowledge!

(Thig. 125–26)

Another bhikkhunī, Uttarā, reported how Paṭācārā spoke to a group of nuns about conduct and discipline:

Exert yourselves in the Buddha's Teaching,
Which having done, one does not repent.
Having quickly washed your feet,
Sit down on one side.

Having aroused the mind,
Make it one-pointed and well concentrated.
Examine the formations
As alien and not as self.

(Thig. 176–77)

Uttarā took Paṭācārā's words to heart and thereby attained the three true knowledges.

In the *Therīgāthā* there is a description of how Paṭācārā used to teach other nuns and of the benefits they derived from her counsel. These verses, according to the colophon, are spoken by an unspecified group of thirty elder nuns who declared arahantship in the presence of Paṭācārā:

"Having taken up the pestle,
Young men pound the grain.
Maintaining their wives and children,
Young men acquire wealth.

Practice the Buddha's Teaching,
Which having done, one does not repent.
Having quickly washed your feet,
Sit down on one side.
Devoting yourself to serenity of mind,
Practice the Buddha's Teaching."

Having heard her advice, Paṭācārā's instruction,
They cleaned off their feet and sat down to one side.
Then, devoted to serenity of mind,
They practiced the Buddha's Teaching.

In the first watch of the night
They recollected their former births.
In the night's middle watch
They purified the divine eye.
In the last watch of the night
They sundered the mass of darkness.

Having risen, they worshipped her feet,
"Your instruction has been taken to heart.
As the thirty gods honor Indra,
The one unconquered in battle,
So shall we dwell honoring you.
We are cankerless, bearers of the triple knowledge."

(Thig. 119–21)

Paṭācārā was able to effect the change from a frivolous young girl to a Sangha elder so quickly because in previous births she had already developed the requisite faculties. Under previous Buddhas, it is said, she had been a nun many times. The insights she had thereby gained were hidden beneath her actions in subsequent lives, awaiting the right conditions to ripen. When her Master, the Buddha Gotama, appeared in the world, she quickly found her way to him, spurred on by suffering and by the unconscious urge to find a way to release from the beginningless round of rebirths. Drawn to the Awakened One and his emancipating Dhamma, she entered the homeless life and attained to unconditioned freedom.

AMBAPĀLĪ: THE GENEROUS COURTESAN

A figure that recurs in the early stages of many religions is that of the famous courtesan or hetaera, whose conversion and inner transformation demonstrates the invincible power of truth and goodness in its contest with the lower elements of human nature. Just as in the New Testament we find Mary Magdalene, and Mary the Egyptian in the wilderness of Egypt, and Rabi'a in the early days of Sufism, so we have Ambapālī and Sirimā in the time of the Buddha. To look at their lives is a useful exercise, if only to help free us from prejudice and presumption and to remind us that the potential for wisdom and saintliness is merely concealed, and never obliterated, by a lifestyle that is outwardly wretched and degrading.

Ambapālī's life was unusual from the very beginning.[22] One day the gardener of a Licchavi ruler in Vesālī found a baby girl lying under a mango tree and gave her the name Ambapālī, from *amba* (mango) and *pāli* (line, bridge). As she grew up she became ever more beautiful and charming. Several of the Licchavi princes wanted to marry her, which led to much quarreling and fighting, since each one wanted her for himself. Unable to solve the matter in this way, after lengthy discussions they finally decided that Ambapālī should belong to no one exclusively but to all in common. Thus she was forced to become a courtesan in the original sense of the word: a lady of pleasure at court, a position having little in common with that of an ordinary prostitute. Thanks to the goodness of her character, she exercised a calming and ennobling influence on the Licchavi princes, and she also spent large sums on charitable activities so that she became virtually an uncrowned queen in the aristocratic republic of the Licchavis.

Ambapālī's fame spread and reached King Bimbisāra of Māgadha, who came to feel that his capital too should be graced by a similar attraction. This he found in a young woman named Sālavatī, who later became the mother of Jīvaka, the court physician. First, however, King Bimbisāra went to meet Ambapālī in person. Like everyone else, he was overcome by her beauty and enjoyed the pleasures she could offer, as a result of which she bore him a son.

In the course of his final journey the Buddha stopped at Vesālī and stayed at Ambapālī's Mango Grove. Ambapālī came to pay her respects to him and the Buddha inspired her with a long discourse on the Dhamma, at the end of which she invited the Master and the order of monks to her home for the next day's meal. As she was leaving hurriedly in her best chariot, the Licchavi princes, in their best chariots, drew up alongside her and asked why she was traveling in such a hurry. She answered that the Enlightened One and his monks would be coming to her home for their alms meal on the following day and she had to make sure everything was ready. The noblemen begged her to yield this privilege to them, offering her one hundred thousand gold coins for it, but she replied that she would not sell this meal for the whole of Vesālī and its treasures. So the Licchavis went to the Buddha and invited him to accept the next day's meal from them. The Blessed One, however, refused since he had already accepted Ambapālī's invitation. The Licchavi's then snapped their fingers—an expression of frustration—and exclaimed, "We have been defeated by that mango girl! We have been tricked by that mango girl!" The next day, after the Buddha had finished his meal at Ambapālī's home, Ambapālī drew up close to him and made a gift to the Order of her wonderful park, the Mango Grove, where the Buddha had already preached some sermons in the past.

Ambapālī's son by King Bimbisāra became a monk, with the name Vimala-Kondañña, and achieved arahantship. Later, after listening to one of her son's sermons, Ambapālī entered the order of nuns. She took her own body as a meditation subject, reflecting on its impermanence and vulnerability to pain, and by doing so she attained arahantship. In her verses of the *Therīgāthā,* spoken in her old age, she movingly compares her former beauty with her present withered state:

> My hair was black, the color of bees,
> Each hair ending in a curl.
> Now on account of old age
> It has become like fibers of hemp:
> Not otherwise is the word
> Of the Speaker of Truth.
>
> Covered with flowers my head was fragrant
> Like a casket of delicate scent.
> Now on account of old age
> It smells like the fur of a dog.

Not otherwise is the word
Of the Speaker of Truth.

Formerly my eyebrows were beautiful
Like crescents well painted by an artist's hand.
Now on account of old age
They droop down lined by wrinkles.
Not otherwise is the word
Of the Speaker of Truth.

Brilliant and beautiful like jewels,
My eyes were dark blue and long in shape.
Now, hit hard by old age,
Their beauty has utterly vanished.
Not otherwise is the word
Of the Speaker of Truth.

Formerly my teeth looked beautiful,
The color of plantain buds.
Now on account of old age
They are broken and yellow.
Not otherwise is the word
Of the Speaker of Truth.

Formerly my two breasts were beautiful,
Swollen, round, compact, and high.
Now they just hang down and sag
Like a pair of empty water bags.
Not otherwise is the word
Of the Speaker of Truth.

Formerly my body was beautiful,
Like a well-polished sheet of gold.
Now it is all covered with wrinkles.
Not otherwise is the word
Of the Speaker of Truth.

Formerly both my feet looked beautiful,
Like (shoes) full of cotton-wool.
Now, because of old age

They are cracked and wrinkled all over.
Not otherwise is the word
Of the Speaker of Truth.

Such is this body, now decrepit,
The abode of many kinds of suffering.
It is nothing but an aged house
From which the plaster has fallen off.
Not otherwise is the word
Of the Speaker of Truth.

(Thig. 252–270; selections)

This contemplation, assiduously practiced, gave Ambapālī a progressively deeper insight into the nature of existence. She gained the recollection of previous lives and saw the meanderings she had undergone in her journey through saṁsāra: at times she had been a prostitute, at other times a nun. She saw too that despite the degradation to which she had sometimes plunged, she had repeatedly been capable of acts of unusual generosity, which brought their own rewards in her successive births. Often she had been beautiful, but always her physical beauty had faded, crushed by aging and death. Now in her last life she had finally attained, through the utter extinction of delusion, the imperishable beauty of final deliverance. In the following verses Ambapālī bears testimony to her elevation to the status of a "true daughter of the Buddha":

Attended by millions of creatures
I went forth in the Conqueror's Teaching.
I have attained the unshakable state,
I am a true daughter of the Buddha.

I am a master of spiritual powers
And of the purified ear-element.
I am, O great sage, a master of knowledge
Encompassing the minds of others.

I know my previous abodes,
The divine eye is purified,
All my cankers have been destroyed,
Now there is no more re-becoming.

(Ap.ii, 4:9, vv. 213–15)

SIRIMĀ AND UTTARĀ

The story of Sirimā, as recorded in the Pāli commentaries, begins with a woman named Uttarā, the daughter of the wealthy merchant Puṇṇa in Rājagaha. Both Puṇṇa and Uttarā were followers of the Buddha.[23] A rich merchant named Sumana, who in earlier times had been Puṇṇa's benefactor, wished to marry his son to Uttarā. Puṇṇa, however, was unwilling to accept the proposal. The merchant reminded him that for many years Puṇṇa had been in his employment and that his present wealth had been accumulated during those years of service. Puṇṇa answered him: "You and your family follow wrong systems of belief, but my daughter cannot live without the Three Jewels." The merchant appealed to other members of their class, who came to plead with Puṇṇa to give his daughter to the merchant's son. In the end, moved by the entreaties of his respected fellow citizens, Puṇṇa had no choice but to yield his daughter.

The marriage took place at the very beginning of the rainy season, when the monks enter upon their annual three months' rains retreat. After moving into her husband's house, Uttarā no longer had any opportunity to meet monks or nuns, let alone to give them alms and listen to the Dhamma. For two and a half months she endured this privation, but then she sent her parents this message: "Why have you thrown me into such a prison? It would have been better to have sold me as a slave than to have married me into a family of unbelievers. In all the time I have been here I have not been allowed to perform a single deed of merit."

Puṇṇa was terribly upset when he received this message. Out of compassion for his daughter he devised the following scheme to help her achieve her objective. He sent his daughter fifteen thousand golden coins along with the following message: "Sirimā, the courtesan in our town, charges a thousand golden coins for a night of pleasure. Offer her the enclosed sum of money to entertain your husband for a fortnight while you go and perform whatever meritorious deeds you like." Uttarā followed this advice and brought Sirimā to the house. When her husband saw the beautiful courtesan, he readily agreed to let her take his wife's place for a fortnight, so that Uttarā would be free to give offerings and listen to the Teaching as much as she wanted.

This was the last fortnight before the end of the rains retreat, after which the monks would again start their wanderings. For this two-week period, Uttarā begged the Buddha and his monks to come for alms every day at her home. The Buddha, out of sympathy, agreed to this invitation, and thus she was able to listen to many teachings. On the next to last day, the day before the closing ceremony of the rains retreat, Uttarā was constantly busy with preparations in the kitchen. Seeing her scurrying about, her husband could not help being amused at what he considered sheer foolishness. As he watched her running here and there, covered with sweat and soot, he thought: "This silly fool does not know how to enjoy her wealth in comfort. Instead, she rushes blindly about, happy that she is serving that bald-headed ascetic." He smiled to himself and walked away.

When Sirimā, the courtesan, saw him smile, she wondered what had evoked it. Seeing Uttarā near by, she jumped to the conclusion that they had shared a moment of intimacy. This made her angry and upset. For two weeks she had enjoyed the feeling of being the mistress of the house, and now this incident reminded her that she was only a guest. She felt intensely jealous of Uttarā and wanted to hurt her. So she went into the kitchen, took a ladleful of boiling oil, and approached Uttarā. The latter saw her coming and thought to herself: "My friend Sirimā has done me a great service. The earth may be too small, the Brahma-world too low, but my friend's virtue is very great, for it is through her help that I have been enabled to give offerings and listen to the teachings. If now there is any anger in me, let the oil burn me, but if I am free of anger it won't burn me." And she suffused Sirimā with loving-kindness. When the courtesan poured the oil over her head, it flowed off harmlessly, as if it were cool water.

Sirimā, infuriated, scooped up another ladleful of boiling oil, hoping this time it would burn. At this point Uttarā's maids intervened. They grabbed hold of Sirimā, threw her to the floor, and beat and kicked her. Uttarā first tried in vain to stop them, but finally she placed herself between the maids and Sirimā and asked her quietly: "Why did you do this evil thing?" Then she cleaned her with warm water and anointed her with the finest perfume. Sirimā, coming to her senses, remembered that she was indeed only a guest in the house. She thought: "I have indeed done an evil thing, pouring boiling oil over her, just because her husband smiled at her. Not only did she endure this without anger, but when her maids attacked me she held them back and protected me. Let my head split into seven pieces if I do not beg her forgiveness." She fell to Uttarā's feet and begged to be forgiven. Uttarā said: "My father is still living. If he forgives you, so will I." Said Sirimā, "I shall go to your father, the rich guild master, and ask him to forgive me."

Uttarā replied, "Puṇṇa is the father who brought me into the round of suffering. If the father who is bringing me out of the round forgives you, then so will I."

"But who is the father who is bringing you out of the round of suffering?"

"The Buddha, the Fully Enlightened One."

"But I don't know him. What shall I do?"

"The Teacher will be coming here tomorrow, together with his monks. Come yourself, bringing whatever offering you can, and ask his forgiveness."

Sirimā agreed gladly and went home. She told her many servants to prepare all sorts of foods and the next day brought them to Uttarā's house. She, however, still ashamed of her bad behavior, did not dare to serve the monks herself. Uttarā took charge of everything. When everyone had eaten, Sirimā knelt at the Buddha's feet and begged forgiveness. "What for?" he asked. Sirimā told him about the whole incident. The Enlightened One asked Uttarā to confirm what had happened and inquired what her thoughts had been when she saw Sirimā coming toward her with the boiling oil. "I suffused her with loving-kindness," said Uttarā, "and thought to myself: 'My friend Sirimā has done me a great service…'"

"Excellent, Uttarā, excellent!" said the Blessed One. "That is the right way to overcome anger." And he added the following verse:

> Overcome anger by non-anger,
> Conquer evil by goodness,
> Conquer the niggardly with a gift,
> And the liar with truth.
>
> (Dhp. 223)

Then the Master expounded the Dhamma to all those present and explained the Four Noble Truths. At the end of this instruction Uttarā attained the fruit of once-returning. Her husband, until then an unbeliever, as well as her equally skeptical parents-in-law, all attained the fruit of stream-entry.

Sirimā too attained the fruit of stream-entry. Unwilling to continue as a courtesan, she devoted herself to looking after the order of monks and performing other meritorious works. She invited the Sangha to send eight monks to her house every day for their meal, distributing invitation vouchers that could be shared out within the Order. She always served the monks who came to her with her own hands, and her food offerings were so abundant that each portion would have been enough for three or four people.

One day, one of the eight monks who had eaten at Sirimā's house went back to his monastery three miles away. When he arrived there, the elders asked him whether there had been enough to eat. He explained to them the arrangement whereby eight monks were fed every day. When they asked whether the food had been good he went into raptures. The food, he said, was indescribable; only the best of everything was served, and the helpings were so generous that they would each be enough for three or four persons. But, he went on, Sirimā's looks surpassed her offerings: she was beautiful and graceful and radiant with charm.

As the new arrival spoke, one of the monks listening to his description was struck with love for Sirimā, despite the fact that he had never set eyes on her. Anxious to see her on the very next day, early in the morning he contrived to obtain one of the vouchers. It so happened that just on that day Sirimā had fallen ill and had taken off all her finery and gone to bed. When she was told that the monks had arrived, she did not have the strength even to get up but left it to her maids to serve them. Once all the bowls had been filled, and the monks had started eating, she made an effort to rise from her bed and, supported by two maids, came painfully into the room to pay her respects to the monks. She was so weak that her whole body shook. The lovesick monk, seeing her thus, thought: "She looks radiantly beautiful even when she is ill. Imagine how great her beauty must be when she is well and wearing all her jewelry!" Passion long suppressed arose mightily in him, and he could not even eat. So taking his bowl, he wandered back to his monastery, where he covered the bowl and lay down on his bed. Though his friends tried to coax him to eat, they did not succeed.

That same evening Sirimā died. King Bimbisāra sent a message to the Buddha: "Sir, Jīvaka's younger sister has died."[24] The Buddha sent him a message to the effect that Sirimā's body should not be cremated at once but placed in the charnel ground, where it was to be guarded to prevent carrion crows and other beasts from devouring it. This was done. After three days the putrefying corpse was all swollen and crawling with worms, so that it looked like a pot of rice boiling on the fire with bubbles rising to the surface. Then King Bimbisāra decreed that all adult inhabitants of Rājagaha were to file past the body, to see Sirimā in her present condition. Failure to do so would be punished with a fine of eight gold coins. At the same time he also sent a message to the Buddha inviting him to come to the charnel ground with his monks.

The lovesick monk had not eaten for four days and the food in his bowl was by now also crawling with worms. His friends came to him and said: "Brother, the Teacher is going to see Sirimā." At the word "Sirimā" the monk was galvanized, and forgetting his weakness and hunger he jumped up, emptied and rinsed his bowl, and joined the others who were going to look at Sirimā. There, a large crowd had congregated. The Buddha with his monks stood to one side, then came the nuns, then the king with his retinue, then the male and female devotees.

The Buddha asked King Bimbisāra: "Who is this, great king?" "Jīvaka's younger sister, sir, Sirimā by name." "This is Sirimā?" "Yes, sir." "Then let it be proclaimed with beating of drums that whoever pays the sum of one thousand coins may have Sirimā."

But no man wanted Sirimā now, not even at a lower price, not even for one penny, not even for free.

Then the Buddha spoke: "Here, monks, you see a woman who was loved by the world. In this same city, in the past, men would gladly pay a thousand gold coins to enjoy her for just one night. Now, however, no one will have her, even for nothing. This is what the body comes to, perishable and fragile, made attractive only through ornaments, a heap of wounds with nine openings, held together by three hundred bones, a continuing burden. Only fools attach fancies and illusions to such an evanescent thing." And he concluded with this verse:

> See this skinbag all adorned;
> It is just a mass of wounds.
> Diseased, an object of desires,
> It has nothing stable or lasting.
>
> (Dhp. 147)

After the Buddha had given this "funeral oration," a teaching with a practical object lesson, the lovesick monk was freed from his passion. Concentrated on the contemplation of the body, he cultivated insight and attained arahantship.

Sirimā, however, had attended her own funeral. After her death she was reborn as a devatā in the heaven of the Thirty-three. Looking down upon the human world, she saw the Buddha with his monks and the assembly of people standing near her corpse. In a blaze of glory she descended from heaven, accompanied by five hundred celestial maidens in five hundred chariots. Then she dismounted and saluted the Blessed One.

The Venerable Vaṅgīsa, the foremost poet in the Sangha, addressed her in verse, asking her from where she had come and what meritorious deeds she had performed to obtain such success. Sirimā replied to him in verse:

In that excellent, well-built city among the hills,
I was an attendant of the excellent, splendid king.
I was perfectly trained in dance and in song;
In Rājagaha they knew me as Sirimā.

The Buddha, the lord of seers, the guide,
Taught me the origin, suffering, impermanence;
The unconditioned, eternal cessation of suffering;
And this path, unbent, straight, auspicious.

Hearing of the deathless state, the unconditioned,
The Teaching of the supreme Tathāgata,
I was perfectly restrained by the precepts,
Established in the Dhamma taught by the Buddha, best of men.

Having known the dust-free state, the unconditioned,
Taught by the supreme Tathāgata,
Right there I reached the serene concentration:
That was my supreme assurance.

Having gained the supreme Deathless that makes for distinction,
I was fixed in destiny, distinguished in penetration.
Free from perplexity, honored by a multitude,
I enjoy abundant sport and delight.

Thus I, a devatā, am a seer of the Deathless,
A female disciple of the supreme Tathāgata;
A seer of Dhamma, established in the first fruit,
A stream-enterer, I am free of the bad bourns.

Respectful towards the splendid King of Dhamma,
I have come to worship the Supreme One
And the inspiring monks who delight in goodness,
To revere the auspicious assembly of ascetics.

I was joyful and elated when I saw the Sage,
The Tathāgata, best charioteer of tamable men.
I worship the supremely compassionate one,
The cutter of craving, the guide who delights in goodness.

(Vv. 137–49)

ISIDĀSĪ: A JOURNEY THROUGH SAṀSĀRA

In Pāṭaliputta, which was to become the capital of King Asoka, there lived two Buddhist nuns, Isidāsī and Bodhī, both skilled in contemplation, well versed in the Teaching, free from all defilements.[25] One day after they had gone on their alms round and had finished their meal, the two friends sat in the shade, and their conversation drifted towards their personal histories. The older nun, whose name was Bodhī, had apparently undergone much suffering before she joined the Order, and she wondered why her younger companion Isidāsī had decided to renounce the world. The latter was still in the flush of youth. She had a cheerful countenance, and it hardly seemed conceivable that life could have left bitter traces on her. So how, the older nun wondered, had the suffering of existence revealed itself to her and impelled her to a life of renunciation?

You are lovely, noble Isidāsī,
And your youth has not yet faded,
What was the flaw that you had seen
That led you to pursue renunciation?

(Thig. 403)

Isidāsī told her story. She had been born in the south, in Ujjeni, the capital of the kingdom of Avantī. Her father was a wealthy citizen, and she was his only, much-loved daughter. A business friend of his, a wealthy merchant, asked him to give his daughter in marriage to his son, and Isidāsī's father was glad for his daughter to marry into the friend's family. Isidāsī was an upright, well-disciplined young woman. The deep respect for her parents that she had learned at home she extended equally to her parents-in-law, and she entertained a warm, friendly relationship with all her husband's relatives, maintaining always a deliberate attitude of proper modesty. She was also a very industrious and conscientious housewife. She served her husband with great love, even cooking his meals with her own hands rather than leaving this task to the servants:

By myself I cooked the rice,
By myself I washed the dishes.
As a mother looks after her only son,
So did I serve my husband.

I showed him devotion unsurpassed,

I served him with a humble mind;
I rose early, I was diligent, virtuous—
And yet my husband hated me.

(Thig. 412–13)

Isidāsī was indeed one of those ideal wives on the Indian model who selflessly serve their husbands, and her husband had every reason to rejoice that he had found such a life companion; for even amongst Indian women, generally known for their gentle disposition, she excelled and was truly a treasure. Yet, strangely, her husband could not tolerate her, and he went to his parents and voiced his complaint. His parents, however, praised her virtues and asked the young man, with great bewilderment, why he did not like her. He explained that she certainly had done nothing to hurt him, nor had she ever displayed any aggression against him, but he simply did not like her, he was tired of her, he had had enough of her, and he was ready to leave the house so that he would not have to set eyes on her any more (Thig. 414–16).

The parents were very upset and could not understand their son. So they asked Isidāsī to come to them, sadly told her how matters stood, and begged her to tell them what she had done, assuring her that she could speak in full confidence. They must have imagined that their son had for some reason been reticent about speaking up, and they hoped that their beloved daughter-in-law would tell them what was amiss so that they could take steps to reconcile her husband to her. The whole affair was conducted on all sides in a calm and dignified manner. Neither the parents nor the son were at all violent or aggressive, and the son was even ready to leave the house and go his own way rather than do anything against Isidāsī. The parents too were ready to forgive their daughter-in-law for any wrong that she might have done. But she answered quite truthfully:

I have done nothing wrong,
I have done him no harm,
I have not spoken rudely to him.
What have I done that my husband hates me?

(Thig. 418)

In fact, nothing whatsoever had happened. Even her husband himself did not know why he hated her and could give no rational explanation for his antipathy. As Isidāsī's in-laws could not remedy the situation, and as they did not want to lose their son, they had no choice but to send her back to her parents. Such an exemplary woman, they thought, would surely find another husband with whom she could be happy. For Isidāsī, of course, this was an absolutely humiliating experience. Returning to her parents as a rejected wife, she was almost devastated:

> Rejected, overcome by suffering,
> They led me back to my father's house.
> "While appeasing our son," they exclaimed,
> "We have lost the beautiful goddess of fortune!"
>
> (Thig. 419)

Her father took his only daughter back under his protection. Though what had happened was beyond his comprehension, he started looking for another husband for her. Among his acquaintances he found a virtuous and wealthy man who was so happy at the prospect of marrying Isidāsī that he offered to provide half the usual marriage fee. But although Isidāsī served her new husband with the utmost love and affection, after barely a month the same strange pattern once again repeated itself. The second husband lost his affection for her, became irritated with her mere presence, and sent her back to her parents, the marriage annulled.

Now both she and her father were totally at a loss. Shortly thereafter a mendicant came to the house in quest of alms. The man did not seem too happy with his ascetic condition, and it suddenly occurred to Isidāsī's father to offer him his daughter. The father suggested to the ascetic that he discard his robe and begging bowl and settle into a more comfortable lifestyle, with a splendid mansion for his home and the beautiful Isidāsī for his wife. The ascetic readily agreed to this tempting offer, which was beyond his wildest expectations. But after only two weeks he came to his father-in-law and begged him to return his robe and bowl: he would rather starve as the poorest of beggars than spend one more day in Isidāsī's company. The whole family pleaded with him to tell them what he wanted; they would fulfill his every wish if he only agreed to remain, for he was a virtuous man. But he refused every inducement. He was, he said, sure of one thing only: he could no longer stay with Isidāsī under one roof. And with these words he left (Thig. 422–25).

Isidāsī was utterly miserable and considered committing suicide rather than having to go on bearing such suffering. Now it so happened that on that same day a Buddhist nun named Jinadattā came to her father's house on her alms round. Seeing the nun's peaceful countenance, Isidāsī thought that she should become a nun herself. She made her wish known, but her father, reluctant to lose his only daughter, pleaded with her to stay at home. Here, he said, she could perform meritorious deeds that would lead to her future welfare. But Isidāsī wept and begged her father to let her go forth. By this time she had realized that her incomprehensible fate must be due to some deeper cause, some evil kamma created in a former life. Finally her father relented:

> Then my father said to me,
> "Attain enlightenment and the supreme state,
> Gain Nibbāna which the best of men
> Has himself already realized."
>
> (Thig. 432)

Thus Isidāsī took leave of her parents and her circle of relatives. She followed the elder nun to the monastery and went forth into the homeless life.

After her ordination she spent seven days in utmost exertion, and by the end of the week she had realized the three higher knowledges—the recollection of past lives, the knowledge of the passing away and rebirth of beings, and the knowledge of the destruction of defilements. Through her ability to remember previous lives Isidāsī found the underlying causes behind her marital failures in this life, and much else that lay hidden in the dim recesses of saṁsāra.

Looking past into the past Isidāsi saw that eight lives ago she had been a man—a goldsmith, handsome and rich, full of the intoxication of youth. Dazzled by physical beauty, this dashing goldsmith had seduced the wives of others, with no regard for decency and morality. He loved to conquer other men's wives, one after another, like a butterfly flitting from flower to flower. Like Casanova or Don Juan he played with love and felt no compunction over the damage he could cause. All he wanted was the thrill of conquest, the titillation of lust, but never any responsibilities, any commitment, any obligation to love. He wanted to take his pleasure, again and again, and he wanted change. He broke his victims' hearts, and did not care in the slightest what happened to them. Whether he broke hearts or marriages was for him a matter of indifference. And so he danced for a while, as it were, on the top of a volcano—until his time was up.

Then he fell into the dark abyss that he had dug out for himself by his own reckless conduct. He was reborn in hell, where there is wailing and gnashing of teeth, and there he experienced a thousand times over the suffering that he had inflicted upon others. He had been infinitely ruthless in deed and in intention, so in hell he was subjected to infinitely ruthless punishment, without pity and without mercy, just as he himself had been pitiless and cruel on earth. The special punishment for adulterers and lechers in hell, they say, is an excursion without respite through a forest where every leaf is a sword. They see a beautiful woman in the distance, run after her, and are cut on all sides by the razor-sharp sword edges. And the woman, like Fortune on her sphere, runs ahead and beckons but can never be reached. Yet the lecher, impelled by obsessive desire, cannot help himself: time and again he throws himself into the forest and is cut to shreds by the sharp leaves. "And I suffered torment for a long time," says Isidāsī the nun (Thig. 436). She clearly remembered her human existence as the goldsmith and knew full well why he had to undergo such bitter atonement.

After completion of this hellish punishment, he moved on in saṁsāra. In his next life he had forgotten everything and was reborn in the womb of a monkey. As he had worked through the worst consequences of his misdeeds, he was beginning to rise slowly from the depths. After having done penance for the hate that was in him when he coarsely rejected the women he had seduced and despised their deceived husbands, he still retained the drives of a purely animal craving, and through the influence of these tendencies he assumed the form of an animal. This is a literal manifestation of the saying of Dionysius the Areopagite: "The nature of desire is such, that it turns a man into the thing he desires." That man—who had indulged his lustfulness without scruples or inhibitions—now became a being not subject to the rule of reason, an animal, and precisely the animal that is nearest to man: a monkey. Only seven days after his birth, however, the leader of the monkey tribe bit off the newborn's sexual organs, to prevent future rivalry:

> A great monkey, leader of the troop,
> Castrated me when I was seven days old.
> This was the fruit of that kamma
> Because I had seduced others' wives.
>
> (Thig. 437)

After dying as a monkey, he was reborn as a sheep, the offspring of a lame one-eyed ewe. Further, he was made a gelding, unable to satisfy the sexual urge. He lived in misery thus for twelve years, suffering from intestinal worms and constantly obliged to transport children. His third animal existence was as an ox, castrated, and forced to pull the plow and cart throughout the year, with hardly any rest (Thig. 440–41). Hard work was precisely what the licentious goldsmith had always avoided, and now hard work was precisely what he could not escape. He had many duties to perform and very little pleasure, not only because he was castrated, but also because he had to pull heavy loads all day long and, at one point, also lost his eyesight.

In the next life, he who had been successively goldsmith, hell dweller, monkey, sheep, and ox, again arrived at human status—but as a hermaphrodite, a cross between male and female (Thig. 442). Because in his earlier existence he had been so obsessed with sexual organs, both his own and those of women, now he found himself having both at the same time—which, of course, again precluded all satisfaction, making of him an outsider in society, especially since he was the son of a slave girl and had been born in the gutter. He eked out an unhappy existence for thirty years and then died.

In the next existence, the being who had gone from manhood to a life in hell, from hell to animal life, and from animal to hermaphrodite, was reborn as a woman. This completed the sex change. He had now become what was formerly the object of his desires: a woman. Indeed, desire turns a man into the things he desires. The newborn girl was the daughter of a man in the lowest social caste, an impecunious carter who failed in everything he undertook and ended up owing everybody money. As his creditors were constantly harassing him and he had nothing to give them, he offered to one of them, a wealthy merchant, his daughter as a slave. The merchant released him from his debts, gave him some money as a bonus, and took the girl. She wept and grieved, but all to no avail—she was taken from home into slavery. When she was sixteen years old, and an attractive virgin, the son of the house fell in love with her and took her as his secondary wife. He was already happily married to an honorable, virtuous wife, who loved him above everything. She was naturally very distressed when her husband took another wife and felt rejected. The younger woman, however, did everything in her power to defend her newly won position and succeeded in sowing discord between husband and wife. Having known the misery of utter poverty and the burdens of a slave's life, she was determined to defend her position as the wife of a rich man, and thus she did everything possible to displace her rival. This brought about much feuding and quarreling, until she finally managed to sever the tie between her husband and his first wife (Thig. 443–46).

After that life, in which she had again misused the opportunities for happiness offered by human birth, she was reborn as Isidāsī. The fruit of her earlier bad actions having now been exhausted, she was born as a perfect human being. But because in her preceding life she had driven another woman away from her home and enjoyed taking her place, she now had to suffer the contempt and neglect of three successive husbands. None of the three men she held dear wanted her, she was despised and rejected as wife by all of them, apparently without justification but actually as a consequence of her own earlier actions. Since, however, she did not react with anger and aggression, but endeavored at all times to be a model wife, she was able to build on this virtuous foundation. After becoming a nun she attained the meditative absorptions with unusual rapidity and quickly penetrated the key to her mysterious fate.

Once Isidāsī had understood all these connections, once she had realized the evil consequences of unrestrained craving and seen how this leads time and again to self-assertion at the expense of others, the wish arose in her to turn away altogether from the whole cycle of suffering. She understood the interplay of inclinations in her earlier lives and in her present life, and she saw with the divine eye that the same holds true for other beings as well. And thus, having experienced the Teaching in actual practice, she finally attained the third higher knowledge, the full and complete understanding of the Four Noble Truths, which brings release from saṁsāra forever. Thus she became one of the holy ones, an arahant. Having wandered from lecher to hell dweller, then through three lives as a male animal to rebirth as a hermaphrodite, then as a poor slave child who rose to wealth, and finally as a rejected wife—eight lives full of confusion, full of craving and hate—she had had enough. Now, free at last, she could say:

> This was the fruit of that past deed,
> That although I served them like a slave,
> They rejected me and went their way:
> Of that, too, I have made an end.
>
> (Thig. 447)

CHAPTER 8

AṄGULIMĀLA

A Murderer's Road to Sainthood

Hellmuth Hecker

THE MAKING OF A SERIAL KILLER

AṄGULIMĀLA IS ONE of the best known figures of the Buddhist scriptures. The dramatic story of his transformation from a serial killer into a peaceful and enlightened arahant is known to every child in Buddhist lands, and pregnant women look upon him almost as their own patron saint whose protective verse of blessing ensures a successful delivery. The Buddha had often warned his disciples not to judge others on the basis of their appearance and external behavior. Only a Buddha, endowed with his unique faculties, can see into another's heart with impeccable accuracy. In Aṅgulimāla's case, the Buddha had seen his hidden potential to win freedom in this very life, not only from rebirth in the lower worlds but from all the suffering of the beginningless round of existence.

In Christianity, too, we find instances of a radical change in the moral character of people: there is the "thief on the cross" at Golgatha, whom Jesus promised would be with him in Paradise that same day; and the chief of a gang of robbers who was converted by St. Francis of Assisi and became a monk. Cases like these have always moved the hearts of the devout, but for the skeptical they raise the question how such changes are possible. Aṅgulimāla's story might suggest an answer to that question.[1]

In the Buddha's time there was a learned brahmin named Bhaggavā Gagga who served as the royal chaplain in the court of King Pasenadi of Kosala, one of the kingdom's highest offices. One night his wife, Mantānī, gave birth to a son. The father cast the boy's horoscope and to his consternation found that his son was born under the "robber constellation," indicating that the boy had an innate disposition to a life of crime. One can well imagine what the father must have felt when confronted with that shocking and unexpected revelation.

In the morning the brahmin went to the palace as usual and asked the king how he had slept. "How could I have slept well?" replied the king. "I woke up in the night and saw that my auspicious weapons lying at the end of my bed were sparkling brightly, so I was too frightened and perturbed to fall asleep again. Could this mean danger to the kingdom or my life?"

The brahmin said: "Do not have any fear, O king. The same strange phenomenon has taken place throughout the city, and it does not concern you. Last night my wife bore me a son, and unfortunately his horoscope has the robber constellation. This must have caused the weapons to sparkle."

"Will he be a lone robber or the chief of a gang?"

"He will be a loner, your majesty. What if we were to kill him now and prevent future misdeeds?"

"As he would be a loner, teacher, let him be raised and properly educated. Then, perhaps, he may lose his evil propensities."

The boy was named Ahiṁsaka, which means "Harmless." The name was given to him with the hope it would plant in his mind an ideal toward which to strive. When he grew up he was physically strong and powerful, but he was also quite well behaved and intelligent. As he was diligent in his studies, his parents had good reason to think that his evil proclivities were being held in check by his education and by the religious atmosphere of their home. This, of course, made them very happy.

In due course his father sent Ahiṁsaka to Takkasilā, the famous ancient university of India, to pursue his higher education. He was accepted by the foremost teacher at that seat of learning, and he continued to be so studious that he surpassed all his fellow students. He also served his teacher so faithfully and humbly that he soon became his teacher's favorite pupil. He even received his meals from his teacher's family. This made his fellow students resentful and envious. They discussed the problem among themselves: "Since that young Ahiṁsaka came we are almost forgotten. We must put a stop to this and cause a break between him and the teacher." The well-tried way of calumny was not easy, for neither Ahiṁsaka's studiousness nor his conduct and noble ancestry gave an opportunity for denigrating him. "We have to alienate the teacher from him and thus cause a break," they thought, and so they decided that three groups of people should approach the teacher at intervals.

The first group of pupils went to the teacher and said, "Some talk is being heard around the house." "What is it, my dears?" "We believe it is about Ahiṁsaka plotting against you." Hearing this, the teacher became excited and scolded them: "Get away, you miserable lot! Do not try to cause dissension between me and my son!" After some time, the second set of pupils spoke to him in a similar way. So also a third group, who added: "If our teacher does not trust us, he may investigate for himself."

Finally the poisonous seed of suspicion took root in his heart, and he came to believe that Ahiṁsaka, so strong in body and mind, actually wanted to push him out. Once suspicion is roused, one can always find something that seems to confirm it. So the teacher's suspicion grew into conviction. "I must kill him or get him killed," he thought. But then he considered: "It will not be easy to kill such a strong man. Besides, if he is slain while living here as my pupil, it will harm my reputation and students may no longer come to me. I must think of some other device to get rid of him as well as punish him."

It happened that soon afterwards Ahiṁsaka's course of studies had come to an end and he was preparing to go home. Then the teacher called him and said: "My dear Ahiṁsaka, for one who has completed his studies, it is a duty to give a gift of honor to his teacher. So give it to me!" "Certainly, master! What shall I give?" "You must bring me a thousand human little fingers of the right hand. This will then be your concluding ceremonial homage to the science you have learned."

The teacher probably expected that Ahiṁsaka, in his attempt to complete that deed, would either be killed himself or would be arrested and executed. Perhaps the teacher may also have secretly cast Ahiṁsaka's horoscope, seen from it his latent propensity to violence, and now tried to incite it.

Faced with such an outrageous demand, Ahiṁsaka first exclaimed: "O master! How can I do that? My family has never engaged in violence. They are harmless people." "Well, if the science does not receive its due ceremonial homage, it will yield no fruit for you." So, after suitable persuasion, Ahiṁsaka finally consented. After worshipping his teacher, he left.

The sources on which this present narrative is based do not tell us what had finally convinced Ahiṁsaka to accept his teacher's macabre demand without any stronger protest. One of his motivations may have been the belief that an unquestioning obedience to the guru was the first duty of a pupil, this being an echo of the higher principles that governed his earlier life. But the stronger factor behind his decision was probably his innate disposition to violence. His teacher's words may have aroused in him a strange attraction to a life of violent adventure, which he might also have seen as a challenge to his manly prowess.

Tradition reports that in one of his former lives Ahiṁsaka had been a powerful spirit, a so-called yakkha, who used his superhuman strength to kill human beings to satisfy his appetite for human flesh. In all his past existences that are reported in the Jātakas, two traits are prominent in him: his physical strength and his lack of compassion. This was the dark heritage of his past which broke into his present life, submerging the good qualities of his early years.

So, in his final response to his teacher's demand, Ahiṁsaka did not even think of the alternative: to gather the fingers from corpses thrown into India's open charnel grounds. Instead he equipped himself with a set of weapons, including a large sword, and went into the wild Jālinī forest in his home state, Kosala. There he lived on a high cliff where he could observe the road below. When he saw travelers approaching, he hurried down, slew them, and took one finger from each of his victims. First he hung the fingers on a tree where birds ate the flesh and dropped the bones. When he saw that the bones were rotting on the ground, he threaded the finger bones and wore them as a garland. From that he received the nickname Aṅgulimāla, "Finger Garland."

AṄGULIMĀLA BECOMES A MONK

As Aṅgulimāla continued to launch his gory attacks, people shunned the forest and soon nobody dared to go there, not even the firewood gatherers. Aṅgulimāla now had to approach the outskirts of villages and, from a hiding place, attack people who passed, cutting off their fingers and threading them to his necklace. He even went so far as to enter houses at night, killing the inhabitants just to take their fingers. He did this in several villages. As no one could resist Aṅgulimāla's enormous strength, people abandoned their homes and the villages became deserted. The homeless villagers, having trekked to Sāvatthī, camped outside the city and went to the royal palace where, weeping and lamenting, they told King Pasenadi of their plight. Now the king saw that firm action was necessary and he had the drum of royal announcements beaten to proclaim: "Quickly, the robber Aṅgulimāla must be captured. Let an army detachment gather for instructions!"

Apparently, Aṅgulimāla's true name and descent had remained unknown, but his mother intuitively sensed that it could be none other than her son, Ahiṁsaka, who had never returned from Takkasilā. So, when she heard the public announcement, she was sure that he had fallen into those evil ways predicted by his horoscope. She went to her husband, the brahmin Bhaggavā, and said: "That fearful bandit is our son! Now soldiers have set out to capture him. Please, dear, go find him! Plead with him to change his way of life and bring him home. Otherwise the king will have him killed." But the brahmin replied, "I have no use for such a son. The king may do with him as he likes." A mother's heart, however, is soft, and out of love for her son she set out alone for the forest area where Aṅgulimāla was reported to have been hiding. She wanted to warn him and save him, and to implore him to renounce his evil ways and return with her.

At that time Aṅgulimāla had already gathered 999 fingers, and only one more was needed to complete the target of a thousand set by his teacher. To bring his task to an end he may well have killed his mother, who was drawing ever closer along the road. But matricide is one of the five heinous offenses that produce, irreversibly, an immediate rebirth in hell. Thus, without knowing it, Aṅgulimāla was hovering close to the rim of hell.

On just this occasion—it was the twentieth year of the Buddha's teaching career—the Master, when surveying the world with great compassion, became aware of Aṅgulimāla. To the Buddha, with his faculty of remembering former existences, this person was not unknown. In many lives they had met before, and often the Bodhisatta had conquered Aṅgulimāla's strength of body by his strength of mind. Once Aṅgulimāla had even been the Bodhisatta's uncle (Jāt. 513). Now, when their lives had crossed again and the Buddha saw the grave danger toward which Aṅgulimāla was heading, he did not hesitate to walk the thirty miles to save him from irreparable spiritual disaster.

The *Aṅgulimāla Sutta* (MN 86) says:

> Cowherds, shepherds, and ploughmen passing by saw the Blessed One walking along the road leading to Aṅgulimāla and told him: "Do not take that road, recluse. On this road is the bandit Aṅgulimāla, who is murderous, bloody-handed, given to blows and violence, merciless to living beings. Villages, towns, and districts have been laid waste by him. He is constantly murdering people and he wears their fingers as a garland. Men have come along this road in groups of ten, twenty, thirty, and even forty, but still they have fallen into Aṅgulimāla's hands." When this was said, the Blessed One went on in silence. For a second time and a third time those people warned him, but still the Blessed One went on in silence.

From his lookout Aṅgulimāla first saw his mother approaching. Though he recognized her, so steeped was his mind in the heartless thrill of violence that he still intended to complete the thousand fingers by killing the very woman who had brought him into this world. Just at that moment the Buddha appeared on the road between Aṅgulimāla and his mother. Seeing him, Aṅgulimāla thought: "Why should I kill my mother for the sake of a finger when there is someone else? Let her live. I will kill the recluse and cut off his finger." The sutta continues:

> Aṅgulimāla then took up his sword and shield, buckled on his bow and quiver, and followed close behind the Blessed One. Then the Blessed One performed such a feat of supernormal power that the bandit Aṅgulimāla, though walking as fast as he

could, could not catch up with the Blessed One, who was walking at his normal pace. Then the bandit Aṅgulimāla thought: "It is wonderful! It is marvelous! Formerly I could catch up even with a swift elephant and seize it; I could catch up even with a swift horse and seize it; I could catch up even with a swift chariot and seize it; I could catch up even with a swift deer and seized it. But now, though I am walking as fast as I can, I cannot catch up with this recluse who is walking at his normal pace." He stopped and called out to the Blessed One, "Stop, recluse! Stop, recluse!"

"I have stopped, Aṅgulimāla. You stop, too."

Then the bandit Aṅgulimāla thought: "These recluses, followers of the Sakyan scion, speak truth, assert truth; but though this recluse is walking yet he says, 'I have stopped, Aṅgulimāla. You stop, too.' Suppose I question the recluse?"

Then he addressed the Blessed One in stanzas thus:

"While you are walking, recluse, you tell me you have stopped;
But now, when I have stopped, you say I have not stopped.
I ask you now, O recluse, what is the meaning of it;
How is it that you have stopped and I have not?"

And the Blessed One replied:

"Aṅgulimāla, I have stopped forever,
I abstain from violence towards living beings;
But you have no restraint towards things that breathe:
So that is why I have stopped and you have not."

When Aṅgulimāla heard these words, a second and greater change of heart came over him. The suppressed current of his nobler and purer urges broke through the dam of hardened cruelty to which he had become habituated in all those last years of his life. He realized that the ascetic standing before him was no ordinary bhikkhu but the Blessed One himself, and he knew intuitively that the Master had come to the forest entirely on his account, to pull him back from the bottomless abyss of misery into which he was about to tumble. Moved to the very roots of his being, he threw away his weapons and pledged himself to adopt a totally new way of life:

"Oh, at long last this recluse, a venerated sage,
Has come to this great forest for my sake.

Having heard your stanza teaching me the Dhamma,
I will indeed renounce evil forever."

So saying, the bandit took his sword and weapons
And flung them in a gaping chasm's pit;
The bandit worshipped the Sublime One's feet,
And then and there asked for the going forth.

The Enlightened One, the sage of great compassion,
The teacher of the world with all its gods,
Addressed him with these words "Come, bhikkhu,"
And that was how he came to be a bhikkhu.

Although none of the traditional sources gives us any insight into the inner side of Aṅgulimāla's metamorphosis, we might suppose that the presence of the Buddha before him enabled him to see, in a flash, the unfathomable suffering in which his life had become enmeshed and the even graver misery that lay in store for him when his evil kamma would ripen. He must have realized how he had been victimized by his own blind ignorance, and it must have become clear to him that the only way he could escape the dark consequences that perpetually hung over him was to extricate the very root of all rebirth and suffering. Seeing that there was no hope for him within the world, he had to entrust himself to the prospect of final deliverance from the world, by the conquest of his own self-delusion. This impelled him to take the radical step of complete renunciation by entering the Sangha and becoming a spiritual son of the Awakened One, his redeemer and refuge.

Not long afterwards, the Buddha, together with a large number of monks and with Aṅgulimāla as his attendant monk, set out to wander to Sāvatthī, Aṅgulimāla's home territory. They arrived there in stages. The people of Sāvatthī, however, did not yet know about Aṅgulimāla's great transformation, and they complained that the king had hesitated too long in sending out troops to track down and capture the bandit. Now King Pasenadi himself, at the head of a large unit of his best soldiers, set out toward Aṅgulimāla's haunt, the Jālinī forest. On his way he passed the Jetavana monastery where the Buddha had just arrived. Since for many years he had been a devoted follower of the Buddha, he stopped on his way to pay his respect to the Master.

The Buddha, seeing the soldiers, asked King Pasenadi whether he had been attacked by a neighboring king and was going to war. The king said that there was no war; rather, along with his soldiers, he was after a single man, the murderous Aṅgulimāla. "But," he added ruefully, "I shall never be able to put him down."

Then the Blessed One said: "But, great king, suppose you were to see that Aṅgulimāla had shaved off his hair and beard, had put on the saffron robe, and had gone forth from the home life into homelessness; that he was abstaining from killing living beings, from taking that which is not given, and from false speech; that he was refraining from eating at night, ate only in one part of the day, and was celibate, virtuous, of good character. If you were to see him thus, how would you treat him?"

"Venerable sir, we would pay homage to him, or rise up for him, or invite him to be seated; or we would invite him to accept the four requisites of a monk, and we would arrange for his lawful guarding, defense, and protection. But, venerable sir, he is an immoral man, one of evil character. How could he ever have such virtue and restraint?"

Then the Master extended his right arm and said to King Pasenadi: "Here, great king, this is Aṅgulimāla."

The king was now greatly alarmed and fearful, and his hair stood on end. He had entirely lost his composure, so terrifying was Aṅgulimāla's reputation. But the Buddha said: "Do not be afraid, great king. There is nothing for you to fear."

When the king had regained his composure, he went over to the Venerable Aṅgulimāla and asked him for the clan name of his father and mother, thinking it unsuitable to address the monk by the name that was derived from his cruel deeds. On hearing that his father was a Gagga by clan and his mother a Mantāni, he was greatly surprised to find that this Aṅgulimāla was the son of his own royal chaplain, and he remembered well the strange circumstances of his birth. It moved him deeply that the Buddha had been able to turn this cruel man into a gentle member of the Sangha. The king now offered to support "the noble Gagga Mantāniputta" with all the monk's requisites, that is, robes, food, shelter, and medicine. But Aṅgulimāla had taken upon himself four of the strict ascetic observances (*dhutaṅga*): he was a forest dweller, lived on alms round, was a refuse-rag wearer, and restricted himself to one set of three robes. Hence he replied: "I have enough, great king, my triple robe is complete."

Then King Pasenadi turned again to the Buddha and exclaimed: "It is wonderful, venerable sir! It is marvelous how the Blessed One subdues the unsubdued, pacifies the unpeaceful, calms the uncalm. This one, whom we could not subdue with punishments and weapons, the Blessed One has subdued without punishments or weapons."

As soon as Aṅgulimāla had taken up going on alms round people fearfully ran from him and closed their doors. So it was in the outskirts of Sāvatthī, where Aṅgulimāla had gone first, and it was the same in the city where Aṅgulimāla had hoped he would not be conspicuous. He could not get even a spoonful of food or a ladle of gruel during his alms round.

The Vinaya (1:74) records that some people, seeing Aṅgulimāla in robes, resented it and said: "How can these recluses, the monks of the Sakyan scion, ordain a notorious criminal!" Monks who heard this told it to the Buddha, who then proclaimed the rule: "Monks, a notorious criminal should not be ordained. He who ordains such a one commits an offense of wrongdoing (*dukkaṭa*)." The Buddha knew well that though he himself was able to perceive the potential for good in a criminal, those after him might not have that capacity nor the authority to carry out whatever they understood. An acceptance of former criminals might also have induced unrepenting criminals to use the Order as a sanctuary to escape arrest and punishment.

A few people, trusting the Buddha's judgment, may have changed their attitude and given alms to Aṅgulimāla when he stood before their door, but most were still hostile. Although Aṅgulimāla realized it was futile to walk on alms round in his home town, he continued the practice as a duty.

"BORN WITH THE NOBLE BIRTH"

Once, on his alms round, Aṅgulimāla saw a woman in labor who was having much difficulty in bringing forth her child. Compassion immediately arose in him and he thought: "How much do beings suffer! How much do they suffer!" On his return to the monastery he reported this to the Master, who told him: "Then go into Sāvatthī, Aṅgulimāla, and say to that woman: 'Sister, since I was born, I do not recall that I have ever intentionally deprived a living being of life. By this truth may you be well and may your infant be safe!'"

But Aṅgulimāla protested: "By saying that, Lord, wouldn't I be telling a deliberate lie? For I have intentionally deprived many living beings of life."

"Then, Aṅgulimāla, say to that woman: 'Sister, since I was born with the noble birth, I do not recall that I have ever intentionally deprived a living being of life. By this truth may you be well and may your infant be safe!'"

Aṅgulimāla had it announced to that woman that he would be coming. People put up a curtain in the woman's room, and on the other side of the curtain a chair was placed on which the monk was to sit. When

Aṅgulimāla arrived at the woman's house, he made the "asseveration of truth" as instructed by the Buddha. His words were indeed true, for he had undergone a noble birth—a spiritual rebirth—when the Buddha ordained him as a monk. The conversion of the heart gave him a power to help and to heal even stronger than his previous power to hurt and destroy. Thus, through the power of his asseveration, both mother and infant had a safe delivery.

Generally, the Buddha did not engage in "raising the dead" or in "spiritual healing." He knew that those revived would still one day die. He showed greater compassion when he taught beings about the true state of deathlessness and the way to acquire it. But why did the Buddha make an exception in the case of Aṅgulimāla and instruct him to use the power of truth for the purpose of healing? Here is a reflection by the teachers of old, recorded in the commentary to the *Aṅgulimāla Sutta*:

> There may be those who ask: "Why did the Blessed One make a monk do a physician's work?" To that we answer: That is not what the Buddha did. An act of truth is not a medical function; it is done after reflecting on one's own virtue. The Blessed One knew that Aṅgulimāla had been short of almsfood because people became frightened when they saw him and ran away. To help him in that situation, he let Aṅgulimāla perform an act of truth. Thereby people would think: "Having aroused a thought of loving-kindness, the Elder Aṅgulimāla can now bring safety to people by an act of truth," and they would no longer be afraid of him. Then Aṅgulimāla will not go short of almsfood and will be fit to do a monk's work.
>
> Until then, Aṅgulimāla had not been able to focus his mind on his basic meditation subject. Though he practiced day and night, always there would appear before his mind's eye the place in the jungle where he had slain so many people. He heard their plaintive voices imploring him: "Let me live, my lord! I am a poor man and have many children!" He saw the frantic movements of their arms and legs when in fear of death. When he was faced with such memories, deep remorse gripped him and he could not remain sitting comfortably on his meditation seat. Therefore the Blessed One let him perform this act of truth about his noble birth. He wanted to make Aṅgulimāla consider his "birth" as a monk to be something very special, so that he would be inspired to strengthen his insight and attain arahantship.

The episode proved to be of great help to Aṅgulimāla, and he showed his gratitude to his Master in the best way possible, namely, by perfecting the task set him by the Buddha:

> Before long, dwelling alone, withdrawn, diligent, ardent, and resolute, the Venerable Aṅgulimāla, by realizing it for himself with direct knowledge, here and now entered upon and dwelt in that supreme goal of the holy life for the sake of which noble sons rightly go forth from the home life into homelessness. He knew directly: "Birth is destroyed, the holy life has been lived, what had to be done has been done, there is no more of this to come." And the Venerable Aṅgulimāla became one of the arahants.

At last his earlier name, Ahiṁsaka, the Harmless One, fully befitted him. Since the episode with the ailing woman, most of the people had gained full confidence in his inner transformation and there was also no lack of support when he went on alms round in Sāvatthī. However, a resentful few could not forget that Aṅgulimāla the bandit was responsible for the deaths of their loved ones. Unable to win revenge through the law, they took matters into their own hands and attacked Aṅgulimāla with sticks and stones as he walked for alms. Their assault must have been quite brutal, for Aṅgulimāla returned to the Buddha seriously injured, with blood running from his head, with his bowl broken, and with his outer robe torn. The Master saw him coming and called out to him: "Bear it, brahmin! Bear it, brahmin! You are experiencing here and now the result of deeds on account of which you might have been tortured in hell for many years, for many hundreds of years, for many thousands of years."

Being an arahant, Aṅgulimāla remained firm and invulnerable in mind and heart. But his body, the symbol and fruit of previous kamma, was still exposed to the effects of his former evil deeds. Even the Buddha himself, as a result of former deeds, had to suffer a slight injury at the hands of his evil cousin Devadatta. The two chief disciples also had to experience bodily violence: Sāriputta was hit on the head by a mischievous demon and Moggallāna was brutally murdered. If even these three great ones could not avoid bodily harm, how could Aṅgulimāla escape such a fate—he who in his present life had committed so much evil? Yet, it was only his body that received these blows, not his mind, which remained in inviolable equipoise. As an arahant, he was also in no need of consolation or encouragement. Hence we may understand the Buddha's words to Aṅgulimāla as a reminder of the kammic concatenation of causes and effects, which still had to be endured, though greatly ameliorated by his inner metamorphosis.

AṄGULIMĀLA'S VERSES

There is no other record about the later period of Aṅgulimāla's life than what he himself said in the verses from the *Theragāthā* that follow.[2] These tell us that he lived in such solitary places as forests, caves, and mountains, and that, having finally made the right choice in his life, he spent his days in happiness.

Who once did live in negligence
And then is negligent no more,
He illuminates the world
Like the moon freed from a cloud.

(871)

Who checks the evil deeds he did
By doing wholesome deeds instead,
He illuminates the world
Like the moon freed from a cloud.

(872)

The youthful bhikkhu who devotes
His efforts to the Buddha's Teaching,
He illuminates the world
Like the moon freed from a cloud.

(873)

Let my enemies but hear discourse on the Dhamma,
Let them be devoted to the Buddha's Teaching,
Let my enemies wait on those good people
Who lead others to accept the Dhamma.[3]

(874)

Let my enemies give ear from time to time
And hear the Doctrine as told by men who preach forbearance,
Of those who speak as well in praise of kindness,
And let them follow up that Dhamma with kind deeds.

(875)

For surely then they would not wish to harm me,
Nor would they think of harming other beings,
So those who would protect all beings, frail or strong,
Let them attain the all-surpassing peace.
(876)

Conduit-makers guide the water,
Fletchers straighten out the arrow,
Carpenters straighten out the timber,
But wise men seek to tame themselves.
(877)

There are some that tame with beatings,
Some with goads and some with whips;
But I was tamed by such alone
Who has no rod nor any weapon.
(878)

"Harmless" is the name I bear
Who was dangerous in the past.
The name I bear today is true:
I hurt no living being at all.
(879)

And though I once lived as a bandit
With the name of "Finger-garland,"
One whom the great flood swept along,
I went for refuge to the Buddha.
(880)

And though I once was bloody-handed
With the name of "Finger-garland,"
See the refuge I have found:
The bond of being has been cut.
(881)

While I did many deeds that lead
To rebirth in the evil realms,
Yet their result has reached me now;
And so I eat free from debt.
(882)

They are fools and have no sense
Who give themselves to negligence;
But those of wisdom guard diligence
And treat it as their greatest good.

(883)

Do not give way to negligence
Nor seek delight in sensual pleasures,
But meditate with diligence
So as to reach the perfect bliss.

(884)

So welcome to that choice of mine
And let it stand, it was not ill made;
Of all the Dhammas known to men,
I have come to the very best.

(885)

So welcome to that choice of mine
And let it stand, it was not ill made;
I have attained the triple knowledge
And done all that the Buddha teaches.

(886)

I stayed in forests, at the root of a tree,
I dwelt in the mountain caves—
But no matter where I went
I always had an agitated heart.

(887)

But now I rest and rise in happiness
And happily I spend my life.
For now I am free of Māra's snares—
Oh! for the pity shown me by the Master!

(888)

A brahmin was I by decent,
On both sides high and purely born.
Today I am the Master's son,
My teacher is the Dhamma-king.

(889)

Free of craving, without grasping,
With guarded senses, well restrained,
Spewn forth have I the root of misery,
The end of all taints have I attained.

(890)

The Master has been served by me full well,
And all the Buddha's bidding has been done.
The heavy load was finally laid down;
What leads to new becoming is cut off.

(891)

CHAPTER 9

ANĀTHAPIṆḌIKA

The Buddha's Chief Patron

Hellmuth Hecker

ANĀTHAPIṆḌIKA BECOMES A DISCIPLE

"THUS HAVE I HEARD. On one occasion the Blessed One was dwelling at Sāvatthī, in Jetavana, the monastery of Anāthapiṇḍika..." Numerous discourses of the Buddha begin with these words, and hence the name of that great lay devotee, Anāthapiṇḍika, is well known to readers of Buddhist literature. His name means "one who gives alms (*piṇḍa*) to the helpless (*anātha*)," and is the honorific of the householder Sudatta of the city of Sāvatthī. Who was he? How did he meet the Buddha? What was his relationship to the Teaching? The answers to these questions may be found in the many references to him that occur in the traditional texts.

Anāthapiṇḍika's first encounter with the Buddha took place shortly after the Master's third rains retreat following his Enlightenment. In this early period of his ministry the Buddha had not laid down any regulations regarding dwelling places. The bhikkhus lived wherever they wished—in the woods, at the roots of trees, under overhanging rocks, in ravines, caves, charnel grounds, and the open air. One day a wealthy merchant of Rājagaha, capital of the kingdom of Magadha, became a faithful lay follower of the Buddha. Seeing how the monks lived, he suggested to them that they ask their Master whether he would allow them to accept a permanent residence. When the Buddha gave his permission, the merchant at once set about to erect no fewer than sixty dwellings for the monks, explaining that he needed to gain merit. With the building of that first Buddhist monastery, the foundation was laid for the spread of the Dhamma, for now there would be a training center for the Order.[1]

This merchant had a brother-in-law, named Sudatta but always called Anāthapiṇḍika, who was the richest merchant in Sāvatthī. One time, when Anāthapiṇḍika was traveling on business in the neighboring state of Magadha, he came to Rājagaha. As usual, his way led him first to his brother-in-law, to whom he was bound by a warm friendship. When he entered the house he found to his astonishment that the household hardly noticed him. Previously he had been accustomed to his brother-in-law's full attention and to a rousing welcome from the other residents of the house. But now he saw that they were all very busy, eagerly making elaborate preparations. He asked his preoccupied brother-in-law what this meant: "A wedding? A major sacrifice? A visit from the king?" But the brother-in-law explained: "I have invited the Enlightened One and the order of monks here for tomorrow's meal."

Anāthapiṇḍika became attentive: "Did you say 'the Enlightened One'?"

"Indeed," answered the brother-in-law, "tomorrow the Enlightened One is coming." And Anāthapiṇḍika, hardly able to believe his ears, asked a second and a third time: "Did you say 'the Enlightened One'?" Then, breathing a deep sigh of relief, he said, "Even the sound alone of these words is indeed rare in this world—the Enlightened One. Can one really see him?" His brother-in-law answered: "Today would not be suitable, but you can go early tomorrow morning."

That night, as Anāthapiṇḍika lay down to sleep, he was moved by tumultuous thoughts and feelings. So strong was his anticipation of the next day's meeting that he woke up three times in the night, thinking it was already daytime. Finally, he arose even before dawn and went out of the city toward the monastery. In the darkness, fear overcame him, doubt and uncertainty stirred within his heart, and all his worldly instincts told him to turn back. But an invisible spirit named Sīvaka urged him to continue on:

A hundred thousand elephants,
A hundred thousand horses,
A hundred thousand mule-drawn chariots,
A hundred thousand maidens
Adorned with jewelry and earrings—
These are not worth a sixteenth part
Of a single step forward.

"Go forward, householder! Go forward, householder! Going forward is better for you, not turning back again."

And so through the rest of the night Anāthapiṇḍika walked resolutely on. After a while he saw in the misty dawn a figure walking silently back and forth. Anāthapiṇḍika stopped. Then the figure called to him in an indescribably melodious voice: "Come, Sudatta!"

Anāthapiṇḍika was startled at being addressed in this manner, for no one there addressed him by his given name. He was known only as Anāthapiṇḍika, and besides, he was unknown to the Buddha and had come unexpectedly. Now he was certain that he was in the presence of the Enlightened One. Overwhelmed by the gravity of the encounter, he fell at the Master's feet and asked him in a stammering voice: "Did the Blessed One sleep well?" With his answer to this conventional question the

Buddha gave Anāthapiṇḍika a glimpse of his real stature:

Always indeed he sleeps well,
The brahmin who is fully quenched,
Who does not cling to sensual pleasures,
Cool at heart, without acquisitions.

Having cut off all attachments,
Having removed care from the heart,
The peaceful one indeed sleeps well,
For he has attained peace of mind.

Then the Blessed One, leading Anāthapiṇḍika step by step, spoke to him of giving, of virtue, of the heavens; of the perils, vanity, and defiling nature of sensual pleasures; of the benefits of renunciation. When he saw that Anāthapiṇḍika was ready in heart and mind—pliable, unobstructed, uplifted and serene—he explained to him the teaching that is unique to the Enlightened Ones: the Four Noble Truths of suffering, its cause, its cessation, and the path. With that, the dust-free, stainless eye of truth (*dhamma-cakkhu*) opened for Anāthapiṇḍika: "Whatever has the nature of arising, all that has the nature of cessation." Anāthapiṇḍika had understood the truth of the Dhamma, had overcome all doubts, and was without any wavering; certain in his mind, he was now self-dependent in the Master's Dispensation. He had realized the path and fruit of stream-entry (sotāpatti).

He then invited the Blessed One for a meal the next day at the home of his brother-in-law, and the Master accepted. After the meal, Anāthapiṇḍika asked the Buddha if he might build a monastery for the Order in his hometown of Sāvatthī. The Buddha answered: "The Enlightened Ones love peaceful places."

"I understand, O Master, I understand," answered Anāthapiṇḍika, overjoyed with the acceptance of his offer.[2]

When Anāthapiṇḍika returned to Sāvatthī, he encouraged the people along the route to receive the Buddha in a respectful manner. Once he arrived in Sāvatthī, he immediately searched for an appropriate location for the monastery. The site had to be neither too close to the city nor too far; it should not be overrun by people in the daytime or noisy at night; it should be accessible to devoted visitors and also fit for those bent on seclusion. At last, in the chain of hills surrounding the city, he found a beautiful forest glade, ideal for the purpose. This was Jetavana—Jeta's Grove—a glade belonging to Prince Jeta, a son of King Pasenadi.

Anāthapiṇḍika visited Prince Jeta in his palace and asked if the forest were for sale. The prince answered that he would not sell it even for the appropriate price of eighteen million gold coins. "I will give you that much, right now," replied Anāthapiṇḍika, but they were not able to come to terms and went to an arbitrator. The arbitrator ruled that the price should amount to as many gold coins of the eighteen million as could be laid next to each other on the land, and on this basis an agreement of sale was drawn up.

Anāthapiṇḍika brought many carts filled with gold coins and had the coins spread out upon the site. Finally only one small patch of ground at the entrance remained bare. He gave instructions for more gold to be brought, but Prince Jeta announced that he was prepared to build a mighty gate and tower on that spot at his own expense. This imposing bastion and gate protected the monastery from the outside world, shielding it from the noises of the road and emphasizing the dividing line between the sacred and the mundane. Anāthapiṇḍika then spent another eighteen million for buildings and furnishings. He built individual cells, a meeting hall, a dining hall, storerooms, walkways, latrines, wells, and lotus ponds for bathing as well as a large surrounding wall. Thus the forest glade was transformed into a monastery and stood apart as a religious sanctuary (Vin. 2:158–59). To honor both parties to its establishment, the texts always refer to it by two names: "Jeta's Grove" and "Anāthapiṇḍika's monastery."

When all the preparations had been completed, the Buddha and his monks came to Sāvatthī to take up residence at the new monastery. On their arrival Anāthapiṇḍika invited them for a meal, after which he asked the Buddha: "How should I proceed with the offering of this Jetavana?" "You may dedicate it to the Sangha of the four quarters, present and future." And so Anāthapiṇḍika did. Then the Buddha expressed his appreciation to him in the following verses:

They ward off cold and heat and beasts of prey from there
And creeping things and gnats and rains in the wet season.
When the dreaded hot wind arises, that is warded off.
To meditate and obtain insight in a shelter and at ease—
A dwelling place is praised by the Awakened One
As chief gift to an Order.

Therefore a wise man looking to his own weal,
Should have dwelling places built, so that
Learned ones can stay therein.

To these food and drink, raiment and lodgings,
He should give, to the upright, with mind purified.
Then these will teach him Dhamma dispelling every ill;
He, knowing that Dhamma, here attains Nibbāna, cankerless.

(Vin. 2:147–48; 2:164–65)[3]

The alms meal for the monks was followed by a sumptuous celebration for the laity, with gifts for everyone. This cost another eighteen million, so altogether Anāthapiṇḍika spent fifty-four million on the headquarters for the Order. Therefore the Buddha declared him to be the foremost patron of the Sangha (AN 1, chap. 14).

THE WEALTHY PATRON

After establishing the monastery Anāthapiṇḍika was assiduous in his support for the resident Sangha. He provided the monks dwelling there with all necessities. Each morning he sent rice gruel, and each evening he supplied all the requirements of clothing, almsbowls, and medicines. All repairs and upkeep in Jetavana were undertaken by his servants. Above all, several hundred monks came daily to his home—a seven-story mansion—to receive the forenoon meal. Every day at mealtime his home was filled with saffron robes and the ambiance of saintliness.

When King Pasenadi learned of Anāthapiṇḍika's generosity, he wished to imitate him, and so he supplied alms for five hundred monks daily. One day, as he was on his way to talk with the monks, he learned from his servants that the monks were taking the food away with them and giving it to their supporters in the city, who would offer it back to them. The king was mystified, for he had always provided very tasty food, and so he asked the Buddha about the reason for the monks' behavior. The Buddha explained to the king that in the palace the courtiers distributed the food without any inner feeling, just following orders as if they were cleaning out a barn or taking a thief to court. They lacked faith and had no love for the monks. Many of them even thought the monks were parasites living by the labor of the working population. When anything was given in that spirit, no one could feel comfortable accepting it—even when the meal was made of the most delicious food. In contrast, the faithful householders of the city, like Anāthapiṇḍika and Visākhā, welcomed the monks and regarded them as spiritual friends who lived for the welfare and benefit of all beings. A humble meal provided by a friend would be worth much more than the most sumptuous meal offered by someone who did not give in the right spirit. The Buddha added a verse for the king to remember:

> A dish may be insipid or savory,
> The food may be meager or abundant,
> Yet if it is given by a friendly hand,
> Then it becomes a delicious meal.
>
> (Jāt. 346)

Not only were Anāthapiṇḍika and Visākhā the foremost donors in Sāvatthī (Jāt. 337, 346, 465), but their help was frequently solicited by the Buddha whenever something needed to be arranged with the lay community. Yet even Anāthapiṇḍika's wealth was not inexhaustible. One day treasures worth eighteen million were swept away by a flash flood and washed into the sea. Moreover, he had lent about the same amount of money to business friends who did not repay him, and he was reluctant to ask for the money back. Since his fortune had amounted to about five times eighteen million, and he had already spent three-fifths of this for the monastery, his wealth was now running out. Anāthapiṇḍika, the millionaire, had become poor. Nevertheless, despite the hardship, he still continued to provide some food for the monks, even though it was only a modest serving of thin rice gruel.

At that time a spirit lived in Anāthapiṇḍika's seven-storied palace above the gate. Whenever the Buddha or a holy disciple entered the house, the spirit, following the law of his realm, was obliged to step down from his place in order to honor them. This, however, was very inconvenient for the spirit, and so he tried to think of a way to keep the monks out of the house. He appeared to a servant and suggested stopping the almsgiving, but the servant paid no attention. Then the spirit tried to turn the son of the house against the monks, but this also failed. Finally, the spirit appeared in his supernatural aura to Anāthapiṇḍika himself and tried to persuade him that since he was now so impoverished it would be prudent to stop giving alms. The great donor replied that he knew of only three treasures: the Buddha, the Dhamma, and the Sangha. He said he was intent on looking after these treasures, and he told the spirit to leave his house as there was no place in it for enemies of the Buddha.

Thereupon the spirit, again following the law of his realm, had to abandon that place. He went to the deity who was the divine protector of the city of Sāvatthī and requested an assignment to a new shelter. The deity referred him to a higher court, that of the Four Divine Kings, the deities who collectively ruled over the lowest heaven. But these four also did not feel qualified to make a decision and sent the homeless spirit to Sakka, the king of the devas.

In the meantime, however, the spirit had become aware of his wrong conduct and asked Sakka to seek forgiveness on his behalf. Sakka required that as a penance the spirit help Anāthapiṇḍika to regain his fortune. First the spirit had to retrieve the sunken gold; then he had to procure unclaimed buried treasure; and finally he had to persuade Anāthapiṇḍika's debtors to repay their debts. With a great deal of effort the spirit fulfilled these tasks. In doing so, he appeared to the debtors in dreams and demanded repayment. Before long Anāthapiṇḍika again had fifty-four million and was able to be as generous as he was formerly.

The spirit appeared now before the Buddha and asked forgiveness for his malevolent behavior. He received forgiveness, and after the Enlightened One had explained the Dhamma to him he became a disciple. The Buddha taught him, moreover, that a person who strove for perfection in giving could not be kept from it by anything in the world, neither by spirits, nor gods, nor devils, nor even by threat of death (Jāt. 140, 340).

After Anāthapiṇḍika had regained all his wealth, a brahmin became jealous of his good fortune and decided to steal from him what, in his opinion, had made him so wealthy. He wanted to abduct the manifestation of Sirī, the goddess of fortune, because he thought that fortune would then leave Anāthapiṇḍika and come to him, bound to do his bidding. This strange perception was based on the idea that the so-called favors of fate, while a reward for earlier good deeds, are nevertheless dispensed by deities dwelling in the beneficiary's house, who draw such favors to their master.

So the brahmin went to Anāthapiṇḍika's house and looked around to see where the goddess of fortune might be found. Like many Indians of his day he had clairvoyant powers and he saw Fortune living in a white cock which was kept in a golden cage in the mansion. He asked the master of the house to give him the cock to waken his students in the morning. Without hesitation the generous Anāthapiṇḍika granted his wish. However, just at that moment, Fortune wandered into a jewel. The brahmin requested this too as a present and received it. But then the spirit hid in a staff, a weapon used for self-defense. After the brahmin had successfully begged this, the manifestation of Sirī settled down on the head of Puññalakkhaṇā, Anāthapiṇḍika's wife, who was truly the good spirit of this house and therefore had the protection of the gods. When the brahmin saw this, he recoiled in fright: "His wife I cannot request from him!" He confessed his evil intentions, returned the presents, and, deeply ashamed, left the house.

Anāthapiṇḍika went to the Enlightened One and told him of this strange encounter, which he had not understood. The Buddha explained the connection to him—how the world is changed through good works and how, for those with right insight through moral purification, everything is attainable, even Nibbāna (Jāt. 284).

Every time the Buddha stayed in Sāvatthī, Anāthapiṇḍika visited him. At other times, however, he felt bereft without a tangible support for worship. Therefore one day he told Ānanda of his wish to build a shrine. When Ānanda reported this to the Enlightened One, the latter declared that there were three types of shrines: the corporeal, the memorial, and representations. The first type was a corporeal relic, which, after the Buddha's Parinibbāna, was deposited in a stūpa; the second was an object which had a connection with the Enlightened One and had been used by him, such as the almsbowl; the third was a visible symbol. Of these three supports for worship, the first was not yet a possibility as long as the Blessed One was still living. The third would not be appropriate for those who could not content themselves with a mere picture or a symbol. There remained only the second.

The Bodhi tree in Uruvelā seemed the best object to serve as a memorial to the Blessed One. Under it he had found the door to the Deathless, and it had provided him with shelter during the first weeks after his Enlightenment. So it was decided to plant a small shoot of this tree in Sāvatthī. Mahāmoggallāna brought a cutting from the original tree, which was to be planted at the gate of Jetavana in the presence of the court and the most distinguished of the monks and laity. Ānanda presented the sapling to the king for the ceremonial planting. But King Pasenadi replied, with princely humility, that he served in this life merely as a steward for the office of the king. It would be far more appropriate for someone with a closer relationship to the Teaching to consecrate the tree. So he presented the shoot to Anāthapiṇḍika, who was standing next to him.

The tree grew and became an object of devotion for all the pious laity. At the request of Ānanda, the Buddha spent a night sitting under the tree in order to bestow on it another more distinguished consecration. Anāthapiṇḍika often sought out the tree and used the memories associated with it and the spiritual upliftment which he received there to focus his thoughts on the Blessed One (Jāt. 479).

ANĀTHAPIṆḌIKA'S FAMILY

Anāthapiṇḍika was happily married. His wife, Puññalakkhaṇā, lived up to her name, which means "one with the mark of merit," and as the good spirit of the house she took care of the servants and of the monks who came at midday. She, too, was devoted to the Dhamma, as was her brother, who had been one of the Buddha's first lay disciples.

Anāthapiṇḍika had four children, three daughters, and a son. Two of the daughters, Big Subhaddā and Little Subhaddā, were steeped in the Dhamma like their father and had attained stream-entry. And just as they took after their father in spiritual matters, so they did in worldly affairs; they were both happily married. But the youngest daughter, Sumanā, surpassed even the rest of her family in her deep wisdom. Upon hearing a discourse from the Buddha she had quickly attained the second step of purification, becoming a once-returner. She did not marry, but not because she had renounced marriage. In fact, when she saw the happiness of her two sisters, she became sad and lonely. Her spiritual strength did not suffice to overcome her depression. To the deep sorrow of her family, she wasted away, eating nothing, starving to death. She was reborn in the Tusita heaven, one of the highest heavens in the sensual realm, and there she had to purge herself of the residue of dependency on other people, her last desire directed outwardly.[4]

The only son of Anāthapiṇḍika, Kāla the Dark One, was at first a strain on his father's house. He did not want to know anything of the Dhamma but immersed himself completely in his business affairs. Then one day his father urged him to observe a holy day, offering him one thousand pieces of gold if he would keep the Uposatha. Kāla consented, and soon found it relaxing to take one day of the week off from business to enjoy himself in the company of his family. Because of this, the fasting regulations of the Uposatha did not weigh too heavily on him. Then his father made a second request and offered him another thousand if he would go to the monastery and learn a stanza of Dhamma by heart in the presence of the Master. Kāla gladly agreed. This became the turning point of his life. Each time that Kāla learned a verse, the Buddha made him misunderstand it, so that he had to listen repeatedly with keen attention. While attending to the meaning he suddenly became profoundly inspired by the Teaching and attained to stream-entry right on the spot. Thereby his daily life became richly ennobled, just as in his father's case, and he also became a major benefactor of the Order, known by the name of "Little Anāthapiṇḍika."[5]

Kāla was married to Sujātā, a sister of the famous lay devotee Visākhā. Sujātā was very proud of her family background and her wealth on both sides. Because her mind revolved around nothing else but these trifles, she was inwardly unfulfilled, dissatisfied, and peevish, and she vented her unhappiness on others. She treated everyone harshly, beat her servants, and spread fear and terror wherever she went. She did not even follow the rules of propriety in her relationships with her parents-in-law and her husband, so important in Indian society.

One day after an alms meal at their house, the Buddha was giving a discourse when loud shouts and yelling were heard from another room. The Master interrupted his talk and asked Anāthapiṇḍika the reason for this commotion, which sounded like the noisy shouts of fisherfolk. The householder answered that it was his own daughter-in-law scolding the servants. She was a shrew, he said, who did not behave properly toward her husband or his parents, who did not give alms, who was faithless and unbelieving, and who was forever causing conflict.

Then an unusual thing happened: the Buddha asked that she be called. When she appeared before him, he asked her which of the seven types of wives she wanted to be. She replied that she did not understand the meaning of this, and asked for more explanation. So the Enlightened One described the seven kinds of wives to her in verse:

> With hateful mind, cold and heartless,
> Lusting for others, despising her husband;
> Who seeks to kill the one who bought her—
> Such a wife is called *a slayer.*
>
> When her husband acquires wealth
> By his craft or trade or farm work
> She tries to filch a little for herself—
> Such a wife is called *a thief.*
>
> The slothful glutton, bent on idling,
> Harsh, fierce, rough in speech,
> A woman who bullies her own supporter—
> Such a wife is called *a tyrant.*
>
> One who is always helpful and kind,
> Who guards her husband as a mother her son,
> Who carefully protects the wealth he earns—

Such a wife is called *a mother.*

She who holds her husband in high regard
As younger sister holds the elder born,
Who humbly submits to her husband's will—
Such a wife is called *a sister.*

One who rejoices at her husband's sight
As one friend might welcome another,
Well raised, virtuous, devoted—
Such a wife is called *a friend.*

One without anger, afraid of punishment,
Who bears with her husband free of hate,
Who humbly submits to her husband's will—
Such a wife is called *a handmaid.*

The types of wives here called a slayer,
A thief, and the wife like a tyrant,
These kinds of wives, with the body's breakup,
Will be reborn deep in hell.

But wives like mother, sister, friend,
And the wife called a handmaid,
Steady in virtue, long restrained,
With the body's breakup go to heaven.

(AN 7:59)

Then the Blessed One asked her pointedly: "These, Sujātā, are the seven kinds of wives a man may have. Which of them are you?"

Deeply moved, Sujātā replied that from then on she would strive to be a handmaid to her husband. The words of the Enlightened One had shown her how to conduct herself as a wife. Later she became a faithful disciple of the Buddha, to whom she was ever grateful for her salvation.

News of the conversion of Sujātā quickly spread. One evening when the Buddha came into the lecture hall and asked the monks what they were discussing, they reported that they were speaking about "the miracle of the Dhamma," shown by the Awakened One's skill in making such a charming wife out of the former "house dragon" Sujātā. Thereupon the Buddha told them how he had already tamed her once in an earlier existence. That time she had been his mother, and he had stopped her from scolding and domineering others through a comparison between the odious crows and the sweet songbirds (Jāt. 269).

Finally, mention is made of a nephew of Anāthapiṇḍika. He had inherited a fortune of forty million but lived a wild life, drinking and gambling and squandering his wealth on entertainers, women, and obliging friends. When he had exhausted his inheritance he asked his rich uncle for support. Anāthapiṇḍika gave him a thousand gold pieces and told him that he should use this to start a business. But again he wasted all of his money and appeared once more at his uncle's home. This time Anāthapiṇḍika gave him five times as much as before, without a single condition, but as a severance. However, though Anāthapiṇḍika warned him that this would be the last handout he would get, the nephew still did not change his wasteful ways. The third time he begged his uncle for money Anāthapiṇḍika gave the young man two pieces of clothing, but he squandered these, too, and was shameless enough to call on his uncle for a fourth time. This time, however, he was told to leave. If he had come as a common beggar and not as a demanding nephew, he certainly would not have left the house of Anāthapiṇḍika empty-handed. But this he did not do, for it was not alms that he wanted but money to squander.

Because he was too lazy and stubborn to earn his own living, yet was not willing to beg, he died wretchedly. His body was found at the city wall and was thrown into the refuse pile. When Anāthapiṇḍika heard of this he asked himself whether he could have prevented this sad ending. He told the Buddha the story and asked if he should have acted differently. The Buddha, however, resolved his misgivings, explaining how that nephew belonged to the fortunately small number of insatiable people who are like bottomless vats. He had perished because of his own reckless behavior, as had already happened to him in an earlier life (Jāt. 291).

ANĀTHAPIṆḌIKA AND HIS FRIENDS

Once Anāthapiṇḍika had attained stream-entry he was unswervingly committed to observing the precepts, to purity of mind, and to the endeavor to uplift those around him. So he lived in purity among like-minded people. Not only his immediate family but also his employees and servants strove to practice generosity, to keep the Five Precepts, and to observe the Uposatha days (Jāt. 382). His home became a center of kindness and goodwill, and this attitude spread to his environment, to his friends and associates. He did not force his ideas on them, nor did he evade the problems of everyday life. Some details of his life in those days are reported in the texts.

Once a group of drinking companions in Sāvatthī ran out of money. As they pondered how they could get more brandy, one of them thought of drugging the wealthy Anāthapiṇḍika and then, when he had become unconscious, robbing him. They knew that he always took a particular route to visit the king, and so they set up a small brandy shop along the way. When Anāthapiṇḍika came along, they invited him to have a drink with them. But thinking to himself, "How can a devout follower of the Exalted One drink brandy?", he declined the invitation and continued on his way to the palace.

The depraved drinkers, however, tried to entice him once again on his return trip. Then he faced them directly and said that they themselves did not want to drink their own brew since it stood just as untouched as on the earlier trip. Were they planning to make him unconscious and then rob him? When he bravely confronted them with these words, they fled in terror (Jāt. 53).

Anāthapiṇḍika knew how to distinguish between his own observance of the precept not to drink alcohol and the behavior of others. For example, one of Anāthapiṇḍika's friends dealt in spirits. In spite of this, Anāthapiṇḍika maintained their friendship. Once, when the wine dealer suffered a major loss of merchandise through the carelessness of an employee, Anāthapiṇḍika was entirely sympathetic and treated his friend no differently than any other friend who had met with misfortune. He himself set a good example, but he did not force his ways on others or reproach them for their shortcomings (Jāt. 47).

Once, when Anāthapiṇḍika was in a region where there was danger of falling into the hands of robbers, he preferred bearing up with the inconvenience of traveling all night to exposing himself to the risk of an attack (Jāt. 103). He was true to the Buddha's advice that one should overcome some things by fleeing from them without making a display of false heroism (see MN 2).

Anāthapiṇḍika avoided being robbed in other ways. He had a friend with the unfortunate name Kālakaṇṇī, "Unlucky Bird," who had been his friend since childhood. When this friend needed money Anāthapiṇḍika helped him generously and appointed him to a job in his own household. His other friends criticized him for this—the fellow had an inauspicious name and he came from rather low origins. But Anāthapiṇḍika rebuffed them, "What's in a name? The wise pay no attention to superstition." When Anāthapiṇḍika went on a business trip he entrusted his house to this friend. Some thieves heard that he was gone and planned a burglary. When they had surrounded the house, the vigilant "Unlucky Bird" beat drums and made so much noise that it sounded as if a celebration were in progress. This convinced the thieves that the head of the house had not really left, so they threw away their tools and fled. When Anāthapiṇḍika heard of this he said to his friends, "See, that 'Unlucky Bird' has done me a great service. Had I listened to you, I would have been robbed" (Jāt. 83, 121).

Most of Anāthapiṇḍika's friends were religious people, although some of them revered the various wandering ascetics who represented the many sects and diverse beliefs prevalent in India at that time. One day Anāthapiṇḍika suggested that a large group of his friends go to listen to the Buddha. They went willingly and were so stimulated by the Enlightened One's discourse that they professed themselves to be his followers. From then on they regularly visited the monastery, gave donations, and observed the precepts and the Uposatha days. But as soon as the Buddha left Sāvatthī, they deserted the Dhamma and once again followed the other ascetics with whom they had daily contact.

Several months later, when the Buddha had returned to Sāvatthī, Anāthapiṇḍika again brought his friends to see him. This time the Awakened One not only presented the edifying aspects of the doctrine but also warned the apostates that there was no better or more comprehensive protection against suffering in the world than the Threefold Refuge in the Buddha, the Dhamma, and the Sangha. This opportunity was seldom available in this world, and whoever forfeited it would be extremely sorry. Those, however, who sincerely went for refuge to the Three Jewels would escape the hell regions and would attain to one of the three happy destinies: a good human rebirth, one of the heavenly abodes, or Nibbāna.

The Buddha challenged these merchants to reconsider their priorities, to recognize that faith in the Triple Gem was not a dispensable luxury that could be casually cast aside when it no longer suited their convenience. He spoke to them of the futility of the many false refuges to which people turn, which cannot offer genuine protection but only symptomatic relief. When their minds became receptive to what he was saying he revealed to them the unique teaching of the Awakened Ones—the Four Noble Truths of suffering, its origin, its cessation, and the path—and at the end of the discourse they all attained stream-entry. In this way, Anāthapiṇḍika's attainment also became a blessing for his friends (Jāt. 1).

DISCOURSES BY THE BLESSED ONE

Of the forty-five rainy seasons of his life as a teacher, the Buddha spent nineteen in Sāvatthī in Anāthapiṇḍika's monastery in the Jeta Grove. Whenever he spent the three or four months of the rainy season there, Anāthapiṇḍika would usually visit him twice a day, often just to see him but frequently to hear a discourse. Anāthapiṇḍika was reticent about asking the Blessed One questions. As the most generous benefactor of the Order, he did not want to create the impression that he was merely bartering his contributions for personal advice. The donations were for him a matter of the heart, given without any thought of reward—the sheer joy of giving was in itself sufficient reward for him. He thought that the Buddha and the monks would not regard the instruction as an obligation or a compensation for the benefactor but would share the gift of the Dhamma as a natural expression of their kindness and compassion.

Therefore, when Anāthapiṇḍika came to the Buddha, he would sit quietly to one side and wait to see whether the Blessed One would give him any instruction. If the Awakened One said nothing, Anāthapiṇḍika would sometimes relate one of the episodes of his life, of which several have been recounted. He would wait to see whether the Blessed One had any comments to make, approving or criticizing his behavior, or whether he would use that incident as a point of departure for a discourse. In this way he connected all that he experienced in his everyday life with the Teaching.

Many of the occasions when the Buddha gave instructions to Anāthapiṇḍika have been recorded in the Pāli Canon. These teachings form a comprehensive code of lay Buddhist ethics, and by eliciting them from the Blessed One Anāthapiṇḍika has also become a benefactor to countless generations of Buddhist laypeople conscientiously trying to follow the Dhamma. The discourses, which are contained in the Aṅguttara Nikāya, range from the simplest message to the most profound.[6] A few are mentioned here, beginning with the basic words of advice to the laity:

> Householder, possessed of four things, the noble disciple has entered on the householder's path of duty, a path which brings good repute and leads to the heavenly world. What are the four?
>
> Herein, householder, the noble disciple waits upon the order of monks with the offer of a robe, almsfood, lodging, and medicines for use in sickness. These are the four things.
>
> (AN 4:60)

Householder, there are these four kinds of bliss to be won by the householder: the bliss of ownership, the bliss of wealth, the bliss of debtlessness, the bliss of blamelessness.

What is the bliss of ownership? A man has wealth acquired by energetic striving, gathered by the strength of his arm, won by the sweat of his brow, justly obtained in a lawful way. At the thought: "Wealth is mine acquired by energetic striving…lawfully gotten," bliss comes to him, satisfaction comes to him. This, householder, is called the bliss of ownership.

What is the bliss of wealth? A man by means of wealth acquired by energetic striving…both enjoys his wealth and does meritorious deeds. At the thought: "By means of wealth acquired…I both enjoy my wealth and do meritorious deeds," bliss comes to him, satisfaction comes to him. This, householder, is called the bliss of wealth.

What is the bliss of debtlessness? A man owes no debt, great or small, to anyone. At the thought: "I owe no debt, great or small, to anyone," bliss comes to him, satisfaction comes to him. This, householder, is called the bliss of debtlessness.

What is the bliss of blamelessness? The noble disciple is blessed with blameless action of body, blameless action of speech, blameless action of mind. At the thought: "I am blessed with blameless action of body, speech, and mind," bliss comes to him, satisfaction comes to him. This, householder, is called the bliss of blamelessness.

Such are the four kinds of bliss to be won by the householder.

(AN 4:62)

There are, householder, five desirable, pleasant, and agreeable things which are rare in the world. What are those five? They are long life, beauty, happiness, fame, and (rebirth in) a heaven. But of those five things, householder, I do not teach that they are to be obtained by prayer or by vows. If one could obtain them by prayer or by vows, who would not do so?

For a noble disciple, householder, who wishes to have long life, it is not befitting that he should pray for long life or take delight in so doing. He should rather follow a path of life that is conducive to longevity. By following such a path he will obtain long life, be it divine or human.

For a noble disciple, householder, who wishes to have beauty …happiness…fame…(rebirth in) a heaven, it is not befitting that he should pray for them or take delight in so doing. He should rather follow a path of life that is conducive to beauty...happiness...fame...(rebirth in) a heaven. By following such a path he will obtain beauty, happiness, fame, and (rebirth in) a heaven.

(AN 5:43)

Householder, there are five reasons for getting rich. What five?

...A noble disciple with riches gotten by work and zeal, gathered by the strength of his arm, won by the sweat of his brow, justly obtained in a lawful way, makes himself happy, glad, and keeps that happiness; he makes his parents happy, glad, and keeps them so; so likewise his wife and children, and his servants.

...When riches are thus gotten, he makes his friends and companions happy, glad, and keeps them so.

...When riches are thus gotten, ill-luck...is warded off, and he keeps his goods in safety.

...When riches are thus gotten, he makes the five oblations to kin, guests, spirit, kings, and deities.

...When riches are thus gotten, the noble disciple institutes offerings of lofty aim, celestial, ripening in happiness, leading heavenward, for all those recluses and brahmins who abstain from pride and indolence, who bear all things in patience and humility, each mastering self, each calming self, each perfecting self.

Now if the wealth of that noble disciple, heeding these five reasons, comes to destruction, let him consider thus: "At least I've heeded those reasons for getting rich, but my wealth has gone!"—thus he is not upset. And if his wealth increases, let him think: "Truly, I've heeded those reasons and my wealth has grown!"—thus he is not upset in either case.

(AN 5:41)

The importance of the preceding discourses is further emphasized by the fact that the Buddha impressed them again on Anāthapiṇḍika on another occasion in a slightly different form. On that occasion he said to him:

Householder, there are these four conditions (to realize which is) desirable, dear, delightful, hard to win in the world. What four? (The wish:) "May wealth by lawful means come to me!" "Wealth being gotten by lawful means, may a good report attend me

> along with my kinsmen and teachers!" "May I live long and reach a great age!" "When the body breaks up, after death may I attain a heavenly world!"
>
> Now, householder, to the winning of these four conditions, four conditions conduce. What four? Perfection of faith, perfection of virtue, perfection of generosity, and perfection of wisdom. (AN 4:61)

The Buddha explained: Faith can only be won if one fully acknowledges the Blessed One and his message about the nature of existence. One can attain virtue only if one fulfills the basic Five Precepts for the moral life. Generosity is possessed by one who is free from the defect of avarice. One achieves wisdom when one realizes that if the heart is overcome by the five hindrances—worldly passions, malevolence, lassitude, agitation, and doubt—then one does what should not be done and fails to do what should be done. One who does evil and neglects good will lose his reputation and his good fortune. On the other hand, one who constantly investigates and observes his inner impulses and motives begins to overcome the five hindrances. Hence their conquest is a consequence of wisdom. If the noble disciple—through faith, virtue, generosity, and wisdom—is well on the way to obtaining the four desired things, namely, wealth, good reputation, long life, and a good rebirth, then he uses his money to accomplish four good deeds. He makes himself, his family, and his friends happy; he avoids accidents; he performs the five above-mentioned duties; and he supports genuine ascetics and brahmins. If one spends one's wealth in ways other than these four, those riches have not fulfilled their purpose and have been senselessly squandered. But if one has diminished one's wealth because of spending it for these four purposes, one has used it in a meaningful way.

On yet another occasion the Buddha explained the difference between right and wrong conduct for the lay disciple. In this discourse (AN 10:91) he says: "The most foolish kind of person is one who, having obtained possessions in dishonest ways, does not even enjoy the use of them himself, nor does he use them to benefit others. Slightly more sensible is the person who at least derives happiness and joy for himself from ill-gotten gains. Still more sensible is the one who uses them to make others happy." Even on these lowest planes of forcible and illegal acquisition of money and goods, which the ordinary person indignantly and indiscriminately condemns, the Awakened One sees fine distinctions in the behavior and attitudes of people. The person who recognizes that the elementary purpose of grasping for wealth is at least to obtain some comfort for himself, could be made to see how, through having an honest income, he can obtain more benefit. And one who derives additional pleasure by giving some pleasure to others, too, will readily understand that he has obviously given no joy to those whom he has cheated or robbed, while by making money honestly, he does not hurt anyone.

The second group of people are those who earn money partly in dishonest ways but partly through honest work. Among these, too, are those who bring joy neither to themselves nor to others; those who at least enjoy their wealth; and those who also gladden others. Finally, the third group consists of those people who earn their living entirely in honorable ways, who likewise fall into the same three groups. But in this last case there are two additional types: those who are strongly attached to their wealth and, being infatuated with it, are unaware of its inherent danger and do not seek a way out of it; and those who are not attached to their wealth and not infatuated by it, but are aware of its inherent dangers and know the way out of it. So there are ten types of people who enjoy worldly pleasures concerned with wealth.[7]

Once the Buddha asked Anāthapiṇḍika whether alms were provided in his house. This refers, according to the commentary, only to alms given to the needy, for the Buddha knew that in Anāthapiṇḍika's house alms were generously given to the Sangha. From this arose a talk on the qualitative grades of excellency in giving. The Buddha explained: "Whether one gives coarse or choice alms, if one gives it without respect and politeness, not with one's own hand, gives only left-overs, and gives without belief in the result of actions, then wherever one is reborn as a result of giving alms, one's heart will have no inclination for fine food and clothing, for fine vehicles, for the finer five sense-objects. His children, wife, servants, and laborers will not obey him, nor listen to him, nor pay attention to him. And why is that so? Because this is the result of actions done without respect."

In connection with this, the Buddha told how in an earlier life, as a rich brahmin named Velāma, he himself had distributed an enormous amount of alms but none of the recipients had been worthy of the gifts. Far more meritorious than large donations to unworthy people would be a single feeding of noble disciples, from stream-enterers to arahants. Even more meritorious would be the feeding of a paccekabuddha or of a hundred paccekabuddhas, and even more so the giving of alms to a Buddha or the building of a monastery. But better yet would be going for refuge to the Buddha, the Dhamma, and the Sangha. And this deed would be perfected if one observed the Five Precepts. It would be still better if one could imbibe a slight fragrance, if only for a moment, of an all-encompassing radiation of loving-kindness (*mettā*). Best of all, however, would it be to cultivate, even for the time of a finger-snap, the insight into impermanence (AN 9:20).

This speech shows the gradations of practice: giving, virtue, the meditation on universal love, and finally, the unwavering realization of the impermanence of all conditioned things. Without making efforts in giving, in virtue, and in impartial love for all fellow creatures, the concentrated contemplation of impermanence is not possible; for in the peace and quiet which this practice requires, pangs of conscience or other dark thoughts may arise.

This exposition on the kinds of giving recalls another short discourse. It is the only one in which Anāthapiṇḍika himself asks a question, namely, "How many are worthy of receiving gifts?" The Buddha answered that there are two kinds: those who are on the way to liberation and those who have already attained it (AN 2:27).

While in the talks mentioned thus far the purification of the heart has been more or less indirectly stressed, on other occasions the subject was approached directly. Thus once the Buddha said to Anāthapiṇḍika: "If the heart is corrupted, then all actions, words, and thoughts are tainted too. Such a person will be carried away by his passions and will have an unhappy death, just as the gables, rafters, and walls of a badly roofed house, being unprotected, will rot when drenched with rain" (AN 3:107–8).

Another time Anāthapiṇḍika went with several hundred lay followers to the Master, who spoke to them thus: "To be sure, you householders provide the monastic community with clothing, food, shelter, and medicine, but you should not be satisfied with that. May you also from time to time strive to enter and abide in the joy of (inner meditative) seclusion!"[8]

After these words the Venerable Sāriputta added the following: "At a time when the noble disciple dwells in the joy of (meditative) seclusion, five things do not exist in him: there is no pain and grief connected with the senses; no pleasure and gladness connected with the senses; no pain and grief connected with what is unwholesome; no pleasure and gladness connected with what is unwholesome; no pain and grief connected with what is wholesome" (AN 5:176).[9]

On another occasion when Anāthapiṇḍika and many lay followers again visited the Buddha, the Blessed One said to Sāriputta:

> A white-clad householder who is restrained in his actions according to the Five Precepts and who can, easily and without difficulty, obtain at will the four lofty mental abidings which bring happiness in the present—such a householder may, if he so wishes, declare of

> himself: "Destroyed for me is (rebirth in) hell, destroyed is animal rebirth, destroyed the realm of ghosts: destroyed for me are the lower worlds, the unhappy destinies, the abysmal realms: I have entered the stream, no more subject to fall into the states of woe, affirmed, assured of final enlightenment."
>
> In what Five Precepts are his actions restrained? A noble disciple abstains from killing, from taking what is not given, from wrong sensual behaviour, from lying, and from intoxicants that cause indolence.
>
> And what are the four lofty mental abidings bringing happiness in the present, which he can obtain at will? A noble disciple has unshakable faith in the Buddha, unshakable faith in the Dhamma, unshakable faith in the Sangha; and he is possessed of virtues beloved by the nobles—virtues that are unbroken, unviolated, untarnished, without blemish, bringing freedom, praised by the wise, ungrasped, conducive to concentration. These are the four lofty mental abidings bringing happiness in the present, which purify the impure mind and cleanse the unclean mind. These he obtains at will, easily and without difficulty. (AN 5:179)

At another time the attainment of stream-entry was explained to Anāthapiṇḍika in three different ways—but to him alone. The Buddha said:

> When in the noble disciple the five fearsome evils have disappeared, when he possesses the four attributes of stream-entry, and if he understands wisely and well the noble method, then he can regard himself as a stream-enterer. However, one who kills, steals, engages in sexual misconduct, lies, and takes intoxicants, generates five fearsome evils both in the present and in the future, and experiences pain and grief in his mind. Whosoever keeps away from the five vices, for him the five fearsome evils are eliminated. Secondly, he possesses—as attributes of stream-entry—unshakable trust in the Buddha, in the Dhamma, and in the Sangha, and he observes the precepts flawlessly. And thirdly, he has fully seen and penetrated the noble method, that is, dependent origination. (AN 10:92)[10]

One morning Anāthapiṇḍika wanted to visit the Buddha, but because it was still too early he went to the monastery of some wandering ascetics.

Since they knew him as a follower of the Buddha, they asked him what views the ascetic Gotama held. He replied that he did not know all the views of the Blessed One. When they asked him what views the monks held, he replied again that he did not know all their views. Thereupon he was asked what view he himself held. He replied: "What view I hold, honorable sirs, would not be difficult for me to explain. But may I first ask the honorable ones to present their own views. After that it will not be difficult for me to explain what kind of view I hold."

The ascetics explained their notions of the world. One held it to be eternal, another held it not to be eternal; one held it to be finite, another held it to be infinite; one believed that body and life were identical, others supposed them to be distinct; some believed that Enlightened Ones endured after death, others said that they were destroyed.

Then Anāthapiṇḍika spoke: "Whichever of these views one held, it could come only from one of two sources: either from one's own unwise reflections, or through the words of another. In either case, the view has arisen conditionally. Conditioned things, however, are transitory; and things of a transitory nature involve suffering. Hence, one who holds views and opinions clings to suffering, succumbs to suffering."

Then the ascetics wished to know what views Anāthapiṇḍika held. He answered: "Whatever arises is transitory; the transitory is of the nature of suffering. But suffering does not belong to me, that is not I, that is not my self."

Seeking a rebuttal, they argued that he himself was involved in clinging as he clung to the view he had just expressed. "Not so," he replied, "for I have perceived these things in accordance with reality, and besides, I know the escape from this as it really is"—in other words, he used the view only as a means and in time would also discard it. Thereupon the wanderers were unable to respond and sat in silence, aware they had been defeated.

Anāthapiṇḍika went quietly to the Blessed One, reported the conversation to him, and received the Buddha's praise: "You were right, householder. You should guide those deluded ones more often into harmony with the truth." And then the Master delighted and encouraged him with a discourse. After Anāthapiṇḍika had left, the Blessed One said to the monks that even a monk who had lived one hundred years in the Order would not have been able to reply to the wanderers better than Anāthapiṇḍika the householder had done (AN 10:93).

Finally, two other incidents may be reported: Anāthapiṇḍika was ill and requested a visit from a monk in order to receive consolation. Because Anāthapiṇḍika had done so much as a benefactor of the Order, there was no question that his request would be fulfilled. The first time, the Venerable Ānanda came to him; the second time, the Venerable Sāriputta. Ānanda said that one of untrained mind was afraid of death and of the afterlife because he lacked four things: he did not believe in the Buddha, the Dhamma, and the Sangha, nor did he possess the virtues dear to the noble ones. But Anāthapiṇḍika replied that he had no fear of death. He possessed unshakable trust in the Buddha, the Dhamma, and the Sangha, and as for the precepts for householders, he knew of none which he was still violating. Then Ānanda praised him and said that he had just declared the fruit of stream-entry (SN 55:27).

When the Venerable Sāriputta visited, he told Anāthapiṇḍika that unlike the untrained worldling for whom hell was imminent, he had faith in the Three Jewels and had not broken the precepts. If he were now to concentrate very strongly on his faith in the Buddha, the Dhamma, and the Sangha, and on his own virtue, then his sickness might disappear through this meditation. He did not, like those who were untrained, have wrong views, wrong intentions, wrong speech, wrong action, wrong livelihood, wrong effort, wrong mindfulness, wrong concentration, wrong knowledge, or wrong liberation. If he would consider the fact that he, as a stream-enterer, was in possession of the ten noble factors, flowing in the direction of right liberation, then through this meditation his illness would vanish. Through the strength of this contemplation, Anāthapiṇḍika recalled his great fortune to be a noble disciple, and by the power of this excellent spiritual medicine the disease disappeared immediately. He stood up, invited the Venerable Sāriputta to partake of the meal prepared for himself, and carried on a further discussion with him. At the end Sāriputta taught him three verses to remember:

When one has faith in the Tathāgata,
Unshakable and well established,
And good conduct built on virtue,
Dear to the noble ones and praised—

When one has confidence in the Sangha
And view that has been rectified,
They say that one is not poor,
That one's life is not vain.

Therefore the person of intelligence,
Remembering the Buddha's Teaching,

Should be devoted to faith and virtue,
To confidence and vision of the Dhamma.

(SN 55:26)

Eighteen discourses to Anāthapiṇḍika have been briefly recounted. Fourteen were given at the Blessed One's own instigation; one arose when Anāthapiṇḍika posed a question; in another he reported how he had taught others; and in two he was instructed by Ānanda and Sāriputta. These eighteen discourses reveal how the Buddha made the Teaching clear to the laity and inspired them to joyful endeavors.

THE DEATH OF ANĀTHAPIṆḌIKA

The death of the great patron is related in the *Anāthapiṇḍikovāda Sutta,* Advice to Anāthapiṇḍika (MN 143). The householder fell ill a third time with very strong pains which were getting worse and not abating. Again he asked the Venerable Sāriputta and the Venerable Ānanda for assistance. When Sāriputta saw him, he knew that Anāthapiṇḍika was nearing death and gave him the following instructions: "Do not cling, householder, to the six sense faculties and do not attach your thoughts to them. Do not cling to the six sense objects and do not attach your thoughts to them. Do not cling to the six types of consciousness, to the six sense contacts, to the six feelings, to the six elements, to the five aggregates, to the four formless realms. Do not cling to anything that is seen, heard, sensed, thought, perceived, and investigated in the mind, and do not attach your thoughts to this."

Anāthapiṇḍika must have followed this detailed presentation with his heart, so that even as he listened he was already practicing in the way the wise and holy Sāriputta had instructed him. At the end of the instructions, tears came to Anāthapiṇḍika's eyes. Ānanda turned to him compassionately and asked if he were sinking. But Anāthapiṇḍika replied: "I am not sinking, O worthy Ānanda. I have served the Master and the spiritually accomplished monks for a long time, yet I have never before heard such a profound discourse."

Then Sāriputta said: "Such profound talk, householder, will not be clear enough for white-clad lay followers; it is clear enough for renunciants."

Anāthapiṇḍika answered: "Venerable Sāriputta, let such talks on the Dhamma be given to white-clad lay followers, too. There are those with just a little dust on their eyes. If they do not hear such teachings they will be lost. Some may be able to understand."

The difference from the previously presented teaching of the Buddha is significant. Here we are concerned with ultimate questions, with the highest deliverance, not just on a theoretical basis but as practice. As a disciple who possessed the fruit of stream-entry, Anāthapiṇḍika was aware of the transitory nature of the five aggregates of clinging, and he himself had spoken on the three characteristics of existence: impermanence, suffering, and nonself. But there is a great difference as to whether one merely hears these things and ponders them, or whether one actually practices and applies them to oneself. In this distinction lies the essential difference between the methods the Buddha used to teach householders and those he used to teach monks.

For the laity, insight into the nature of existence was presented as a matter of knowledge, and this teaching was given at first to the monks as well. But for the many monks who had progressed further, the Buddha introduced the practice that would lead to complete liberation even in this life. Only if one sees that Sāriputta's exposition was a practical step-by-step approach to Nibbāna can one understand that Anāthapiṇḍika had never heard the core of the Teaching presented in quite such a manner. In his dying hour he was already far removed from worldly concerns and, while thinking of the Dhamma, had renounced attachment to worldly possessions as well as his body; thus he found himself in a situation comparable to that of the most advanced monks. Under these circumstances Sāriputta was able to give him such instructions as would have the most far-reaching effects.

After advising Anāthapiṇḍika in this way, the two elders left. Shortly thereafter the householder Anāthapiṇḍika died and was reborn in the Tusita heaven, where his youngest daughter had preceded him. Yet he was so genuinely devoted to the Buddha and the Sangha that he appeared in the Jetavana monastery as a young deva, filling the whole area with heavenly light. He went to the Buddha and, after paying homage to him, spoke the following verses:

> This indeed is that Jeta's Grove,
> The resort of the Order of seers,
> Dwelt in by the Dhamma King,
> A place that gives joy to me.
>
> By action and knowledge and righteousness,
> By virtue and an excellent life:
> By this are mortals purified,
> Not by clan or by wealth.

Therefore a person who is wise,
Out of regard for his own good,
Should carefully examine the Dhamma:
Thus he is purified therein.

Sāriputta truly is endowed with wisdom,
With virtue and with inner peace.
Even a bhikkhu who has gone beyond
At best can only equal him.

Having spoken thus, the deva paid homage to the Blessed One and, keeping him on the right, disappeared right there.

The next day the Buddha informed the monks what had happened. Immediately Ānanda spoke up: "Venerable sir, that young deva must surely have been Anāthapiṇḍika. For Anāthapiṇḍika the householder had full confidence in the Venerable Sāriputta."

And the Master confirmed this: "Good, good, Ānanda! You have drawn the right inference by reasoning. For that young deva was Anāthapiṇḍika" (SN 2:20; MN 143).

THE HOUSEHOLDER CITTA

ON ONE OCCASION THE BUDDHA enumerated for the benefit of his bhikkhus the names of twenty-one eminent lay disciples (upāsakas) who had attained realization of the paths and fruits. Fourth on this list we find the householder Citta of Macchikāsaṇḍa, near Sāvatthī (AN 6:120). On another occasion the Blessed One said to his bhikkhus: "Should a devoted mother wish to encourage her beloved only son in a proper way, she may tell him: 'Try to become like the householder Citta, my dear, and like the householder Hatthaka of Ālavi.' These two, Citta and Hatthaka, are models and guiding standards for my lay disciples. The mother may then continue: 'But if you should decide to become a monk, my dear, then try to imitate Sāriputta and Mahāmoggallāna.' These two, Sāriputta and Mahāmoggallāna, are models and guiding standards for my bhikkhus" (SN 17:23).

Thus the Buddha stressed that a devoted lay disciple should foster the wish to become like Citta and Hatthaka, while devoted bhikkhus should aspire to equal Sāriputta and Mahāmoggallāna. Here different models are set for laypeople and for monks. A lay follower is not to choose a bhikkhu as his model but a lay disciple; and a bhikkhu should not choose a lay disciple but a bhikkhu. The modes of living of the two types are quite different and an example taken from one's own background is bound to prove more effective. A lay disciple aspiring to be like Sāriputta should take the robe; but if he wants to permeate his life with the Dhamma while still living as a householder, he should look up to householders like Citta and Hatthaka as his models.

In enumerating his foremost disciples, the Buddha mentioned three persons who excelled in expounding the Dhamma: the bhikkhu Puṇṇa Mantāṇiputta, the bhikkhunī Dhammadinnā, and the householder Citta (AN 1, chap. 14). There is no record of any other lay disciple who was so well gifted in this respect. This Citta, a teacher of the good Dhamma, the model for Buddhist lay disciples, was a wealthy merchant who owned a whole hamlet, Migapathaka, and nearby a large wood, Ambātakavana. This he presented to the Sangha, building a spacious monastery there, where many bhikkhus often dwelt. His devotion to the Blessed One is explained by the fact that he had been a servant of the Bodhisatta in a former life and had followed him into homelessness (Jāt. 488). There are no less than eleven accounts of the life of this devoted upāsaka, from which may be gathered a distinct outline of his personality.

Citta particularly appreciated a certain bhikkhu, the Venerable Sudhamma, and always consulted him before proffering an invitation to other bhikkhus. One day Sāriputta, Moggallāna, Anuruddha, Ānanda, and several other wise and learned elders arrived at Macchikāsaṇḍa in the course of a journey. At once Citta approached them, and Sāriputta granted him a Dhamma talk of such profundity that Citta attained to the second stage of sanctity, that of once-returner (sakadāgāmī). Citta immediately invited the illustrious gathering for the next day's meal. Afterwards it occurred to him that in this one instance he had forgotten to inform Sudhamma in advance, and he hastened to let him know of the invitation.

When the Venerable Sudhamma learned of this, he grew jealous and crossly reprimanded Citta for not having told him beforehand. Although Citta had cordially invited him to join the meal offering, Sudhamma scornfully declined. Citta repeated his civil request twice more, but in vain. So, thinking in his heart that Sudhamma's obstinacy had no bearing on his deed and the deed's fruit, he went home and joyfully began preparations for the auspicious event.

The next day, however, the Venerable Sudhamma could not bring himself to stay away. He joined the gathering as if nothing had happened and praised the bounty and refinement of Citta's hospitality. "But real consummation," he added sarcastically, "would have been achieved by serving cream cakes to round off the meal." Citta replied that his friend's ill-advised behavior reminded him of a story he had heard. Some people known to him once bred a hybrid from a crow and a hen, but the resulting chick was afflicted with a grotesque defect. Whenever it wanted to crow like a cock, it cawed like a crow; and when it tried to caw like a crow, it crowed like a cock. By this, Citta intended to say that Sudhamma had not only failed in correct behavior as a bhikkhu but in proper civility as a layman too. Refusing an invitation out of jealousy was hardly right for a monk, and criticizing the food was poor manners for a householder. Sudhamma was deeply offended by these words and wanted to leave. Thereupon Citta offered to support him for the rest of his life, but the bhikkhu rejected his offer. Citta then kindly asked him to visit the Buddha and relate what had occurred to him. When Sudhamma left abruptly, Citta said: "Till we meet again."

The Buddha said to Sudhamma: "Foolish man, what you did was unseemly, improper, discourteous, not the way of an ascetic. How could you meanly insult and show disdain for a devoted, faithful lay disciple, a benefactor and supporter of the Sangha?" And at a meeting of the Sangha it was decided that Sudhamma should call on the householder Citta and ask his forgiveness.

Sudhamma accordingly set out, but on reaching Macchikāsaṇḍa he felt so deeply embarrassed that he could not force himself to do what he had come for. So he turned back without having seen Citta. When his fellow bhikkhus asked him whether he had performed his duty, and learned that he had not, they informed the Buddha. The Master then advised another bhikkhu to accompany Sudhamma on his difficult errand, and so it was done. Sudhamma asked Citta for forgiveness and Citta pardoned him.[1]

Of the ten instructive discourses contained in the Citta Saṁyutta, three deal with questions posed by Citta to bhikkhus, three with queries put to Citta by bhikkhus, and four refer to personal events.

Once Citta invited a group of elder bhikkhus from the monastery he had founded for a meal. Afterwards he requested the senior monk to give an exposition of what the Buddha had said on the variety of elements. The elder was unable to explain, and after he had been requested in vain a second and a third time, the youngest bhikkhu, named Isidatta, asked for permission to reply to Citta's request. The elder consented, and Isidatta, a pupil of the Venerable Mahākaccāna, lucidly explained the variety of elements on the basis of eighteen elements: the six sense faculties, the six types of objects, and the six elements of consciousness.

The bhikkhus then took their leave. On the way back to the monastery the senior bhikkhu commended young Isidatta for his excellent exposition, and said that next time he should not hesitate to speak up in a similar situation. There was no envy in the elder's heart, but on the contrary he felt sympathetic joy (*muditā*) over his young companion's accomplishments and depth of understanding. Isidatta on his part felt no pride, so both complied with the ideals of the monk's life (SN 41:2).

On another occasion Citta posed the question: "From what do wrong views on the world and the self originate?" He asked for an exposition of what the Buddha had taught on this subject in the great *Brahmajāla Sutta.* Again the senior bhikkhu was ignorant of the matter and again Isidatta replied. Wrong views, he said, invariably originate from the view of a self (*sakkāyadiṭṭhi*). Citta then went on to ask from what the view of a self originates, and Isidatta replied that the uninstructed worldling, untrained in the noble Dhamma, takes the five aggregates of personality as being "mine," "I," and "my self." Thus he is continually creating the illusion of selfhood out of what are merely transient, empty phenomena: form, feeling, perception, volitional formations, and consciousness.

Citta was delighted with the discourse and asked Isidatta from where he came. "From the township of Avantī," Isidatta replied. Citta, who did not know his name, then asked whether he knew a certain Isidatta there, with whom he used to correspond, explaining the Dhamma to him and encouraging him to take the robe. As he did not know what had been the outcome, he wished to learn of it. He had never seen Isidatta, and now to his great joy he learned that his former pen-friend had indeed decided upon ordination and was now sitting before him. He asked for the favor of supporting him, but Isidatta, though appreciating the generous offer, declined and took his leave, never to return (SN 41:3).

The commentary does not explain Isidatta's motives for leaving so suddenly. It seems likely that he preferred anonymity, and now that his identity had been disclosed by the conversation with Citta he felt he could no longer reside in that region. He attained to arahantship, and all we hear further of him is a short stanza dealing with the five aggregates (Thag. 120).

On the third occasion when Citta was the questioner, it was a monk called Kāmabhū who replied. Citta put to him no less than eleven abstract questions concerning the three types of formations (*saṅkhārā*) and their cessation (SN 41:6). These were the same as the questions which the householder Visākha put to the nun Dhammadinnā (MN 44).

The first talk in which Citta is found replying to questions occurred when some senior bhikkhus, after the alms round, were sitting together on the porch of the monastery discussing the problem of whether the fetters (*saṁyojana*) and the sense objects are the same or not. Some said they were the same, some said they were different. Citta happened upon the scene and joined the gathering. When invited to comment, he declared that in his view the fetters and the sense objects are different, not only in name but in meaning too. As in a pair of oxen, the white one is not the fetter of the black and the black one is not the fetter of the white, but both are fettered by a single rope or yoke-strap, so the sense faculties had no power to bind the external objects and the external objects had no power to bind the sense faculties, but they were yoked by craving. The bhikkhus rejoiced at the learned lay disciple's answer and declared that Citta must be in possession of the eye of wisdom which ranges over the profound Teaching of the Buddha (SN 41:1).

This same simile is used on two other occasions by Sāriputta and Ānanda (SN 35:191, 192). Its exact import was lucidly explained by the Buddha (SN 35:109, 122) when he said that the six sense faculties and their objects are the things fettered, and that craving, or lustful desire (*chandarāga*), alone is the fetter that binds them. This is an important point to take into consideration in order to avoid a futile fight against the outer sense objects and the inner sense faculties; for it is our internal lust and desire that bind us, not the sense faculties and their objects. The simile aptly assigns black to the six inner domains, since the subject is what is unknown; and white to the outer domains, because the objects are evident.

The second talk showing Citta as a teacher starts when the bhikkhu Kāmabhū recites a stanza spoken by the Buddha, a solemn utterance, and asks Citta to elucidate it:

> The faultless chariot with its one axle
> And white canopy rolls.
> See him coming, without blemish,
> Without ties, the one who has crossed the stream.[2]

Citta first wanted to know whether the utterance was one of the Buddha's, which Kāmabhū confirmed. Obviously, to Citta only a saying of the Buddha's was worthy of deep reflection. Then he asked for a short time to reflect and finally said: the chariot (*ratho*) is the bodily form which moves round (*vattatī*); the one axle (*ekāro*) is mindfulness (*sati*); the smooth, frictionless holding together of the parts is virtue; the white silken canopy (*seta-pacchādo*) is emancipation. So the arahant ("him coming," *āyantaṁ*), without blemish (*anīghaṁ*) or ties (*abandhanaṁ*), has crossed the stream (*chinnasotaṁ*); he has done away with greed, hatred, and ignorance and is safe from the ocean of craving. Kāmabhū then told Citta that he could well be called happy and blessed, as the eye of wisdom had come to him in explaining that profound saying of the Buddha's (SN 41:5).

The third incident relates a conversation in the course of which the bhikkhu Godatta (Thag. 659–72) challenged Citta to expound on this controversy: are the immeasurable liberation of mind, the unattached liberation of mind, the void liberation of mind, and the signless liberation of mind the same in meaning and different only in name or are they different both in name and meaning.[3] Citta replied that they may be considered the same or different, according to the point of view. They are different in meaning and different in name when considered as referring to different types of temporary emancipation, but the same in meaning and different only in name when considered as different aspects of final emancipation. When different in both meaning and name, the immeasurable liberation is the four divine abodes (brahmavihāra), the unattached liberation is the third formless attainment, the void liberation is the insight contemplation of nonself, and the signless liberation is the meditative experience of Nibbāna. When identical in meaning and different only in name, all four signify the arahant's unshakable liberation from greed, hatred, and delusion (SN 41:7).

Elsewhere, more personal events are also related. One time, after some bhikkhus had taken their alms at his house, Citta accompanied them back to the monastery. It was very hot and they were perspiring freely. The youngest of the bhikkhus, Mahaka, remarked to the senior one that wind or rain would certainly be welcome. The observation sounds banal and not worth mentioning, but its import lies in the fact that Mahaka could exercise psychic powers and was asking permission to do so. When he actually did procure rain to refresh his companions, Citta was deeply impressed, particularly since Mahaka was still very young.

At the monastery, therefore, he asked the bhikkhu to display his powers once more. Perhaps it was the first time Citta had seen a paranormal feat of this kind, and he felt a natural curiosity about it. Mahaka complied. A coat and a bundle of hay were placed on the porch, after which Mahaka went inside and closed the door. Creating a beam of tremendous heat he directed it through the keyhole and turned the bundle of hay to ashes without harming the coat.

Filled with enthusiasm, Citta offered to support Mahaka for life. Like Isidatta, however, Mahaka preferred to leave the place and never returned (SN 41:4). Bhikkhus are forbidden to impress laypeople by the exhibition of paranormal powers (Vin. 2:112). Mahaka was young, and these powers were still new and titillating to him, so he could not resist Citta's request; but he recollected himself immediately after and did the right thing by leaving for good.

Citta's town was visited not only by bhikkhus but also by ascetics of other persuasions. One of these was the leader of the Jains, Nigaṇṭha Nātaputta. Citta called upon him as well, for he did not look down on those of other sects and was courageous enough to take up the challenge of dispute (SN 41:8). Nātaputta wanted to know whether Citta believed the Buddha's statement that there is a state of concentration (samādhi) void of thought and examination (*vitakka-vicāra*). Citta answered that he did not believe there is such a thing, and Nātaputta, eager to enlist the renowned Citta in support of his views, was quite pleased with the reply. "Well said!" he exclaimed, and went on to expound his own belief that stilling the flow of thought would be as difficult as stopping the Ganges with one's bare hands: "Impossible it is to make thought and examination cease," he declared.

Nātaputta, however, had failed to catch Citta's exact meaning. Citta now countered with a query: "What do you think is more excellent, venerable sir, belief or knowledge?" "Knowledge," Nātaputta answered. Thereupon Citta explained that he himself had experienced all the jhānas, of which the last three are actually without thought and examination. Hence for him it was no longer a matter of *belief* but of *knowledge* from direct experience that the Buddha's statement was correct.

Thereupon, Nātaputta blamed him severely for the form of his first reply. Citta protested that first he had been praised for being a wise man, and now he was called a fool. Only one of the two opinions could be true, so what did Nātaputta really think of him?

But Citta was not to receive an answer, for Nātaputta preferred to remain silent. This incident shows how even famous philosophers may fall into inconsistencies, especially when their pride is hurt, and Nātaputta claimed to be more than a mere philosopher. He had always failed to attain the higher jhānas, so he conveniently concluded that they are a myth. Now, when an entirely trustworthy man declared that he had actually attained to these jhānas, the baselessness of his own theory was proved, along with the inferiority of his own status. Nātaputta's chagrin must have been increased by the fact that whereas he himself had been for so long a practitioner of extreme asceticism, Citta was still living the household life. It is scarcely to be wondered at that Nātaputta withdrew in confusion.

The third personal encounter related is between Citta and the naked ascetic Kassapa (SN 41:9). This ascetic was an old friend of Citta's family and so, when he visited his old home town for the first time after many years, he called on Citta. Citta asked him how long he had been leading the ascetic life. "Thirty years," he was told. Citta next inquired whether he had attained to superhuman states of bliss or supernormal insight. Kassapa answered, "No, I have just been going about naked, shaving my head, and dusting my seat." That was his life.

Now it was Kassapa's turn to ask questions. How long had Citta been a lay follower of the Buddha? "Thirty years," Citta replied. "Had he attained to superhuman states?" "Well," Citta said, "I have certainly experienced the four jhānas, and should I die before the Blessed One, he would say of me that no fetter bound me any more to the sense-sphere world."

This, as Kassapa knew very well, meant that Citta was a non-returner (anāgāmī), one who had attained to the third of the four stages of awakening. The ascetic, worn by painful austerities, was stunned by the idea that a layman could reach such a high attainment. Justly considering that since this was possible for a layman in the Buddha's Dispensation, even more could be gained by a bhikkhu, he asked Citta to help him in taking the robe. He was duly admitted to the Sangha, and he attained arahantship shortly thereafter.

Three other friends of Citta's also became bhikkhus after discussions of that kind. They were Sudhamma, Godatta, and Isidatta, who, as related before, had been in correspondence with Citta. All three of them attained to ultimate emancipation, leaving Citta, the householder, behind.

The last account we have of Citta relates the circumstances of his death (SN 41:10). When he fell ill devas appeared to him and urged him to set his heart upon becoming a world monarch in his next life.[4] No, Citta answered; he was aiming at something higher, more noble and peaceful than that. He was seeking the Unconditioned—Nibbāna. In recommending Citta to be a world monarch the devas must have been unaware of his attainment, which made it impossible for him to return to the human realm. He had already gone beyond the lure of sensual desire, which is the fetter binding beings to the human world.

His relatives, unable to see the devas, imagined that Citta was in delirium. He reassured them, explaining that he was conversing with invisible beings. Then, at their devout request, he gave them his last advice and admonition. They were to repose trust in the Buddha and his Dhamma always, and they were to remain unswervingly generous toward the holy Sangha.

Thus this noble lay follower of the Buddha passed on to his successors the pattern of conduct which he himself had followed throughout his life with such brilliant success, one that had brought him to liberation from the miseries of the sensuous realm and within sight of the Deathless, the final end of suffering.

THE BHIKKHU CITTA

This Citta was the son of an elephant trainer. When he was still a youth he met an elderly bhikkhu who was returning from his alms round with a particularly tasty item of food in his bowl. The bhikkhu had no desire for it, so he gave it to the young lad. Citta was greatly pleased, and he joined the Sangha thinking that as a bhikkhu he would be fed like that every day without having to work for a living. With such a motivation, however, no ascetic life is possible, and shortly afterwards he discarded the robe and returned to lay life.

All the same, the spirit of the holy Sangha had left a deep and indelible impression on his mind. Soon he felt dissatisfaction with the life of a householder and asked for ordination once more. Having obtained it, after a time he deserted the Sangha again. This happened a third, fourth, and fifth time, after which he married.

One night sometime after his marriage he was unable to fall asleep. While he was looking at his pregnant wife, who was sound asleep, the wretchedness of sensual pleasures was driven home to him so forcefully that he seized a yellow robe and hastened to the monastery at once. On his hurried way through the silent night all the good seeds planted during his previous monkhood blossomed and then and there he attained to stream-entry.

At the monastery, however, his former fellow monks had just agreed among themselves to refuse a possible sixth request for ordination from Citta. They felt that they had been patient enough with him and considered him a disgrace to the Sangha, totally unfit for the holy life. Even while they were so deliberating, they saw Citta himself approaching. His features were aglow with a new bliss, and his manner was so calm and mild that they found it impossible to refuse him another ordination. This time he quickly succeeded in the four jhānas and signless unification of mind.

This filled him with joy, and he felt a great urge to talk about his success. On one occasion some arahants were sitting together in conversation and Citta interrupted them again and again. The senior bhikkhu of the gathering, the Venerable Mahākoṭṭhita, advised him to wait until the senior monks had finished what they had to say. Thereupon Citta's friends said that he ought not to be reprimanded, because he was wise and capable of explaining the Dhamma from his own experience.

Mahākoṭṭhita answered that he could see Citta's heart. Then he went on to explain, by similes, that there are states of mind that may be excellent as long as they last but are still unable to prevent a bhikkhu from giving up the monkhood again. He illustrated this point with a number of similes. A cow securely tied up in the byre seems peaceable enough, but turned loose it quickly tramples down the green crops. Likewise a bhikkhu may be humble and well behaved in the presence of the Master or holy monks, but left on his own he tends to relapse and leave the Sangha. Again, a person may be in possession of the four jhānas and signless unification of mind, and as long as these persist he is safe; but as soon as the bliss wanes he goes among people, talkative and unrestrained, bursting with pride to announce his achievement. Then his heart becomes filled with greed and he gives up the monk's training. He may feel secure in the jhānas, but it is precisely this which leads to his ruin. While a king and army, with drums and chariots, are camping in the woods, nobody can hear the crickets chirping and everybody might think they had been silenced. But after the troops have moved on the crickets can easily be heard again, although one might have been quite sure there were none (AN 6:60).

Later on, Citta actually did leave the Sangha for a sixth time to return to family life. His bhikkhu friends then asked the Venerable Mahākoṭṭhita whether he had himself foreseen that Citta would act thus, or whether devas had told him. He replied that it was both. In astonishment those friends went to the Buddha and related the matter to him. The Blessed One dispelled their apprehensions by telling them that Citta would soon return.

One day Citta went to see the Buddha, accompanied by Poṭṭhapāda, a wandering ascetic of another sect. Poṭṭhapāda posed some deep questions regarding the different modes of arising in the three worlds. Citta followed up with further questions as to the differentiation between these forms of becoming, since, having experienced the jhānas, he was familiar with some of them. The Blessed One's answers satisfied him fully and he requested admission to the Sangha for the seventh time, which turned out to be the last. The Buddha gave his consent, and in a short time Citta too became one of the arahants (DN 9).

In the commentary to the above sutta we are told just why it was that the bhikkhu Citta, in his last life, had to defect from the Sangha so many times before attaining arahantship. It appears that a long, long time ago, when the Buddha Kassapa was teaching the Dhamma, there were two friends who joined the Sangha. One of them became dissatisfied with the hardships of a bhikkhu's life and contemplated returning to his family. His friend encouraged him to make this decision, because in his heart he longed to be able to feel himself superior. This ugly motive had its result much later during the lifetime of the Buddha Gotama. It subjected this false friend, now the bhikkhu Citta, no less than six times to the humiliation of leaving the Sangha and having to petition for readmission.[5]

This shows that there are some kammas so strong that their results cannot be resisted; they can only be lived through with patience and understanding. But since we do not know whether or not certain influences in our lives are the results of such kamma, or, if they are, how close they may be to exhaustion, it behooves us to strive against them. Apart from everything else, such striving has its own value. While it may appear in this life to be futile, ultimately it will bear fruit for our good. The immutable law of cause and effect ensures that no effort is wasted. Here, as elsewhere, the Dhamma urges us to set our face against every form of fatalism—that most enervating and paralyzing view of life—even in its most subtle guises. It encourages us to rise from our failures undaunted and ever ready to try again. Defeats there may be—bitter and heartbreaking setbacks in the battle against craving and ignorance—but the true follower of the Buddha is one who will never admit any defeat as final. Like an old and tried warrior, we must be prepared to lose every battle except the last, confident that by perseverance the final victory will be ours.

FATHER AND MOTHER NAKULA

The town called Suṁsumāragiri (Crocodile Hill) was located in the country of the Bhaggas in the Ganges Valley, and it was here that the Blessed One spent one of the forty-five rainy seasons of his ministry (MN 15). Once, when the Buddha was walking through the streets of the town, a citizen prostrated himself at his feet and cried: "My dear son, why have you never called on us? Now please honor our home, so that your aged mother may lay her eyes on you, too!"

The man was not out of his mind. The fact is that in former births he and his wife had been the Bodhisatta's parents not once but five hundred times, and many more times they had been his uncle, aunt, and grandparents. A faint memory of this had lingered on, and at the sight of the Blessed One full recollection had broken forth and overpowered the old man. Incidents of this kind still sometimes happen in Asian countries even today.

This old man was the householder Nakulapitā (Father Nakula); his wife was known as Nakulamātā (Mother Nakula). They are mentioned together by the Buddha as being among the foremost of his lay disciples, particularly for their unfaltering faithfulness to each other. The brief account of them in the Pāli Canon depicts a conjugal love of divine stature, accompanied by absolute trust based upon their common faith in the Blessed One.

When the Buddha received an invitation to their home, Father Nakula gave him an account of their marriage. Although he had been married very young, he said, he had not once broken faith with his wife throughout the years, not even in thought, let alone in deed. And Mother Nakula made the same declaration on her part. Neither husband nor wife had ever deviated for a moment from their mutual fidelity.

In their devotion, both of them expressed a longing to be together again in their future lives, and they asked the Master what they could do to ensure that they got their wish (AN 4:55). The Buddha did not reject the question or criticize their aspiration. He replied: "Should a husband and wife wish to enjoy each other's company in this life and afterward to meet again in the next, they should cultivate the same faith, the same virtue, the same generosity, and the same wisdom. Then they will meet again in their next lives." And the Buddha added these stanzas:

When both are faithful and bountiful,
Self-restrained, of righteous living,
They come together as husband and wife
Full of love for each other.

Many blessings come their way,
They dwell together in happiness,
Their enemies are left dejected,
When both are equal in virtue.

Having lived by Dhamma in this world,
The same in virtue and observance,
They rejoice after death in the deva-world,
Enjoying an abundance of pleasure.

How a man of lofty aspirations may live with a woman his peer, guarded by virtue, is explained by the Blessed One elsewhere. There he says that not only do both consorts abide by the Five Precepts, but over and above this they are virtuous and noble-minded; when asked for help they never refuse, and they never despise or insult ascetics and brahmins (AN 4:54). In the light of these words it can easily be seen how much is expected of a couple like that: not religious piety only, but also a heart staunch enough to be detached from the petty events of everyday life and everything that is low and base. It is frequently said of the white-clad lay follower that he does not refuse requests and easily forgoes his own wishes or pleasures. This shows a detachment from persons and things, a capacity for letting go and relinquishment. From this comes inner freedom, the only sound basis for the cultivation of wisdom. Virtue in action, renunciation in the heart, wisdom in the mind—these factors make for harmonious and gentle life together.

Knowledge concerning rebirth and of ways to obtain a favorable one was common in India at that time. In the case of the couple Nakula, since they actually remembered some of their previous lives, it was not necessary to enlarge on the subject. The Blessed One's concise reply was all they needed.

The prerequisites for harmonious married life are explained by the Buddha in more detail in the *Sigālovāda Sutta* (DN 31).[6] There we read that the husband—who is responsible for taking the initiative—should relate to his wife in five ways: he should treat her with respect; he should not disdain her; he should be faithful to her; he should allow her authority in the household; and he should provide her with all necessities and adornments according to his means. If he conducts himself thus, his wife will take pride in looking after his needs; the household will run smoothly; she will treat callers and servants politely; she will be faithful; she will protect his property and carry out her tasks skillfully and dutifully.

The Nakulas were not solely concerned with a favorable rebirth: they also took interest in the lawfulness governing human life and in the deeper problems of existence. Once Father Nakula asked the Blessed One why it is that some people attain to emancipation and others do not. The answer was: "Whosoever clings to the objects perceived by the senses cannot gain liberation. Whoever stops clinging will be liberated" (SN 35:131). This is a reply which, in its concentrated terseness, can be fully comprehend only by one well versed in the Dhamma, but Nakula grasped its implications at once.

On another occasion Father Nakula went to pay homage to the Buddha. He was now aged and infirm, he said, and only on rare occasions could he see the Blessed One. Would the Buddha out of compassion give him a word of spiritual guidance to hold and treasure? The Buddha replied: "The body is subject to sickness and decay, a burden even in the best circumstances. Hence one should train oneself thus: 'Though my bodily frame is ill, my mind shall not be ill.'"

Soon afterwards, Nakula met the Venerable Sāriputta, who addressed him with the words, "Your deportment is calm, householder, and your features serene. Did you hear a Dhamma discourse from the Master today?"

"So it is," Nakula answered. "The Blessed One has this very day comforted me with his ambrosial words." Upon hearing this, Sāriputta gave a full explanation of the Buddha's concise words, expounding on the way to overcome physical sickness by not identifying with the five aggregates. When the time comes—as it inevitably does—that the evanescence of things becomes evident, the well-trained person does not despair but coolly looks on with equanimity. His body may wither, but his heart remains sound (SN 22:1).

It was not only Father Nakula who strove for wisdom to overcome death. His wife resembled him in this respect, as can be seen by another report (AN 6:16). When her husband fell dangerously ill, Mother Nakula consoled him thus:

> Do not harbor distress at the thought of my being left behind. To die like that is agonizing, so our Master has advised against it. For six very good reasons you need not be concerned about me: I am skilled at spinning, and so shall be able to support the children; after having lived the home life chastely with you for sixteen years

> I shall never consider taking another husband; I shall never cease seeing the Master and his bhikkhus, but rather visit them even more frequently than before; I am firmly established in virtue and have attained to peace of mind; and lastly, I have found firm footing in the Dhamma and am bound for final deliverance.[7]

Encouraged by these words, Father Nakula recovered from his illness. As soon as he was able to walk he went to the Buddha and recounted his wife's words. The Lord thereupon confirmed that to have such a wife was indeed a blessing. He said: "You are truly blessed, householder, in having Mother Nakula as a mentor and adviser who is solicitous and concerned for your welfare. Mother Nakula is indeed one of the white-clad female devotees who are perfect in virtue, stilled of mind, and firmly established in the Dhamma."

Here a solution is given for reconciling the seemingly opposite tendencies of life: the deep affection between husband and wife on the one hand, and the striving for deliverance on the other. Looking sympathetically at this story of the Nakula couple, one may come to think that a life of renunciation may not be necessary if a married life is led in such an exemplary way, or that one can even combine attachment and detachment. But if one looks more closely one will see that it is far from easy to follow faithfully the life led by that noble couple. It is not enough that there is concern and solicitude for one another. The conditions for a married life in chaste companionship must not be overlooked. The spouses who in their youth had led a married life of sensual fulfillment did not abstain from physical contact only in old age, when the senses were quieted, but they voluntarily lived a celibate life much earlier. In the case of the Nakula couple, they had lived without physical connection for sixteen years, as their words to the Master testify.

Hence the individual wishing to take the first steps on the road to emancipation should make a personal decision: to remain in the home environment and try to outgrow its sensual temptations, or to overcome worldliness as a member of the Sangha in the congenial company of exemplary fellow celibates. As long as the Enlightened One himself, the incomparable guide of those to be trained, was at the head of the Order, the decision was not so difficult. But even today those who do not feel fitted for life in a monastic community may also lack the strength of character to renounce sexual relations in a married life devoted to progress on the path. Both ways of life will demand acts of renunciation.

Notes

Editor's Introduction

1. On the Buddha's ten "powers of knowledge," see MN 12, "The Greater Discourse on the Lion's Roar."

2. For a fuller discussion of the Buddhist picture of the cosmos within the developed Theravāda tradition, see Bhikkhu Bodhi, ed. *A Comprehensive Manual of Abhidhamma*, chap. 5, secs. 2–17 (BPS, 1993).

3. See Bodhi, *Comprehensive Manual of Abhidhamma,* chap. 5, secs. 18–33.

4. In the suttas the expression *ariyasāvaka* seems to be used in two senses: in a broad sense to mean "a disciple of the Noble One," i.e., of the Buddha, referring to any earnest lay disciple; and in a narrower, more technical sense to denote the eight types of noble individuals, i.e., those disciples who have attained the planes of spiritual nobility. It is in this second sense that I use the expression here.

5. See SN 13:1.

6. Detailed information about the twenty-four Buddhas preceding Gotama can be found in the *Buddhavaṁsa.* The story of the Bodhisatta's encounter with Dīpankara is at Bv. 2A, 37–108. The preceding three Buddhas are mentioned at Bv. 27, 1.

7. For a detailed discussion, see Bhikkhu Bodhi, *The Discourse on the All-Embracing Net of Views* (BPS, 1978), part 4.

8. A paccekabuddha is one who attains enlightenment without the aid of a teacher, like a supreme Buddha, but unlike a supreme Buddha does not establish a Dispensation. Paccekabuddhas, it is said, arise only during periods when the teaching of a supreme Buddha is not known in the world. See Ria Kloppenborg, *The Paccekabuddha: A Buddhist Ascetic* (BPS, Wheel No. 305/307, 1983).

9. The source for these distinctions is the Suttanipāta Commentary, pp. 48–52 (PTS ed.). An aeon (*kappa*) is the amount of time needed for the cosmos to evolve and dissolve; for a simile, see SN 15:5, 6. I have not been able to find an exact specification of the duration of an *asaṅkheyya.*

10. Dr. Hecker's original profiles have in some cases been enlarged by Ven. Nyanaponika. See credits page for details.

11. See Vism. 7.89–100.

12. For details, see Russell Webb, *An Analysis of the Pāli Canon* (BPS, 1991).

CHAPTER ONE: SĀRIPUTTA: THE MARSHAL OF THE DHAMMA

1. The following account of Sāriputta's early life is taken from AN Comy. (to AN 1, chap. 14: Etadaggavagga), with passages from the parallel version in Dhp. Comy. (to vv. 11–12). See BL, 1:198–204.

2. According to the *Cunda Sutta* (SN 47:13) and SN Comy., the name of his birthplace was Nālaka, or Nālagāma, which may be an alternative. It was probably quite close to the famous town of Nālandā. Sāriputta's father was a brahmin named Vaganta (Dhp. Comy. to v. 75).

3. The source for the following is Vin. 1:39 ff.

4. The Pāli of the stanza is as follows:

   Ye dhammā hetuppabhavā
   tesaṁ hetuṁ tathāgato āha,
   tesañ ca yo nirodho
   evaṁvādī mahāsamaṇo.

   This stanza was later to become one of the best known and most widely disseminated epitomes of Buddhism, standing for all time as a reminder of Sāriputta's first contact with the Dhamma and also as a worthy memorial to Assaji, his great teacher.

5. That is, monks, nuns, and male and female lay followers.

6. *Dīghanakha Sutta*, MN 74.

7. The fact of his attainment to the *paṭisambhidā-ñāṇa*, or analytical knowledges, which has here been added to the commentarial text, is mentioned by Sāriputta himself at AN 4:173.

8. The group of five disciples were the five ascetics to whom the Buddha preached his first sermon in the Deer Park at Benares. The others referred to are the successive groups converted to the Dhamma at the outset of the Buddha's ministry. For details see Vin. 1:15–35.

9. This account is also taken from AN Comy. to Etadaggavagga. See also Editor's Introduction, p. xv.

10. A slightly different version of this is found in Thag. Comy. where it deals with Sāriputta's verses.

11. Snp. vv. 316 ff. (also called *Dhamma Sutta*).

12. The incident is recorded at AN 9:11 and at Dhp. Comy. (to v. 95). See Nyanaponika Thera, trans. *Aṅguttara Nikāya: An Anthology*, part 3 (BPS, Wheel No. 238/240), sec.10.

13. See below, p. 55.

14. Conceit (*māna*) and restlessness (*uddhacca*) are two of the five fetters (*saṁyojana*) which are destroyed only at the stage of arahantship. Worry (*kukkucca*), however, is removed already at the stage of non-returner (*anāgāmī*).

15. The commentary to the sutta explains that although Buddhas are able to divine such matters themselves, they ask questions for the instruction and illumination of others.

16. See *The Greater Discourse on the Elephant's Footprint* (BPS, Wheel No. 101, 1981).

17. See the *Discourse on Right View* (BPS, Wheel No. 377/379, 1991).

18. Thag. Comy. quotes from the *Niddesa* and attributes it to Sāriputta (*dhammasenāpati*).

19. On the character of the *Niddesa*, see E. J. Thomas, "Buddhist Education in Pāli and Sanskrit Schools," in *Buddhistic Studies*, ed. B. C. Law (Calcutta, 1931), pp. 223 ff.

20. A translation by Bhikkhu Ñāṇamoli is published under the title *The Path of Discrimination* (PTS, 1982). The section on mindfulness of breathing is included in the same translator's anthology, *Mindfulness of Breathing* (BPS, 1964).

21. *Atthasālinī* (PTS ed.), pp. 16–17. See *The Expositor*, 1:20–21.

22. *Atthasālinī*, p. 17; *Expositor*, 1:21.

23. A world monarch (*cakkavatti-rājā*) is the ideal world ruler of Buddhist texts, who rules on the basis of righteousness.

24. See *Mahāparinibbāna Sutta*, chap. 2, "Last Days of the Buddha" (BPS, 1988). It was during his stay at Beluvagāma that the Master fell gravely ill.

25. See above, pp. 11–12.

26. The Four Great Kings are the presiding deities of the lowest heaven of the sensual realm. Each deity rules over one of the four quarters.

27. The younger brother of Sāriputta.

28. Verse translation from the Pāli by Nyanaponika Thera.

29. *Stūpa*: a reliquary monument, in which are deposited relics of the Buddha or

of eminent monks. In Buddhist countries these are found in almost every temple and monastery and are treated as objects of veneration. They are also known as *caityas* and, in Sri Lanka, as *dagobas.*

30. This is according to the commentary to the *Ukkacelā Sutta.*

31. Mil. 204. Horner, trans. *Milinda's Questions,* 1:295. See also above, p. 15.

32. These texts are translated in *The Way of Wisdom* (BPS, Wheel No. 65/66).

CHAPTER TWO: MAHĀMOGGALLĀNA: MASTER OF PSYCHIC POWERS

1. Sources for sections 1 and 2 are AN Comy. and Dhp. Comy. See chap. 1, note 1.

2. DN 2; adapted from the translation by T. W. Rhys Davids.

3. Source: Vin. 1:39 ff.

4. For the Pāli text, see chap. 1, note 4.

5. Here it is of interest to note that the three monks who were closest to the Buddha, Ānanda and the two chief disciples, did not attain to stream-entry by the Buddha's own instruction but through the guidance of others: Ānanda through his teacher, the arahant Puṇṇa Mantāniputta; Upatissa through the arahant Assaji; and Kolita through Upatissa, one who at the time was not even an arahant but only a stream-enterer. For such an attainment to be possible, Kolita needed to possess strong confidence in his friend as well as in the truth; and Kolita did have this confidence.

6. Vin. 1:42–43.

7. AN 7:58.

8. "Signless concentration of mind" (*animitta-cetosamādhi*): The commentary to this sutta explains it as a high level of insight-concentration (*vipassanā-samādhi*) that keeps the mind free from such delusive "signs" as those of permanence and of greed. This explanation appears plausible in view of the fact that Moggallāna was "liberated in both ways," through concentration and insight. On the related term "signless deliverance of mind" (*animitta-cetovimutti*), see MN 43.

9. The distinction between the two types of arahants is explained at MN 70 (1:477–78). See also DN 15 (2:70–71).

10. *Mahā-abhiññatā.* This refers to the six supernormal knowledges, on which see below, p. 89.

11. See AN 4:167–68.

12. SN 35:202.
13. The following quotations are from SN 17:23 and MN 141.
14. This incident is reported at SN 6:10 and Snp. 3:10; see above p. 29.
15. See above, p. 21.
16. See above, pp. 28–29.
17. Examples of such discourses given by Mahāmoggallāna are MN 15 and MN 37, AN 10:84, SN 35:202, SN 44:7–8.
18. Ud. 3:4–5. Translations by John Ireland, *The Udāna.*
19. The Uposatha is the day of special religious observance. The major Uposathas fall on the full-moon and new-moon days of the lunar month, when the monks collectively recite their code of disciplinary rules (*Pātimokkha*) and lay Buddhists undertake additional precepts, listen to sermons, and practice meditation. Minor Uposathas are observed on the two half-moon days. This incident is reported at: AN 8:20; Ud. 5:5; Vin. 2:236–37.
20. SN 8:10.
21. SN 19:1–21; Vin. 3:104–8.
22. This incident is recorded in the *Māratajjanīya Sutta* (MN 50).
23. According to the Buddha in the *Mahāparinibbāna Sutta*, those who have mastered the four roads to psychic power can, if they wish, extend their life span to the end of the aeon, a full period of cosmic evolution and dissolution.
24. See BL, 2:304–8.
25. SN 47:14.

Chapter Three: Mahākassapa: Father of the Sangha

1. He had attained mastery over the nine meditative absorptions and the six supernormal knowledges (*abhiññā*), which include arahantship. See below, p. 123.
2. According to the *Gopaka-Moggallāna Sutta* (MN 108) there are ten qualities of a monk that inspire confidence (*pāsādanīya-dhammā*): he is (1) virtuous, (2) learned, (3) content with his requisites; (4) he can easily obtain the four jhānas; he possesses (5) psychic powers, (6) the divine ear, (7) penetration of the minds of others, (8) recollection of former lives, (9) the divine eye, and (10) destruction of the cankers, i.e., arahantship.
3. This account of Mahākassapa's early life is taken from SN Comy. (to SN 16:11). A similar version is found in AN Comy. to Etadaggavagga.

4. It should be noted that the reply of the laborers is not consistent with the Buddhist understanding of kamma. According to the Buddha, kamma is created by volition, and where volition to take life is absent there can be neither the kamma of killing nor moral responsibility.

5. Bhikkhunī Vibh., Saṅghādisesa 1; Pācittiya 10, 12, 13. Vin. 4:227, 267, 269, 270.

6. Bhikkhunī Vibh., Pācittiya 33. Vin. 4:290.

7. Bhikkhunī Vibh., Pācittiya 35. Vin. 4:292.

8. This account is based on the commentary to SN 16:11. Baddhā is not mentioned here, but at Ap. ii, 3:7, v. 245, she states that she was his wife at the time Vedeha formed his original aspiration to great discipleship before the Buddha Padumuttara, and the account of her own original aspiration is given in the AN Comy. to Etadaggavagga.

9. *Paccekabuddha*: see Editor's Introduction, note 8. This incident and the following lives are related in the commentary to SN 16:11.

10. The story resumes with the commentary to SN 16:11.

11. See Nyanatiloka, *Buddhist Dictionary*, s.v. *dhutaṅga*, and especially Vism., chap. 2, which is devoted entirely to this subject.

12. Dhp. Comy. (to v. 118); BL, 2:265–67.

13. Dhp. Comy. (to v. 56); BL, 2:86–89. See Ud. 3:7.

14. See above, p. 38.

15. By walking about without proper care he destroyed the "young corn" of the Sangha. By allowing unrestrained young monks to come into contact with supporting families, he made the latter disaffected.

16. The account of the First Council is at Vin. 2:284 ff.

17. Although the commentaries say that Mahākassapa was 120 years old at the time of the First Council, this chronology is hardly plausible, for it would mean that he was forty years older than the Buddha and thus already an old man of at least seventy-five at their first meeting.

18. This chronicle is reproduced in full in the *Aśokāvadāna* and in extracts in the *Divyāvadāna* and other works, including the Sanskrit Saṁyuktāgama, the Northern Buddhist counterpart of the SN. The summary given here is based on Etienne Lamotte, *History of Indian Buddhism*, pp. 206–7. Although the sources use Sanskrit, for consistency with the rest of this biography we have used the Pāli equivalents.

19. See the bibliography.

20. The sentences introducing sections of the verses are derived from Thag. Comy.

21. Lit., "a man of the four directions"; that is, he is satisfied with the conditions he finds wherever he lives.

22. *Alaṁ me atthakāmassa.* As Mahākassapa had already arrived at the goal of arahantship, his verse must be interpreted either as exhortative in force or as indicating that he desires to enter into the direct meditative experience of Nibbāna.

23. We find here one of the few allusions to the idea of a Buddha-field in canonical Pāli literature.

24. This verse is stock and is also found among Moggallāna's verses above.

CHAPTER FOUR: ĀNANDA: GUARDIAN OF THE DHAMMA

1. *Sekha,* lit. "a learner" or "trainee." This refers to a disciple who has reached one of the lower three stages of awakening, i.e., a stream-enterer, once-returner, or non-returner.

2. SN 16:11. See above, pp. 128–29. The fact that Kassapa calls Ānanda a youngster seems to contradict the commentarial tradition that Ānanda was born on the same day as the Buddha; in such a case he would then be an old man of eighty and would hardly need to point to a few gray hairs to prove that he was no longer a youngster.

3. What follows is a summary of MN 122. See *The Greater Discourse on Voidness* (BPS, Wheel No. 87, 1982).

4. The knowledges of past lives, of the arising and passing away of beings according to their kamma, and of the destruction of the cankers.

5. *Āneñja-samādhi.* Comy.: This is the concentration connected with the fruition attainment of arahantship, based on the fourth jhāna or immaterial absorptions.

6. Even recently in Burma there have been monks who could recite from memory the entire Tipiṭaka, which fills forty-five volumes!

7. See above, p. 31.

8. It seems that the Buddha did not absolutely refuse Mahāpajāpatī Gotamī but perhaps wished to test her determination. It would have been very difficult for aristocratic women in those days to become nuns and live a hard life in the forest, subsisting on almsfood.

9. The commentaries, as well as other later Buddhist writings, try to explain the

Buddha's statement so that it is not inconsistent with the continued existence of Buddhism long after the five-hundred-year period was over.

10. See above, pp. 127–28 and p. 129.

11. But obviously there are many discourses of the Buddha which were not recorded, for instance, the detailed exposition of his "graduated talk," which he gave so many times; also many occasions in the account of his last days when only the subject headings are mentioned.

12. Instances of this are found at MN 81, MN 83, AN 5:180, and Jāt. 440.

13. This account is taken from AN Comy. to Etadaggavagga.

14. See chap. 2, note 19.

15. See Sister Vajirā and Francis Story, *Last Days of the Buddha* (BPS, 1988).

16. See above, p. 48–54.

17. *Animitta-cetovimutti*: a deep state of meditation that transcends the signs, or marks, of conditioned existence.

18. See above, p. 90.

19. DN Comy. and Mil. 141 explain *kappa* here as meaning *āyukappa*, the full length of the natural human life span, i.e., 120 years (see *Last Days of the Buddha*, p. 106, n. 21). In the canon, however, *kappa* is always used, in relation to time, to signify an aeon, the full duration of a world system, and there seems no reason to ascribe another meaning to it, not justified by the context, in the present passage. Surely the Buddha's mastery over the four roads to power gave him the ability to extend his life span far longer than a mere forty years.

20. For a discussion of the nature of this dish, see *Last Days of the Buddha*, p. 109, n. 38.

21. See chap. 1, note 29.

22. See chap. 1, note 23.

23. The "companion" referred to in the first verse is Sāriputta. "The old ones" are the older generation of monks such as Sāriputta and Moggallāna; "the new ones," the younger generation of monks, some of whom must have caused trouble in the Sangha.

24. This account of the First Buddhist Council is derived from Vin. 2:284 ff.

25. It is possible that the actual order of the discourses within the various collections was also standardized at this Council.

26. See AN 4:111.

CHAPTER FIVE: ANURUDDHA: MASTER OF THE DIVINE EYE

1. In the Dhp. Comy. the anecdote occurs twice, in the stories to v. 17 and v. 382; see BL, 1:231–32, 3:267–68.
2. This account is based on Vin. 2:180–83.
3. See chap. 4, note 4.
4. Nandiya has a verse at Thag. 25, Kimbila at Thag. 118. See also AN 5:201, 6:40, 7:56; SN 54:10.
5. The inner light (*obhāsa-saññā*) is the inner vision of light preparatory to full concentration (Comy.: *parikammobhāsa*). The vision of forms (*rūpānaṁ dassana*) is the seeing of forms with the divine eye.
6. "The non-diffuse" (*nippapañca*) is Nibbāna, the final freedom from the vast multiplicity and complexity of phenomenal existence. "Diffuseness" (*papañca*) accordingly means existence in its aspect of enormous variety.
7. For a detailed description of the divine eye from the standpoint of the later literature, see Vism. 13. 95–101.
8. The full system of *satipaṭṭhāna* meditation is explained at DN 22 and MN 10. For an excellent contemporary account, see Nyanaponika Thera, *The Heart of Buddhist Meditation* (London: Rider, 1962; BPS, 1992).
9. Ibid., pp. 181–82; p. 207, n. 45.
10. These are the stream-enterer, the once-returner, and the non-returner.
11. *Ābhassarā devā.* Their realm within the fine-material sphere (*rūpadhātu*) corresponds to the level of the second jhāna.
12. The Five Precepts (*pañcasīla*) are the foundation of lay Buddhist morality: abstinence from killing, stealing, sexual misconduct, false speech, and intoxicants.
13. Source: Dhp. Comy. (to v. 221); see BL, 3:95–97.
14. Source: Dhp. Comy. (to v. 382) and AN Comy. to Etadaggavagga. See BL 3:264.
15. Ibid. The summary here draws on the version in AN Comy. The version in Dhp. Comy. differs in details. See BL, 3:264–67.
16. Source: Dhp. Comy. (to v. 382); BL, 3:269–70.

CHAPTER SIX: MAHĀKACCĀNA: MASTER OF DOCTRINAL EXPOSITION

1. The Buddha assigns Mahākaccāna to this position at AN 1, chap. 14, Etadaggavagga.

2. This sketch is taken from AN Comy. to Etadaggavagga, which is partly paralleled by Thag. Comy. to vv. 494–501.

3. Ap.i, 4:3.

4. Ap.i, 54:1.

5. The offering of the golden brick is mentioned in AN Comy.

6. The account here resumes as in AN Comy.

7. His parents' names are mentioned at Ap.i, 54:1, v. 21.

8. According to the commentary, at the moment the Buddha invited them to join the Order their hair and beards disappeared and they were spontaneously provided with bowls and robes, created by the Buddha's psychic power.

9. Vin. 1:194–98. The story of Soṇa is also related at Ud. 5:6, but without the passage on the modification of the monastic rules.

10. At Vin. 2:299, in describing the preparations for the Second Council, it is said that eighty-eight arahants from Avantī gathered on the Ahogaṅgā mountain slope. They are described as "mostly forest dwellers, mostly almsmen, mostly rag-robe wearers, mostly wearers of the three robes," and are contrasted with sixty arahant bhikkhus from Pāvā, all of whom observe these ascetic practices. Although any conclusions drawn from this passage are speculative, these monks may have belonged to Mahākaccāna's pupillary lineage, and the reason they were "mostly" observers of the ascetic practices (rather than entirely such) is that he inspired his disciples to undertake such practices by personal example without making them mandatory.

11. Isidatta is mentioned at SN 41:1, 2. In the first sutta he answers a question on the diversity of elements, a topic that Mahākaccāna also discusses (see below, pp. 231–32); in the second sutta he answers a question on speculative views. To escape the fame and admiration which came to him on account of these replies, he disappeared into obscurity. See below, p. 368.

12. Dhp. Comy. (to v. 94); BL 2:202–3.

13. Dhp. Comy. (to v. 43); BL 2:23–28.

14 MN Comy. (to MN 108).

15. See above, pp.39–41.

16. See above, pp. 45–46.

17. For a detailed and insightful discussion of the *Madhupiṇḍika Sutta*, see Bhikkhu Ñāṇananda, *Concept and Reality in Early Buddhist Thought* (BPS, 1971), pp. 2–9.

18. MN contains four suttas, nos. 131–34, dealing with the Bhaddekaratta verses.

The title phrase is itself a riddle: Ven. Ñāṇamoli had rendered it "one fortunate attachment," Ven. Ñāṇananda as "the ideal lover of solitude." Both take the word *ratta* to be the past participle of *rajjati* and to mean "attached" or "in love with." But it seems more likely that the word *ratta* here is an equivalent of *ratti,* "night," so that the expression *bhaddekaratta* means "one excellent night," referring (as the poem suggests) to a complete day and night of fruitful meditation practice. In the translation of the poem just below I follow this last interpretation.

19. The four *viññāṇaṭṭhiti* are mentioned at DN 33 (3:228). See also SN 22:53, 54.

20. DN 21 (2:283). See *Sakka's Quest* (BPS, Wheel No. 10). The DN text does not include the words *seṭṭhā devamanussānaṁ,* "best among devas and humans," appearing in the SN quotation.

21. See Vism., chaps. 4 and 5.

22. Sinhala script and PTS editions read here *ādi,* though the Burmese script edition reads *assāda.* The latter reading may result from the assimilation of an uncommon reading to the standard triad of *assāda, ādīnava, nissaraṇa.*

23. This verse occurs also as Dhp. 6.

24. Bhikkhu Ñāṇamoli's translation of the *Peṭakopadesa* is published as *The Piṭaka Disclosure* (PTS, 1964); of the *Nettippakaraṇa,* as *The Guide* (PTS, 1962).

25. For a discussion of the *Netti* methodology, see Ven. Ñāṇamoli's introduction to *The Guide.*

26. For a translation of the *Netti* analysis of the first sutta of the Dīgha Nikāya, see Bhikkhu Bodhi, *The Discourse on the All-Embracing Net of Views* (BPS, 1978), part 3.

27. *The Guide,* pp. xxvi–xxviii.

28. G. P. Malalasekera, *The Pāli Literature of Ceylon* (1928; repr., BPS, 1995), pp. 180–82.

CHAPTER SEVEN. GREAT WOMEN DISCIPLES OF THE BUDDHA

1. The main source for the story of Visākhā's early life and marriage is Dhp. Comy. (to v.53) and AN Comy. (to Etadaggavagga). See BL, 2:59–84.

2. At that time it was customary in India to give a certain amount of gold to the bride's parents before marriage.

3. Stale leftovers were eaten by low caste people, servants, and beggars. Visākhā

intended to point out that Migāra consumed the result of his previous kamma but neglected to produce further good kamma for future benefit.

4. The Eight Precepts (*aṭṭhasīla*) observed on Uposatha days are an extension of the basic Five Precepts observed on a daily basis by the lay Buddhist (see above chap. 5, n. 12). In the Eight Precepts the third precept is changed to complete sexual abstinence. The three additional precepts are (6) abstaining from food after midday, (7) abstaining from dancing, singing, music, and shows, and from personal ornamentation with garlands, jewelry, and cosmetics, and (8) abstaining from high and luxurious beds and seats.

5. The five spiritual faculties (*pañcindriya*) and five powers (*pañcabala*) are faith, energy, mindfulness, concentration, and wisdom. The seven enlightenment factors (*satta bojjhaṅga*) are mindfulness, investigation of phenomena, energy, rapture, tranquillity, concentration, and equanimity.

6. Source: Jāt. 415.

7. Dhp. Comy. (to v. 151); see BL, 2:340–42.

8. Sources: Dhp. Comy. (to v. 347), Thig. vv. 139–44 and Comy.; Ap.ii, 2:8. See BL, 3:225–26.

9. Translation by H. T. Francis, in Cowell, ed. *The Jataka* 3:110.

10. Sources: Dhp. Comy. (to vv. 102–3); Thig. vv. 107–11 and Comy.; Ap.ii, 3:1. See BL, 2:227–32.

11. The five aggregates, the twelve sense bases, and the eighteen elements. See Nyanatiloka, *Buddhist Dictionary*, for definitions.

12. Sources: Dhp. Comy. (to v. 114), Thig. vv. 213–23 and Comy.; Ap.ii, 3:2. See BL, 2:257–60.

13. Sources: Thig. vv. 102–6 and Comy.; Ap.ii, 3:6. See also Dhp. Comy. (to v. 115), BL, 2:260–61; the story here about a nun named Bahuputtikā is modeled on Soṇā's story as told in Thig. Comy. but differs slightly in details.

14. In both the Dhp. Comy. and Thig. Comy. versions, the verse the Buddha cites in her praise is Dhp. 115. But Dhp. 112 is cited in the Ap. version, and this seems more appropriate as Soṇā was best known for her energy.

15. *Animitta*; that is, devoid of the "signs" of conditioned formations. This can be taken as either a state of insight contemplation on impermanence or as the supramundane path arisen through contemplation of impermanence.

16. Sources: Thig. vv. 82–86 and Comy.; Ap.ii, 3:5.

17. The meditation on the repulsive nature of the body, developed by reflection on the various bodily organs and tissues or by the contemplation of a decaying corpse.

18. The following account is based mainly on Dhp. Comy. (to vv. 21–23) and AN Comy., Etadaggavagga. See BL, 1:266–93.
19. *The Itivuttaka: The Buddha's Sayings*, trans. by John D. Ireland (BPS, 1991).
20. But see the story of the death of Mahāmoggallāna, above, pp. 101–5.
21. Sources: Dhp. Comy. (to v. 113); Thig. 112–16 and Comy.; Ap.ii, 2:10. See BL, 2:250–56.
22. Sources: Vin. 1:231–33; DN 16; Thig. 252–72 and Comy.; Ap.ii, 4:9.
23. Sources: Dhp. Comy. (to v. 223); Vv. 137–49 and Comy. See BL, 3:99–107; *Vimāna Stories*, pp. 110–22.
24. Sirimā's family connections are as follows: Prince Abhaya, a son of King Bimbisāra, had had a love affair with a courtesan named Sālavatī of Rājagaha. From their union Jīvaka was born, the future court physician of Magadha. At a later time Sālavatī gave birth to Sirimā, of an unknown father. Thus Jīvaka was an illegitimate grandson of King Bimbisāra, and Sirimā, indirectly, an illegitimate step-granddaughter. This may explain the king's interest in her.
25. Sources: Thig. 400–47 and Comy.

CHAPTER EIGHT: AṄGULIMĀLA: A MURDERER'S ROAD TO SAINTHOOD

1. The primary source for the story of Aṅgulimāla is the *Aṅgulimāla Sutta* (MN 86). Additional details are provided by MN Comy. and Thag. Comy. Passages from the *Aṅgulimāla Sutta* cited here are taken from *Middle Length Discourses of the Buddha*, pp. 710–17; this includes the translation of Thag. 871–86, verses that also appear in the Majjhima Nikāya.
2. Verses 871–72 are paralleled by Dhp. 172–73; v. 873 by Dhp. 382; v. 877 by Dhp. 80; vv. 883–84 by Dhp. 26-27 (with a slight variation).
3. Comy. says that Aṅgulimāla spoke vv. 874–876 after he had been injured during his alms round.

CHAPTER NINE: ANĀTHAPIṆḌIKA: THE BUDDHA'S CHIEF PATRON

1. Source: Vin. 2:146 ff.
2. The story of Anāthapiṇḍika's meeting with the Buddha is related at SN 10:8 and at Vin. 2:154 ff., and in the *Jātaka Nidānakathā.*
3. Translated by I. B. Horner, *The Book of the Discipline*, 5:206.
4. Dhp. Comy. (to v. 18); BL, 1:242–44. No explanation is given in this

source as to why she did not marry. Since during this period, in Middle India, marriages were generally arranged, it seems a marriage for the daughter should not have been a problem.

5. Dhp. Comy. (to v. 178); BL, 3:28–30.
6. See *Aṅguttara Nikāya: An Anthology*, trans. Nyanaponika Thera.
7. The same analysis is also found at SN 42:12, addressed to the headman Rāsiya.
8. *Pītiṁ pavivekaṁ*. Joy (*pīti*) is present in the first and second meditative absorptions (*jhāna*).
9. "Connected with the senses," i.e., with sense *desire* and the sense *objects*. Of the last three items, the first refers to the pain and grief that arise when unwholesome aims fail; the second, to the pain and grief that arise when unwholesome aims succeed; and the last, to the pain and grief that arise when wholesome aims fail.
10. The same text is also found at SN 12:41 and SN 55:28.

CHAPTER TEN: SHORTER LIVES OF THE DISCIPLES

1. Source: Vin. 2:15–18.
2. *Neḷaṅgo setapacchādo, ekāro vattatī ratho*
   Anīghaṁ passa āyantaṁ chinnasotaṁ abandhanaṁ.

   The verse was spoken at Ud. 7:5 with reference to the Venerable Bhaddiya the Dwarf, an arahant with great psychic powers who was ugly and deformed.
3. The Pāli terms are: *appamāṇā cetovimutti, ākiñcaññā cetovimutti, suññatā cetovimutti*, and *animittā cetovimutti.*
4. See chap. 1, n. 23.
5. DN Comy (to DN 9).
6. See Nārada Thera, *Everyman's Ethics* (BPS, Wheel No. 14, 1985).
7. By the remark "having lived the home life chastely" (*gahaṭṭhakaṁ brahmacariyaṁ samāciṇṇaṁ*) she indicates that they abstained from sexual relations during this period. By the last remark she shows her attainment of stream-entry.

Bibliography

Pāli Sources in English Translation

Aṅguttara Nikāya: *The Book of the Gradual Sayings.* Trans. F. L. Woodward and E. M. Hare. 5 vols. PTS, 1932–36. *Anguttara Nikāya: An Anthology.* Trans. Nyanaponika Thera; 3 parts. BPS, 1970–76.

Atthasālinī: *The Expositor.* Trans. Pe Maung Tin; 2 vols. PTS, 1920–21.

Buddhavaṁsa: *The Chronicle of Buddhas.* Trans. I. B. Horner. In *Minor Anthologies of the Pāli Canon,* part 3. PTS, 1975.

Dhammapada: *The Dhammapada: The Buddha's Path of Wisdom.* Trans. Acharya Buddharakkhita. BPS, 1985.

Dhammapada Aṭṭhakathā: *Buddhist Legends.* Trans. E. W. Burlingame. 3 vols. Cambridge: Harvard University Press, 1921; repr., PTS, 1969.

Dīgha Nikāya: *The Long Discourses of the Buddha.* Trans. Maurice Walshe. Boston: Wisdom Publications, 1995.

Itivuttaka: *The Itivuttaka: The Buddha's Sayings.* Trans. John D. Ireland. BPS, 1991.

Jātaka: *The Jātaka, or Stories of the Buddha's Former Births.* Trans. under the editorship of E. B. Cowell. 6 vols. Cambridge, 1895–1905; repr. in 3 vols., PTS, 1972; Delhi: Motilal Banarsidass, 1990.

Mahāparinibbāna Suttanta: *Last Days of the Buddha.* Trans. by Sister Vajirā and Francis Story. Rev. ed. BPS, 1988.

Majjhima Nikāya: *The Middle Length Discourses of the Buddha.* Trans. Bhikkhu Ñāṇamoli and Bhikkhu Bodhi. Boston: Wisdom Publications; BPS, 1995.

Milindapañha: *Milinda's Questions.* Trans. I. B. Horner. 2 vols. PTS, 1963–64.

Paṭisambhidāmagga: *The Path of Discrimination.* Trans. Bhikkhu Ñāṇamoli. PTS, 1982.

Saṁyutta Nikāya: *The Book of the Kindred Sayings.* Trans. C. A. F. Rhys Davids and F. L. Woodward. PTS, 1917–30. *Saṁyutta Nikāya: An Anthology.* Trans. John D. Ireland, Bhikkhu Ñāṇananda, and Maurice Walshe. 3 parts. BPS, 1967–85.

Suttanipāta: (1) *The Sutta-Nipāta.* Trans. H. Saddhātissa. London: Curzon, 1985. (2) *The Discourse Collection.* Trans. K. R. Norman. PTS, 1992.

Theragāthā: (1) *Psalms of the Brethren.* Trans. C. A. F. Rhys Davids. PTS, 1913. (2) *Elders' Verses,* vol. 1. Trans. by K. R. Norman. PTS, 1969.

Therīgāthā: (1) *Psalms of the Sisters.* Trans. C. A. F. Rhys Davids. PTS, 1909. (2) *Elders' Verses,* vol. 2. Trans. by K.R. Norman. PTS, 1971.

Udāna: *The Udāna: Inspired Utterances of the Buddha.* Trans. John D. Ireland. BPS, 1990.

Vimānavatthu: *Vimāna Stories.* Trans. Peter Masefield. PTS, 1989.

Vinaya Piṭaka: *The Book of the Discipline.* Trans. I. B. Horner. 5 vols. PTS, 1938–66.

Visuddhimagga: *The Path of Purification.* Trans. Bhikkhu Ñāṇamoli. Colombo: Semage, 1956; BPS, 1975.

Reference Works

Lamotte, Étienne. *History of Indian Buddhism from the Origins to the Sakra Era.* Trans. by Sara Boin-Webb. Louvain-Paris: Peeters Press, 1988

Malalasekera, G. P. *Dictionary of Pāli Proper Names.* 2 vols. London, 1937–38; PTS, 1960.

Nyanatiloka Thera. *Buddhist Dictionary: Manual of Buddhist Terms and Doctrines.* 4th ed. BPS, 1988.

Webb, Russell. *An Analysis of the Pāli Canon.* BPS, 1991.

Contributors

Bhikkhu Bodhi is an American Buddhist monk from New York City who was ordained in Sri Lanka in 1972. He is currently the president and editor of the Buddhist Publication Society. His books include *The All-Embracing Net of Views*, *A Comprehensive Manual of Abhidhamma*, and (as co-translator) *The Middle Length Discourses of the Buddha.*

Hellmuth Hecker is a leading German writer on Buddhism and a translator from the Pāli Canon. His books include a German translation of the *Saṁyutta Nikāya* (parts 4 and 5), a two-volume chronicle on Buddhism in Germany, and a biography of Ven. Nyanatiloka Mahāthera, the first German Buddhist monk.

Nyanaponika Thera (1901–94) was one of the foremost interpreters of Theravāda Buddhism in our time. Born in Germany, he entered the Buddhist Order in Sri Lanka in 1936 under Ven. Nyanatiloka Mahāthera, and spent fifty-eight years as a monk until his death in late 1994. He was the founding president and longtime editor of the Buddhist Publication Society in Kandy. His books include *The Heart of Buddhist Meditation, The Vision of Dhamma*, and *Abhidhamma Studies.*

Index

Mahāmoggallāna (*continued*)
wandering and spiritual search, 71–75; youth, 69–71
Mahāmoggallāna's psychic powers, 88–96; divine ear (clairaudience), 93; divine eye (clairvoyance), 93; power of transformation, 96; telekinesis (supernormal locomotion), 95–96; thought reading, 92; travel by mind-made body (astral travel), 94–95
Mahānāma, 185–86
Mahānisabha, 114
Mahāpajāpatī Gotamī, 154–55; verse on Dhamma, 155
mahāpurisavitakka (truly great man), 190
Mahinda, 42
Majjhima Nikāya, 59–61, 224–29
malicious demon (*yakkha*), 36, 93
Mallas, 167, 175, 178
Mallikā, 255–63; builds hall for the Sangha, 257; former lives, 261–62; queen of Kosala, 256; transgression of, 262–63; wins husband over to the Dhamma, 257–58
Mansion of Migāra's Mother, 95, 220, 252
Mantānī, 319
Māra, 33, 100–1, 169–71, 266, 278
Māra's daughters, 232–33
Marshal of the Dhamma. *See* Sāriputta
Master of Doctrinal Exposition. *See* Mahākaccāna
Master of the Divine Eye. *See* Anuruddha
Master of Psychic Powers. *See* Mahāmoggallāna
Mātali, 150
meditations for inducing concentration (*kasiṇa*), 191, 196, 233–34
meditations on universal love, compassion, altruistic joy, and equanimity (*brahma-vihāra*), 23, 60
meditative absorptions. *See* jhānas
meditative attainments, 35, 54, 65
Meṇḍaka, 247–48
mettā (meditation on loving-kindness), 45, 288, 293, 355
Middle Country, 216, 218–19
Middle Way, 118
Migapathaka, 365
Migāra, 248, 250–51
mindfulness (*sati*), 151, 152, 189, 369. *See also* four foundations of mindfulness
mindfulness of the body (*kāyagatā sati*), 239
miserable ghosts (*petas*), 94
Moggallāna. *See* Mahāmoggallāna
monastic discipline, code of (Pātimokkha), 92, 131
monk. *See* bhikkhus
Mother Nakula, 377–78
Mount Kukkaṭapāda, 132–33
Mudgala, 69

nāgas, 15, 96, 97
Nakulamātā, 375. *See also* Mother Nakula
Nakulapitā, 375. *See also* Father Nakula
Nālaka, 49, 51, 52

Wisdom Publications

Wisdom Publications, a not-for-profit publisher, is dedicated to making available authentic Buddhist works for the benefit of all. We publish translations of the sutras and tantras, commentaries and teachings of past and contemporary Buddhist masters, and original works by the world's leading Buddhist scholars. We publish our titles with the appreciation of Buddhism as a living philosophy and with the special commitment to preserve and transmit important works from all the major Buddhist traditions.

If you would like more information or a copy of our mail order catalogue, please write to us at:

Wisdom Publications
199 Elm Street
Somerville, Massachusetts 02144
USA

The Wisdom Trust

As a not-for-profit publisher, Wisdom Publications is dedicated to the publication of fine Dharma books for the benefit of all sentient beings and dependent upon the kindness and generosity of sponsors in order to do so. If you would like to make a donation to Wisdom, please contact our Somerville office.

Thank you.

Wisdom Publications is a non-profit, charitable 501(c)(3) organization and a part of the Foundation for the Preservation of the Mahayana Tradition (FPMT).

The Buddhist Publication Society

The Buddhist Publication Society is an approved charity dedicated to making known the Teaching of the Buddha, which has a vital message for people of all creeds.

Founded in 1958, the BPS has published a wide variety of books and booklets covering a great range of topics. Its publications include accurate annotated translations of the Buddha's discourses, standard reference works, as well as original contemporary expositions of Buddhist thought and practice. These works present Buddhism as it truly is—a dynamic force that has influenced receptive minds for the past 2,500 years and is still as relevant today as it was when it first arose.

A full list of our publications will be sent upon request. Write to:

The Honorary Secretary
Buddhist Publication Society
P.O. Box 61
54, Sangharaja Mawatha
Kandy, Sri Lanka

Teachings of the Buddha Series

The Middle Length Discourses of the Buddha: A New Translation of the Majjhima Nikāya

Translated by Bhikkhu Ñanamoli & Bhikkhu Bodhi

1995 Outstanding Academic Book Award —Choice Magazine

Tricycle Prize for Excellence in Buddhist Publishing for "Dharma Discourse"

This collection—among the oldest records of the historical Buddha's original teachings—consists of 152 *suttas*, or discourses, of middle length. The *Majjhima Nikāya* might be concisely described as the Buddhist scripture that combines the richest variety of contextual settings with the deepest and most comprehensive assortment of teachings.

"...remarkable both in its scope and in its contemporary rendering of the Buddha's words."—*Tricycle: The Buddhist Review*

ISBN 0-86171-072-X, 1424 PAGES, $60.00

The Long Discourses of the Buddha: A Translation of the Dīgha Nikāya

Translated by Maurice Walshe

This collection consists of thirty-four longer length *suttas.* These suttas reveal the gentleness, compassion, power, and penetrating wisdom of the Buddha. Included are teachings on mindfulness; morality, concentration and wisdom; dependent origination; on the roots and causes of wrong views; and a long description of the Buddha's last days and passing away.

"[These suttas] are not meant to be 'sacred scriptures' that tell us what to believe. One should read them, listen to them, think about them, contemplate them, and investigate the present reality, the present experience with them. Then, and only then, can one insightfully know the truth beyond words." —Venerable Sumedho Thera

ISBN 0-86171-103-3, 656 PAGES, $34.95